Feeling the heat

International perspectives on the prevention of wildfire
ignition

Janet Stanley
University of Melbourne
Alan March
University of Melbourne
James Ogloff
Swinburne University of Technology
Jason Thompson
University of Melbourne

Series on Climate Change and Society
VERNON PRESS

www.vernonpress.com

In the Americas:	*In the rest of the world:*
Vernon Press	Vernon Press
1000 N West Street,	C/Sancti Espiritu 17,
Suite 1200, Wilmington,	Malaga, 29006
Delaware 19801	Spain
United States	

Series on Climate Change and Society

Library of Congress Control Number: 2020934225

ISBN: 978-1-64889-068-0

Also available: 978-1-62273-828-1 [Hardback]; 978-1-64889-010-9 [PDF, E-Book]

Cover design by Vernon Press. Cover image by Vik Dunis.

The Powerful Owl, *Ninox strenua*, is Australia's largest owl with a wingspan of up to 140cm. It occurs in Eastern and South-Eastern Australia, mostly in large forested areas. The Powerful Owl mates for life, which can be over 30 years, and nests in large tree hollows in eucalypt trees that are at least 150 years old. The Powerful Owl is threatened with extinction and would have been severely impacted by the recent wildfires in Australia. It is also adversely affected by high-frequency prescribed burning, as this reduces its food supply of smaller birds and mammals.

Table of contents

List of figures

List of tables

Acknowledgements

The authors of the book would like to thank the following organisations who assisted with research funding: the Australian Research Council (project LP160100661), Crime Stoppers Victoria Limited, and The Bushfire and Natural Hazards Cooperative Research Centre. Many organisations have cooperated with this project, for which the authors are very grateful. These include, the Victorian Police, the Victorian Department of Environment, Land, Water and Planning and 226 strategic who produced many of the figures and tables. Professor Brendan Gleeson and staff of the Melbourne Sustainable Society Institute, School of Design, University of Melbourne, have always provided much appreciated on-going support and encouragement for wildfire research. Janet would also like to thank her family and husband John who edited some chapters and tolerated her frequent absences allowing her to remain hunched over a computer.

Preface

This book aims to join up the story on wildfires to provide a strategic perspective on the vital but internationally neglected topic: the prevention of wildfire. Wildfire is commonly considered and addressed in three segments, comprising: pre-fire planning, suppression of the fire, and post-fire recovery. However, there is a stage before this – prevention of ignition. The term 'prevention' is sometimes linked with pre-fire planning, but the idea of 'planning' commonly carries the tacit assumption that something is going to happen. While, of course, not all wildfires can be prevented, overlooking preventative actions promotes a belief of an inevitability that no wildfires can be prevented.

There is possibly a range of reasons for this oversight. The agency responsible for wildfire in industrialised countries, fire services or fire brigades, have historically been tasked with undertaking fire suppression. They have become specialised in dealing with the fire occurrence itself, rather than the much broader issues in relation to wildfire, such as: What is the cause of wildfire? Why is wildfire increasing? What is the impact of wildfire? What is the best way to prevent wildfire? Who should be involved in decision-making around wildfire? What values are under threat by wildfire? At the same time, other disciplines have been reluctant to add their contribution to the wildfire conversation. This is perhaps due to the competence of fire services in the task of extinguishing fires, but also the speed of change in numbers and severity of wildfires now experienced, has caught people unprepared. Linking multiple voices is complex, especially when the structures for such a process are not in place. It is also difficult to bring about major changes when complexities around power, gender, politics, ideology and hierarchical systems are present, as has evolved in some fire services, some government departments, and some lobby groups.

This book seeks to highlight the dichotomy between the situation that a significant proportion of wildfires are caused by humans, while the great majority of actions in relation to wildfire involve changes to the natural environment. This is undertaken in the context of climate change, species extinction, and emergencies, due to fossil fuel use and land clearing, leading to conditions that will be inhospitable to current human societies. In the words of climate scientists, a deep transformation based on a fundamental reorientation of human values, equity, behaviour, institutions, economies, and technologies, is required.

While an international perspective has been attempted in this book, the complexity and size of the topic, the widely different situations and approaches taken between countries, as well as the lack of empirical knowledge in many associated areas, creates considerable difficulties in coming to grips with the field of wildfire. Much information sits in grey literature and the media, which is both difficult to access and of variable quality. Some areas of wildfire occurrence are almost totally over-looked, especially wildfire in industrialising countries associated with land-use change, economic gains and conflict. However, despite the limitations, it is hoped that this book offers a much wider perspective than is traditionally given around wildfire, such that it will stimulate a broader inter-disciplinary involvement in the field and encourage researchers to begin to fill in the multiple knowledge gaps. Indeed, it is argued that such an approach is vital if there is to be any hope of reducing the occurrence of wildfire as the planet becomes hotter.

The authors of this book come from widely different disciplines. The difficulties associated with an integrated approach to the prevention of ignition, as well as the need for this, is evident in this book. The integrated story is only just beginning. In part due to some differences in disciplinary approaches, the chapters have been written so that each chapter can be read as a body of work on a particular subject, as well as part of a more complete story.

Finally, while this book was being published, the catastrophic wildfires in Australia continued to devastate the country. The world was watching. One positive outcome to be taken from this disaster was a call by many Australians for greater action on climate change and to a lesser extent, for protection of the natural environment. At the same time, the shortcomings of the current responses to wildfire in Australia was revealed. This was in terms of confusion about fire ignition and prevention, the extent of ideology rather than evidence that is influencing opinions and policy, and the need for more resources for fire suppression. It is yet to be seen as to whether these deficits are addressed in the future. It is hoped that this book will encourage a more effective response in Australia and internationally.

Section 1:
The current picture

The first four chapters of this book explore issues in the present position of wildfire. Chapter 1 looks at the extent of the problem. Chapter 2 gives an overview of the causes of ignition, revealing the poor state of knowledge on this issue. Chapter 3 positions our latest knowledge of people who light malicious fires. Finally, chapter 4 gives an overview of the patterns that are present in wildfire ignitions.

Wildfires: We have a problem

Introduction

This book is about the prevention of wildfires, that is, avoiding the ignition that leads to a wildfire. It is argued that this is a topic that, internationally, is given little consideration in research, policy and practice. When it is discussed and put into practice, a narrow approach is commonly taken. Often this narrow approach is accompanied by confusion as to the purpose of the activity, as well as neglect of a wide range of opportunities that could contribute to prevention. This book endeavours to offer a broad perspective on the prevention of ignition of wildfires, drawing in the many components of the wildfire story. It hopefully reveals interplays between multiple, highly complex systems. In particular, the book includes material on the malicious lighting of wildfires, which, although it is believed to account for about half of all wildfires, is little understood and even more rarely considered in approaches to prevention.

This first chapter presents a broad overview of why this book has been written. It introduces the subject of wildfire, its increasing severity and frequency, and how wildfire can be severely disruptive at best but more often heart-breaking, leading to personal and societal change. It introduces the major compounding drivers that lead to, and interact with, wildfire: climate change, population growth, urban and spatial planning, and the major knowledge gaps about wildfire. There is discussion on how prevention is currently viewed and the failure to address the prevention of ignition.

A wildfire is defined in the Cambridge Advanced Learner's Dictionary (2017) as a fire in an area of combustible vegetation that occurs in the countryside or rural area. Definitions vary, as some include the speed of burning and whether the wildfire is under control or not (Johns 2014). However, the authors of this book argue that a wildfire should be viewed as any spreading fire that is associated with vegetation and starts outside a dense urban area (although it may threaten urban areas). This holds whatever the character or source of ignition of a fire. The term 'wildfire' is used in this book, except where bushfire is part of a title or in a quote. Other terms are sometimes used internationally, such as 'wildland fire' in the US, 'bushfire' in Australia, and 'forest fire' in Europe and at times in Northern America. Although these terms can be used where a forest is involved, and/or as a broad descriptor of a vegetation fire, the different use is not always made clear.

Wildfire events as this book is written

As this chapter is being written (mid-2018), an unprecedented heatwave is occurring across the northern hemisphere. Unusually high temperatures, often accompanied by low rainfall, started in May 2018 and extended into August. Unprecedented wildfires have accompanied this heat in many countries, in terms of the number of fires, their size, the difficulties extinguishing them, and their impact. As well as occurring in countries traditionally more prone to wildfire, such as Portugal, Spain, Greece, Russia, Canada and California, the fires extended to traditionally cooler climate locations. Wildfires have been rare occurrences in Sweden, Lapland, Arctic Circle and Alaska, the current fires also impacting Norway, Denmark and Latvia. In July 2018 Greece experienced many severe wildfires, leaving 102 people dead and 187 people hospitalised with injuries[1]. In July and August 2018, Sweden struggled to extinguish some 4,000 wildfires in the context of a 250-year record of high temperatures (Johnsen 2018). On August 9, there were 465 fires burning across British Columbia, with the fire danger rating as 'high' or 'extreme' in virtually every part of the province (Judd 2018). Wildfires in 2018 in California, reported by CALFIRE (The Department of Forestry and Fire Protection) and US Forest Service, were said to be the most destructive on record. A total of 7,571 fires burnt 676,312 hectares or 6,763 square kilometres, the largest annual burnt area recorded (California Department of Forestry and Fire Protection 2018). The Insurance Institute recorded slightly more: 8,054 wildfires in 2018, covering 737,804 hectares (Insurance Information Institute 2019). The Camp Fire in Northern California, which started on 8 November 2018, said to be the most destructive fire on record in the state, lead to 88 deaths and burnt 18,800 structures, including 14,000 houses (Insurance Information Institute 2019).

In 2018, Texas had 2,387 more fires than California. California was followed by North Carolina, Georgia, Florida and Oregon (Insurance Information Institute 2019). In 2017, while California sat at the top of the list, extensive wildfires occurred in differing states to those in 2018, suggesting that wildfire risk is fairly widespread in the USA. Indeed, in early August 2018, 14 states in the USA reported large fires from Alaska to New Mexico (Irfan 2018a). While the total area burnt in the USA in 2018 was below the total area burnt in 2017, the fires in 2018 were 30% larger than the average over the past decade, making them the most destructive fires on record.

---

[1] Wikipedia referring to a Greek newspaper, May 2019, https://en.wikipedia.org/wiki/2018_Attica_wildfires.

Most countries found these 2018 wildfires difficult to extinguish as they did not have the standby resources on the scale needed. Internationally, other resources are sometimes brought to the firefighting task, both from within and between countries. The military and prisoners were deployed in 2018 to assist with the suppression of severe wildfires in California (Fathi 2018; US Forest Fire Services 2019). Both military and passenger planes were used to dump fire-retardants on flames (Irfan 2018b). Loans of planes and helicopters from neighbouring countries assisted firefighting in Sweden (Smith, Vonberg & Miller 2018). Firefighting in the UK was assisted by the military and police (BBC News 2018a).

The impacts of these recent fires are already being seen in terms of deaths and injuries, loss of homes and property, and loss of commercial forests and farm animals. Air pollution is said to be causing respiratory illnesses, nosebleeds, coughs and eye problems in the UK (BBC News 2018a). However, the less visible losses are rarely formally itemised. These include personal suffering; loss of valued belongings and pets; loss of employment; increase in relationship breakdowns and domestic violence; and loss and change in natural ecosystems, including the decline and loss of species. Press reports of 2,000 acres (809 hectares) of moorland being destroyed emerge in the UK, pointing out the heavy toll of wildlife, birds and farm animals (Cox 2018; Halton 2018). One wildlife expert in the UK said the effects of the fire could last for up to fifteen years (Halton 2018). Later in this book, it is noted that in some countries, such as Australia, the adverse impact may be permanent where locations are subject to repeat fires.

As with the impact of wildfire, the cause of the fires is given little attention in the media. However, a clear link has been made between climate change and wildfire. World Weather Attribution (2018) has found that the probability of the 2018 heatwave, associated with the northern hemisphere fires, is more than two times higher today than if human activities had not altered climate. Such heatwaves will become less exceptional in the future. The Economist magazine (2018a) had a lead article entitled, In the line of fire: The world is losing the war against climate change. Other journals include articles that reflect a similar call to action, such as in Salon: "On climate change, it's time to start panicking: The crisis over global warming warrants an unparalleled response" (Rozsa 2018).

The frequency and size of wildfires

The incidence of wildfires is increasing, along with the risk of a fire lit in a forest or grass area becoming large and dangerous or becoming a 'catastrophic' fire (Dutta, Das & Aryal 2016; Hughes & Alexander 2017). The descriptions of wildfire severity vary between authors and sources; however, the terms 'catastrophic' or 'extreme' wildfire are often used in an attempt to differentiate it from a 'normal' wildfire (Tedim et al. 2018). A catastrophic or extreme fire is all but impossible to extinguish without a natural suppressant, such as heavy rain, and the spread of the fire is difficult to predict (Sharples et al. 2016). Sometimes the impact of the wildfire is also used as a differentiating point (Tedim et al. 2018). Williams and colleagues (2019) suggest that the growth in fire will be exponential over the next 40 years.

In western USA, the number of large wildfires and size of the area burnt has continued to increase with each decade since the 1970s, despite improved firefighter coverage and resources (Paton, Buergelt & Flannigan 2015; Westerling 2016). The increase in the area burnt each decade averages about 390% above the previous decade. Canada evacuated 90,000 people in December 2016, the fire reported as still burning 17 months later (Balch et al. 2017; Nuccitelli 2017). The 2017 and 2018 fires in Canada were the largest ever recorded since the 1950s, with 1.2 million hectares and 1.4 million hectares of forest burnt, respectively. The alpine fires in Victoria, Australia, were close to this size, the 2003 fire covering 1.2 million hectares (DELWP 2019; Jia et al. 2019).

Europe has been experiencing very large fires since the early 1990s that overwhelm resources and firefighting capacity. Wildfires are predicted to increase in number in the future, also moving northwards (Paton et al. 2015). The large and increasing numbers of extensive wildfires in Russia pose particular difficulties around extinguishing the fires, due to the remoteness of many areas and access difficulties (Paton et al. 2015).

Africa is said to have the greatest frequency of wildfires, particularly in northern Angola, the southern region of the Democratic Republic of the Congo, southern Sudan and the Central African Republic. Fire is used to clear forests for agriculture in these countries (United Press International 2006). While wildfire is a frequent occurrence in some Asian countries, it is an emerging problem in others, such as Taiwan and India (IPCC 2019; Paton et al. 2015). Indonesia has, and continues to experience very large wildfires (Sagala, Sitinjak & Yamin 2015). China does not have many wildfires, said to be due to deforestation, although it has experienced some severe ones (Lawson 2019).

Australia is among the most fire-prone countries in the world (Paton et al. 2015). According to the Australian Steering Committee for the Review of Government Service Provision, there were 101,867 fires reported to Australian fire service agencies in the year 2013-2014 (SCRGSP 2016). This comprised 19,524 'structural' fires (a fire within a building or man-made structure) 43,646 'landscape' fires (a fire in a forest or grass area, known as wildfire) and 38,697 'other' fires (these include vehicle, other property, and the burning of rubbish that got away). Thus, about 43% of the fires recorded were categorised as landscape fires.

These figures relate to officially recorded fires and are likely to be an under-estimate of actual fires, especially fires that are small and/or extinguished quickly. Most fires are under five hectares (Parliament of Victoria 2017). Indeed, it seems that this is an under-estimation, revealed using hot-spot estimation based on satellite imagery (Dutta, Das & Aryal 2016). This technique found that in 2013 Australia experienced a weekly average of 4,495 wildfires, representing about 238,940 wildfires for the year, over five and a half times the officially recorded landscape fires in Australia for 2013/4 (SCRGSP 2016). A few of these will be fires that have been deliberately lit by an authority in order to reduce fuel in a particular area, especially in autumn when most prescribed[2] burning takes place.

The above research found that wildfires have increased in Australia by 40% over the five years to 2016 (Dutta, Das & Aryal 2016). This is associated with a long-term increase in extreme fire weather, and an increase in the length of the fire season, across large parts of Australia and many other countries (World Meteorological Organization 2018).

The impact and cost of wildfires

Wildfires have led to many adverse impacts. These include loss of life; physical and emotional injury; loss of structures, products and goods; biodiversity alteration and loss. The latter includes an increase in forest fragmentation and weed penetration, soil erosion, and loss of landscape and recreation values (Martinez, Vega-Garcia & Chuvieco 2009). While these impacts are mentioned in the literature, the full impact of wildfire on the environment, people, and economies has not been fully calculated, nor yet fully understood (Barron 2018).

Environmental impact of wildfire

Fire has always been part of human civilisation, whether on a small scale for activities like cooking and heating or on a larger scale, such as used as a weapon of war or to manage vegetation. Indeed, many landscapes have been formed and shaped by human burning activity. There may be an ecological dependence on the continuation of a fire regime, as in some Australian ecosystems where particular plant species will only propagate after a fire. Thus burning, as

---

[2] The term 'prescribed burning' is used in this book. It is defined as "the controlled application of fire under specified environmental conditions to a predetermined area and at the time, intensity, and rate of spread required to attain planned resource management objectives" (AFAC 2012). This process is also referred to as 'cool burning'.

historically undertaken by many Indigenous Australian communities, may be important to continue in selected ecosystems (Gammage 2011).

The impact will also depend on the heat, size and frequency of fire, as well as local weather conditions. This applies to both unintended wildfire and prescribed burns. Fires may promote new seed growth but may also lead to environmental damage. Damage may occur where burning is too frequent for the plants and animals to recover, where the fire does not offer an escape route for animals, or where wildfire occurs in an area that doesn't have a historical record of fire, such as areas in Western Tasmania (Zylstra 2016). In Canada, northern ecosystems based on balsam fir, white spruce and white cedar, have no special adaptations to fire, being historically subject to fire only every few centuries. Thus, these forests have difficulty recovering from more frequent burns (Natural Resources Canada 2019). Indeed, frequent burning combined with climate changes is leading to widespread conversion of forests to scrubland in many countries, thus accelerating ecosystem conversions or losing pre-existing ecosystems (Jaffe 2019; Johns 2014; Kitzberger et al. 2017). These land conversions are said to be one of the main reasons for the world's decline of mammals, birds, fish and reptiles by 60% since 1970. The World Wildlife Fund believes that this species decline is now jeopardizing the future of people (WWF 2018).

Social, health and economic impacts

Wildfire can lead to the deaths of residents and firefighters, although the loss of firefighters is less common in countries with more developed firefighting systems. Worldwide, 273 people were killed by wildfires in 2018, with the fires in the USA accounting for 108 fatalities and 100 in Greece (Löw 2019). Despite 27,000 residents being evacuated due to the 2018 Camp Fire, California, 86 people were killed (Löw 2019). The year before, wildfires in Portugal that resulted in 66 deaths were described by the Portuguese Prime Minister as "the greatest tragedy of human lives that we've witnessed in our country in years" (reported in DW 2017). The January 2009 fires in Victoria, Australia, (Black Saturday) led to 173 deaths.

Fire-related injuries and illness are not always counted, yet more people are injured in Australia by wildfires than by all other natural disasters combined (Tomison 2010). The Productivity Commission (2018) in Australia estimates that 3,416 hospitalisations occurred due to direct fire injury in 2015-16, equating to a rate of 14.3 per 100,000 people. Internationally, wildfires are said to indirectly cause 330,000 premature deaths a year (The Economist 2018b). Particulates in the wildfire smoke can exacerbate breathing problems, especially among children, older people and those with asthma (Hamers 2018). This can impact people living considerable distances from the fire, as happened in Nevada and large areas of California. Wildfires in Indonesia regularly result in Malaysia and northern Australia being blanketed in smoke for several months, with a substantial negative impact on respiratory health (Frankenberg, McKee & Thomas 2005). The impact of smoke from wildfires in the UK in 2018, was noted earlier (BBC News 2018b).

Impacts on people also may arise due to psychological stress and trauma (McCaffey et al. 2014). Stress will occur where there are deaths and injuries to family members or neighbours. Disturbed behaviour is more common after a severe fire, where substance abuse, family violence, self-harm, and suicides can rise as much as 8% (Doherty & Clayton 2011). Both children and adults may suffer post-traumatic stress and lingering behavioural issues associated with fear or anxiety. Significant stress may occur with the need to evacuate from dwellings and settlements in the face of a wildfire. Over 50,000 people were evacuated in the 2018 Northern Californian fires (BBC News 2018c). Those in poorer and industrialised countries may not have emergency accommodation available (Paton, Buergelt & Flannigan 2015). Homelessness may turn into a longer-term problem in poorer countries and where people held no housing insurance, in industrialised countries. While positive feelings may arise from inter-personal support offered and an increase in connection with the community, there is a risk that this is short-lived, and disputes may arise about how the fire was managed and post-fire reconstruction. The 2018 Californian fires burnt 1.7 million hectares, necessitating 12,000 people to fight the fires, which in turn lost business and personal time.

As well as people's homes, wildfires can destroy and damage other infrastructure, businesses, and farms. It can affect soil quality through the impact of heat and cover of ash, thus damaging agriculture and food production. While there are said to be substantial knowledge gaps in the understanding of water quality impacts following wildfires, some impacts are known. The major 2009 wildfires in Victoria had the effect of depressing Melbourne's water catchment yield by 20% to 30% for about 30 to 50 years (Skinner, then Managing Director of Melbourne Water, reported by Ker 2009). Rivers and farm dams may develop elevated levels of suspended sediment, nutrients and metals, as well as blooms of cyanobacteria (blue-green algae). These events can eliminate both oxygen and sunlight in freshwater and produce potent toxins, thus threatening water quality in rivers and dams (Smith et al. 2011).

Wildfires can create additional hazards, such as increases in water run-off, flash floods, landslides and mudslides on fire de-vegetated land, causing soil depletion and the water-sediment noted above (Smith et al. 2016). Indeed, an observed pattern (by one of the authors) may occur where exceptionally heavy rainfall follows a wildfire. Very hot, large fires can change local weather conditions, creating storms and lightning (Badlan et al. 2017). Such conditions, described as a firestorm, create intense heat up to 15 kilometres in the air and can trigger thunderstorms and wind conditions that override ground conditions and move the firestorm unpredictably (Badlan et al. 2017; Evans 2019).

Munich Re (in a partial assessment of cost) concluded that the most expensive 'natural' catastrophes in 2018 were the wildfires in California (Löw 2019). The most expensive of these fires was the Camp Fire in northern California (Löw 2019). This fire, together with the Carr Fire in July/August 2018, and the Woolsey fires in November 2018, resulted in losses of US$24 billion, insurance covering 75% of this loss. Balch and colleagues (2017) place the accrued direct and indirect impacts of wildfire on infrastructure and communities as possibly US$60 billion.

Possibly the most comprehensive assessment of loss from wildfire in Australia has been undertaken by the consultancy firm, Deloitte Access Economics (2016) in relation to the 2009 Black Saturday wildfires in Victoria. Black Saturday describes a series of about 400 wildfires, many of which joined together, that occurred between the 5th and 9th February 2009. The fires proved a landmark in Australia's response to fires, with the death of 173 people; 2,029 homes lost, 61 businesses, 5 schools and a number of small towns lost, as well as 400,000 hectares of land burnt, much on the interface between rural and urban landscape.

Deloitte Access Economics took the unusual step of estimating the social costs, said to be AUD$3.9 billion. This included death, physical injury and disability, mental health, alcohol misuse, ill-health including chronic disease, family violence and relationship breakdown. They also included crimes (apart from looting directly after the fire), loss of pets, social dislocation and loss of energy and communication networks, loss of heritage and culture, and on-going social costs. Deloitte found that the long-term costs of natural disasters may be under-estimated by over 50%. However, as Deloitte omitted some shorter-term costs in their calculations, the authors of this book suggest that the under-estimation is likely to be more than 50%. The cost of disaster recovery relating to government and community infrastructure, as well as personal donations of time and money, appear excluded in the calculations. National Economics (NIEIR 2014) have modelled the adverse impact of wildfire on local economies and investment decisions, based on a Black Saturday fire that had a severe impact on a Victorian township.

Fighting fires also incurs considerable costs. In 2015, the US Department of Agriculture, responsible for wildfire in the USA, was spending 50% of the budget on wildfire suppressions. This necessitated a transfer of funds from other programs, such as recreation and the economical use of forests (US Department of Agriculture 2015). Suppression of wildfires in 2017 was said to again exceed available funding (US Department of Agriculture 2019), Bach and colleagues (2017) estimating it to be US$2 billion. Congress in March 2018 decreed that fighting fires would not mean restrictions in prevention, maintenance and restoration costs, although President Trump felt that the suppression expenses were due to the mismanagement of forests (Holpuch & Anguiano 2018; The Economist 2018c).

The Country Fire Authority (CFA), the rural fire service in Victoria, had 2,507 paid staff, 35,263 operational volunteers and 18,821 volunteer support staff in 2017, supported by total assets of approximately $A1.5 billion (CFA 2017). Public servants from the Victorian Departments of Environment, Land, Water and Planning (DELWP) and Parks Victoria, also engage in fire management. The Victorian Police undertakes investigative and surveillance work of those suspected of fire lighting as well as emergency response work during a wildfire. As noted in the media reports, discussed in this chapter, severe fires are also fought by the military and police in many parts of the world.

In 2016-17, for Australia as a whole, fire service organisations attended a total of 394,054 emergency incidents, of which about one-quarter were fire event incidents (Productivity Commission 2018). Associated organisations with emergency responsibilities attended a total of 77,832 incidents (this figure excludes Queensland), of which approximately 20% were fire-related. This data excludes the other fire-related activities undertaken by fire and related services, such as prescribed burning, education and training. 20,008 full-time equivalent paid personnel were employed by fire service organisations, of which 77% were paid firefighters, and 152,883 were volunteers (Productivity Commission 2018). While paid firefighter personnel numbers increased very slightly in the year to 2016-17, volunteer numbers decreased more than the increase in paid staff. Estimates undertaken by National Economics suggest that the number of firefighters overall needs to double by 2030 in order to keep pace with climate change (NIEIR 2013).

Wildfire ignition

A repeated perspective covered in this book is the need to clearly define terms, especially in relation to wildfire 'ignition' and wildfire 'spread'. Ignition refers to the start or point of combustion of a fire. For combustion to take place, a source of heat (such as a lit match), oxygen and fuel are needed. Thus, ignition occurs when a source of heat (which can include embers or flames) is applied to fuel that has air around it. The major supplier of heat is through direct or indirect human behaviour. Spontaneous combustion, or material catching fire through the creation of heat, rather than an external agent, is rare, although not unknown. It can occur with coal, grain stores, oily rags, garbage, compost and fermentation in some products.

Once ignition has occurred, the spread of a fire is determined by the amount, dryness and continuity of fuel; the local weather conditions; geographical features, such as the steepness and direction of slopes; current and past land-use practices; and features of suppression, such as response time, equipment and approach taken by firefighters. Fuel and weather are interconnected, with various views on their relative importance. High temperatures, especially where associated with strong winds and a lack of rainfall, can create the conditions for a wildfire to be more ferocious, travel faster and cover a much larger area of land (Bradstock et al. 2014). The interface between weather and fuel is complex. A good rainfall season can encourage vegetation growth, which may, in turn, increase the risk of a fire spreading in subsequent years if the weather is hot and dry, and especially if there are also strong winds. At the same time, rainfall and moisture reduce the chance of wildfire ignition in the short term. Coen, Stavros and Fites-Kaufman (2018) have modelled very localised impacts of wind and weather conditions created by the fire itself, such as lowering air pressure causing winds stronger than official measurements taken nearby. They argue that such conditions may have a bigger impact on fire on some slopes than fuel reduction strategies.

A person with positive or negative intentions may directly ignite a wildfire. The consequences of this action may result in positive or negative outcomes for the firelighter, other members of society, and the environment. For example, a fire may be lit with the intention of reducing a fuel load so a subsequent wildfire may be less severe. Alternatively, a person may wish to impress peers by participating in delinquent activities, such as setting alight a dumped car, the fire travelling to adjacent vegetation, creating a wildfire. Neither may necessarily wish to cause a large and dangerous wildfire. A wildfire may also be lit indirectly and unmaliciously by the use of machinery that sparks, or by leaving an outdoor cooking fire unattended. Lightning strikes may cause a wildfire. Burning embers may blow from a wildfire and start a fire in a new location.

The official record of a wildfire might state the source of ignition of a fire. Although this may change if the fire is directly investigated, the official record is not always amended. Often, official records have a large 'unknown' category. The media may make suggestions about the cause of the fire, and again this tends not to be corrected if subsequently found to be different. Some uncertainty about the cause can be seen in the examples of wildfires outlined earlier in this chapter. In Sweden, the media reports that several of the 2018 fires were started by people illegally using disposable barbeques (bans on use were in place due to the weather conditions). Other suggestions were that the wildfires were started by lightning strikes. A damaged cable at a utility pole reportedly started the 2018 wildfire in eastern Attica, Greece. There were said to be strong indications that arson was the cause for the 2018 fires in Kineta and Penteli, in Greece[3]. In the UK, a 22-year-old man was arrested in connection to the moorland fire at Winter Hill; several people were seen lighting fires close by (BBC News 2018c). The Barnsley fire in South Yorkshire, UK, was thought to be deliberately lit, as was the Saddleworth Moore fire, as people were seen lighting fires shortly before the fire broke out (BBC News 2018c; Cox 2018; Lewis 2018). In the USA, a 51-year-old male was arrested and charged with two counts of arson in Orange County, California, the fire resulting in the evacuation of 20,000 residents (Robinson 2018). As of mid-2018, the causes of the large 2015 and 2017 fires in California have not been determined (Atleework 2018).

While these fires are reported in the media, other wildfires receive less attention as they occur regularly, perhaps every year over the past few decades, and are often outside the major industrialised countries. Such fires can be ascertained through NASA's real-time satellite data. In Indonesia, 11,254 fires were recorded over a week in August 2018 (Global Forest Watch Fires 2018). While it is illegal to set fires to clear land in Indonesia, the practice is common, with 99% of fires in Sumatra and Kalimantan said to be deliberately lit (NASA Earth Observatory 2014). Over the same week, there were 164,919 fires in the Democratic Republic of Congo, and 109,137 in Zambia (Global Forest Watch Fires 2018). Although the numbers and extent of these fires far outstrip those reported in Europe and North America, they tend to be largely overlooked in the media and academia in the western world.

Internationally, it is reported that most wildfires occur as a result of human activity. The exact proportion varies for many reasons, particularly due to the lack of a rigorous investigation of the cause of many fires. Lovreglio and colleagues (2010) reports that the Food and Agricultural Organisation Fire Management and Global Assessment 2006 Report estimates that the Mediterranean region accounts for the largest proportion of human-caused fires in the world (95%) followed by South Asia (90%), South America (85%) and Northeast Asia (80%). A study published in the Proceedings of the National Academies of Science found that humans cause 84% of wildfires in the USA, whether igniting directly or indirectly (Balch et al. 2017). Wildfires started by human activity, in the context of dangerous fire conditions have tripled the length of the fire season, burning an area seven times greater than that affected by lightning fires, and being responsible for nearly half of all area burnt. The causes of ignition are considered further in chapter 2.

---

[3] Stergiou 2018 Wikipedia referring to a Greek newspaper, 26 July 2018.

The compounding factors that raise the risk of wildfire after ignition

As noted above, wildfires are now occurring more frequently, along with adverse impacts. Research suggests that much of western USA will experience an increase in the area of land burnt, with greater severity, over the next 30 years (King 2017; Kitzberger et al. 2017; Stambaugh et al. 2018). There is likely to be a number of causes for this. If the proportion of people who light fires remains unchanged, then the numbers of fire lighters would increase with population growth. At the same time, under the influence of climate change, the chances of a successful ignition of wildfire and the risk of it becoming large, greatly increase. These are all complex issues that make fire prediction very difficult under our present state of knowledge (Bradstock et al. 2014; Pausas & Fernández-Muñoz 2012). The fire risk is also exacerbated by inadequate prevention responses. The present approach to the prevention of fire lighting can be summarised "as small in scale, uncoordinated, lacking a comprehensive approach and rarely evaluated" (Stanley & Read 2016, p.153).

Climate change influences on wildfire

It's hard to know where to start with a discussion on climate change. The science is clear and unequivocal, and evidence is available that climate change now plays a role in every extreme heat event. Yet an adequate response to this knowledge is not occurring (Lewis & Perkins-Kirkpatrick 2018). Given the current climate change policies, the world is on track to have a temperature rise of 3.1°C to 3.7°C by 2100 (Climate Action Tracker 2018). However, a recent publication by the Potsdam Institute reports that even if the carbon emission reductions called for in the COP21[4] are met there is still a risk of the planet entering 'Hothouse Earth' conditions (Steffen et al. 2018). A Hothouse Earth climate will, in the long term, stabilize at a global average of 4°C to 5°C higher than pre-industrial temperatures. December 2018 and January 2019 were Australia's hottest-ever months on record, and low rainfall levels have continued through 2019 for many states (Bureau of Meteorology 2019). Tasmania had its driest January on record, with destructive wildfires (World Meteorological Organization 2018). These severe impacts have occurred at the low end of the predicted temperature rise.

Work by Weitzman (2010, 2012) queries whether it is wise to only view temperature rises in averages, noting that a central factor of any credible economic analysis of climate change has to be its extreme uncertainty.

---

[4] COP21 is a United Nations agreement to reduce greenhouse gas emissions, adopted in December 2015 and ratified by 185 countries in January 2019.

Weitzman argues that it is important to know the shape of probabilities under a distribution curve. Both known risks, and also unknown risks, need to be taken into account. However, the shape of this probability curve of temperature rises is uncertain.

Weitzman's work has shown that as the temperature rises, the fatness of the upper limit tail of the probability curve increases, so the known risk of moving to even higher temperatures increases. An example of the implication of this is as follows. If the tail of the normal curve is fat, at 408.71 parts per million (ppm) of greenhouse gasses (GHGs) (as present at August 2018), then there is a 0.9% chance of the temperature rising to 6°C or more. At the current trend of the temperature rising to 3°C, then the probability of the temperature rising to 6°C or more if the tail is fat, is 6%. At 4°C, there is a 14% to 15% chance of reaching 6°C, whatever the size of the tail. While this work is debated, Weitzman is not the only eminent climate scientist to point out the uncertainty of currently used climate models. They argue that they underestimate the social and economic costs of climate change and the value of decarbonisation (Roberts 2018). This problem can be recognised with the failure to fully account for the costs of wildfires, as noted earlier in this chapter.

Unfortunately, the extent of this potentially catastrophic risk is not recognised by some countries where politicians are not providing adequate policy to reduce GHG emissions. While most countries have signed on to the agreement to meet lower emission targets, this total is insufficient, and action on the ground is often limited. In particular, the USA and Australia could be described as two outlier countries in relation to their attitude to climate change. President Trump exclaimed that: "We love beautiful, clean West Virginia coal" and Prime Minister Morrison, brought and stroked a lump of coal in Parliament in 2017. Morrison's second but one predecessor, Abbott, claimed that climate change is "absolute crap", likening it to killing goats to appease a volcano god (Secombe 2018, p.10).

While the USA has withdrawn from the Paris agreement and is reversing emission reduction policies, Australia tenuously holds onto the Paris agreement but fails to put in place policies to achieve it (Wentz 2018). During the peak of the Californian wildfires in August 2018, President Trump tweeted that the fires were being made worse by bad environmental laws leading to a lack of water to fight fires, a situation strongly refuted, with climate change clarified by fire experts as the reason for the severe fires (Robinson 2018). California had experienced its hottest single month in 124 years of recordkeeping, preceded by a four-year drought. The Re-insurer, Munich Re, places climate change as the cause of the extreme Californian wildfires in 2017 and 2018 (Löw 2019). Australia has similarly experienced many years of severe drought.

Australia is not on track to achieve its modest emission target of a 26–28% reduction below 2005 levels by 2030, which was committed to in Paris and ratified on 6 November 2016. Indeed, Australia's emissions continue to grow under a vacuum of emissions policies (Climate Action Tracker 2018). On the 24 August 2018, right-wing factions and climate deniers within his own Conservative Party removed the sitting Australian Prime Minister, Malcolm Turnbull. While this political destruction was underway, questions were being asked about drought-stricken farmers struggling to keep their animals alive, supported by government handouts of $A1.8 billion (Seccombe 2018). In a survey of 1,300 farmers, 90% said they were concerned about the damage done to the climate, 88% saying they wanted their political representatives to do more about climate, and 85% expressing some level of concern about the increased risk of wildfire (Farmers for Climate Action 2016). Seccombe notes that while Parliament House smelled Turnbull's blood, "elsewhere in the country, people smelled other things: dust and death and smoke" (Seccombe 2018, p.4). That day, some 70 fires were burning in New South Wales in the middle of winter. The entire state was officially in drought. A total fire ban had been imposed, the earliest declaration ever.

The climate/wildfire system

The occurrence and severity of wildfires increase with the effect of climate change, while at the same time, the wildfire itself increases the risks of climate change. Increasing temperatures, along with more frequent and severe droughts and associated conditions, are increasing the risk of wildfires, particularly in the southwest and southeast of Australia (Hughes & Fenwick 2016). Higher temperatures increase evapotranspiration, reducing moisture on the ground and in vegetation, increases lightning activity and lengthens the fire season (Paton, Buergelt & Flannigan 2015). Yet the increase in numbers and intensity of wildfires has grown significantly even on the passage up to the current global average temperature rise of 1°C in 2018 (with a margin of error of ±0.13°C), above the pre-industrial baseline (1850-1900) (World Meteorological Organization 2018). If global temperatures reached 3°C above pre-industrial levels, the area burnt in southern Europe would double in size. In California, the average fire season is 84 days longer than it was in the 1970s. Without climate change, only half as much land would have burnt between 1984 and 2015 (The Economist 2018b & c). Wildfires were said to have abruptly increased in western USA forests in the mid-1980s, due to warming and earlier spring snowmelt and an associated reduction in moisture levels (Westerling 2016).

Wildfires emit greenhouse gases, including carbon dioxide, nitrous oxide and carbon monoxide. Two large fires in the Australian Alps in 2003 and

2006/7 were found to result in the emission of 132 million tonnes of carbon dioxide (Bowman & Murphy 2015), the equivalent of about a quarter of Australia's annual emissions for 2003. The US Department of the Interior (2018) reports the 2018 wildfire season in Californian is estimated to have released 68 million tons of carbon dioxide, about 15% of California's total annual emissions, or enough CO2 to endanger the state's progress toward meeting its greenhouse gas reduction targets (Berwyn 2018). International forest destruction accounts for about 17% of emissions, roughly the same as all forms of international transport (The Prince's Rainforest Project 2009). Emissions from tropical forest clearing may be responsible for 20% to 60% of fossil fuel burning emissions (Crutzen & Andeae 1990 reported by Ekayani 2011). As the world's largest tropical rainforest, the Amazon plays a vital role in mitigating climate change by absorbing and storing carbon dioxide. When cut or burnt, the forest not only ceases to fulfil this function but also releases back into the atmosphere the carbon dioxide it had previously stored. Sixty percent of the Amazon is located within Brazil, and deforestation accounts for nearly half of the country's GHG emissions, according to government data.

However, the exact amount of emissions from wildfires is complex, resulting in variable estimates. For example, mega-fires may increase overall emissions, as emissions from decomposing dead wood often greatly surpass the direct emissions of the fire itself. Growing trees use carbon dioxide. Aerosols from wildfires have short term cooling impacts, but particulates from fires can increase ice-melt (Berwyn 2018; CBC radio Canada 2018). The usefulness of prescribed burning as a tool to reduce the size of wildfires and thereby, carbon emissions, is questioned by some researchers in both Australia and the US (Bowman et al. 2013). These issues are discussed further in chapter 8.

At the same time, tropical forests can store up to 10% of annual emissions; storage capacity lost when the forest is destroyed. A recent report from the United Nations, drawn from some 7,000 scientific papers, found that in order to keep global warming under 2°C a significant reduction in land sector emissions is needed. These emissions come from agriculture, forestry and land clearing (Howden 2019). The report states that all land-based ecosystems, including agricultural land, forests and wetlands, absorb about 22% of carbon emissions. Thus, fire in rural and forested areas that degrades land and risks changing the water, moisture and evaporation systems, is a circular occurrence that both arise from climate change and also promotes climate change. Fire damage that also contributes to the growth of drought in drylands has increased by 40% since 1961 (Howden 2019).

Population growth

The current world population of 7.6 billion is expected to reach 8.6 billion in 2030, 9.8 billion in 2050 and 11.2 billion in 2100 (United Nations Department of Economic and Social Affairs 2017). This equates to about 83 million people being added to the world's population every year. The greatest growth is occurring in the poorest countries. This trend in population size is expected to continue, even assuming that fertility levels will continue to decline, as the life expectancy is increasing.

As noted earlier, one implication of this is that if it is assumed, as noted earlier, that the proportion of the population of people who light fires, directly or indirectly, is constant, then the supply of firelighters will increase as the population grows. However, as discussed in chapter 3, disadvantage increases the risk of malicious fires. Inequality within countries has been rising since 1980 (Dervis & Qureshi 2016). For example, the average income of the richest 10% of the population is about nine times that of the poorest 10% across the OECD, up a multiple of seven just 25 years ago. Dervis and Qureshi argue that the sharply rising inequality within many countries and the shrinkage of the middle class in advanced economies are of great concern. There are other concerns about trends that may increase the occurrence of wildfire. For example, the 'historic' levels of migration experienced by many countries, as is the case in Australia, may also be raising the risk of wildfire (OECD, IOM & UNHCR 2018, p.5). New migrants may bring their old experiences and habits into their new country. Leaving campfires unattended, burning rubbish, and being unaware of fire regulations, may lead to wildfire in high-risk fire locations, as is anecdotally reported as being the case in Victoria.

Urban Planning for population growth

An outcome of this population growth, in many countries, is an increasing footprint of cities and urban settlements. Increasing sprawl may penetrate into forested and/or grassland areas, where many wildfires are ignited. Urban planning has allowed this development in many parts of the world, rather than accommodating increasing population through greater urban density sufficient to accommodate the growing population. However, some cities, such as Vancouver, Canada, have managed to densify the central and middle parts of the city to better absorb population increases. Other pressures are facilitating this sprawl. One example of this is the need to raise finance to support the supply of services in new housing developments on the urban edge. This has led to increased housing approvals to enable local government to increase their rates or tax revenue (The Economist 2018c). The pressures of post-wildfire reconstruction of housing have at times, led to waived building rules. Houses have been allowed to be constructed closer together and with narrower streets in fire-prone locations, leading to greater access difficulties in firefighting and risk of embers moving from one house to the next (Gonzalez-Mathiesen, March & Stanley 2019). Thus internationally, urban and land-use planning has not responded sufficiently to the many increasing pressures of population growth and climate change and the associated challenges of wildfire in countries with high wildfire risks (The Economist 2018c). Since 1990, 60% of new homes in California, Washington and Oregon, have been built in locations abutting natural areas. Thus in 2017, 28% of houses in California were deemed to be at high or extreme risk of wildfire (Irfan 2018a; Löw 2019). In Victoria and NSW, many of the urban sprawl suburbs on the cities' edges have extensive lags in infrastructure provisions, such that employment opportunities and public transport are scant (Brain, Stanley & Stanley 2018). The mix of social exclusion and high levels of youth unemployment, together with urban penetration into fire-prone areas is potentially a volatile combination for maliciously lit wildfires, an issue discussed further in chapter 4 (Stanley 2020). Youth is the largest group of people who light fires (Tomison 2010). High levels of youth unemployment can be found in many countries experiencing wildfires. In May 2019, youth unemployment levels in Greece were 40.4%, in Spain, 31.7% and in Italy, 30.5% (Statista 2019). Disillusionment, disadvantage and boredom create a ripe breeding ground for fire lighting.

The failure to address prevention of wildfire

How prevention is understood

The physical characteristics of wildfire, particularly through the use of fire behaviour and spread models, has been available in the United States, Canada, Australia, Spain, Greece since the 1950s and 60s (Lovreglio et al. 2010). In contrast, preventing ignition in the first place is largely overlooked. Few resources are allocated to improve understanding of the drivers of wildfire ignition, or for action to prevent ignition (Lovreglio et al. 2010; Stanley & Read 2013). The term 'prevention' is sometimes used in relation to wildfire but tends to be variously understood. Preference is given to use of the term 'mitigation', again usually not defined and also used inconsistently. Coughlan and Petty (2012) make two very important links that are emphasised in this book. They talk about two aspects of the role of human activity in wildfires, firstly as a source of ignition of wildfire (thus prevention of ignition), and secondly in relation to the determination of the severity, frequency, extent and intensity of wildfires worldwide (thus mitigation or preventing the fire becoming larger). It is important to make this distinction clear, as the authors of this book believe it is leading to many lost opportunities to reduce the number of wildfires.

Language is powerful, encompassing how issues are defined, attitudes, values and behaviours (Saunders 2017). Such context prescribes how people should regard and respond to the ideas (Hartley 1982). Different words create different ideas and suggest different approaches. Other wildfire-related words are also defining how issues should be viewed. An example is where forests are often narrowly described as 'fuel loads', rather than complex ecosystems that support many species and have widely different flammability dynamics and dependency on fires (Zylstra 2017). 'Fuel loads' suggest forest are uniformly dangerous and provide "a single answer to every question of fire risk reduction" (Zylstra 2017, p.26).

The Sendai Risk Reduction Framework report, developed by the United Nations Office for Disaster Risk Reduction, mentions prevention but has a preference for the notion of risk reduction for all 'natural' hazards (UNISDR 2015). Disaster risk is seen as encompassing "vulnerability, capacity, exposure of persons and assets, hazard characteristics and the environment" (UNISDR 2015, p.14). The report goes on to say that this knowledge can be used for the purpose of pre-disaster risk assessment, for prevention (almost not discussed further) and mitigation, preparedness, and in response to disasters.

The Australian Productivity Commission Inquiry Report (Productivity Commission 2015) on all 'natural' hazards, talks a lot about mitigation, but again doesn't define the term. A submission to the Inquiry talked about mitigation in terms of preparedness, education and awareness programs. The National Institute of Building Sciences in the USA (2017) has studied the cost/benefits of pre-disaster mitigation. It refers to this work as preparing in advance for future hazardous events, to better assure that the event will have a shorter life and more manageable outcomes. The report largely refers to building regulations to improve the building's durability. European literature adopts a similar perspective, where "measures and policies aiming actually at enhancing preparedness are labelled as prevention" (Sapountzaki et al. 2011, p.1470). Sapountzaki and colleagues (2011) note that while prevention is widely acknowledged as the first priority in risk management, most agencies responsible for risk management focus on emergency planning rather than prevention, a situation particularly true in Italy and Greece. This omission is also evidenced on an international basis through the use of short-term horizons and limited funds allocated to prevention, in comparison to funds directed to the suppression of the fire and the amount of discussion on risk management and mitigation.

Wildfires that are maliciously lit have been largely overlooked in conversations about the prevention of ignition. Muller (2009a) suggests that the ignition of many fires that have been deliberately lit may be preventable, using knowledge about the prevention of other crimes. Three components are generally understood as comprising a *crime triangle*: a motivated offender, a suitable target, and the absence of a capable guardian (Muller 2009a). The suitability of this approach is raised further in later chapters of this book. While prevention offers a hope that a potential disaster can be avoided, part of the problem is that prevention isn't emotional, visual or flamboyant, and prevention success is very hard to measure (Henkey 2018; Stanley 2013). How do we know that what hasn't occurred was prevented by the quiet, background work that addressed the causes of the ignition of fire? Despite this difficulty, preventing a fire occurring in the first place is an area that the authors suggest is highly important if wildfire incidences are not going to continually increase over time.

Henkey (2018) offers some hope, reporting that there is increasing interest in the prevention phase of wildfire, with the US Department of Homeland Security and the Federal Emergency Management Agency increasingly placing prevention on equal footing with other areas of emergency management – planning, response and recovery. However, closer investigation of the report suggests that this interest still sits with preventing the wildfire from becoming large, with emphasis on the protection of critical assets, such as transportation, and food and agricultural sectors. This is not to say that there is no attention given to the prevention of ignition, which occurs mainly in the form of surveillance of those suspected to be a firelighter.

Some confusion is present with other wildfire-related concepts. There is a current trend for research and policy application on natural hazards to centre around the concept of resilience. "Despite this contested academic discourse, resilience is increasingly the foundation of public policies and programmes in natural hazard and disaster management" (Parsons et al. 2016, p. 1). Parsons and colleagues believe that this resilience perspective is here to stay. However, the wide predominance of this concept has probably reduced the space for other aspects, such as prevention. While the term 'resilience' (again) has many meanings, Parsons and colleagues argue that it refers to the capacity of communities to prepare for, and recover from, natural hazard events, as well as the capacities of communities to learn, adapt and transform towards resilience. Thus, these issues assume a 'natural' event will take place, that is, it skips over prevention, and it could be argued, acts as a diversion. The resilience term also tends to generalise, such as commonly overlooking equity issues in its application. While talking about resilient communities, it places responsibility on individual coping capacities, even where resource distribution is unequal.

There is a prevailing view that wildfires are a 'natural' event, with the connected assumption that ignition cannot be stopped, even although the great majority of wildfires are caused by humans (Lovreglio et al. 2010). This situation is not aided by the fact that the cause of most wildfires is not comprehensively investigated. Given that only one in five wildfires is reported in Australia (a similar ratio that is likely to be repeated in other countries), and not all reported fires are investigated, it is hard to get an accurate picture of the importance of different causes of ignition. Investigative priority is usually given to the larger and more dangerous wildfires, although the outcome of a wildfire, is not directly related to the ignition source. Often the evidence as to the cause is difficult to ascertain; thus, the cause may be classified as unknown or the most likely cause documented. Data handling can obscure ignition causes. The information recorded in a data set is likely to be collected by many different people; thus, the use of categories of data may not be consistent, data may not be updated when new information comes to hand, and the data may not be shared between relevant authorities. While this situation is not helped by difficult and complex wildfire situations (Muller 2009b), this approach has little changed since it was recognised in Australia ten years ago. Data management is discussed further in chapters 2 and 9.

There are many conditions related to wildfire ignitions that encompass human behaviour and government policies. They bring in a wide range of prevention possibilities, most, it is argued, under-utilised. Where these options are put in place, they remain largely unrecorded and not evaluated for effectiveness and utility. This book aims to expand the suite of prevention options, recommending integration of policies and processes to achieve a comprehensive and inclusive approach that covers the broad aspects of wildfire.

What is spent on prevention?

The costs associated with prevention do not appear to be available, although there is some work on the costs of mitigation. According to the Productivity Commission (2015) in Australia, governments over-invest in post-disaster reconstruction and under-invest in mitigation. Thus, natural disaster costs have become a growing, unfunded liability for governments. Between 2009–10 and 2012–13, $A11 billion was spent in Australia on recovery from all disasters, while $A225 million was spent on mitigation (Productivity Commission 2015). The Commission recommends that the Federal government increase allocations for mitigation to each Australian state, from $A26 million to $A200 million a year, this figure is matched by the states. The Australian Business Roundtable recommends a $A250 million annual fund (Gough 2018). It should be noted that the Productivity Commission and the Australian Business Roundtable are referring to all 'natural disasters', not only wildfires. The mitigation being referred to is in the categories of preventing the size and impact of natural disasters through National Emergency Management projects and programs relating to volunteer support, education, research and infrastructure investment. Neither prevention in terms of addressing climate change, or stopping ignition, is mentioned, critical oversights.

The California Department of Forestry and Fire Protection spent $US3.8 billion fighting fires in 2018 in California state, more than it spent in the previous 30 years combined (The Economist 2018c). In the USA, the National Institute of Building Sciences (2018) found that mitigation grants by the Federal Government saved about $US4 for every $US1 spent to protect from wildfire. However, the mitigation referred to relates to building codes in structural planning regulations. Work by one of the authors found that adherence to new post-2009 Black Saturday building regulations in Victoria resulted in a fourfold increase in survival rates when compared to older houses built prior to the new regulations (Holland et al. 2013).

Too many fires to extinguish

The world appears to be totally unprepared for the increase in the number and intensity of wildfires and the implications of this paradigm change. By way of example, some years ago, the Australian research institute, NIEIR, was commissioned by the United Firefighters Union of Australia to undertake an estimate of the future need for firefighters in paid employment in Australia (NIEIR 2013). The job was difficult for a number of reasons, one of which was the inconsistencies present in the data on the number of firefighters in Australia. For example, in Victoria, the Productivity Commission data (SCRGSP 2012) and the Census data (ABS 2013) were different by more than half. The poor collection of wildfire data is a theme that will be repeatedly returned to in this book. The research revealed that over half (52% of 547) of the Local Government Areas in Australia don't have an employed firefighter associated with a fire brigade or government. The growth rate of employment of all sources of firefighters nationally, from 2006-07 to 2010-11, was less than 2.4%, although this may have changed in subsequent years. Based on population growth (lives that need protection) and property assets growth, NIEIR found that the total number of employed firefighters will need to increase by approximately 50% by 2030. The rate of recruitment suggests that capacity is diminishing rather than increasing. Accounting for climate change, on top of population increase, Australia would need an extra 3,566 to 4,350 professional firefighters in 2020, and 8,095 to 10,024 by 2030, on a baseline of 2012. These calculations relate to wildfire only, not the 'all-hazards' and emergency response approach increasingly being undertaken by traditional firefighters.

It would seem that Australia is not the only country experiencing problems around fire suppression. As noted earlier, there was a need to draw on other people to fight many of the 2018 fires in some countries, such as the army and prisoners. A reduction of firefighter numbers in Spain, in 2012, due to cost, coincided with the worst forest fires for a decade (Salvador 2016). Given the extent of wildfires and the extensive, and growing costs incurred, the authors of this book suggest that while increasing firefighting operations will always be required, greater investment in the prevention of ignition could reduce the total costs of wildfires and is vital in wildfire management. The Australian Productivity Commission notes that the "current government natural disaster funding arrangements are not efficient, equitable or sustainable. They are prone to cost shifting, ad hoc responses and short-term political opportunism… Governments overinvest in post-disaster reconstruction and underinvest in mitigation… As such, natural disaster costs have become a growing, unfunded liability for governments" (Productivity Commission 2015, p.2).

The book contents

This book largely focuses on the prevention of ignition, particularly linking the issue of deliberate lighting of wildfire with what is commonly perceived to be mainstream wildfire issues: planning, preparation, mitigation, suppression and recovery. The book argues that a more comprehensive approach to the prevention of wildfire that includes a better understanding of ignition is likely to produce an improved outcome for society and the environment. However, this will not be sufficient of itself, as attention is also urgently needed to the underlying drivers of fire: climate change, population growth, and improved urban planning that dovetails with the emergency services approach.

While the book content overviews an international perspective (as far as material is available), there is an emphasis on the situation in the state of Victoria, Australia. There are a number of reasons for this. Victoria is said by some to be the most vulnerable part of the most fire-vulnerable continent in the world; therefore, it is vital to adopt best practice (Buxton et al. 2011; Gill, Stephens & Cary 2013). Every country has its specific understanding and approach to wildfire. Also, as in Australia, each state or government division within a country usually has its own localised approach. This book aims to give an overarching perspective that links many issues rather than presenting detailed variations present in many countries. Besides, the authors live in Victoria, thus seek to take advantage of a deeper localised knowledge!

A word of caution is expressed in relation to this book. As noted, the field of prevention of wildfires has not been comprehensively addressed. Research is scant and is rarely subject to a systematic and comprehensive approach to understanding the field. There is a more recent growth in academic interest in the broad area of wildfires, especially in relation to the response. Many of the works on wildfire are a decade or more old and, even if only a few years old, given the rapid change in climatic conditions, population growth and urbanisation, there is a risk that they may not reflect the current or future situations. This said, important issues were explored in early research, some of which have not had recent development, so this older literature should not be overlooked.

This book is divided into three sections. Section one (chapters 1 to 4) overviews specific issues in relation to wildfire that are important to understand if the prevention of wildfire is to be successful. Chapter 2 explores what is currently understood as the causes of ignition. Chapter 3 looks at the issue of wildfire arson, while chapter 4 examines the patterns around location and time that are associated with wildfire events. Section two (chapters 5 to 9) addresses prevention in more detail. Chapter 5 overviews the current approaches to prevention and raises a discussion of the broad areas of knowledge and responses associated with prevention. Chapter 6 gives a case-study of the role and place of local government in Victoria in relation to wildfire. Chapter 7 talks about the role and place of community in preventing wildfire. Chapter 8 explores the impact of wildfire on the environment, and chapter 9 examines the current shortcomings of officially collected wildfire data. Section 3 consists of two chapters. Chapter 10 sets out a broad overview of the position and role of prevention, while chapter 11 offers more detail on possible prevention projects and programs.

Chapter 2

Why do wildfires happen?

Introduction

Lovreglio et al. (2010) succinctly directs us to the problem of our limited knowledge about wildfire ignition with two quotes: "It is next to impossible to design specific fire prevention campaigns if one cannot identify the causes of wildfires in a systematic way" (FAO 1999 reported in Lovreglio et al. 2010, p.8). And again: "Until our ability to determine the causes of forest fires improves, our efforts at prevention will essentially remain shots in the dark" (Environment Policy 2003, reported in Lovreglio et al. 2010, p.8).

While chapter one provided an overview of the various causes of ignition of wildfires, this chapter offers a more comprehensive appraisal of the causes of ignition. It examines how each cause is generally perceived, as well as some of the context and issues about the ignition source. The chapter starts with an overview of some of the complications around understanding the causes of ignition. It revisits the discussion about how fire is perceived, introduced in chapter 1. This is followed by a discussion of which ignition causes are recorded, defined and classified. It illustrates how the lack of standardisation in datasets, both within and between countries, is holding back understanding about ignition and thus the prevention of ignition.

Overview of ignition

Internationally, wildfires are differentially viewed. While some countries don't yet have a wildfire data collection system, those that do commonly only record where wildfire is ignited in particular ways. The reliability of this record also varies, with a large disparity in the percentage of wildfires investigated to ascertain (where possible) the cause of ignition. This appears to be a common problem arising in many countries, as is the recording of wildfires. For example, the collation of fire situation reports in the USA found 71,499 reports on individual wildfires in 2017 and 58,083 in 2018. However, the number of wildfires that occurred does not appear to be available (National Interagency Fire Centre 2019). This is especially concerning given the recent occurrence of catastrophic fires, unprecedented for their deep and long-lasting social, economic, and environmental impacts. Chapter 9 also offers further discussion on the difficulties the field has in recording wildfire data.

As noted in chapter one, there is a strong belief that wildfire is a 'natural event' that cannot be stopped. For example, the final report of the Inquiry into Fire Season Preparedness in Victoria noted that: "It has been made clear throughout the inquiry that bushfire is not a preventable natural phenomenon. It is part of the Australian landscape" (Parliament of Victoria 2017, p. 2). This chapter seeks to raise evidence to counter this belief. It argues that it is not helpful to describe wildfire as a 'natural' phenomenon, as the implication is that nothing can be done to prevent wildfire, as stated in the above Inquiry Report. Back in 2010, this issue was raised by Lovreglio and colleagues. The authors were 'surprised' that wildfires are still considered as natural hazards, even by some authoritative sources, such as NASA and in official documents of the European Union. The authors note that: "Forest fires are neither a natural occurrence nor a natural disaster, with the exception of those fires started by natural agents. They are, on the contrary, an anthropogenic phenomenon which exclusively and directly depends on social behavior" (Lovreglio et al. 2015, p.8). Daniel Calleja Crespo, Director-General for Environment to the European Commission, said in the foreword to the report, Forest fires in Europe, Middle East and North Africa 2017: "In the vast majority of the cases, it is human intervention that ignites fires, which, under extreme weather conditions spread uncontrollably. …Fire prevention is thus key in tackling wildfires" (San-Miguel-Ayanz et al. 2018, p.6). However, despite this statement, the report appears to narrowly view preventative measures. It cites activities such as forest thinning, grazing, and planting climate-resilient species to create diversified forests, with no mention back to human activities.

While many North American and Australian ecosystems evolved under the influence of fire, the current wildfire regimes are a very different phenomenon (US National Park Service 2017). Past wildfires rarely burnt all vegetation; instead, they left a mosaic pattern of burnt and unburnt patches across the landscape. This offered new growth, nesting sites and additional food sources from insects colonising dead wood. Historical records of Australian Indigenous people reveal that they used fire to encourage the growth of grass to attract kangaroos to enable them to be speared for food (Gammage 2012). Early white settlers recorded that these fires were low heat, out by the next day, and left unburnt patches.

There are a number of ways that a wildfire can start. Balch et al. (2017) examined 1.5 million USA government records, from 1992 to 2012, of wildfires that were extinguished or managed by state or federal agencies, excluding prescribed burns and managed agriculture burns. This data recorded that: "Human-started wildfires accounted for 84% of all wildfires, tripled the length of the fire season, dominated an area seven times greater than that affected by lightning fires, and were responsible for nearly half of all area burned.

National and regional policy efforts to mitigate wildfire-related hazards would benefit from focusing on reducing the human expansion of the fire niche" (Balch et al. 2017, p. 2,946). Balch and colleagues (2017) concluded from this analysis that the direct role of people in increasing wildfire activity has been largely overlooked.

A person, with positive or negative intentions, can directly light a wildfire. The consequences of this action may result in good or bad outcomes for the firelighter and other members of society. For example, a fire may be lit with the intention of reducing a fuel load, so a subsequent wildfire may be less severe. Alternatively, a person may wish to impress peers by participating in delinquent activity, such as setting alight a dumped car. Neither may wish to cause a large and dangerous wildfire, although this may be the outcome. A wildfire may also be lit indirectly or unmaliciously by the use of machinery that sparks, or by leaving an outdoor camp-fire unattended. Lightning strikes may cause a wildfire, where no human is directly involved, although, as discussed below, human-caused climate change is increasing the occurrence of lightning. A wildfire may occur due to burning embers blowing from another fire, starting a wildfire in a new location.

Complications in understanding the cause of wildfire ignition

Varying categorisations

Many factors complicate our understanding of wildfire ignition. Most of these complications are common internationally, thus making both within and between-country comparisons difficult. Without a comprehensive understanding of details around the ignition: where, what, how and by whom, something is ignited, it is difficult to understand why the particular building, car or forest burnt and thus what prevention approaches are needed.

An important distinction is between urban and structural fires and a fire in a rural or forest setting, although it is recognised that this differentiation can blur with some fires that occur in the rural/urban interface. In the USA, official records tend to differentiate between urban fires and wildfires, while this distinction is not usually made in Victoria with regard to malicious fires. The European Union reports on the date, size and location of forest fires for 33 European and Northern African countries, compiling the data collected by these countries (San-Miguel-Ayanz et al. 2018). Forest fires are defined by the European Union as fires that spread wholly or in part in a forest or other wooded land, as distinct from other rural or an urban location. Fires that occur in rural locations that fall outside this defined location don't appear to be collected by the European Union. For example, the Former Yugoslav Republic of Macedonia records that 1,787 fires occurred in 2017, 301 (17%) of these being forest fires, the nature of other fires are not explained. However, Greece appears not to differentiate forest fires from other fires in their section of the report, suggesting that the forest fire definition is variably used. The cause of the forest fire is described in different ways between the countries. Some countries do not give a cause, such as Cyprus and Belgium, other countries offer only limited information. Prescribed burns appear to be largely unrecorded in most countries.

In Australia, what is burnt is usually classed as 'vegetation', 'structural' and 'other', which leaves aside the question as to whether the fire could be described as an urban fire or a rural wildfire. For example, where 'vegetation' fires are reported, as in the Productivity Commission Report (2018), such fires may occur in a forest, along a roadside, within a sports oval, indeed, anywhere (in an urban or rural setting) with vegetation. A 'structural' fire may occur in an urban or rural area, where it may lead to a 'vegetation' wildfire. Similarly, a burnt vehicle could be in any location, at times (accidentally or purposefully) igniting a wildfire. For maliciously lit fires, it is usually important to differentiate between urban fires and rural wildfires, as there may be a difference in motivation leading to the ignition of the fire. Structural fires may be motivated by a wish for revenge, or to collect an insurance claim, that is, an instrumental reason. A fire may be lit for expressive reasons, such as unresolved trauma or psychopathology, and possibly more likely to be a vegetation fire. These different reasons would lead to different prevention approaches that target these motivational differences.

Variation in perceived causes of wildfire

As suggested above, understanding the reason for the ignition of a fire is very important. The causes of ignition of wildfires in Australia are commonly categorised as accidental (also known as reckless), suspicious, deliberate (or malicious), natural, re-ignition, prescribed burn, other, and unknown (Bryant 2008a). There is often a range of events included within these categories. For example, accidental ignition of a wildfire may be caused by sparks from machinery, from fire lit to burn off stubble from an agricultural crop, or combustion in a waste tip.

Other countries use their own systems of classification, and as in Australia, more detailed identification of wildfire causes tends to vary according to the collection agency. For example, the California Department of Forestry and Fire Protection (2015) uses the categories: undetermined, miscellaneous, debris burning, lightning, arson, electrical power, vehicles, equipment use, campfires, playing with fire and smoking. Keeley & Syphard (2018), who examined historical patterns of wildfire ignition sources in California, expressed confidence in the veracity of very early fire records. They believe that state and federal archives show that managers have always been conscientious about reporting to ensure accuracy and completeness. Although they also note that categories have changed over time, that the issue of urban/rural interface wildfire arson was not recognised, and they ignore 'unknown' and 'miscellaneous' categories of wildfires.

Further uncertainty arises, as allocating the category in which to place the cause of ignition can vary according to who is categorising and is often based on judgment (Muller 2009b; Plucinski 2014). For example, in Australia Bryant (2008a) notes that fire investigators may be suspicious that a fire was deliberately lit by drawing on the evidence of the location, timing or other circumstances, or in the absence of another feasible explanation. A similar problem is present in Italy and Spain, where the cause of a fire is said to be usually based on an opinion by a forestry officer filling in a form (Lovreglio et al. 2010; Salvador 2016). Many countries are also reliant on the information from court records once the accused has been convicted; if they are convicted. Where the information on the cause of the fire subsequently becomes available, the official database is not always updated (personal communication to one of the authors). As an offender who lights a malicious fire is not necessarily immediately apprehended, recorded rates of deliberate fire lighting "must be regarded as partially speculative, and therefore an estimate only" (Bryant 2008a, p. 2).

Despite this uncertainty, data and practitioner opinions suggest that most fires are caused by humans. The US National Park Service (2017) states that people cause 90% of the wildfires in the USA. A recent article and the Californian fire service places the figure at 95% (reported by Arango 2018; Balch et al. 2017). While the European Fires Report states that humans cause forest fires in the vast majority of cases, Hungary believes that 99% of their forest fires are caused by humans. As noted above, the precise cause varies greatly between countries, with negligence, as well as 'unknown' featuring highly in many countries (San-Miguel-Ayanz et al. 2018).

An Australian example

Ten years ago, Bryant (2008a) analyzed the causes of landscape fires in Australia. This data was drawn from 280,000 vegetation fires from 18 major fire and land management agencies responsible for wildfires from all states and territories, covering five years to 2001/02. The Australian Institute of Criminology (2017) collated this information into Australia-wide data (Figure 2.1). Bryant notes that the proportion of vegetation fires designated as deliberate varied between agencies and regions, as well as noting other inconsistencies. Overall, as shown in Figure 2.1, the Australian Institute of Criminology records that approximately 8% of all vegetation fires were recorded as being malicious, and another 22% as suspicious. However, about 40% of recorded vegetation fires did not have an assigned cause. When fires are investigated, it is found that the majority have been due to malicious lighting (Tomison 2010). An analysis in Western Australia placed the rate of malicious fires at 68%. Thus, if half of the unassigned causes in Bryant's analysis were deliberately lit, reflecting the known and suspected malicious fire rates, perhaps 50% of fires were maliciously lit over this time period in Australia.

Figure 2.1: Causes of wildfires from 18 Australian fire and land management agencies, 1997/98 to 2001/2.

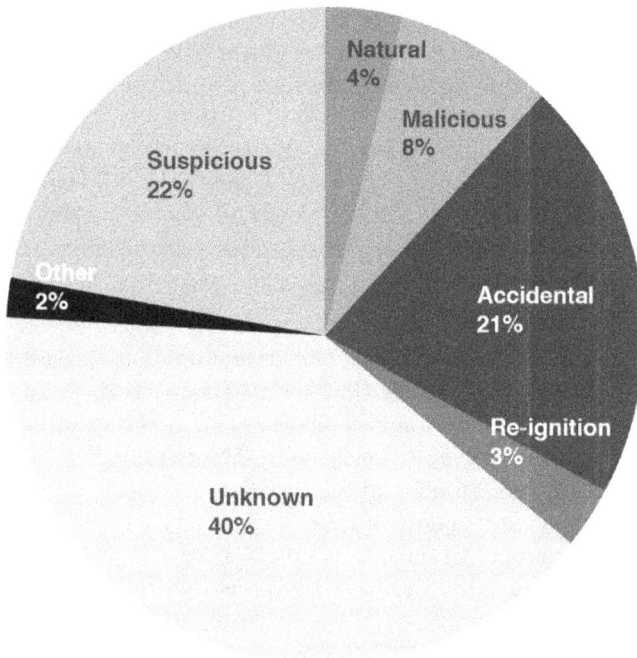

Source: information derived from Australian Institute of Criminology 2017.

Another Australian review of the cause of ignition, undertaken by Muller (2009b), found wide variation in recorded malicious wildfires. They ranged from an annual average of 19% (data from the NSW Rural Fires Services 1999/2000 to 2003/4) to 69% (data from the Department of Fire and Emergency Services, WA, 2000/1 to 2006/7). Muller reports that 29% of wildfires were due to a 'natural' cause. However, Bryant's analysis, concludes that 4% of fires were defined as 'natural'. Bryant notes a point of confusion in that fires defined as 'natural' may be suspiciously lit but fanned by 'natural' causes, such as wind, thus enlarging the fire.

Figure 2.2: 29 year average cause of Victorian wildfires 1987/88 to 2016/17.

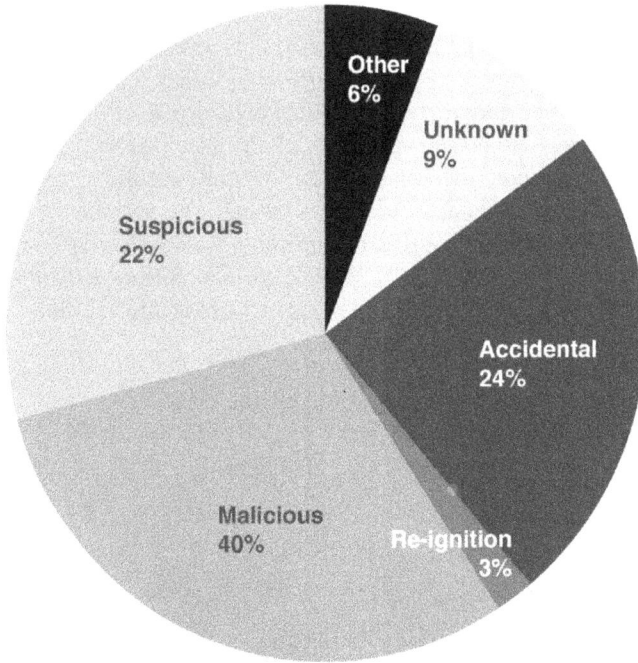

Source: Derived from dataset of Victorian government.

Figure 2.2 summaries 29 years of data on the causes of wildfires in Victoria (1997/98 to 2016/17). The data has been re-categorised into groups comparable with the Bryant data in Figure 2.1, recognising that the two time periods and recorded areas are different. The proportion of fires in each of the categories varies between the two datasets. The Victorian data does not use the category of 'suspicious', recording 30% of fires as deliberate, the total of suspicious and malicious fires in Figure 2.1. It is unclear how 'suspicious' is dealt with by the Victorian dataset. The biggest differences between the datasets are found in the natural and unknown categories. Lightning is reported as occurring seven times as often in the Victorian dataset, when compared with the national data, whereas unknown causes are 4.5 times more common in the national data, in comparison with the Victorian dataset. It could be that a wildfire is attributed to lightning by the Victorian dataset where the cause is unknown.

Internationally viewed causes of wildfire

Figure 2.3 shows the causes of wildfires that occurred in 2010, collated by the California Department of Forestry and Fire Protection (2015) and organised into similar categories to those in Figure 2.1. A note on the report from the California Department states that the data only includes that collected from incident reports, and there is no obligation to provide this data. The low number of fires reported (312) suggests that much information is missing. 'Other' is the largest category with most causes in this category being described as 'miscellaneous'. 10% of the 'other' category was said to be due to smoking, with smaller numbers blamed on power faults and campfires. Only 5% of fires were said to be deliberate. The category of 'suspicious' is not used, but this category may be included in a large number of unknown causes. The year before this, 2009, (Coughlan & Petty 2012) reported that in the South East Coasts of the USA, 'illegally set' fires accounted for 37% of wildfires. A further 38% of fires were described as legally maliciously lit but escaped, turning into a wildfire.

Figure 2.3: Sources of ignition of wildfires in California, 2015.

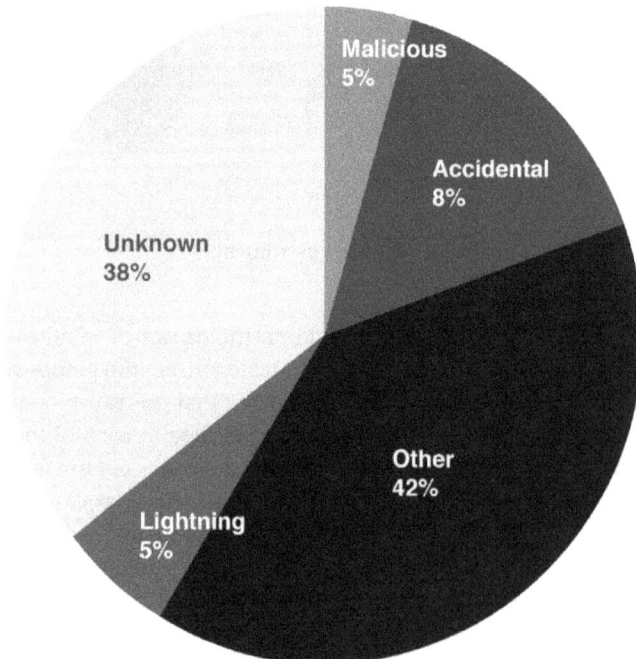

Source: Derived from California Department of Forestry and Fire Protection 2015.

As reported earlier, Balch and colleagues (2019) review of recorded fires in the USA (1992 to 2012) found that 84% of wildfires were human-initiated, 21% due to arson, accounting for some 40,000 wildfires annually. Human lit wildfires caused the fire season to be three times longer than the lightning-caused fire season and were said to be the substantial driver of overall fire risk to ecosystems and economies.

Most recorded wildfires in the fire-prone region of Attica, Greece, (67% in the period 1991-2004) are registered as having an unknown cause (Tedim, Xanthopoulos & Leone 2015). However, other data on wildfires in the Lazio region of Italy, which occurred from 2003-2007, reports the following categories and incident ratio:

- Arson – 77.3%

- Unknown – 11.3%

- Ignorance (defined as not reporting a fire, not extinguishing a bonfire, throwing away a cigarette etc.) – 10.1%

- Accidental (due to lack of knowledge) – 0.8%

- Natural causes – 0.5%

Catry et al. (2007) report that only 3% of the investigated forest fires (fires that occurred fully or partly in a forested area) in Spain, between 2000 and 2005, were naturally caused (lightning). About 49% of the wildfires were maliciously caused, while 37% were due to negligence and 11% were accidentally caused. Padilla and Vega-Garcia (2011) report that in Spain, between 1996 and 2005, people caused 78% of 197,625 wildfires, however, fires, where the cause was unknown, are said to be included in this category. Salvador (2016) reports that 95% of forest fires are caused by humans, although notes that the causes of 67% of forest fires in 2012 in Spain were classified as 'unknown'.

Summary of section

Despite the confidence expressed by Keeley and Syphard (2018) in relation to the wildfire data from California, internationally, most data sets reflect the lack of certainty of the causes of ignition in recorded fires. In 2008, Bryant concluded that the vast majority of vegetation fires arise from human causes, including malicious fires. Despite the revealed uncertainty, Bryant's conclusion is still relevant over a decade later, when she says that reducing wildfires that are deliberately lit can have a significant influence on the total number of fires in Australia. This could be broadened to many causes of wildfires in many countries. Reducing the 'unknown' causes and the uncertainty around causes is highly important, in order to be able to undertake a fully effective approach to prevention of ignition of malicious and other wildfires.

The following sections examine the causes of wildfire in greater detail, using Australian data as examples. They are organised into 'authorised' and 'unauthorised' fires that are usually officially recorded by fire-related agencies, and wildfires that are usually not recorded in official wildfire statistics. The inclusion of fires not usually recorded by fire-related agencies seeks to broaden the conversation about wildfires as to why some fires are excluded, as all wildfires have potentially dangerous outcomes. Presenting material in this way also seeks to illustrate how artificial boundaries are placed around different aspects of the one problem, often formed by embedded historical approaches, tacit value judgements, and ideology.

Wildfire causes that are usually recorded

Particular causes of wildfire tend to be officially recorded by fire agencies and government departments. This section discusses those that are most commonly officially recorded internationally. These wildfires may be deliberately or accidentally lit by a person, neither event receiving a lot of research or policy attention (Balch et al. 2017). Wildfires may also arise as a result of indirect human activity and are usually officially recorded.

Malicious ignition

Unauthorised malicious and suspicious fires are thought to account for up to half of the wildfire ignitions internationally, although, as discussed above, the official recordings of this vary greatly between countries and often within countries, as well as over time. The motives for purposefully and illegal lighting vary widely but are commonly viewed as due to a psychological or pragmatic need in the lighter. These issues are discussed further in chapter 3. Two special cases of malicious fire lighting are also discussed in this book. Firstly, 'copycat arson', where the person seeks to maliciously light a wildfire, their thoughts triggered by representations in the media. They may try to emulate how a prior wildfire was lit; this issue is covered in chapter 11. The second particular group of firelighters are those who are associated with the fire-brigades. This is discussed further in chapter 3.

Accidental or reckless ignition

Accidental or recklessly lit wildfires includes many causes of ignition. Such causes range from unanticipated occurrences, such as sparks from machinery lighting a fire, to wildfires that should not have occurred if the law had been obeyed, such as a bonfire lit on a Total Fire Ban Day. As discussed further below, there can be considerable blurring between what is defined as malicious and what is considered accidental or reckless.

Campfires or BBQ

According to the Victorian dataset, an average of 66 wildfires occurred annually from a campfire or BBQ, from 1987/88 to 2011/12, jumping to an average that is three times this size from 2012/13 to 2016/17. Unattended campfires (that had not escaped from their site) were excluded from Figure 2.2. This information was recorded only in the 2015/6 and 2016/7 and accounted for a disproportionate number of fire records, 676 fires, representing 31.3% of recorded fires over the two-year period. This increase in records is possibly due to a decision in Victoria to more closely monitor campfires in state parks, due to increased concerns about wildfire. A small part may also reflect Melbourne's large migrant intake in recent years; people not necessarily aware of the flammability of the Australian bush. As a result, the Victorian Government has employed more air and vehicle patrols to monitor campfires lit in public forested areas. Ignition due to outdoor BBQs was identified in both the Swedish and UK wildfires that occurred in July and August 2018, referred to in chapter one.

The reporting of unattended campfires by Victorians to emergency services does not appear to reflect the recent official concerns about campfires. Research was undertaken in Victoria on community reporting of wildfire to a responsible authority. The research found that even if the respondent to the research questionnaire was the only witness to an unattended or potentially dangerous campfire, and it was a Total Fire Ban Day, 68% of respondents would not report that campfire (Read & Stanley 2018). However, 66% of those who wouldn't report said they would handle the situation themselves, presumably by seeing that the fire was put out. This still leaves about one-third of respondents who would apparently do nothing.

Other reckless or accidental ignitions

Over 29 years to 2017, the Victorian dataset has recorded an annual average of 39 wildfires arising from burning off grass and scrub, and 22 wildfires due to burning off a windrow or heap of cleared trees. Some of these fires may be due to illegal fires, while others may have had a permit to burn, but the fire got away. Other less frequent causes of wildfires that were recorded in the dataset were:

- domestic waste disposal (annual average of 5 fires)

- industrial waste disposal including logging (5)

- machine exhausts (5.5)

- wildfire due to power transmission lines (6)

- sparks from train or truck (3)

- the burning of buildings or part thereof (2.5)

- fireworks (2).

Uncertain intention

Two categories of ignition from smoking devices 'cigarette, match, pipe' (18 on average annually), and 'burning a vehicle or machine' (27 on average annually), were not placed by the Victorian dataset in the malicious category. Such ignition or fuel sources are at times used by those who light malicious fires. Tomison (2010) points out that many accidental fires are attributed to cigarettes. Given the difficulty in starting a fire with cigarettes, many roadside fires attributed to cigarettes may, in fact, be malicious. Indeed, one of the authors of this book witnessed a fire that burnt vegetation and a building, the cause being put down to an accidental fire due to a cigarette being thrown from a car. However, the author was aware that five fires occurred along a couple of kilometres of highway within a 20-minute timeframe, only one becoming large and dangerous, and thus probably the only one reported. Five fires clustered in time and place are unlikely to be accidental.

In the comprehensive analysis undertaken by Bryant (2008a), there was wide variation in how a wildfire believed to be caused by smoking, was viewed. This varied from 16.8% of smoking-related ignitions in an agency in South Australia recorded as an accidental event, to 100% recorded as accidental in agencies in other states. On the other hand, 0.3% were recorded as an incendiary event in one agency, with 30.5% in another agency. Research in Western Australia (undated) reports that 60% of 1,631 fires over two years were classified as non-deliberate, 38% deliberate, and 2% unknown.

The wider problem of establishing cause and culpability

While both purposeful and unintentional ignition may have very severe consequences, the stated or perceived intention of a person, who is caught lighting a fire outdoors, are important considerations in determining the consequences for that person. In Australia, under the *Victorian Summary Offences Act* (2012), it is illegal to light a fire in the open air that results in destruction, damage or danger to life or property, or leave an unattended fire in the open air. In practice, it is difficult to gain a conviction under the *Victorian Summary Offences Act*, and when an offence is heard at the Magistrate's Court, penalties are low (Gippsland Arson Prevention Program 2017). Magistrates in Victoria can hand down fines of $A37,310, or two years imprisonment, or both. However, in practice, most infringement penalties incurred are largely '*Undertakings of Good Behaviour'* or a penalty in the order of $A200-300 fines. Thus, if the fire was described by the lighter as 'unintentional', and it was put out quickly, then the person may be given a $A300 fine in Victoria.

Alternately, a person who admits that they wanted to create a major wildfire, and if this fire killed people, then an adult may be given a long prison sentence. The true intention of the firelighter is often not known. Thus, the penalty may depend on whether the ignition is deemed to be 'malicious' or 'accidental', and also in some situations if the fire becomes large and dangerous. The firelighter may be at risk of receiving a 15-year prison sentence in a criminal court in Australia, or 25 years if deaths occurred, or may receive a small fine or warning issued by the local government.

For example, Brendan Sokaluk, aged 39, was convicted of killing 10 people by deliberately lighting a wildfire in Victoria on Black Saturday, February 2009. The fire also resulted in 150 homes being lost and 36,000 hectares of land destroyed in 'a catastrophic blaze' (Justice Coghlan, reported by Farnsworth 2012). On that day, the temperature peaked at 46°C, and the fires were fanned by wind gusts reaching 70 kilometres an hour. While Sokaluk maliciously lit at least one fire, he may not have set out to create a catastrophic fire that resulted in many deaths. Sokaluk was given a jail sentence of 17 years and 9 months. In the USA, a person can receive a more severe penalty for an 'accidental' fire. For example, a man in California was incarcerated and paroled after two years, after he started a wildfire that destroyed houses. He was mowing his field in the middle of the day with a temperature of 105 degrees F, despite being advised of the fire danger by a neighbour (Bulwa 2008).

Additionally, it may be that little, if any, intervention of any sort takes place in Victoria, such as reporting to the police or school authorities taking action. Such circumstances may be where a young person lights an intentional fire, such as in a rubbish bin, but the fire is seen and quickly extinguished. Thus, complications such as noted above, have led arson to be described as 'a crime of detection' (Salvador 2016, p.340). In other words, fire lighting is not perceived as a crime, until the police or other official deems it to be so.

Distinguishing between the causes of ignition can be a difficult and time-consuming task, yet one that the authors believe should be undertaken in order to better understand future wildfire risk in order to establish prevention strategies. Indeed, Martinez and colleagues believe that the usual classification of fires as negligent or intentional, though useful for legal purposes, may not be useful in certain locations where the reason why the fire occurred may not be clear, such as is illustrated above (Martinez, Vega-Garcia & Chuvieco 2009).

Martinez and colleagues suggest that in highly subdivided agricultural properties, higher rates of accidental fires may occur due to the greater use of agricultural machinery, a greater risk of conflicts, and the neglect of land. All these causes are potentially difficult to ascertain the reason for the fire.

Ignition indirectly due to human behaviour

Some wildfire ignitions may not be directly attributable to a specific person's activity, but the fire may be indirectly caused by human action or inaction.

'Natural' ignition

Lightning and spontaneous combustion are commonly defined as 'natural' sources of fire. Lightning accounted for 0.55% of wildfires, and combustion 0.48% of wildfires, in research done in Western Australia (Plucinski 2014). Victorian data records an attendance to an average of 199 lightning started wildfires per year. However, as noted in chapter one, the recorded increase in lightning can also be in part associated with humans due to the increased storm activity associated with the failure to adequately respond to climate change (Steffen, Alexander & Rice 2017). Indeed, the Australian Institute of Criminology (2008) notes that, despite these uncertainties, at the time of writing 'natural' fires are actually quite rare. Catry et al. (2007) report that only 3% of the forest fires successfully investigated between 2000 and 2005 in Spain were 'naturally' caused. However, not all reports have this view. Prestemon and colleagues report that, based on official wildfire records, lightning caused 45% of forest fires and 80% of area burnt managed by the US Forest Service and managed by Department of the Interior[1] lands between January 2000 and December 2008 (Prestemon et al. 2013).

It would appear that climate change will result in more lightning strikes. Research predicts that annual mean lightning will increase in the USA by about 12% ±5% SD for every degree of rising in the centigrade global average air temperature (Romps et al. 2014). Given that the average world temperature has risen 0.5°C, over the 29 years of data, and assuming the rate of increase occurs in Australia, as in the USA, it could be expected that there would be a small upwards trend over this time (of about 6%) in the number of recorded

---

[1] The Department of the Interior in the United States is responsible for the management and conservation of most federal land and natural resources. It oversees such agencies as the Bureau of Land Management, the United States Geological Survey, and the National Park Service.

lightning strikes. However, no trend line over time could be fitted to the Victorian 29-year distribution.

Ignition due to power lines

A large inconsistency in data can be found in many countries in relation to fires started by power lines. A Victorian database has recorded an average of six wildfires annually starting this way. The Victorian Parliamentary Inquiry into bushfire preparedness was told that electrical infrastructure starts about 200 wildfires a year (Parliament of Victoria 2017). The California Department of Forestry and Fire Protection (2018) found that power lines started 8% of fires in 2015, burning 149,241 acres, more than twice the amount from any other cause. However, Penn (2017) reports that this problem has increased significantly in the USA since this time, leading to power lines being amongst the top three causes of wildfire.

Fires often not recorded

Authorised fire ignition

In certain circumstances, authority is given to light a fire in a rural setting for fuel reduction, land clearing, agricultural purposes or burning rubbish. While this is an ignition, if the fire is confined, small, and conditions associated with the permit to ignite, it probably wouldn't be classified as a wildfire. However, boundaries around the form of this fire may be blurred. For example, at what point should the fire be recorded if it becomes larger than anticipated, the conditions of the permit are not adhered to, or the true purpose of the ignition varies from the application.

Permits to burn

Australia has a system of rating fire dangerous days. A Fire Danger Period is declared by the fire brigade or a particular local government area, which could last six or seven months, depending on the weather conditions. During this time a permit is needed to light a fire outdoors. Total Fire Bans (TFB) are declared in Victoria by the Country Fire Authority (the main rural fire services agency) on days when fires are likely to spread rapidly and likely to be difficult to control. Thus, on TFB days, activities such as out-door BBQs, campfires, burning-off, and use of a chainsaw or farm machinery that may generate sparks, are not permitted. In particular circumstances, when a TFB is not in place, fires may be permitted in order to burn rubbish, clear debris and burn cleared vegetation. This is allowed when determined by the Local Government to be safe, such as when weather and land conditions do not pose a high wildfire risk, and safety requirements are met, such as a three-metre fire break is prepared, and neighbours notified. Fire may be used to burn unwanted vegetation after logging, as currently occurs in Australia.

Fighting fire with fire

Fire is commonly used in Australia, and in other parts of the world, as a means of reducing the severity of a wildfire or controlling a potential or on-going wildfire. In the absence of an existing wildfire, a low heat ground fire is lit to reduce the fuel load so a wildfire, should it occur, may not be as large and may burn with a lower intensity. This is known as a fuel reduction burn, cool burn or a prescribed burn. These prescribed burns are undertaken by emergency authorities on publicly owned land, large state forests, national parks and roadsides in the USA and Australia (US National Park Service 2017). In the USA, 74% of states utilise some formal process for permitting or authorizing prescribed fire activity (Melvin 2018). In Australia, in particular, they have become highly controversial.

Due to the dry weather conditions and an early start to the fire season, Victoria completed only about 30% of prescribed burning programs planned for the up-coming 2018/19 wildfire season. 66,000 hectares were burnt, 190,000 being planned (Doyle 2018). The 2017 bushfire season ran into early April 2018, and most of the 66,000 hectares of prescribed burning the state managed to achieve was condensed into a 2½ week window. Although there is little information available, anecdotal evidence suggests that in some situations where a wildfire is present in an isolated area, this is controlled by fire authorities but not actively extinguished. Thus, in effect, the fire is turned into a 'prescribed burn', or an 'ecological burn', albeit a fire that has the potential to be a very large and destructive burn (see, for example, Green 1931; Kilgore 1973).

It would seem that quite a few prescribed burns turn into an uncontrolled wildfire. This occurred near Lancefield, a small settlement on the edge of Melbourne, in 2015. A prescribed burn broke containment lines and destroyed four homes, burning more than 3,000 hectares of farmland and state forest (Edwards 2015). While a few prescribed burns are recorded in official data sets, many don't appear to be. Research in Western Australia reported that an average of 2.5% of wildfires in two fire districts in the Perth area from 2004 to 2012 resulted from escaped prescribed burns (Plucinski 2014). Evidence given to the Victorian Parliamentary Inquiry noted that the Victorian government conducted 670 prescribed burns in 2014-15 (Parliament of Victoria 2017). The Victorian database recorded that annually an average of six wildfires were attended due to re-ignition of prescribed burns. The other use of fire, known as back-burning, is where a fire is lit by firefighters to reduce the fuel source and thus reduce or prevent the spread of an existing wildfire. It is likely that such a response would be viewed as part of the original wildfire. Prescribed burns and backburning are discussed further in chapter 8.

Ecological burns

Some ecological systems require fire to open seedpods and facilitate plant reproduction (US National Park Service 2017). Thus, ecological burns are sometimes carried out in forest parks. However, as will be discussed in chapter 8, there is frequently a lack of clarity about the purpose of an authorised fire.

Unauthorised ignition

Certain types of fires tend not to be recorded by fire agencies, although data may be collected in some countries by other authorities, such as the Ministry of Agriculture in Spain (Salvador 2016). This information may not be publicly released. In Europe, while some countries offer data on agricultural-related fires, this information is not included in the European Commission's fire data collection (San-Miguel-Ayanz et al. 2017).

Certain types of wildfires may have agricultural, cultural and historical reasons for ignition, or they may have more antisocial or illegal intentions, such as revenge, and maintaining employment. Thus, it is unclear how they should be categorised. Some of these fires are viewed as 'normal practice', such as fires for agricultural purposes, and others should perhaps be subject to legal prosecution as arson. While some historical or agricultural-related fires may not get out-of-control, they may still have an extensive downside with smoke pollution and damage to the soil etc. The risks associated with such fires are increasing, especially in the context of population growth and climate change.

Fires in landfill sites

Fires in landfill sites may arise due to surface fires, spontaneous combustion or legacy heat. Legacy heat is the inadvertent burial of a heat source. Spontaneous combustion occurs where a buried heat source, resulting from biological decomposition or chemical oxidation, produces a rise in temperature if the waste mass cannot dissipate the heat faster than it is being produced, a process known as 'thermal runaway' (Foss-Smith 2010). For example, spontaneous landfill combustion has been traced to a batch of mercury cell batteries which short-circuited during the final settlement of a landfill, and to cotton rags soaked in aluminium paint. Below surface fires can remain hot for years under starved oxygen conditions. Landfill fires emit a toxic cocktail of fugitive gases including formaldehyde, hydrogen cyanide, hydrogen sulfide, nitrogen oxides, as well as polychlorinated dibenzo-*p*-dioxins and polychlorinated dibenzofurans (Bates 2004; Foss-Smith 2010; Thornton 2002). Thus, such fires can be potentially lethal with well-proven acute and chronic health impacts (Foss-Smith 2010). There is very little research internationally about fires in landfill sites, despite the fact that they occur frequently. In the USA, there are around 8,300 landfill fires a year (US Fire Administration 2004) and in the UK around 280 to 300 a year. Anecdotal information speaks of a large number of fires in landfills in recent years in Sweden and Australia (Lönnermark et al. 2008). An additional problem in Victoria is the occurrence of fires in a number of recycling plants in the last few years, causing toxic smoke over Melbourne suburbs (Preiss 2019). The plants had accumulated large plastic stockpiles at the facilities that posed a real fire risk to local communities and in breach of safety regulations (ABC News 2019). The causes of these fires have not been announced.

Fire in coalmines

Spontaneous heating resulting in fires in coal mines is said to be a major problem worldwide (Singh 2013). This problem is present in most coal-mining countries: USA, China, Australia, South Africa, Germany, Indonesia and India. Fires can be hard to detect and last for decades as they are very hard to extinguish, especially if the fire is allowed to grow. A mine fire under the abandoned town of Centralia, Pennsylvania, has been burning for 52 years (to 2014) (Zhang 2014). There are said to be hundreds of mine fires burning at present and expected to keep burning until the end of the century, with estimates of 20 million to 600 million metric tonnes of coal lost annually to these fires (Munroe 2019). The burning coal releases potentially toxic elements like mercury, methane, carbon monoxide, carbon dioxide, arsenic, fluorine and selenium into the air (Munroe 2019; Singh 2013). They can also cause the surrounding area to become hot and unstable and may lead to sinkholes.

Agricultural burning

'Slash and burn' land clearance of grasslands and forest for agriculture is practised most often in parts of Africa, northern South America and Southeast Asia. Central Africa has a very long tradition of seasonal burning by farmers to remove old crops and weeds and return nutrients to the soil (Jenner 2018). This practice dominates the instances of wildfires seen in Angola in the week to June 21, 2018, where the NASA satellite revealed 67,162 fires were burning. India has a long history of burning agricultural stubble. This contributes to severe air pollution in Delhi. Unfortunately, the practice is said to be increasing due to changes in climate that necessitate a faster turnover in land use to enable a second crop to be grown. Extreme fires double the amount of pollution and increase total particulate levels 12 times higher than WHO recommendations, and even 20 times higher on some days (Jenner 2019). While the practice is illegal, the deterrent isn't sufficient to prevent the practice. Eastern Russia also has a tradition of this form of agricultural burning.

Lovreglio and colleagues examined the motives for fire in three areas in Southern Italy by posing a series of questions to a panel of selected experts (Lovreglio et al. 2010). The most frequent motives for fires were said to be related to historical agricultural use of fire, such as stubble burning. Spain also has a persistence of traditional agrarian approaches and the historical use of fire in agricultural activities (Martinez, Vega-Garcia & Chuvieco 2009). Salvador (2016) notes that fires associated with farming practices or to clear bushes, were the highest cause of fire in 2012, about 22% of fires or about 43,000 fires in Spain.

Indeed, many countries undertook this practice, but it has been discontinued comparatively recently. Australia used fire as a way of clearing animals, such as mice and snakes, as well as burning off excess waste vegetation, prior to harvesting sugar cane. However, fires are still lit in northern Australia to improve grass growth for cattle that roam over vast areas. Such agricultural practices led to fires in the past in rural southern USA (Doolittle & Lightsey 1979). Prestemon and colleagues (2013) consider the reduction in this form of fire lighting in the USA may in part explain their belief in a downward trend in the number of wildfires. However, this report covered fairly old data, from 1972 to 2008.

Institutional and economic fires

Some deliberately lit wildfires to clear forests are undertaken by companies. Land is cleared by fire for palm oil growing in Indonesia (The Prince's Rainforest Project 2009). Local villages are sometimes paid to start the fire for the company (personal communication to one of the authors). Plantation farming practice drains the wet forests, thus creating the circumstances for an increase in fire risk on the dry peat soils.

Salvador (2016) writes that the use of land may be contested; thus, wildfires may be lit to achieve corporate or business outcomes. Such outcomes could be for land clearing and land speculation purposes. Despite a possible 1,000 wildfires being lit for such purposes in 2012 in Spain, very few criminal convictions of company offenders took place. Of the 186 forest-related arson criminal sentences identified between 2008 and 2012, only 12 resulted in a corporation receiving a monetary fine. Salvador (2016, p.348) notes that environmental crimes, including malicious fire lighting, illustrates "a nexus of inequality promulgated by a discriminatory court system and the power of corporations to engage in environmental harms without worries about their criminal consequences".

Large areas of the Amazon forest have been cleared over the past few decades to expand crop growing and beef farming, or to increase the value of farming property (Givetash 2019). Under the current Brazilian government, the number of wildfires in the Amazon has increased 80% from January 1 to the end of August 2019, compared to the same period in the previous year. This has resulted in more than 74,000 fires (Givetash 2019; Human Rights Watch 2019). August 10 was deemed 'fire day', coinciding with the President of Brazil's promise to reduce environmental protections of the forest and promote 'development' of the forest. Illegal logging by criminal networks, and resulting forest fires, are connected to acts of violence and intimidation against forest defenders and the state's failure to investigate and prosecute these crimes. The wildfires are started by people completing the process of deforestation where trees of value have been removed, in order to clear the land.

Anecdotal evidence exists that fires in remote areas in Australia may be occasionally lit by those financially retained to extinguish wildfires. Similarly, the practise of delaying the extinguishing of fires by paid casual firefighters, in order to maximise the higher payment acquired when firefighting, was reported to one of the authors.

Wildfire as a tool of conflict

Fire been used against people and communities as a weapon of violence and warfare (Baird 2006). In Galicia (North-West Spain) and in northern Portugal, arson associated with social conflicts, such as a loss of rangelands used by the local community, is said to be a major problem (Ganteaume et al. 2013). In Spain, wildfires may be used in land disputes, for revenge, used as a form of protest in relation to reforestation or a conservation classification, or they may also be used by groups to create social disruption (Salvador 2016). Land conflicts led to fires in the past in rural southern USA (Doolittle & Lightsey 1979).

In the research in Italy by Lovreglio and colleagues (2010), referred to above, the second most frequent cause of fire after agricultural purposes, was as a result of labour conflicts. These could be as a protest against the declaration of a protected area, revenge against Public Administrations or Public Entities, or ownership or labour conflicts. Of particular importance were fires lit by firefighters. Ironically, Lovreglio and colleagues (2010) note that as a result of these fires concerned citizens demand more firefighting resources, thus creating a vicious cycle. Martinez, Vega-Garcia & Chuvieco (2009) found a similar association in Spain, where the unemployment rate was found to be higher in areas where more fires occurred.

Fire has been used as a weapon. For example, a sustained campaign of burning was used against the ethnic group of Rohingya people living in Myanmar (Human Rights Council 2018). In 2013 and 2014, anti-Muslim violence in Rakhine State, Myanmar, included the burning of mosques. From 25 August 2017 fire was used more comprehensively against the Rohingya people, along with other acts of extreme violence. The Myanmar security forces were said to be actively involved and complicit (Human Rights Council 2018). At least 392 Rohingya villages in Rakhine state were destroyed by fire, as well as the burning of bodies in mass graves, and people who had been locked in structures, burnt alive.

Terrorism and Wildfire

There is a very small amount of literature on terrorism and wildfire, the little material on this issue largely referring to the use of fire in an urban setting. Part of the purpose of terrorism is not only to destroy but also create terror in people and make sure that there is media coverage around this event (Stanley & Goddard 2002). However, some fire lighting by terrorists may serve other purposes. For example, it may be used to divert emergency services away from an attack elsewhere or overwhelm resources (Joint Counterterrorism Assessment Team 2019). These features distinguish this behaviour from most malicious fire lighting, where the firelighter seeks personal gratification from the event and prefers to keep his or her involvement secret. The malicious fire lighter rarely intends to create a large and dangerous fire. However, in some of the terrorism and broader literature, there is a tendency to use the concepts of arson and terrorism inter-changeably, as well as descriptions of wildfire as a 'war zone'. This again creates some confusion as to the cause and purpose of the ignition and again leads to no clear pathway to the prevention of ignition.

Jackson and Frelinger (2007) explored 5,000 records of the weapons used by international and domestic terrorists between 1980 and 2005, held in two databases by the RAND Corporation, USA. They note that there are more records on the more recent events, as domestic terrorism was not historically recorded. They also caution about the quality of the data. While fire is likely to be incidentally part of many terrorist events, Besenyö (2017) reports that 11% of incidents perpetrated by 55 terrorist organisations purposefully used some form of fire, either solely or in combination with other weapons.

While most terrorist incidents were in an urban context, forest fires appear to be part of the agenda for some terrorists. Wildfire is discussed as a method of terror in the USA, Australia and Europe, further noting the location, time of year and weather that would be best suited for such an event (Besenyö 2017). Instructions targeting domestic terrorists about how to make incendiary devices to target wildland areas have been found in terrorist magazines in 2012 and 2017 (Joint Counterterrorism Assessment Team 2019). Due to the low arrests of malicious firelighters, there are suspicions relating to ignition by terrorists in some wildfires, such as in the French Riviera in July 2003, Greece in 2007, Russia in 2012, and in Arizona in 2013. However, it would seem that the publicity component of the terrorist act is absent in these events if terrorism is the cause.

There appears to be more evidence for terrorism events by Palestinian extremists using forest fires in Israel in 2016, the fires travelling to urban areas (Besenyö 2017). This form of terror using forest fires has been used from the 1920s by Palestinian terrorists, said to be responsible for one-third of forest fires in Israel (Baird 2006). In 2016, the fires numbered more than 1,773. They required firefighting aircraft from many countries, including the USA, to enable the fires to be extinguished. As a result, the Israeli Prime Minister stated that all arson would now be viewed as an act of terror and treated accordingly.

Fire used by hunters

In Europe, fire may be used by hunters, or to protest about a limitation of hunting areas, representing about 2.4% of known fires or about 12,000 fires in Spain in 2012. Hunting also results in the ignition of wildfires in Italy (Ganteaume et al. 2013). In the Northern Territory, Australia, wildfires may be lit by recreational pig hunters (Notzon & Damjanovic 2017).

Conclusions

A number of conclusions can be drawn. There are serious data limitations internationally, about recording the cause of fires, which must be addressed. While some inter-country variation is expected in the categorization of causal explanations, the extent of the variations suggests large inaccuracies in the data. The human cause of ignition is recognized as significant but appears to be rarely addressed, and the link between people and prevention is almost totally absent in most wildfire reports. Internationally, there remains a strong belief that prevention exclusively centres on environmental modification. It is unclear why some wildfires are officially reported, and other wildfires are not, perhaps the dominance of the ideology that fire is a 'natural' event, is clouding much thinking. It is possibly the historical and cultural context that has normalized such fires, which goes some way to explaining why the extensive number of wildfires occurring in, for example, Angola, Africa, are largely left out of the wildfire conversations.

The establishment of recording standards is urgently needed in order to better understand the causes of wildfires. These should be international in approach to enable sharing of research and knowledge. At the same time, the causes of wildfire need to be investigated on a localised, nuanced basis, in order to understand specific country, cultural and spatial influencing factors. The tunnel vision of aspects of wildfire can possibly only be overcome through a much wider involvement of disciplines in fire research and on-the-ground applications. Such broader input could offer perspectives around human behaviour, planning, economics, ecologists, climate scientists, demographers and philosophers, to disentangle values and ideology from empirical findings. It is argued in this book that it will be only through these changes that a comprehensive and effective system of prevention of wildfire ignition will be established, with the aim of reducing the occurrence of wildfires around the world. Many of the issues raised here are further discussed in other book chapters.

Chapter 3

Who lights fires and why?[1]

Introduction

The first question many people ask when they hear that someone maliciously lit a fire is – "why would someone do that?" It is indeed difficult to understand why people might maliciously light fires, including those that can have catastrophic results. At its base, all people have some interest in fire and derive enjoyment from it. We enjoy sitting around fires, sitting in front of the fireplace, and watching fire. Children, in particular, have a fascination for fires. Given the importance of fire in the evolution of humans, our interest in fires is unsurprising (Ogloff 2009). What is more difficult to understand, however, is how some people, beyond childhood, continue with an unnatural interest in lighting fires. Unfortunately, we remain somewhat limited in our ability to answer the fundamental question of why some people maliciously light fires. Part of the reason for our lack of understanding of firelighters is because so few firelighters are apprehended. For example, in Victoria, the Crime Statistics Agency reported that of the 4,480 arson offences (with 1,397 unique offenders) identified between 2011 and 2016, only 37% of offences were solved (Crime Statistics Agency 2016).

Questions pertaining to malicious wildfire lighters are even more difficult to answer, given the staggeringly low number of offenders identified for wildfire offences (Ducat & Ogloff 2011). For example, in the Victorian sample over the five-year period from 2011 to 2016, only 46 such offenders were apprehended (Crime Statistics Agency 2016). Of the wildfire offenders, more than half were known to police for prior offending and 16 (34%) had previously committed an arson or criminal damage offence. Unfortunately, such low numbers of identified offenders have hampered efforts at identifying common characteristics or conducting comparative analyses with other arson offenders to determine if those who light malicious wildfires form a distinct group of offenders. The smaller number of wildfire arson convictions may be due to a number of reasons. First, not only is it more difficult to detect malicious wildfires given that such fires can occur in rural and remote areas,

[1] We are grateful to Dr. Lauren Ducat, clinical and forensic psychologist, for her assistance in preparing this chapter.

but it is also harder to identify the perpetrators (Willis 2004). Second, even individuals who are detected may not be charged with specific wildfire offences, but other related offences, which makes the collation of data about these individuals difficult (Doley 2003). For these reasons, what we know about wildfire firelighters is limited; however, more is known about other arson offenders.

This chapter provides an overview of what is known about malicious urban firelighters, and to the extent possible, those who light malicious wildfires, who may share common characteristics (Ducat & Ogloff 2011). We start with a brief mention of the estimated prevalence of fire lighting in the general community. We then consider specific groups of malicious wildfire offenders, such as those with mental illnesses, women, and young offenders. We will also consider the extent to which there are markers that differentiate malicious firelighters from other offenders, what might lead a person to deliberate fire lighting, including a brief discussion of the current theories of adult fire lighting, subtypes of firelighters, and finally, the issue of wildfires set by fire service personnel. The chapter concludes with a discussion of the knowledge gaps and future areas of research to better understand the psychology of wildfire lighters.

Prevalence of Arson

Due to the low rate of identification of maliciously lit fires and the low apprehension rates, even when it is known that fires were deliberately lit, it is not possible to definitively identify the prevalence rate of malicious fire lighting in the community (Ogloff 2009). Some researchers have tried, however, to establish prevalence rates for malicious fire lighting. For example, Gannon and Barrowcliffe (2012), and Barrowcliffe and Gannon (2015), set out to assess the prevalence and characteristics of un-apprehended arsonists. In the first study, 11% (n = 168) of respondents reported a past diagnosis of behavioural problems. In the second study, 158 individuals from the 5,568 households surveyed, reported that they had engaged in malicious fire lighting. This represents a rate of 2.84%. In the USA, the *National Epidemiological Survey on Alcohol and Related Conditions* examined the incidence of fire lighting in the community (Blanco et al. 2010). The research revealed an estimated lifetime prevalence rate of approximately 1% of the adult USA population.

While these findings provide some evidence that the base-rate of deliberate fire lighting among people is low, the numbers nonetheless represent a huge number of maliciously lit fires. For example, the USA findings would indicate approximately 2 million adult Americans deliberately light fires. While informative, these data do not provide an indication of the nature or severity of the fires that people lit. Indeed, the prevalence and nature of malicious fire lighting have been deemed an international public health issue (Tyler et al., in press).

Common characteristics of arsonists

There is a growing body of literature describing the characteristics of firelighters (Ogloff 2009). We begin by describing the common characteristics observed amongst groups of firelighters, discuss emerging evidence about the psychological characteristics that may distinguish them from other offenders, and repeat firelighters from one-time offenders, and briefly explore differences in various groups of firelighters (the young, the persistent, the accidental firelighter, women and those with mentally illnesses).

Background history and demographics

Although firelighters are a heterogeneous lot, existing research points to a range of characteristics that are relatively common among those who have been apprehended (Bell, Doley & Dawson 2018; Dickens et al. 2009; Doley 2003; Ducat, Ogloff & McEwan 2013; Ellis-Smith, Watt & Doley 2019; Gannon & Pina 2010; Martin et al. 2004; Prins 1995; Rix 1994). Findings from the studies cited show that malicious firelighters are overwhelmingly young, single, Caucasian males, with interpersonal difficulties. They often come from deprived childhoods in which they experienced abuse and have poor educational attainment. They typically have lower occupational status and impoverished relationships. As a group, they typically have 'versatile' or diverse offending histories.

The research has largely shown that firelighters target residential properties (Gannon & Pina 2010; Tyler et al. 2015). However, this is most likely an artefact of the types of fires that are identified as arson and reported, and the types of offenders who are apprehended. It is also the case that a disproportionate amount of research has been conducted in jurisdictions, such as the UK, where wildfire is less of an issue.

In 2008, Muller published a study that investigated the population of firelighters (1,099 arson and 133 wildfire arson defendants) from New South Wales, Australia between 2001 and 2006. Virtually all were male (90%) and adults (84%). A disproportionate number of both adults (20%) and adolescents (37%) were Indigenous. More than half of the adult offenders had a prior conviction for some offence, but very few had prior arson convictions (3% arson offenders, 2% wildfire arson offenders had prior arson). Of the 555 individuals who had a prior conviction, only seven (1.3%) were exclusively firelighters; criminal versatility was the rule.

Few studies have examined fire lighting by Indigenous groups, especially in Australia, which is surprising, given the historical and cultural importance of fire in Aboriginal culture (Muller & Bryant 2008a; Willis 2004) and the over-representation of Aboriginal and Torres Strait Island People in the justice system generally. A recent Australian study by Ellis-Smith, Watt and Doley (2019) found that although their sample was overwhelmingly non-Indigenous, there was a significant difference between the expected and observed number of Indigenous Australians as a percentage of the total number of arsonists represented in their sample. They also found some differences in the characteristics of Indigenous and non-Indigenous firelighters. Indigenous firelighters were more likely to have been substance-affected at the time of the offence, and to have impulsively lit fires for expressive reasons. Interestingly, fewer Aboriginal firelighters had received mental health diagnoses than the non-Aboriginal group. The authors postulated that this difference might relate more to the under-utilisation of services by this group than a real difference. Unfortunately, there was no analysis of the targets or the location of the fire lighting (i.e. wildfire, structural, etc.) to determine differences between the groups.

Two Australian studies have examined differences between men and women who deliberately light fires. In a large-scale study comparing the psychiatric and offending variables of all men (909) and women (143) who were convicted of fire lighting in Victoria between 2000 and 2009, Ducat, McEwan and Ogloff (2017) found that men and women reoffended at similar rates, with similar characteristics of the reoffenders between the two groups. Women were found, however, to have been less criminally versatile than men, with fewer past offences, especially violence offences. Women were more often diagnosed with depression, substance misuse and personality disorder (particularly Borderline Personality Disorder) than men.

Ellis-Smith, Watt and Doley (2019) explored characteristics of convicted arsonists by exploring the sentencing decisions for 305 arson offenders across Australia. Consistent with international findings, women accounted for 11% (34) of the sample. Almost half the females (48%) and more than one-third of males (36.5%) had been diagnosed with a mental illness. However, they found no significant differences in the types of diagnoses identified, with depression and schizophrenia being most common. They also found similar rates of exclusive fire lighting, and similar offence characteristics, between males and females. Interestingly, however, they found that the proportion of women sentenced over the 25-year period increased.

Offending

The fire lighting literature is replete with debate over the question of whether firelighters are a unique set of individuals and if they are versatile or exclusive offenders (Ducat, McEwan & Ogloff 2013). Research is increasingly showing that firelighters, and repeat firelighters, in particular, are less likely to be 'exclusive' offenders and much more likely to be versatile offenders, committing malicious fire lighting in the context of diverse offending careers. For example, Soothill, Ackerley and Francis (2004) examined recidivism across four different samples totalling more than 10,000 arsonists convicted in England and Wales between 1951 and 2001. They found an arson recidivism rate of 7.8% to 20.7% of both males and females, but a general recidivism rate of between 52% and 70%.

Regarding criminal versatility, in the study noted previously, Ducat and her colleagues (2013) found only 20% of their sample of more than 1,000 arsonists were 'exclusive' firelighters, whilst 44% had three or more offence types. Exclusive offenders tended to be younger and to have no other offence history. Ellis-Smith and colleagues (2019) recently replicated Ducat and colleague's results, finding that approximately 19% of their sample were exclusive firelighters, with the majority exhibiting criminal versatility. Again, similar to Ducat and colleague's findings, most exclusive firelighters were being sentenced for the first time, had no youth offending history, and were more likely to set fire to their own property. Similarly, older studies have found that most arson offenders are criminally versatile (Barnett, Richter & Renneberg 1999; Muller 2008). These findings indicate that criminal versatility is a key risk factor for future offending, which is the case in other offender groups.

High-consequence fire lighting

Maliciously lit fires can range from small fires in rubbish bins to large fires that destroy property and occasionally result in the death of people. Most research has not considered the nature and severity of fires that have been set. Thus, a number of questions arise regarding more serious fires, including whether the characteristics of high-consequence firelighters are similar to other groups of firelighters, and whether established recidivism rates and factors associated with repeat fire lighting generalise to high-consequence firelighters. The limited literature on high-consequence firelighters indicates that there is little overlap between those who repeatedly set fires and those whose fires result in injury, death or significant destruction.

Geller and colleagues undertook studies to determine the nature of fires lit by patients in a large state hospital in the USA. First, they found that 7% of firelighters who reoffend go on to endanger life by fire lighting (Geller, Fisher

& Moynihan 1992). Similarly, they found that 12.5% re-offend by setting fire to houses (Geller, Fisher & Bertsch 1992). Findings such as those revealed by Geller and colleagues show that few repeat firelighters endanger life or set more serious fires, and these groups represent only a small proportion of all deliberate firelighters.

In their seminal study of 1,346 firelighters in the USA, Lewis and Yarnell (1951) suggested that high-consequence fire lighting and repeat fire lighting were unrelated. For example, they found that those most likely to cause serious injury, or even death were motivated by jealousy; however, they were also the least likely to set further fires. Likewise, in a large study of Canadian arsonists, Rice and Harris (1991) compared one-time firelighters with repeat firelighters, the latter having higher levels of aggression, set fires in domestic settings and rarely attempted to extinguish the fires. More recently, studies on arson-homicides have found that a high proportion of these offences occurred in the homes of victims (65%), occurred at night (61%), and targeted intimate partners (46%) (Drake & Block 2003; Ferguson et al. 2015). Ferguson and colleagues (2015) also found higher rates of mental illness (19.1%), post-homicide suicides (11.2%), and alcohol or drug-related intoxication (19.1%) among perpetrators of arson homicides compared to non-arson-related homicide offenders. These limited studies, therefore, indicated that high-consequence fire lighting might, in fact, arise for different reasons, in different contexts.

Dickens and colleagues (2009) have also argued that the intentions (motives) associated with high-consequence fire lighting may distinguish them from repeat firelighters and have disputed the convention that "a big fire is just a small fire that hasn't been controlled" (p. 32). The suggestion that intentions underlying fire lighting are not linked to consequent harm implies that fire lighting differs from other forms of offending. Certainly, the intentions of firelighters to cause harm and the actual outcomes of their behaviour may not be aligned due to aspects of planning/timing, environmental conditions, population factors and access to fire and rescue services. However, this could also be said of other forms of offending but would not lessen the importance of understanding perpetrators' motives.

Nanayakkara and colleagues (in press, a) conducted a recent study of high-consequence firelighters (n = 114) based on data obtained from the Coroners Court of New South Wales, Australia. In New South Wales, high-value fires lit by arson (exceeding $100,000 damage) and those causing serious injury or death are investigated by the Coroners Court. Among other things, the study investigated the motives for high-consequence fires. The authors identified five types of fire lighting using multi-dimensional scaling: 1) intimate partner violence; 2) hopeless; 3) instrumental gain; 4) vandalism; and 5) fire interest. Notably, the majority of the fires examined were found to involve planning and the use of accelerants, reaffirming the purposeful nature of high consequence fire lighting.

The general paucity of research on firelighters who are responsible for the most harmful and destructive fires highlights a gap in the literature. Consequently, the question of whether recidivistic firelighters are also responsible for high-consequence fire lighting remains largely unanswered. The available literature hints that similar factors that distinguish one-time and repeat firelighters (i.e. major mental illness or violence) might also mark differences between harmful and recidivistic firelighters.

Mental illness

It is well known that mental illness is over-represented among convicted offenders generally (e.g. Schilders & Ogloff 2014); similarly, this appears to be particularly true for both convicted arsonists and firelighters. Just because there is an increased rate of mental illness among firelighters, it does not mean that the link is not necessarily causal. Rather, several authors have contended that, in most cases, the relationship between mental illness and arson is indirect, by moderating pre-existing vulnerabilities (Gannon et al. 2012; McEwan & Ducat 2015; Nanayakkara, Ogloff & Thomas 2015). Also, pyromania, of course, has a direct relationship with fire lighting (Nanayakkara et al. 2015).

Pathological firelighters, known as pyromaniacs, form a distinct, albeit small, group of malicious firelighters. Elements of the diagnosis include: deliberate and purposeful fire lighting on multiple occasions; an inability to resist setting fires; extreme interest in fire-related paraphernalia; increased tension or arousal before the act followed by an intense relief once committed; a lack of other motives or gain (for example, monetary gain, crime concealment, socio-political expression or anger or revenge); and is not better characterised by another disorder (American Psychiatric Association 2013). Rates of pyromania have varied in the literature from one to 60% (Lewis & Yarnell 1951; Nanayakkara, Ogloff & Thomas 2015). Contrary to the popular conceptions of serial arsonists, most are not pyromaniacs. There has been much disagreement in the literature as to the definition, existence and rate of pyromania, with some authors contending that it simply does not exist (Willis 2004). Most researchers and clinicians acknowledge that pyromania does exist, but pyromaniacs form a very small proportion of deliberate firelighters (Nanayakkara, Ogloff & Thomas 2015).

To examine the prevalence of mental illness among firelighters, Ducat, Ogloff and McEwan (2013) conducted a larger scale epidemiological study employing data linkage methods. They compared the mental health diagnoses and mental health service usage of all 1,328 arsonists convicted in Victoria,

Australia between 2000 and 2009 with a matched community control sample and 421 non-fire lighting offenders. The results revealed that 37% of arsonists had formal contact with public mental health services, compared with 29.3% of offenders in the control sample. Overall, firelighters were more likely to have been diagnosed with any mental illness than both control groups. In particular, they were more likely to be diagnosed with depressive disorders, anxiety disorders, childhood behavioural disorders, substance misuse disorders, and personality disorders. The same was true when comparing firelighters and community controls, with the addition of a higher incidence of psychotic disorders in the fire lighting sample. A similar epidemiological study conducted in Sweden, with 1,689 convicted arsonists and 40,560 community controls, found significantly higher rates of schizophrenia in firelighters (Anwar et al. 2011). Recently, Ellis-Smith and colleagues (2019) examined 305 sentencing decisions for arson offences committed in Australia and found that in nearly half (45.5%) of the firelighters had received a mental health diagnosis in their lifetime, while 37.7% were identified as having a current mental health condition. The most commonly identified diagnoses were depression, schizophrenia and personality disorder. The authors note that these diagnoses were reported at sentencing, and thus may not represent true incidence of mental illness. This is especially for personality disorder, which is notoriously under-diagnosed in sentencing reports. However, it provides further support for the prevalence of mental illness amongst firelighters. Community studies in the adult USA population found a proportionally higher incidence of mental illness in those arrested for arson charges (17%) than others, including mood disorders, substance abuse disorders and personality disorders (Blanco et al. 2010).

Nanayakkara and colleagues (in press, a) conducted a study to explore the differences among mentally disordered firelighters who were referred to community forensic mental health services in New South Wales and Victoria, Australia. They also investigated the nexus between mental disorder and fire lighting. The sample included 103 people, and the researchers considered a range of variables, including motives, clinical (diagnostic) and behavioural variables. They found, using multidimensional scaling, that four different groups of mentally disordered firelighters emerged, with each type reflected differences in motive and diagnosis and were distinguished according to the prevailing behaviours and/or psychological states: 1) psychotic struggle; 2) hopeless; 3) dysregulated mood, and 4) fire interest. The Psychotic Struggle Type included variables of psychosis, fire lighting in places of residence, familiar victims and multiple motives including revenge, self-defence and religious-based motives. The motives within this type were primarily derived from persecutory and/or religious delusions. The co-occurring motives captured within this type were also considered to reflect the likely disorganised mental states of the firelighters.

The Hopeless Type included variables of being subject to mental health legislation at the time of fire lighting, being in hospital, the motive of suicide and self-immolation. The inclusion of variables denoting hospitalisation and involuntary treatment within this type reflected the psychiatric morbidity and subjective hopelessness of these individuals and is consistent with treatment protocols that endorse the involuntary admission of individuals who pose a risk to themselves. As in the first study, variables captured in the Hopeless Type highlight the increased risk of suicidal behaviour among those with major mental illness and demonstrates fire lighting as a hazardous means of attempting suicide, particularly during hospital admissions.

The Dysregulated Mood Type included variables of personality disorder, history of abuse, self-harm, mood dysregulation, and the motive of express frustration. These variables were acknowledged as features common to borderline personality disorder. Consequently, fire lighting in this type was inferred as having a functional purpose, similar to that of self-harm in borderline personality disorder.

Finally, the Fire Interest Type included variables of pyromania, serial fire lighting, setting to vegetation and the motive of excitement. These variables indicated that firelighters within this type engaged in serial fire lighting, likely due to a pathological interest in fire, which is pathognomonic of pyromania.

The relationship between mental disorder and fire lighting observed in this study suggests two clinical pathways to fire lighting. Fire lighting manifest in psychosis appeared to indicate a more direct relationship, with people setting fires as a result of their psychotic beliefs. By contrast, fire lighting that arises in the context of personality disorder and pyromania appeared to be moderated by the respective mental disorder.

These findings demonstrated that there were clear differences among mentally disordered fire lighting and that those differences were observed across psychiatric diagnoses, motives, and contexts for fire lighting. The findings also suggest that the relationship between mental disorder and fire-lighting may vary, dependent on mental health conditions.

Deliberate versus accidental fire lighting

There is scant literature exploring the characterological differences between individuals who engage in malicious fire lighting, and those who accidentally light a fire. The evidence available is typically derived from samples of juveniles who have either come to the attention of authorities or their parents for engaging in unsafe fire behaviour. Fire play is common amongst children

(Putnam & Kirkpatrick 2005), but the majority of children do not go on to engage in malicious fire lighting as they age. Authors have reported that it is usually the combination of the curiosity of fire and simultaneous experiences of family difficulty and stressful life circumstances that result in children engaging in more serious forms of fire lighting behaviour (Lambie, Seymour & Popaduk 2012; Mackay et al. 2006). The research examining the outcomes of those programs shows that the majority of children who enter those programs will not go on to light another fire (Faidley 2015; Lambie et al. 2009). Although there is little evidence to support any theories about why that is, it is likely that the level of antisociality would be a predictor in such cases. Mackay and colleagues (2009) examined risk factors for persistence of fire lighting behaviours amongst juveniles. They found that the combination of fire interest and antisociality were the best predictors of both the severity of fire lighting and persistence. Martin and colleagues (2004) similarly reported antisociality to be a significant predictor of future fire lighting behaviour.

It could be hypothesised then, that individuals who accidentally light fires may be less antisocial, and therefore more likely to be deterred from future fire play by the consequences of the fire and the attention it brought upon them. Supporting this, a study of community firelighters, who self-reported having lit fires for which they were not caught, noted that had they had better fire awareness and knowledge of the potential damage caused by fire, they would not have set the fire (Barrowcliffe & Gannon 2015).

Young versus older offenders

Fire lighting by adolescents is an issue worth paying attention to, as trend data from a range of industrialised countries, such as Australia, New Zealand, the USA, the UK and Europe, suggests that roughly half of all maliciously lit fires are lit by young offenders, typically those aged 12 to 17 years (Faidley 2015). Furthermore, studies have reported that up 60% of young offenders who maliciously light fires are recidivist firelighters (Kolko et al. 2001; Kolko & Kazdin 1992; Lambie et al. 2013; MacKay et al. 2006). This compares to community samples of adults where 40-50% of firelighters report having engaged in multiple fire lighting episodes (Del Bove et al. 2008; Mackay et al. 2009). The consensus appears to be that fire lighting by adolescents occurs in the context of severe psychosocial dysfunction and an array of other antisocial behaviours (Lambie & Randell 2011; Stanley 2002). Notwithstanding this, firelighters typically display greater levels of dysfunction and psychopathology than even other antisocial groups. This is true in the adult population, as we have already seen. However, a schism remains between the adult and juvenile fire lighting literature. Examination of the factors linked to juvenile fire lighting and recidivism closely follow trends reported in the adult literature, lending weight to current theories of adult fire lighting and proposed pathways into adult fire lighting.

Lambie and colleagues (2013) followed 182 fire lighting juveniles who had been referred to the New Zealand Fire Awareness and Intervention Program (FAIP) over a ten-year period. They found that while the fire lighting reoffence rate was low (2%), the general reoffence rate was high (59%). This finding is remarkably consistent with adult fire lighting literature (see for example Ducat, McEwan and Ogloff 2015 who reported a fire lighting reoffence rate of 5% and a general reoffence rate of 55.4%). Reoffending was predicted by having a history of fire lighting prior to the FAIP intervention and having experienced abuse. Conversely, living with both parents at this time of intervention decreased the probability of engaging in future offending behaviour. Other significant factors associated with past fire lighting included family stress and a diagnosis of Attention Deficit Hyperactivity Disorder (ADHD), and severity of offending was associated with family violence (either as a victim, complainant or perpetrator).

These findings have been replicated elsewhere in the adolescent literature (see for Lambie & Randell 2011 for a review; Roe-Sepowitz & Hickle, 2011; Stanley 2002; Watt et al. 2015), and the adult fire lighting literature (Bell, Doley & Dawson 2018). Specifically, juvenile firelighters tend to be male, have psychiatric diagnoses (specifically conduct disorder, Attention deficit hyperactivity disorder, and depressive illnesses), engage in drug use and suicidal behaviours, have poor social skills and therefore poor relationships with others, and report greater fire interest than non-fire lighting peers (Watt et al. 2015). They also tend to have experienced dysfunctional and abusive caregiver environments, low socioeconomic status, and having engaged in a range of other antisocial behaviours. It appears that fire lighting in youth may be associated with greater severity and persistence of offending (Kennedy et al. 2006; Stickle & Bleckman 2002).

The combination of antisociality and fire interest or curiosity appears to be important. Martin and colleagues (2004) found that the best predictor of self-reported fire lighting behaviour was serious antisocial behaviours, while others have noted the importance of fire interest or curiosity and previous fire lighting behaviour (Kolko & Kazdin 1992; Mackay et al. 2006). More recently, Watt et al. (2015) compared differences in risk factors and prevalence of fire lighting behaviours between 138 adolescents adjudicated as offenders and 136 non-offenders from two schools in Queensland, Australia. Offenders were more likely to have a history of fire lighting. Repeat fire lighting was predicted by a history of antisocial behaviour, positive affect regarding fire, fire-related interests, and preoccupation with fire. Juveniles who lit fires were most likely to have reported having done so for fun/boredom (67.4%), curiosity (13.2%)

and because friends were lighting fires (9.7%). Interestingly, the contribution of antisocial behaviour was less relevant in the prediction of fire lighting behaviours once fire-specific variables were accounted for. This indicates that specific interest in fire and positive affect associated with fire lighting is likely to predict future fire lighting for adolescents, as with adults, and may be the key distinguishing factor that predicts which juveniles might go on to maintain fire lighting behaviour into adulthood.

These findings support current theories of fire lighting that indicate that childhood adversity and negative developmental experiences, as well as engaging in fire lighting behaviour as a child, is a significant risk factor for future malicious fire lighting, and point toward interventions that may encourage juvenile firelighters to desist from fire lighting. The fact that the risk factors for adult and juvenile fire lighting bear remarkable semblance indicates that early intervention may be the key to reducing reoffending.

Differences between arsonists and other offenders

Although there has been much debate in the literature about whether firelighters form a distinct group of offenders, emerging research suggests two general themes. The first is that firelighters tend to share a number of general characteristics with other offenders, with some notable exceptions, but, secondly, they may have distinct psychological profiles.

Ducat, McEwan and Ogloff (2013) compared 207 arsonists who were convicted in the Victorian County Court between 2004 and 2009 with 197 offender controls on a range of demographic, criminal justice and psychiatric variables. There were no differences in offence histories of the two groups (perhaps unsurprising given that it was a criminal justice sample), but firelighters were more likely to be unemployed and have lower levels of educational attainment, have been diagnosed with a mental illness, particularly depression and personality disorder, to have a history of suicidal behaviour, childhood behavioural problems, and to have engaged in psychological treatment. Firelighters had more prior incidents of fire lighting and were younger when they first engaged in the behaviour.

Tyler and colleagues (2014) examined a range of variables including offence histories, sociodemographic factors, psychiatric history, family and personal background factors in mentally disordered offenders recruited from six secure psychiatric hospitals in the UK. All participants had a current diagnosed mental disorder and at least one criminal conviction. Overall, there were very few differences in the demographic and offence history variables, but firelighters were significantly more likely to have been diagnosed with a schizophrenic illness and to have reported interest in fire.

Similarly, a UK study comparing 243 mentally disordered firelighters with 100 psychiatric inpatients at Oak Ridge Forensic Mental Health Service found that firelighters tended to be less physically aggressive, had greater incidence of fire lighting and fire interest, had more fire-related acts, such as setting false fire alarms or making bomb threats, than others patients, and their family members were more likely to have a history of fire lighting and family members that reported the patient had childhood interest in fire. They were also more socially isolated and less intelligent.

Debate has raged over the past decades about whether firelighters are more similar than property or violent offenders. Wilpert, Van Horn and Eisenberg (2015) compared 55 firelighters with 41 violent offenders from a Dutch forensic outpatient treatment centre on a range of characterological, personal history and criminal behaviour variables. Consistent with the findings reported above, they found that firelighters were more likely to have been diagnosed with personality disorders (narcissistic traits appearing most often), higher levels of social isolation, and inadequate coping skills. However, violent offenders tended to be younger at first offending, and a larger number had prior offending histories and were diagnosed with drug abuse. Interestingly, and lending weight to the argument that firelighters tend to be general offenders, more than specialists, violent offenders were more likely to be specialist offenders. Few other significant differences were noted.

As with the adolescent literature summarised in the previous section, antisociality is important, but the specific prediction of group membership as a firelighter appears to be mediated by the presence of fire-specific variables. Gannon and colleagues (2013) examined the psychological profiles of 68 firelighters and a matched control sample of 68 non-firelighter prisoners. They found that fire interest, interest in serious fires, greater identification with fire, and lower fire safety awareness were important distinguishing features of firelighters (Gannon et al. 2013; Tyler et al. 2015). These studies also found that other more general psychological characteristics were more common in firelighters: greater anger-related cognition (rumination and hostility) and anger related to provocation, greater physiological arousal to anger, external locus of control and lower self-esteem.

Using a novel approach to sample selection, Barrowcliffe and Gannon (2015) recruited community participants through social media to compare the psychological characteristics of unapprehended firelighters and non-firelighters living in the UK. They defined the groups by asking participants if they had ever deliberately ignited a fire. Of the 232 participants, 40 (17.78%) constituted the unapprehended firelighters. People in this group were more likely to have set a fire in childhood or adolescence, experimented with fire before the age of 10 years, and to have experienced a psychiatric illness, especially a diagnosis of a behavioural disorder. They are also more likely to have been suspended from school, have a history of suicide attempts, and had a family member who also had a history of deliberate fire lighting. Using a range of fire-related tools, and personality-related scales measuring factors such as anger and response to provocation, loneliness, assertiveness, locus of control, boredom proneness, and criminal attitudes and associates, they reported a range of psychological differences between the groups. There is scant literature exploring the characterological differences between individuals who engage in malicious fire lighting, and those who accidentally light a fire.

Overall, firelighters tend to be similar to other offenders in terms of broad criminal history and demographic factors. However, the differences point toward greater psychosocial deficit, psychiatric disturbance, and key psychological differences, which provide opportunities for intervention and diversion.

Typologies of firelighters

Several typologies have been developed over the years to categorise and make sense of the heterogeneity amongst those who deliberately set fires. Single-factor theories have been predominant in the thinking around deliberate fire lighting, and indeed continue to hold an important place in informing lay perspectives about deliberate firelighters. Early typologies focused on single characteristics, such as mental illness, specifically pyromania (Lewis & Yarnell 1951), social learning (Kolko & Kazdin 1986; Vreeland & Levin 1980), biological differences (Virkkunen et al. 1987; Virkkunen et al. 1989) and sexual pleasure or catharsis (Macht & Mack 1968) to explain the behaviour. Often these were derived from observed differences in crime scene actions to extrapolate to possible offender characteristics, or proposed motivations for fire lighting, and were not explicitly theory-driven. However, single-factor theories could not account for the vast differences observed in those who lit fires and did not clearly account for the aetiology of the behaviour (Gannon & Pina 2010).

To account for the deficits of single-factor theories for explaining complex human behaviour such as fire lighting, several authors have proposed multi-factor theories. Two earlier theories, Fineman's Dynamic Behavioural Theory (1980, 1995) and Jackson, Glass and Hope's (1987) Functional Analysis Theory, went some way to explaining the complex and varied pathways individuals make take to deliberate fire lighting. Functional Analytic Theory suggests that fire lighting develops, and is maintained, by a complex interplay between antecedents and consequences to the behaviour. These interact with underlying factors, such as psychosocial disadvantage, life dissatisfaction and self-loathing, social ineffectiveness, early experiences with fire, and internal and external fire lighting triggers. The theory also focused on the impact of both positive and negative consequences of fire lighting as reinforcers. Although the theory has real strengths in its development from both the research literature and clinical experience, it was never empirically tested. Similarly, Dynamic Behaviour Theory states that fire lighting is the result of a complex interplay of developmental, biological, cultural, social learning, and contextual factors. The theory was the first to emphasise the impact of cognition and affect before and after fire lighting. However, this theory also lacked empirical validation.

More recently, Gannon and colleagues (2012) developed the Multi-Trajectory Theory of Adult Firesetting (M-TTAF). The theory accounts for the deficits of previous theories by using an approach that brought together empirically validated and clinically meaningful factors from the research base and clinical experience. This theory highlights the various aetiological pathways to fire lighting, and expressions of the behaviour, as well as avenues for reinforcement for persistent firelighters, and desistance. The theory posits that fire lighting behaviour develops as a result of specific experiences in the developmental context of the firelighter (i.e. biology, developmental experiences, cultural factors and social learning), and gives rise to four key psychological processes that underpin fire lighting: inappropriate fire interests/scripts; offence-supportive cognition; self/emotion regulation issues, and communication problems.

The acuteness and interaction between these four key processes are thought to explain the variability in fire lighting behaviour and clinical presentation. When specific proximal factors are present, producing a continuing dynamic interactive influence of life events, contextual factors and affect/cognition, the pre-existing vulnerabilities become primed and increase the likelihood of the individual engaging in fire lighting behaviour. They propose two moderating factors: self-esteem and mental illness. These factors affect the relationships between psychological vulnerabilities and triggers.

The theory first describes the factors and mechanisms that interact to facilitate and reinforce fire lighting and then go further to put these together into prototypical trajectories (patterns of characteristics leading to fire lighting behaviour), explaining particular presentations of fire lighting behaviour. These trajectories are proposed on the basis of the unique combination of developmental context, psychological vulnerabilities and proximal risk factors, including motivation. The presence and relative importance of various risk factors, and presenting clinical features, are thought to determine how the behaviour is expressed, and then provides clinicians with guidance as to interventions that may be most suitable to reduce the risk of recidivism.

The first proposed trajectory is the 'antisocial cognition' group. Fire lighting for this group often arises out of general criminal attitudes and scripts and is likely to be more instrumental in nature. Typical motivators might include vandalism, revenge and boredom. It would be expected that fire lighting would form just one of an array of antisocial behaviours, which may have an early onset. As with the antisocial cognition group, the 'grievance' firelighter is likely to use fire as an instrument but is likely to do so to express anger at a specific individual or group in response to a provocation. Individuals in this trajectory are expected to show problems in the areas of aggression, anger rumination and hostility, and have poor communication skills underpinned by low assertiveness. They are likely to have fire-specific scripts linking fire and indirect aggression; that is, that fire is a powerful tool to send a message. Unlike the two previous trajectories, individuals following the 'fire interest' trajectory are most likely to have inappropriate interest in fire, scripts about fire being a pleasurable activity in and of itself, and to hold fire-supportive attitudes. Fire lighting is proposed to occur in the absence of general antisocial attitudes, and therefore not likely to form part of a more extensive criminal history. Typically, these firelighters may have problems with impulsivity and use fire as an emotion-regulation strategy, for example, as a method of coping, thrill-seeking or relieve boredom.

Although on the surface the 'emotionally expressive/need for recognition' trajectory may appear similar to the grievance trajectory due to the primary issue being communication skills deficits, the underlying scripts about the use of fire are likely to be different. Those following the emotionally expressive subtype are likely to have a range of problems with emotion regulation, such as poor coping, poor problem-solving and impulsivity. Stressful life events place too much load on them, resulting in the individual feeling unheard, unable to communicate needs and hopeless. Fire, then, is seen as a way of meeting and communicating emotional needs. This group are most likely to engage in fire lighting in conjunction with self-harm and may be more associated with female sample and diagnoses such as depression and borderline personality disorder. The 'need for recognition' group may present differently due to their proposed intact good self-regulation and planning and use of fire in a goal-oriented way, but the underlying problems with communication will be the key clinical feature. Fire lighting may be used to gain social attention or 'hero' status. This trajectory is proposed to account for firefighters who set fires. The final group, called 'multi-faceted', are proposed to have a number of complex and serious problems arising from highly aversive developmental experiences, and inappropriate fire interests and scripts about the use of fire. These scripts are proposed to have developed from a natural curiosity towards fire, and early fire play, which is reinforced as an important messenger, natural coping mechanism, and sensation-enhancing tool. Fire lighting is likely to form one part of a pervasive offending history that is repetitive and has little regard for the safety of others. Therefore, it is likely that these individuals will present with both fire-specific and general antisocial attitudes, problems with self- and emotion-regulation, poor communication skills, and trait anger.

The theory was developed to explain the range of observed adult fire lighting behaviour; however, most of the data on which the theory relies is based on samples of structural (urban) fire lighting. Parts of the theory have empirical support, but the theory as a whole has not yet been validated. Studies have examined and lent support to parts of the theory, especially the psychological vulnerabilities (Barrowcliffe & Gannon 2015; Gannon et al. 2013; Tyler et al. 2015). Dalhuisen, Koenraadt and Liem (2017) attempted to validate the subtypes proposed by the M-TTAF by rating variables linked to the M-TTAF in files of all 389 adult firelighters referred for a forensic mental health assessment to a clinic in the Netherlands between 1950 and 2012. The cluster analyses found partial support for some of the subtypes.

Application of this theory to wildfire lighting is problematic, as with extrapolating all research on structural arson, as there are so little data available to determine its validity. Nonetheless, the theory provides a useful framework for understanding the possible pathways into, and expression of fire lighting, as well as how individuals might cease the behaviour, either spontaneously, or with intervention.

Noting the need for a concise malicious wildfire lighting classification scheme, Willis (2004) postulated a typology of wildfire lighters, structured around five principle types of maliciously lit wildfires.

- Wildfires lit to relieve boredom or create excitement: vandalism, stimulation, activity (something to do). The latter sub-category relates to fire-fighters and others who simply light fires for something to do.

- Recognition and attention: heroism (to gain positive recognition); pleading (a 'cry for help').

- Specific purpose or gain: anger (often toward the government or land management bodies); pragmatic (for a purpose such as land clearing), or crime concealment; material (such as fire-fighters seeking overtime pay); altruistic (firelighter believes the fire will benefit others).

- No motive: Psychiatric (no other motive, no control over actions, and no malicious intent); children (play or experimentation but without malicious intent or awareness of the possible consequences).

- Mixed motives: Multiple (a mixture of the above); Incidental (the result of malicious intent such as crime concealment, but no notion that the fire may spread and result in a wildfire).

Note that while many of the categories share some characteristics with the research on structural fire lighting, the specifics vary. This highlights the need to view wildfire lighting as a separate crime to structural fire lighting and target intervention programs accordingly. While this model is an encouraging first step in the classification of wildfire lighting, the author concedes it is a preliminary model and is yet to be evaluated (Willis 2004). Further research is needed to test the application of such a system. Furthermore, it may not be applicable across all age groups as motivations may be age-specific.

What motivates individuals to set fires?

What motivates the firelighter is a question that has been the focus of much research. The question of firelighter motivation has been preeminent in the offender profiling traditions of the FBI, with arson-specific typologies being developed since the 1980s (Davis & Bennett 2016). In more recent times, motivational typing has come to be viewed as a flawed approach to understanding fire lighting, partly because of the heterogeneous nature of fire lighting and firelighters, and partly due to the often conflated terms used in the literature to ascribe motive (Dickens & Sugarman 2012; Ducat & Ogloff 2011; Gannon & Pina 2010). At best, motivation is but one facet that is worthy of exploration when understanding arson, understood best within the developmental and triggering circumstances of the fire lighting event.

Although different samples (i.e., forensic mental health, criminal justice, community) and different definitions of motivations have led to some variability in reported samples, there are consistencies. Summarising, motivations can be considered along two dimensions: instrumental and expressive (Canter & Fritzon 1998; Ducat & Ogloff 2011). Gannon and Pina (2010) summarise the literature in this area, citing that the most commonly reported motivations reported across the literature are revenge (Inciardi 1970; Koson & Dvoskin 1982), vandalism (Icove & Estepp 1987), and excitement (Iciardi 1970; Icove & Estepp 1987), followed by other, less frequently reported motivators: profit, crime concealment, mental illness, extremism, cry for help, self-harm, heroism, and suicide. It is likely that the preponderance of motivations is accounted for by the complex and multi-faceted nature of fire lighting (Ducat & Ogloff 2011; Gannon & Pina 2010).

As noted above, Nanayakkara and colleagues (in press a & b) examined New South Wales Coronial data, and NSW and Victorian Community Forensic Mental Health samples to better understand specific subgroups of arsonists. Their studies focused on the most serious offences which caused significant damage or physical harm, as well as those with mental illness and female firelighters. While looking at a range of individual, situational and offence characteristic variables, as well as motivation, Nanayakkara and colleagues found that the most commonly reported motives were revenge, profit and excitement. A large portion of those who engaged in fire lighting for revenge targeted their ex- or current intimate partners. Several other studies have also pointed to revenge and excitement as two of the most significant motivations for malicious fire lighting (Dalhuisen, Koenraadt & Liem 2017; Gannon et al. 2013; Rix 1994).

Barrowcliffe and Gannon (2015) found that community-based firelighters reported that they were motivated to set fires out of curiosity (65%) and to create fun or excitement (67.5%), while the majority reported multiple motivations. These motivations may be distinct from those reported by other groups of firelighters, such as mentally disordered offenders and offender populations, where revenge and emotional expression are much more commonly reported. These motivations are also likely to be impacted by the fact that the majority of firelighters in their sample reporting fire lighting with friends (72.5%). Interestingly, just under one-third of participants, forming the largest group, reported that they targeted grass, shrubbery or dry leaves. Although it is hard to extrapolate these findings to lighting wildfires, where the risk of causing significant property damage may be present even when lighting seemingly small grass or shrubbery fires, it does provide some hints as to the kinds of individuals who may target natural environments, and for what purpose.

In contrast to structural fire lighting, wildfire lighters are less likely to engage in fire lighting for revenge or profit, and more likely to light fires out of an interest in fire or excitement-seeking (Muller & Bryant 2009). Where revenge is a potential motivator for wildfire lighting, it is more likely to be a diffuse sense of anger and not targeted towards a specific individual (Muller & Bryant 2009). It is more likely that wildfire lighters do so to fulfil a psychological need. Seasonal trends are evident with wildfire lighting, and that Australian data suggests that more wildfires are set on days declared as Total Fire Ban days, provides support for the notion that individuals may be drawn to engage in deliberate wildfire lighting for the excitement. The media build-up to high fire danger days, and the potential for devastating and far-reaching consequences of starting fires on these days, may be the triggering event (Willis 2004). Commonly reported motivators for deliberate wildfire lighting tend to focus more on the emotive, such as thrill-seeking, boredom relief, and fire interest, than on instrumental motivations.

Case study

Tino was a young man who had aspirations of joining the Country Fire Authority (CFA). He had social difficulties all his life, was bullied at school and in his workplace, and felt that joining the CFA would provide him with a sense of belonging, purpose, and community. When he was part-way through his training, he began to make prank calls to report fires so that he could watch the trucks drive past his house. On more than one occasion, he called them in while he was at the CFA on duty so he could observe the excitement of the trucks being prepared for deployment. After several of these instances, the fire chief and a member of the police attended a CFA meeting that Tino was in attendance. They picked him out of the group, and with everyone watching, arrested him for making the false alarm calls. Although Tino recognised that his behaviour was wrong, he was incensed at being targeted in front of his friends and colleagues. He developed deep-seated anger at the CFA, which had become a lightning rod for all the anger and frustration he felt at those who had bullied him, and at the community at large for what he perceived its rejection of him. While he desperately wanted to punish the CFA for this, he felt incapable of specifically targeting it. Instead, he began setting nuisance fires in natural areas, resulting in multiple callouts a day. On more than one occasion, the fires he set spread in an out-of-control fashion, destroying large swathes of forest and risking community property.

Fire personnel who engage in deliberate fire lighting

Although there is little research on the topic, the issue of fire lighting by fire personnel raises its head each fire season. One reason for the attention to the topic is that the notion that an individual, who is paid to fights fires and save lives (or who volunteers to do so), doing the opposite is abhorrent and casts suspicion on the group as a whole. Secondly, they are a highly visible and relatable group (i.e. not 'just offenders'). Nonetheless, there is little research examining the specific traits of firefighters who set fires, which is likely due to the low numbers of such offenders being apprehended. It is most likely that fire personnel who engage in fire lighting have an interest in fires and may demonstrate a need for recognition.

   The research in existence suggests that they may be higher functioning than other firelighters, showing greater capacity for employment, planning, self-regulation and problem-solving. What they may lack, as proposed by the M-TTAF, is the ability to communicate their needs and fire-specific scripts about the usefulness of fire to meet a need. This group of firelighters has the potential to be more dangerous than others, due to their intimate knowledge of fire behaviour, geography and fire personnel responses, and possibly also due to a false belief in their own capacity to contain a fire or set a specific type of fire. Muller and Bryant (2009) hypothesise that firefighters may be motivated by the need for recognition and social status, excitement and in some cases, to gain employment or jobs. Willis (2004) summarises the literature in this area and suggests that firefighters who engage in malicious lighting are usually relatively new to the job but come from more dysfunctional backgrounds.

Predictors and risk factors for fire lighting

Having examined the possible psychological reasons underlying the decision to light malicious fires, we now turn to the predictors and risk factors that may assist in differentiating those firelighters who are at risk for setting additional fires and those who will not repeat the offending. Importantly, as revealed in the previous section, fire lighting should not be thought of as a unitary construct due to the complex and varying range of behaviours, motivations and antecedents associated with fire lighting (Palmer, Caulfield & Hollin 2005).

A review of 24 studies drawn from the international literature on the incidence of fire lighting reoffence indicates the rate varies from 4% to 60% based on subsequent arsons (Brett 2004). While it is difficult to identify an average rate, it is generally accepted at least 30% of arsonists will go on to subsequently set fires. As with the research on motives, there are few reported predictors that could be used to differentiate malicious firelighters from other offenders, let alone one-off firelighters and serial firelighters. The reported predictors for malicious fire lighting offenders tend to be similar to those for other offenders, and thus render very little predictive validity.

Most studies agree that firelighters, in general, tend to be young males with both interpersonal difficulties and alcohol or drug addictions; show evidence of unstable childhoods and some form of mental health issue (Prins 1995). Based on an analysis of crime scene characteristics noted by investigators, Canter and Fritzon (1998) noted a few common characteristics of repeat fire offender, including making several false alarm fire calls, personality disorder, prior fire lighting offences, and contact with social services.

In analysing the characteristics of repeat firelighters at the Oak Ridge forensic mental health facility in Ontario, Canada, Quinsey and colleagues (2006) found a number of factors that were predictive of repeat fire lighting. These included a traumatic childhood and unstable home life; poor school adjustment; low intelligence; an extensive fire lighting history, particularly with an early onset of the behaviour; and a history of aggression.

Dickens and colleagues (2009) examined case files of 167 adult arsonists to identify factors that differentiated single episode and repeat arsonists. They also considered whether factors could differentiate those firelighters who set fires that caused more serious injury, loss of life or extensive damage. All of the firelighters were referred for a forensic mental health assessment, which is the norm in the UK. One limitation of the study is that rather than following firelighters over time to see whether they reoffended, the researchers were only able to identify from the file material whether they had one or more incidents of malicious fire lighting in the past.

Dickens and colleagues (2009) found that almost half (49%) of the firelighters had lit malicious fires before. These people were found to be younger and more likely to be single. They commenced their criminal offending earlier and experienced school adjustment problems. They were also more likely to have had a learning disability and personality disorder. The repeat firelighters were also more likely to have more extensive histories of property crime and spent a longer period in prison. Although rare, those who experienced feelings of tension and excitement when engaged in fire lighting behaviour were more likely to be repeat fire offenders.

Importantly, and perhaps surprisingly, Dickens and colleagues (2009) did not find any relationship between repeat fire lighting and lighting fires that resulted in injury, extensive danger, or loss of life. In this regard, the authors concluded that we "consider that it may be a mistake to conflate recidivism and dangerousness; our data suggest that a repeat firelighter is not necessarily one who causes the most harm, and the assumption that the concepts of recidivism and dangerousness among firesetters are interchangeable should be challenged" (p. 635).

Ducat, McEwan and Ogloff (2015) conducted a study of more than 1,000 arsonists convicted in Victoria, Australia to: 1) determine the rate of malicious fire lighting recidivism in a representative sample of firelighters before the courts; 2) determine the psychiatric and criminogenic factors that are related to fire lighting recidivism, and 3) develop a clinically meaningful triage tool for identifying fire lighting at increased risk of recidivism. Using a data linkage methodology, they linked the offenders convicted of arson between 2000 and 2009 with the criminal offending database. They then compared the characteristics of those who reoffended by committing arson and arson-related offences with those who went on to reoffend in other ways but not arson, over a follow-up period of 2.5 – 11 years. Results revealed that the rate of malicious fire lighting recidivism was very low (5.33%) compared with the rate of general recidivism (55.4%); the vast majority of fire lighting recidivists were mixed (criminally versatile) offenders (91%). The study found that general criminality, fire lighting history, and psychiatric disorder were associated with fire lighting recidivism. When assessing the risk of fire lighting recidivism, clinicians need to consider general criminality in addition to fire-specific history, and the potential impacts of mental disorder on recidivism (Nanayakkara et al. in press, b).

Given the number of adolescents who offend by deliberate fire lighting (some figures suggest 50% of malicious fires are lit by children (Palmer, Caulfield & Hollins 2005) some discussion of the risk factors for juveniles is warranted. Among adolescents, fire lighting is often part of a broad array of anti-social behaviour. There is a seeming overlap between children who experience severe child abuse, have a mental illness, and engage in antisocial activities (fire lighting being one facet of this) (Stanley 2002). Many of the factors found in adult firelighters (externalising problems; heightened aggression; drug use; poor interpersonal skills; conduct disorder/antisocial personality disorder; family dysfunction and instability; poor academic record; and some evidence of physical or sexual abuse) can also be observed in young firelighters. The overlap between adult and juvenile offenders can be simply explained by the fact that often fire lighting begins in childhood or adolescence and may, therefore, continue on to adulthood. Nevertheless, some of these factors have found some discriminant validity in distinguishing between non-offenders and some other juvenile offenders who do not light fires.

All of these profiles offer some indicators for firelighters in general but not for those who light wildfires, in particular. Unfortunately, the literature in this area is limited. One study examining the offending and reoffending rates of wildfire arson in New South Wales found that the 'average' offender was male; with a mean age of 26.6, although 31% were under the age of 18 at the time of the offence; and were overwhelmingly non-Indigenous. Moreover, prior offence histories were more likely to feature personal crimes, followed by property and drugs offences (Muller 2008, pp. 4-5). However, there was little else found to distinguish these offenders, nor were there any differences found in these factors between convicted structural arsonists and wildfire arsonists. For this reason, it has been suggested that the focus should not be on developing profiles of the 'typical' wildfire lighters as in doing this an important range of characteristics may be overlooked, limiting the utility of the profile (Muller 2008; Shea 2002).

Conclusion

Although limited due to the low apprehension rate of malicious firelighters, a picture is beginning to emerge about the characteristics of firelighters and the types of people who set fires. We know that the prevalence of fire lighting is high, with few people continuing to ignite fires and even fewer ever being caught. This is particularly true of those who lite wildfires, due to difficulties identifying such fires, and then apprehending the perpetrators. Studies of those who have been apprehended, show that approximately half of the firelighters are children or adolescents. Among adults, most are young, single, Caucasian males, with interpersonal difficulties. Within Australia, a disproportionate number of both adolescent and firelighters are Aboriginal or Torres Strait Islanders. Indigenous firelighters have been found to be more likely to have been substance-affected at the time of the fire lighting. They are also more likely than others to have impulsively set fires for expressive reasons. While mental illness is over-represented among firelighters, fewer Aboriginal firelighters have been found to be mentally ill. When compared to male firelighters, women who light fires have been found to reoffend at similar rates, and they share similar characteristics; however, they were found to be less criminally versatile to men, with fewer past offences, especially offences. The women were also more likely to be diagnosed with depression, substance misuse, and personality disorders than men.

As noted, high rates of apprehended firelighters have mental illnesses; although, the relationship between mental illness and fire lighting is less clear. The relationship between mental illness and fire lighting may vary dependent upon the mental health condition. Researchers have identified two possible pathways to fire lighting. First, psychotic disorders, including schizophrenia, have been found to often have a more direct relationship with fire lighting, with people setting fires as a result of their psychotic beliefs. By contrast, fire lighting that arises in the context of personality disorder and pyromania appeared to be moderated by the respective mental illness.

Although many malicious firelighters are criminally versatile (i.e. engage in a range of offences beyond fire lighting), a number of differences have been found between arsonists and other offenders. Firelighters have been found, for example, to be more likely to be unemployed and to have lower levels of educational attainment than other offenders. In addition, the arsonists are more likely to have been diagnosed with a mental illness, particularly depression and personality disorders, to have a history of suicidal behaviour, childhood behavioural problems, and to have engaged in psychological treatment than other offenders.

A number of different typologies have been identified for firelighters; however, some key types have emerged. Gannon and colleagues' (2012) Multi-Trajectory Theory of Adult Firesetting (M-TTAF) brings together empirically validated and clinically meaningful factors from the research base and clinical experience. This theory highlights the various aetiological pathways to malicious fire lighting, and expressions of the behaviour, as well as avenues for reinforcement for persistent firelighters, and desistance. The theory posits that fire lighting behaviour develops as a result of specific experiences in the developmental context of the firelighter (i.e., biology, developmental experiences, cultural factors and social learning), and give rise to four key psychological processes that underpin fire lighting: inappropriate fire interests/scripts; offence-supportive cognition; self/emotion regulation issues, and communication problems. These factors contribute to five proposed trajectories for firelighters, including: (1) the antisocial cognition group, (2) the grievance firelighters, (3) fire interest, (4) emotionally expressive/need for recognition, and (5) multi-faceted. It is unclear how well this theory applies to those who light wildfires, with further research being required to investigate this question.

Sadly, some of the people who deliberately light fires are also those who are tasked with fighting fires. Although there is little research on the topic, the issue of fire lighting by fire personnel arises each fire season. It is likely that these people have an interest in fires and may also demonstrate a need for recognition. They could be more dangerous than other malicious firelighters, given their expertise with fires and their ability to better conceal the cause of fires.

Existing research shows that relatively few people convicted of arson go on to have further convictions for arson. For example, in Victoria, only one in twenty arsonists have later convictions for arson – although more than half went on to commit some other offences. Also, the likelihood of lighting further fires should not be conflated with the likelihood of setting more serious fires or harming people. Moreover, as noted, most firelighters were found to be criminally versatile (i.e. committing a range of offences). Generally speaking, past general criminality, fire lighting history, and having psychiatric disorders increase the risk for reoffending among convicted firelighters.

Given the high percentage of fires that are maliciously ignited, more research is required to understand, explain, and ultimately prevent and treat this problem. To the extent possible, it is important to increase the sample of people studied. For example, some researchers have been able to obtain samples of people who have admitted to maliciously igniting fires, but not been caught or apprehended. Investigating such people in greater detail, at the very least, can help us determine the extent to which 'captured' firelighters share characteristics with those who have not been caught in the criminal justice system.

Chapter 4

Ignition patterns

Introduction

While there has been quite a lot of research on aspects of wildfire in the rural/urban interface, there is a lot more work needed on the interaction between location and cause of ignition. Other important spatial patterns have received little attention, such as the interaction between socio-economic factors and malicious wildfire lighting. The association between disadvantage and crime is discussed in the field of environmental criminology. While the association between disadvantage and fire lighting was recognised a decade ago (Muller 2009a), it remains rarely discussed. This book emphasises the importance of fully understanding the patterns of wildfire ignition in association with cause, if the prevention of ignition is to be successful.

This chapter looks at current knowledge about wildfire ignition patterns and what is known about why these patterns occur. It makes initial steps at linking research from other disciplines to offer some new insights into this body of knowledge and thereby opens up other opportunities for prevention of wildfire. The international literature reports fairly similar fire patterns. In summary, the majority of wildfire ignitions occur where humans interface with the natural environment, due to urban development, farming activities, and where access into forested areas is promoted through roads and tracks. Ignitions in the rural/urban interface are largely human-caused, as a result of malicious or reckless/accidental activities. Fires in these interface areas have a tendency to be smaller, as they are more quickly extinguished due to the danger they pose to humans and structures. Prescribed burning tends to be utilised less often in denser human habited places, again due to the risks involved, with mowing and clearing of vegetation more often practised as a fuel reduction approach. While fewer numbers of ignitions occur in the more isolated and forested areas, such fires usually burn a much larger area and are more ferocious, thus harder to suppress. Forest fires may be ignited by lightning as well as caused by malicious and accidental fires, the latter particularly as a result of recreational activities in forested areas. Prescribed burning is a frequent tool used in forested areas, and at times the fires may not be actively extinguished due to opportunities for fuel reduction or ecological burning.

The research literature reviews spatial patterns of fire at considerably different scales, from regional patterns, down to small-scale locations. This creates difficulties in comparing research findings. Analysis by Genton and colleagues (2006) found that wildfire clustering is evident in all spatial scales, except in very small areas. However, a difficulty in understanding spatial patterns of crime, in general, can again be associated with data, where fine-grained location information is typically not recorded, so coarser data is used, which may impact accuracy. The lack of differentiation in many fire datasets between urban structural, vegetation fires and vehicle fires, adversely impacts understanding of fire patterns, as the cause of the different forms of ignition, can vary. While there has been some spatial and temporal mapping of different forms of crime, their accuracy in forecasting future crime has not been tested (Prestemon et al. 2013). However, temporal data shows greater predictive accuracy (Prestemon, Butry & Thomas 2013).

This chapter is based on a review of the literature. Unfortunately, it does not offer a methodical and comprehensive overview of the issues at the strategic level, rather more random snapshots. There is a need to also rely on rather dated research and relatively small studies at a large scale, all problematical given the rapidly evolving concerns about wildfire.

Wildfire locations

As discussed in chapter 2, most wildfires are caused by human activity. A similar spatial and temporal distribution of human-caused wildfires (malicious and reckless) can be found in Australia (Collins et al. 2015), south-western Europe (Oliveira et al. 2014), the west coast of the USA (Syphard et al. 2007) and Canada (Gralewicz, Nelson & Wulder 2012). Balch and colleagues (2017) note that humans have vastly expanded the spatial distribution and seasonal occurrence of wildfires. Since the fundamentals of both socioeconomic and environmental dynamics change slowly, maliciously lit wildfires have the tendency to occur in the same location and at the same time, each year (Muller 2009b).

Increased migration is an increasing international feature; with people moving between countries due to conflict, climate change impacts or seeking a better life. Within a country, there is movement of people from rural locations to a city, often the more affordable edges of a city. At the same time, there is a trend in industrialised countries for wealthier people to move towards a more rural/environmental or coastal lifestyle, yet close to amenities, with access to either a major or secondary city (Eriksen & Prior 2011; Gill 2005; Llausàs Buxton & Bellin 2016; Lucas et al. 2007). Thus, the rural/urban interface areas have a wide mix of people. These include people who have moved to new, more affordable housing on the edge of urban areas; rural farms; full-time residents (tree-changers); part-time residents (weekend and holidays, hobby farmers), and tourist establishments (Eriksen & Prior

2011). These movements are increasing the person/environment interface and thereby increasing the wildfire risk.

There is a larger literature from Europe and the USA on the rural/urban interface, than from Australia. It is suggested that this may be due to the different geography between Europe and Australia, with perhaps North America sited in the middle. Europe, with a population of 743 million, carries on average 185 people per square kilometre. North America, with a population of 364 million, has approximately 15 people per square kilometre, while Australia, with a population of 25 million, has about three people per square kilometre. This, of course, does not account for the distribution of this population, nor the flammability of the environment. However, it reminds us that Australia, and to a lesser extent, Northern America, does have larger unpopulated areas than Europe. Thus, Australia and North America are likely to have proportionately fewer areas that could be described as urban/rural interface. Hence forested and moorland/grassland areas in Europe are usually more likely to be close to an urban settlement, especially in Western Europe and the UK.

This highlights the need to understand the spatial context in order to understand wildfire patterns. With Europe being more populated, there could be said to be more opportunities for human causes of fire per unit of space. Also, with greater unpopulated areas, it could be surmised that lightning is possibly a more frequent cause of fire in low populated forested areas of Australia and North America. However, this may not hold for arid areas of land, the presence and development of agriculture, and the use of fire by Indigenous people, as well as the size of state and national parks. This suggests that spatial and temporal ignition issues could be a little different between Europe, North America and Australia.

While much of the wildfire literature, in general, originates from Europe, North America and Australia, many fires occur in other countries, such as Africa, South America and Russia. As evidenced by satellite data and, as noted in chapter one, wildfires are increasingly occurring in countries traditionally not fire-prone. The causes of ignition need to be understood in the geographical and cultural context of the region, as well as in the context of the rate and impact of climate change.

Spatial patterns of fire ignition in Europe

The rural/urban interface

Europe, along with other countries, is facing an increasing rural/urban interface wildfire risk (Biasia et al. 2015; Tedim, Xanthopoulos & Leone 2015). Indeed, increasing population density and road access is found in many countries. The southern region of Europe is most affected by wildfires, particularly due to the growth of population over the last three decades (Sapountzaki et al. 2011; Xanthopoulos et al. 2012). Although it needs to be kept in mind that wildfire data vary in accuracy, human-caused wildfires in this Mediterranean region are said to account for 95% of fires, the largest proportion of human-caused fires in the world (Leone et al. 2009, reported in Tedim, Xanthopoulos & Leone 2015). Ganteaume and colleagues (2013) report that in Northern Europe, about 14% of wildfires are deliberately lit, with 79% being accidental or due to negligence, totalling 93% direct human ignition. The centre of Europe has 56% of fires deemed to be deliberate, with 43% being accidental or due to negligence, thus 99% direct human ignition. In Southern Europe, 56% are deliberate, with 40% being accidental or due to negligence, totalling 96% direct human ignition.

As well as population growth, as noted earlier, the desire for a better living environment with less air and noise pollution has also seen a movement into more rural/forested areas (the lifestyle push) (Tedim, Xanthopoulos & Leone 2015). The authors believe that this has led to an increase in roads, offering greater access to more rural areas. This spread of population has increased the risk of reckless/accidental wildfires, such as associated with construction works, garbage burning, car parking on grasses, open barbeques, and children playing with matches.

Catry and colleagues (2007) analyzed 127,492 fires recorded in Portugal during the period 2001-2005. They examined variables such as population density, proximity to urban areas and roads, land cover types, altitude, causes of fire and the area burnt. It was found that wildfire ignitions were concentrated in the most populated municipalities and tended to be maliciously caused. Most fires were also located very close to the main roads (85% at less than 500 metres away and 98% at less than two kilometres). Most ignitions were located in agricultural areas (60%) or in rural/urban areas (25%). About 80% of ignitions occurred at elevations below 500 metres. Most (85%) wildfires were small, less than one hectare, with only 0.3% large wildfires of 500 hectares or more. Ganteaume and colleagues (2013) supported many of these findings, fires being lit between 50 and 250 metres from urban areas and less than 50 metres from roads.

As noted earlier, the above findings may have changed over time, given the changing climatic conditions and changes in populations. This appears to be the case in Europe in the recent past. Tedim, Xanthopoulos & Leone (2015) document that wildfires in the rural/urban interface are relatively recent, the first one starting in 1981. Poor urban planning leading to urban sprawl that may also be associated with illegal development and ad hoc housing increased the risk of wildfires (Tedim, Xanthopoulos & Leone 2015). The situation in Greece illustrates the evolution of the rural/urban wildfire problem. From 1981, when the first rural/urban interface fire in Greece spread through the high-class northern suburbs of Athens, fires in Attica have gradually become more commonplace. Chapter one of this book talks about severe fires in Eastern Attica, that occurred in 2018. Sapountzaki and associates raised the risk of wildfire in this location in an article published in 2011. The risks entailed rapid population growth in the region, acute land-use conflicts around legal, illegal, and disputed land ownership rights, and urban sprawl around Athens, especially along the Eastern coastline with "a mixed forest-housing spatial pattern" (p.1451). The authors noted that fire arose from both intentional lighting and infrastructure neglect, as well as recreational activities and poor electrical wiring.

Research in Spain examined the association between fire danger rating indices and spatial variables (Padilla & Vega-Garcia 2011). A model was developed using a 10-kilometre grid, that examined daily fire weather (rainfall, minimum and maximum temperature, and humidity), vegetation type, landscape features (elevation and slope), fuel levels, human-related geographic measures, 15 fire danger rating indices, and fire records, for the period from 2002 to 2005. The modelling showed that the higher the density of roads, the higher the probability that a fire would occur. Similarly, increasing distance from a town led to a lower probability of ignition. The results were also interpreted according to 53 regions. Four of these areas in North West Spain had nearly all fires ignited by humans (99% compared with 78% in the rest of Spain). Fire was often associated with agricultural burning and pasture improvement. Importantly, the authors concluded that regional differences in human activities might influence fire occurrence patterns, more than biophysical characteristics of the fire environment.

Wildfires away from the rural/urban interface area

Although wildfires largely occur in the rural/urban interface, wildfires in Europe do occur in less population-dense areas. According to Tedim, Xanthopoulos and Leone (2015), forested areas cover about 27% of Europe, but only about 8.5% of wildfires occur in these areas. The authors believe that recent growth in fire problems, particularly in Eastern Europe, is due to extensive abandonment of traditional villages by young people, along with agriculture ceasing over huge tracts of land. The farm abandonment is said to have led to an increase in fuel load. It is also due to fewer people gathering firewood from the forest floor, thus increasing the risk that an ignited fire will spread. However, the causes of ignition, the size of the fires, and the comparative problems between past land fires and current wildfires are not discussed in the article. In other parts of Europe, such as southern Italy, fire is lit in farming areas, mainly related to the traditional practice of burning spent crops, or it is associated with hunting (Tedum, Xanthopoulos & Leone 2015). Ganteaume and colleagues (2013) also mention hunting as a cause of fires and also include other recreational activities such as barbecues and campfires linked to picnicking and hiking in Finland, Sweden, and Poland. Recreational issues were noted in the recent Swedish fires in 2018, referred to in chapter one.

Conclusions about fire in Europe

The European literature strongly suggests that wildfire is highly associated with human activity, the higher the population living close to, and accessing, fire-prone land areas, the greater the occurrence of wildfire. However, farming practices (or a change in them) are also seen as a cause of wildfire ignition.

Spatial patterns of fire ignition in North America

The growing trend of people moving to a rural/urban interface location is also reported in the USA and Canada. Housing within 10 kilometres of the urban/rural interface, was predicted to increase by 80% by 2030 in California (Miller et al. 2011). The population is also increasing in more isolated areas. This is due to people seeking to live in areas with natural amenity values, resort developments in the mountains, and the presence of resource-dependent communities.

Faivre and colleagues (2016) modelled the relative importance of causes of wildfire ignitions in Southern California, from 1980-2009, using United States Forest Services data. The model was based on a 3 x 3 kilometre land size grid and explored 15 explanatory variables in relation to whether a fire had occurred in this area, and if so, the frequency of occurrence. The 15 variables, as with many other studies, examined both the ignition and environmental conditions that would impact the spread of the fire. The factors relating to ignition were accessibility, distance to major and minor roads and housing, and the impact of population and road density. The research found that the most influence on fire occurrence was the presence of populated areas and major infrastructure and highways. A high density of fires occurred where housing meets undeveloped land. Five per cent of the land area produced 40% of ignitions. Approximately 60% of all ignitions occurred within one kilometre of a major road. Seventy-five per cent of ignitions occurred within 5 kilometres of areas with a density of housing greater than 6.2 housing units/km2. The frequency of fires rapidly decreased in areas further away from housing.

The importance of population and road density to human ignition is supported by research in other areas in the USA (e.g. Cardille, Ventura & Turner 2001). This association is expected, as the more people with access, the more likely fires will be ignited. Fires would also be more likely to be noticed and reported if there are more people present to alert authorities. There are also more likely to be fire services in close proximity to where people and structures are dense, due to the risk that wildfire poses. The analysis by Faivre and colleagues (2016) (discussed above) excluded fires that were small – less than 0.1 acres in size; however, the size is not really relevant if it is the number of ignitions that are being counted. The size of the fire is likely to reflect the response time of the fire services and the environmental conditions.

Lightning, malicious, accidental and rail-based wildfire ignitions were shown to have specific clustering patterns in 18 North Eastern Florida counties in data examined from 1981 to 2001 (Genton et al. 2006). As expected, rail fires showed strong clustering along the tracks due to friction sparks. Malicious fires were clustered around the major cities, particularly in two of the five major cities, St Augustine and Gainesville. Lightning, and particularly accidentally caused wildfires, showed fewer clustering patterns.

Wang and Anderson (2010) explored spatial patterns of both human-caused fires and lightning fires in Alberta, Canada. Malicious wildfires were not considered. They examined accidental/reckless fires, largely due to activities in forested and more isolated areas, caused by recreational activities (camping, hiking and hunting) and industrial activities (timber production, transportation, and oil and gas exploration). While about two-thirds of fires were said to be human-caused, and the remainder said to be due to lightning, there was wide variation between regions. In the more southern areas, transport routes were associated with wildfire, particularly where roads increased accessibility to forests, increasingly allowing recreational use. The increase in oil and gas exploration also proved to be a fire risk. Human-caused fires occurred in areas where agriculture, forest, and forest industries coexist. They found that while lightning fires often occurred in clusters, human-caused fires showed stronger clustering patterns for distance scales less than 50 kilometres. The lightning patterns were influenced by geographical conditions creating thunderstorm conditions, commonly in higher elevation areas and areas where boreal[1] forests dominate. Ten per cent of the fires ignited by lightning occurred in what the authors call maritime provinces.

McGee, McFarlane and Tymstra (2015) also point out how extensive the area under forest is in Canada, with most wildfires occurring in the large areas of boreal forest. They also note a trend of an increase of wildfires beyond

---

[1] Boreal forests occur across North America consisting of confers, largely pines, spruces and larches, interspersed with vast wetlands and bogs.

Canada's forested regions, into grassland areas. McGee and colleagues are of the opinion that about half of Canada's fires are human-caused and half caused by lightning, but also note the wide variation between regions. The human-caused wildfires are discussed in terms of accidental fires, the causes of ignitions being associated with the oil and gas industries (flaring from gas wells, brush burning and the use of all-terrain vehicles), the forest industry, transport, and power lines. Malicious fires are not mentioned. However, it is noted that no people have died as a result of wildfire and few homes have been lost since a severe fire in 1938. However, since 2015 there have been extensive and damaging wildfires in Canada every year, the fire in 2016 covering about 1.5 billion acres (600,000 hectares) and destroying 3,244 buildings, but fortunately only two deaths. Many Aboriginal communities in Canada live in forested areas, and with their rapidly growing population, are facing greater risk from wildfire.

Conclusions about fire in Northern America

There appears to have been fewer studies examining the spatial patterns of wildfire ignitions in Northern America. The rural/urban interface wildfire risk is increasingly acknowledged in relation to the recent spate of wildfires occurring, particularly in California. The human cause of fire ignition is recognised, although there is less discussion on malicious fires. Lightning is seen as a bigger problem in Northern America, although the reporting on the incidence of lightning varies greatly.

Spatial patterns of fire ignition in Australia

As in Europe and Northern America, a common finding in Australia is that most ignitions of wildfires occur near urban areas and settlements, particularly on the rural/urban fringe (Bryant 2008a; Muller 2009b). Buxton and colleagues (2011) believe that Melbourne's rural/urban fringe is among the most vulnerable in the world to wildfire hazard. As in other countries, this rural/urban interface comprises urban sprawl and peri-urban housing developments, as well as 'lifestyle' living, often in forested areas close to secondary and smaller settlements (Bryant 2008a; Price 2013). Collins and colleagues (2015) examined spatial patterns of ignition in New South Wales from 2001/2 to 2008/9 and in Victoria from 1997/8 to 2008/9. They covered a total of 113,026 recorded ignitions. As expected, the incidence of human-caused wildfires increased with the numbers of people on the rural/urban interface. The authors noted that what they called 'undetermined' ignitions more closely aligned with the pattern of malicious ignitions rather than accidental ignitions, suggesting many of the undetermined ignitions were due to malicious fires.

The literature from Australia largely examines the population spread due to those seeking a more rural lifestyle, rather than examining sprawl arising from lower-cost housing developments on the edge of major cities and larger rural towns. Buxton and colleagues (2011) consider the rural/urban interface around Melbourne as extending for about 160 kilometres. This area comprises an inner interface area between the defined metropolitan urban growth boundary and an outer peri-urban area towards a rural boundary. Lifestyle housing tends to be spatially spread across these interface areas with accompanying roads that increase access to previously more remote areas including forested areas. It also leads to landscape fragmentation.

Figure 4.1: Location of approved planning permits in the study area between July 2007 and July 2013 by type.

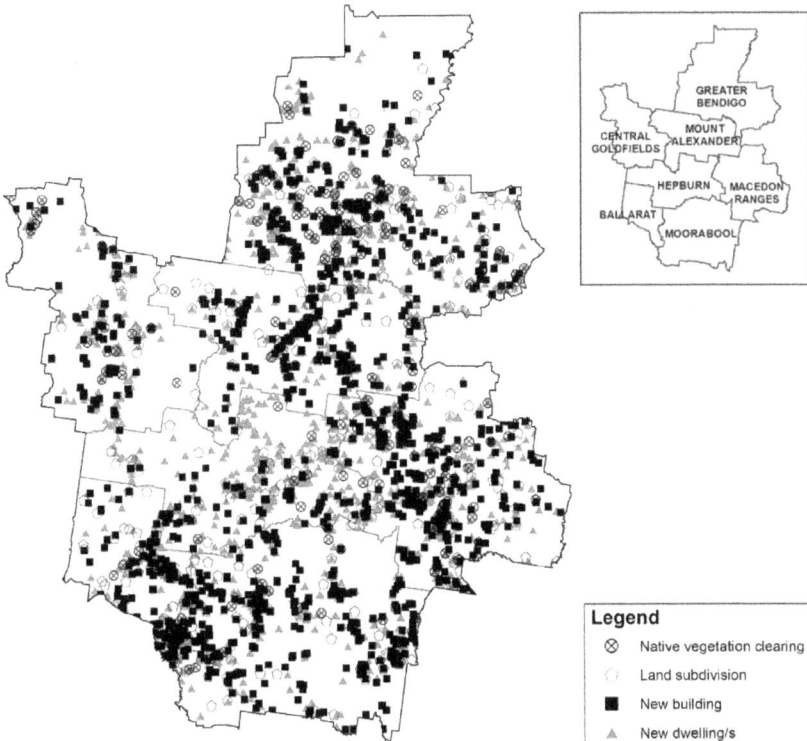

Source: Llausàs, Buxton & Bellin (2016, p. 1314).

Llausàs, Buxton and Bellin (2016) examined a study area comprising seven municipalities within the interface areas located north-west of Melbourne:

Ballarat, Central Goldfields, Greater Bendigo, Hepburn, Macedon Ranges, Moorabool and Mount Alexander (Figure 4.1). They comprised a combined population of over 300,000 people unevenly distributed throughout an area of approximately 12,130 km^2. Figure 4.1 shows land subdivided between July 2007 and July 2013. It reveals the spatial distribution of more than 4,000 planning permits granted outside established townships for new dwellings and buildings. The wide dispersal of dwellings shown in Figure 4.1 clearly illustrates the problem of the mix between people and vegetation, thus the potential risk of wildfires in this area. It also reveals failures in spatial planning and the accompanying lack of attention in planning to the prevention of wildfires.

Llausàs, Buxton and Bellin (2016) believe that, given the proximity of housing and other structures to vegetation in the urban/rural interface, fire risks lie in the inexperience of newcomers and their preference for maintaining the environment as distinct from "more experienced" (p.1308) residents who argue for prescribed burns. However, this greatly oversimplifies the situation. It may be that some of those choosing to live in a natural setting are aware of wildfire risk but prefer to take this risk rather than burn the environment (Reid & Bellin 2015).

A further problem identified by researchers is the form and application of the *1987 Planning and Environment Act of the State of Victoria* (Llausàs, Buxton & Bellin 2016). Zones define the intended uses of land and impose conditions, thresholds and restrictions for various activities, while overlays (such as environment significance, vegetation protection, significant landscape, fire, flood, heritage, erosion and salinity) comprise requirements about specific developments, but not uses. In 2013, rural conservation zones allowed smaller lot sizes (from eight to two hectares) and the requirement for planning permits for structural developments was relaxed. Local Government variously implements overlays, as they often overlap, thus providing inconsistency and the scattered construction seen in Figure 4.1. The study authors believe that the use of zones and overlays in the study area's seven local planning schemes promote development rather than anticipating the consequences of climate and socio-ecological change (Llausàs, Buxton & Bellin 2016). There is also a problem with approvals for land clearing, some 252 approvals being given over the study area in the six-year period. Spatial planning is discussed more thoroughly in chapter 5.

The authors conclude that, as noted by other researchers: "The current planning framework does not offer a clear, unified, strategic vision for rural areas that addresses future challenges... By being anchored in a model of planning that is focused on individual permit applications instead of a planning policy framework effectively matched to land characteristics, the land-use system is unable to anticipate long-term needs, increase landscape resilience and improve adaptive capacity to fundamental change" (Llausàs, Buxton & Bellin 2016, p.1317).

Christensen (2008) examined data reporting fire lighting in forestry plantations in Queensland since 1922, with the advantage that all wildfires within ten forestry areas were investigated by forestry workers trained in gathering, analysis and recording wildfire event evidence. He found that intentional fire lighting occurred six times as often in one forest area than occurred in the second-highest location (633 fires compared with 135 fires). He concluded that the area was particularly vulnerable to wildfire lighting due to its location near a highly-populated area. The forest was highly accessible with multiple access opportunities and heavily used for recreational purposes. Thus, the area attracted crime, with many opportunities for dumping, stripping and torching stolen vehicles, with low guardianship and poor place management practices.

Conclusions about fire in Australia

While the research is limited, the rural/urban interface pattern of a high occurrence of wildfire ignitions again holds. However, again there is little discussion about malicious fires. The increasing population numbers in the rural/urban interface and the associated need for road access, plus the failure to address climate change, suggests there will be an increase in human-caused wildfires in Australia in the future (for example, Bryant 2008a; Collins et al. 2015; Llausàs, Buxton & Bellin 2016). Again, this is a similar issue to what appears to be the case in parts of Europe and Northern America.

Mega or catastrophic wildfires

There is recent interest in researching reasons for the growth in the occurrence of mega-fires that are extremely large and difficult to extinguish (Williams et al. 2019). There is no record of mega-fires in the USA prior to 1970, and their occurrence is expected to increase over time (Patel 2018). Mega-fires are said to account for 1% to 2% of wildfires in the USA. Yet they absorb 85% of total suppression related expenditures and account for 95% of total acres burnt (Williams & Hyde 2009). Examination of mega-fires in Western USA found no pattern between the fires occurring on private or public land (Patel 2018). Of eight mega-fires studied that occurred in forests from 1997/8 to 2010, all were human-caused: three maliciously lit, three ignited due to negligence, for two the human cause was unknown, and one had electrical failure also involved (William & Hyde 2009). Mega-fires were said to be exacerbated by either altered forests, such as tree removal, or forests, other than wet tropical forests, that are less likely to burn left in their natural state. William and Hyde argued for prescribed burning. However, they provided no supporting evidence as to how this would impact the eventual mega-fire, and in an apparent contradiction, also noted that there is some evidence that prescribed burning is ineffectual against a mega-fire. The NASA Observatory reports some evidence that many fires are occurring in areas that have already experienced fires, known as burn-on-burn effects (Patel 2018).

As the mega-fires examined were in forested areas, problems of distance and delayed response, as well as smaller populations and limited emergency response capacity, may well impact on the ability to suppress the fire. William and Hyde noted that until the causes and contributory factors that lead to mega-fires are understood, and acted upon, success with these fires will be uncertain. One of the authors writing this book, on visiting the forests of Kalimantan in Indonesia, observed a range of factors that could exacerbate the growth of a fire to a mega-fire. Suppression of fire was difficult due to the building of water channels to drain the forest land, usually on peat, and there was a lack of water supplies and equipment, such as pumps and vehicles with which to fight the fire.

Drawing the spatial information together

The evidence from the preceding material highlights that the urban/rural interface is a location of considerable fire risk internationally. A critical element is a need for improved land-use planning in order to reduce the human interface with what might be both a high fire risk area and an area of high environmental value. Land-use planning is able to integrate social, environmental and economic issues to reduce the risk of wildfire ignition, yet it is rarely used for this purpose, with the available evidence on spatial patterns and fire risk, not taken into account (Sapountzaki et al. 2011). Sapountzaki and colleagues believe that a lack of spatial planning accounts for ineffective wildfire prevention approaches in Greece and Italy. Wildfire risks cannot be tackled only through measures that only 'prepare' for wildfire. They believe there is a need to enhance the conventionally static planning system with more flexible tools, able to meet the needs of rural/urban development, both in Australia and internationally. This approach is echoed by others, who believe that land-use planning needs to play a central role in reducing risk to populations from wildfire through wise locational decisions for dwellings and other developments in areas of medium and high fire hazard (Buxton et al. 2011).

There appears to be even less research on fires outside the rural/urban interface, where fewer ignitions occur, but they commonly result in larger and more severe fires. However, human activities are often connected with these fires, an increasing trend again, as population penetrates in the more isolated areas, due to industry and resource development and recreational purposes, as well as the risks associated with the current methods of fire as a fuel reduction tool. The environment, Indigenous settlements, and tourism will experience the most adverse consequences of these fires in more remote areas. The use of burning as a farming practice suggests that agricultural agencies need to support farmers to develop other approaches to farming.

Temporal patterns of wildfire

Most vegetation fires in Australia, irrespective of cause, coincide with the wildfire danger period at that location, that is, wildfire is significantly impacted by weather conditions (Bryant 2008b). The fire danger time is increasing in many countries, extending over an eight-month time period in some locations. A more nuanced understanding of the timing of wildfires will vary depending on the cause of the ignition. For example, wildfires that arise from an escaped prescribed burn peak just before and just after the bushfire danger season, when prescribed burning is undertaken (Bryant 2008b). Fires started by lightning tend to occur in a hot and dry season, potentially at any time of the day, but most coincide with the hotter conditions conducive to thunderstorm activity, between midday and 6 pm. Some people may be more inclined (encouraged) to light a malicious fire when the conditions are more favourable for the ignition to turn into a wildfire.

Many crimes occur in time as well as space clusters (Johnson 2014). The suggested reasons for this vary widely. Research on burglaries shows that those that occur close in time and space are more likely to be the work of the same person (Goodwill & Alison 2006; Johnson, Summers & Pease 2009; Summers, Johnson & Rengert 2010). There are suggestions that this may also be the case with malicious lighting of fires (Read & Stanley 2018). Some researchers have investigated fire patterns in relation to the day of the week and the time of day, although this work is mainly urban-based. As with spatial considerations, the timing of human-caused wildfires is related to the timetables of people, their day-to-day activities and cultural patterns (Bryant 2008b; Cohen & Felson 1979; Muller 2009b). Based on data from 24 fire agencies in NSW, from 1997–98 to 2001–02 (55,730 records), both accidental fires and deliberately lit wildfires often occur on the weekend, as do fires with an unknown cause (Bryant 2008b).

Deliberate urban fires largely occur between 1 pm and 4 pm on weekends (Prestemon, Butry & Thomas 2013). Fires are also more likely to occur in school holidays, although the author is talking about fires in an urban setting (Maciak et al. 1998). Other researchers have found that a higher proportion of malicious wildfires occur between 6 pm and 6 am compared with non-malicious fires. In many jurisdictions, night-time fires are principally a feature of Friday and Saturday nights, but the timing of fires is highly location-dependent (Australian Institute of Criminology 2006). Malicious fires that occur on a weekday peak between 3 pm and 6 pm, while accidental fires peak slightly earlier, between 1 pm and 4 pm (Bryant 2008b). The window between 3 pm and 6 pm on weekdays reflects the time when youth often travel unaccompanied by an adult. Indeed, lack of adults present appears to reflect many of these times when fires are lit. In contrast, fires recorded as re-ignition fires, 'natural' and classified as 'other causes', present as constant over the week.

A recent study found that in Florida, when looking at repeat, maliciously lit urban fires over a longer period of time, they are typically clustered over periods of up to 11 days. Although also researching malicious fires in an urban setting, Grubb and Nobles (2016) found that for an ignition that occurred during the day or night, the risk of a repeat fire could occur within a one to two housing blocks, with the risk lasting up to 28 days. These patterns may be due to serial offending or copycat fire lighting.

As with the cause of ignition, there is often uncertainty about the precise time that ignition occurred, especially with wildfires (Bryant 2008b). Records of the time of occurrence of a fire may vary between agencies, fire brigades and jurisdictions. The record may depend on how and when the information is recorded, and also on the different ways specific causes are classified, such as fires started by children (Bryant 2008b). The time when the fire was detected, or the time an alarm sounds may be recorded as the time the fire started, although the fire may have been smouldering for a long time, especially in a remote region.

Serial and copycat arson

Two other forms of clustering in relation to wildfire should be mentioned here. Malicious wildfire lighting may occur with multiple offences committed in a short space of time, or multiple fires may be lit in one location, or the one type of ignition may be repeated at different times and locations. While there is said to be some evidence of serial malicious wildfire ignitions, research by the Australian Institute of Criminology using NSW court data (Muller 2008b) found very low levels of repeat offending over time for urban and wildfire firelighters. This may be associated with the problem that with such a low apprehension rate, it may be that the person is not apprehended for prior fire lighting events. There is some evidence for this. It could be that the firelighter became more careless, spoke about his activities or involved peers in the activity. Repeat malicious firelighters are likely to be young, have a substance abuse problem and a criminal history (Doley et al. 2011). Grubb and Nobles (2016) conclude that there is a case for giving greater attention to research in this area to improve prevention strategies, with particular reference to offender decision-making and victimization risk factors.

Considerable attention in the media is given to wildfire. Wildfire may be presented in the media in a sensational form with heightened emotions. It is common to find media messages conveying a hero or champion status associated with firefighters, who are usually male, as are most malicious firelighters. Indeed, malicious firelighters may join the fire-brigade, seeking this attention. This behaviour has been found to occur with other crimes, where about a quarter of serious offenders have been found to copy crime techniques from the media (Heller & Polsky 1976; Surette 2002).

Conclusions on spatial and temporal patterns of fire

In conclusion, it could be said that there appears to be some evidence for 'hot spots' and the clustering of malicious fires, particularly in an urban setting (Bryant 2008b). Clusters of fires can occur on a temporal basis, as well as on a locational basis, usually occurring from one day to one week after the first fire; however, the authors are again discussing urban-based ignitions (Grubb & Nobles 2016). A person may light more than one fire in a similar location at the same time, they may light fires in close proximity over time or may be using the same method of lighting the fire as observed elsewhere (Australian Institute of Criminology 2017). Serial firelighters are likely to operate relatively close to their residence (Curman 2004; Grubb & Nobles 2016; Kocsis & Irwin 1997).

What can be learned from car fires?

The burning of vehicles has come under little investigation, and again, poor data inhibits understanding. However, the behaviour occurs fairly frequently in many parts of the world and can lead to a wildfire. Little attention is given to reporting the exact location of the burn. While it may be urban or rural-based, it would seem to largely occur in the rural/urban interface areas, either close to an urban parkland or the car is driven to a more rural area. This behaviour may also account for the development of hotspots where a number of burnings may occur over a short period of time in close locations. The burning of stolen vehicles commonly occurs within 24 hours from the theft (Ransom 2007). The burning of stolen vehicles occurs in low socio-economic areas with high rates of general crime. While insurance fraud and hiding forensic evidence are reasons for burning the car, thrill-seeking to watch the car burn is also a motivator. The ignition of vehicles (stolen or not) most commonly is undertaken at night.

The cars burnt are commonly stolen or else abandoned, but vehicles may be ignited where they are parked, suggesting a more urban offence. In Victoria, 1,312 cars were recorded by the police as burnt in the 12 months to September 2018. It is estimated that in 2005/6, 11% of stolen vehicles were burnt when recovered in NSW, while in South Australia, the figure is 8.6% (Ransom 2007). This represents 3,125 stolen vehicles burnt in NSW and 659 in South Australia, but the authors report an increasing trend of thefts and car ignitions over time. Australian Capital Territory Fire and Rescue responded to 291 car fires (including non-suspicious fires) in 2017-18, an increase on the previous two years, with about one-quarter of stolen cars ignited (Lindell 2019).

In the first three months of 2019, eight cars were burnt in an urban suburb of Ballarat, a secondary city in Victoria, six of these in a two-week time period (Kirkhim 2019). Over 50 cars were ignited in rural/urban interface areas in northern and southern areas of Canberra, mostly in bushland locations (Lindell 2019). A car that had been burnt in a forested area close to the edge of Canberra, and close to the city's water catchment area and dam, led to a large wildfire and spot fires in the previous month, requiring eight water-bombing aircraft to extinguish the fire (Sibthorge & Lowrey 2018). Up to 700 homes were alerted to remain on 'standby' in case evacuation was needed.

In the USA, from 2008 to 2010, 14% of all fires were vehicle fires, half of which were deliberately lit (US Fire Administration 2014). From 2003 to 2012, an average of 14,737 vehicle burns were reported, representing 26.5% of all annual malicious fires, a figure that most likely would account for both urban and rural fires. In the USA, two-thirds of maliciously set vehicle fires occur at night (US Fire Administration 2014). The location of ignition and the entailing risks of wildfire are not known.

Theories on spatial and temporal arson

As noted in chapter one, often formal fire data records collect all fire events (structural, vehicle, landscape and urban). There is little attempt to disaggregate this information, although it is possible that different types of ignition are associated with different behavioural characteristics, particularly in relation to malicious fires. While there are some general features across most criminal activities and there may be some commonalities between the forms of malicious fires, it is important to understand where the specific commonalities and differences lie, especially if ignitions are to be prevented. As noted above, there has been little research on a combination of spatial and temporal characteristics of malicious fires, and the available research has largely been undertaken with urban-based fires. Grubb and Nobles (2016) list theories that have been used to explain the spatial and temporal aspects of urban fire lighting. They are outlined below, together with other theories referred to in the literature:

- Rational Choice Theory (Cornish & Clarke 1986; Prestemon, Butry & Thomas 2013). This theory analyses the circumstances that promote crime in a particular place, such as ease of access and the ability to be anonymous.

- Routine Activity Theory (Cohen & Felson 1979; Stahura & Hollinger 1988). This theory proposes a crime triangle: convergence of time and space of likely offenders, a suitable target, and the absence of a capable guardian to deter crime. A person undertaking routine activities over time is likely to identify a suitable target for fire lighting. This is similar to Brantingham and Brantingham's (1981) Crime Pattern Theory, referred to in the context of wildfire by Cozens and Christensen (2011), and discussed further below.

- Broken Windows Theory (Thomas, Butry & Prestemon 2012; Wilson & Kelling 1982). This theory describes how the physical deterioration in a place may encourage crime, and the community may not self-police the area, creating further vandalism and further community withdrawal.

- Situational Crime Prevention is another important crime theory, relevant to spatial issues (Christensen 2008; Clarke 1992; Cozens & Christensen 2011). This approach examines the circumstances of the environment to understand why crime, including a malicious fire, occurred in the location and how the environment could be modified to reduce the likelihood of crime occurring.

Grubb and Nobles point out that there is little integration and/or consensus between the theories and most of these are based on urban fire lighting, where there may be different patterns and different causes to rural related malicious fires.

The research literature has a small amount of discussion on spatial decision-making by different types of offenders, as many crimes are committed close to home (e.g. Rossmo 2000; Townsley & Sudebottom 2010). Grubb and Nobles (2016) report findings from the literature that show that a difference between instrumental firelighters (those who light a fire for a purpose, such as to remove evidence of a robbery) and expressive firelighters (those who light a fire responding to personal emotions, such as excitement around watching flames) (Canter & Fritzon 1998; Wachi et al. 2007). Instrumental firelighters are likely to travel further from home to commit their crimes and are also likely to have a greater distance between their own fire lighting offences when compared to expressive firelighters. Urban fire lighting is more closely associated with instrumental behaviours, such as revenge, an insurance claim, than those who light wildfires.

Other theories of crime don't specifically refer to fire but may be of relevance to wildfire:

- Geo-spatial Decision-making examines issues such as the journey to the crime, the sequential nature of decisions, the direction of the offence/s from home, and the dispersion of crimes (Goodwill 2014).

- Crime Pattern Theory (Brantingham & Brantingham 1993, 1995) describes how everyday activities influence spatial decision-making by offenders through the development of mental maps and cognitive scripts. These will be based on routine activities and familiar places such as home, work and places of recreation. This spatial awareness overlaps with opportunity for crime, where the offender needs to have both a suitable target and an absence of a capable guardian (Christensen 2008; Cohen & Felson 1979; Townsley & Sudebottom 2010).

As far as can be ascertained, mental mapping and decision-making around crime are yet to be examined with people who commit malicious fires in general, and specifically light wildfires. There is an assumption with this work that the offender makes choices about the crime in a rational way that maximises their returns and reduces their chances of being caught (Goodwill 2014). This may be so in some cases but not in others, especially where the offence is wildfire. Young people who light wildfires may be dealing with strong emotions, such as anger or another emotional arousal component to fire lighting, or they may have an intellectual disability. However, this said, the spatial decision-making by the fire lighting offender is important to consider.

As spatial patterns do occur, it is important that the above theories need to be understood better in the context of wildfire. Testing these theories in association with wildfire crime is a critical step towards the development of prevention programs. The next section offers some thoughts on environmental criminology theories that link spatial disadvantage, commonly found on the edges of larger cities and settlements, with the propensity to light fires.

Growing inequality as a spatial concern for wildfire ignition

This section draws on a small amount of research from a range of disciplines, which may offer some pathways into future research with a view to prevention of wildfire programs. Research has shown that some communities disproportionately contribute to the overall number of wildfires (Muller 2009a). Nicolopoulos (1997) found that nine postcodes in Sydney account for nearly a quarter of all fires in the Sydney region.

The Australian population is presently growing at a faster rate than most industrialised countries, with Melbourne and Sydney having the bulk of the growth. The total population of Greater Melbourne increased by a quarter over the 2006-16 decade, averaging 2.3% annually between 2011 and 2016. Population growth rates of some local government areas (LGAs) in Melbourne are well above these rates, particularly those on the outer urban fringe (Brain, Stanley & Stanley 2019). This growth in the outer fringe suburbs tends to mainly comprise young families, attracted by more affordable housing. Despite Melbourne having a 'green belt' and city boundaries designed to restrict urban sprawl, Melbourne continues to push the boundary outwards into grasslands, farmlands, bushland and forest, and what were once small settlements. At the same time, infrastructure spending has greatly lagged in these new outer suburbs, particularly in relation to the provision of public transport. If this trend continues, then approximately $A376 billion will need to be spent to remedy this shortfall by 2031; thus, the problem is far from insignificant (Brain, Stanley & Stanley 2019).

The impact of this infrastructure shortfall can be seen in the lagging Gross Regional Product per capita of the working-age population in the LGAs where the population had an annual average growth over 2% for the 1992-2017 period. Not only was the capacity to earn income reduced in many fringe suburbs, when compared to the rest of Victoria, but social outcomes, such as in the areas of social capital, were also diminished in comparison with the rest of Melbourne. These poorer outcomes reflect social and economic outcomes that align with measures shown to be important for social inclusion and wellbeing. Modelling the drivers of social exclusion resulted in the following features as being highly statistically related to inclusion: having adequate levels of income; accessible transport; good social capital; self-esteem and confidence; and control over your personal environment (such as capabilities to make choices and problem solve) (Stanley et al. 2011; Stanley, Stanley & Hansen 2017).

The fastest-growing LGAs on the fringe of Melbourne showed higher levels of education disadvantage (lower scores in literacy and numeracy), early school leaving, developmental delays at school entry, and high levels of youth unemployment. Where unemployment, under-employment and disengagement (not in education or looking for work) are counted, some LGAs have over one in three youth struggling with employment issues. There are considerably fewer jobs available in the fringe areas when compared with other parts of Melbourne. This is in association with poorer accessibility in general, with low or absent public transport options to gain access to work, services and recreation.

Two fields of research can be linked here, noted but not significantly researched in Australia, USA and the UK. These are the disadvantage found in fringe areas of cities, and the impact this has on fire lighting by youth (Arson Control Forum 2004; Muller 2009a; Prestemon & Butry 2005). As discussed in chapter 3; wildfire arson is predominately perpetrated by those experiencing disadvantage, predominately by young males. The disadvantage takes the form of social exclusion, a low socio-economic background, poor academic achievement, often anti-social behaviour and, for many, a childhood experience of child abuse and neglect (Dolan & Stanley 2010; Stanley 2002). Problematic psychological attributes can accompany this difficult upbringing, such as low self-esteem, anger, frustration, cutting off emotions, a strong interest in fire, and external locus of control (Doley Dickens & Gannon 2016; Stanley 2002; Stanley, Stanley & Hansen 2017; Twenge & Baumeister 2005). Measured using the Psychological Wellbeing Scale (Ryan & Deci 2001), on a scale from 1 to 5, with 5 being the highest level of negative emotions, the average of those who have no social exclusion risks is 1.7 in Victoria. Those at high risk of social exclusion rate an average of 4.8 on negative affect. All this is not helped by the way unemployed youth are labelled and stigmatised (Whiteford 2019). Schemes that offer hardly a living wage for unemployed youth (Newstart), drug-testing, online compliance schemes, and terms such as 'leaners, not lifters' give the perception of unworthiness.

Disillusionment, disadvantage and boredom create a ripe breeding ground for lighting malicious fires (Tomison 2010). Communities with a high propensity for malicious fire lighting often have a high proportion of children under 15 and lower: education levels, employment rates and household income, than the national average (Muller 2009a). Communities on the fringe of cities in Australia are commonly characterised by relatively low median age and/or a high proportion of young persons who are socioeconomically disadvantaged (Nicolopoulos 1997). As these fringe communities are new, with people arriving from many other places, there is a risk of alienation occurring, associated with a disconnect from previous community and support groups. As noted above, the absence of public transport to enable youth to undertake social connections and activities further isolates those who move to fringe suburbs, especially those who leave school early and can't find work (Stanley, Stanley & Hansen

2017). As a result, a greater concentration of other problematic and antisocial behaviours can occur (Pease 1998).

Research undertaken by an author of this book found that disadvantages were also present in some rural areas in Victoria and South Australia, particularly for children and youth. As on the fringe of Melbourne, this was reflected in poor attendance at pre-schools, lack of employment for youth and considerable problems gaining access to services and employment (Stanley & Stanley 2018). A study of rural transport found that youth in South Western Victoria experience the highest levels of transport disadvantage and wellbeing levels are lower than those found in urban Melbourne as a whole (Stanley & Banks 2012). Of great concern is the discrepancy found between self-assessed perception by the youth of their future, where the average score for urban Melbourne was 7.2 on a 10-point scale and 5.6 in rural Victoria. Rural youths were often not able to take advantage of education initiatives designed to keep youths at schools, such as Vocational Education and Training and Victorian Certificate of Applied Learning schemes, due to an absence of transport to access these opportunities. Similarly, a lack of transport prevented the take-up of job opportunities on rural farms. Youth who have never experienced being in the workforce full time, and those unable to get work, risk longer-term disadvantage through the loss of motivation and a reduction in 'employability'.

Examination of the literature on ignition targets suggests that young people particularly light fires where urban structures are in close proximity to a natural setting, such as behind schools, on public access cycle and walking paths, and in rubbish bins (Christensen 2008). As noted above, fires in the rural/urban interface are often lit close to where the firelighter lives, the literature reporting studies finding this to be from half a kilometre to ten kilometres, a walk or comfortable bicycle ride away (Catry et al. 2007; Davidson 2006; Price & Bradstock 2013).

Links with these issues and criminology theories can be made, particularly with Social Learning Theory in the context of deliberate fire lighting (Bandura 1976; Kolko & Kazdin 1986; Macht & Mack 1968; Singer & Hensley 2004; Vreeland & Levin 1980). Social learning theorists view fire lighting as a result of learning from a range of sources. For example, an interest in fire may be triggered through early exposure in childhood, through fire being used as a form of punishment or a parent who was interested in fire lighting. It may be the excitement around the response to a fire that reinforces the behaviour. Poor socialization in early childhood and associated personality outcomes such as "(p)erceived failure, aggression, poor coping, and low assertiveness … may increase an individual's propensity to light fires in an attempt to gain some level of environmental control" (Gannon et al. 2012, p. 110, drawing on

Vreeland & Levin 1980). Poor social learning is likely to be associated with some level of place-based spatial disadvantage and re-enforced by this environment, Other issues, such as rural isolation and social exclusion may compound the family's predisposition to poorer quality parenting.

Outside Australia, a number of authors link low wages and unemployment with the ignition of wildfires, called 'social disorder', defined as the presence of neglected and vacant buildings and a high incidence of petty crimes, as referred to above (for example, Thomas, Butry & Prestemon 2012). Reducing this 'disorder' was found to also reduce the incidence of fire lighting. Ganteaume and colleagues (2013), in a review of the literature, found a frequent reference to the link between socio-economic indicators reflecting disadvantage, such as the unemployment rate, have also been shown to be clearly linked to fire occurrence in many areas of southern Europe.

Conclusions

The discussion in this chapter suggests that understanding the locational and temporal patterns of wildfires could be useful in the development of programs that prevent fire lighting. This knowledge is already being used as a prevention tool in some locations, for example, the fast removal of dumped cars, thus reducing the chance that they will be torched. It is likely that there are many other opportunities for prevention as our knowledge on fire patterns increases. It is particularly important to understand local patterns and to apply local, targeted prevention actions for specific fire hot spots.

Potentially, a lot more could be learned from greater application of crime theories to the issue of malicious fire lighting. There is a great deal more work to be done on the planning side to reduce rural/urban interface vulnerability, an issue further discussed in chapter 6. This will involve some major changes in approaches, including strong involvement with the community (chapter 7). For many reasons, including fire prevention, far greater attention is needed to reducing disadvantage on the urban fringes, a problem that seems to have international currency. The cost of this neglect is too high. Work by Wilkinson and Pickett (2009) has shown that the greater the increase in inequality within countries, the greater the social problems faced by that country, covering issues such as crime, single parenthood, life expectancy, trust, mental illness, imprisonment and literacy.

Section 2:
Prevention approaches

The promotion of health and wellbeing in all people is based on the wellbeing of individuals, organisations and communities, all interconnected in "a tight web of reciprocal influences" (Prilleltensky & Prilleltensky 2006, p.1). Unfortunately, the authors left out another critical component, the wellbeing of the environment. Section 2 of this book explores some of the components of how issues associated with wildfires are, and could be, managed to reduce risk while maintaining societal wellbeing. Chapter 5 explores how the prevention of wildfire is currently understood. Chapter 6 offers a case study on the place and role of local government in Australia. Chapter 7 examines the participation of the community in the prevention of wildfire. Chapter 8 offers a perspective on the neglected environment in the wildfire story. Finally, chapter 9 re-visits the thorny issue of the management of wildfire data.

Chapter 5

Current prevention approaches

Introduction

Prevention is one of the four key components to achieving health and wellbeing, along with strengths and empowerment approaches, as well as changing the context that isn't working (Prilleltensky & Prilleltensky 2006). Prevention has proved to be a difficult area in many fields, the preference being for a reactive response to the problem after it has occurred. For example, only 1% of the health budget is spent on the prevention of mental health problems in Canada and the USA, yet a lot is known about how to prevent mental illness in the first place. Similar comments could be made about the high cost of child abuse and the cost of crime to society, as can be made about the prevention of wildfire, where there is largely a reactive response with little thought about preventing ignition. However, the difference with wildfire is that there is scant research on prevention models and little evaluation of the effectiveness of existing programs. There is a need for a paradigm shift from 'fixing' individual fires, to 'fixing' the broader societal context that leads to the ignition (Prilleltensky & Prilleltensky 2006, p.14).

This chapter overviews the current approaches to wildfire prevention. It first offers a brief look at the development of the organising concept of 'risk', followed by an overview of a commonly used theoretical structure for management, governance and decision-making. It overviews a model to prevention promulgated by the United Nations that sits under a risk management approach, which has largely been adopted internationally. An overview is given of the approach to prevention adopted by some continents. The chapter then offers a study of some of the prevention programs adopted in Victoria, together with a comment on what is known of their effectiveness.

The development of a risk framework

A dawning recognition of a new order in relation to the increasing incidence of extreme events around the world has led to the development of international guidance on strategies to address such issues. A recent report from the European Union (EU) notes how three times as many wildfires have occurred in Europe in the decade starting 2010 when compared to the 1980s (Tidey 2019). This change has also encompassed a trend from smaller sized wildfires to the dominance of mega-fires that cover much larger areas. An average of approximately 4500 km² burnt every year in Mediterranean Europe, resulting in suppression being a much more challenging task (Faivie 2018; Turco et al. 2018).

Buxton and colleagues (2011) draw attention to two important events in the 1990s that helped raise awareness about natural disasters and risk. The United Nations General Assembly nominated the 1990s as the 'International Decade for Natural Disaster Reduction', and in 1992, Beck's *Risk Society* book was published in English and subsequently translated into 20 other languages. Beck viewed a risk society as applying: "a systematic way of dealing with hazards and insecurities induced and introduced by modernisation itself" (Beck 1992, p.21). An outcome of this attention has been that risk has become a central organising concept for 'natural' hazards internationally, particularly around wildfires. The interest has widened to also include related organising ideas, such as the concept of resilience, now widely used (Buxton et al. 2011). It has also led to growing research on wildfire, particularly the literature on mitigation and planning, using a socio-ecological system framework. Under this framework, some environmental conditions, such as fuel loads and some social issues, such as living location, are examined to develop a risk profile (see, for example, Ager et al. 2016; Kolden & Henson 2019). However, this research, and application of the ideas, is still very much under-developed, the authors of this book view this work as, at times, both narrow and lacking clarity, points that will be taken up again in chapter 11.

International approach to risk and disaster reduction

The *Sendai Framework for Disaster Risk Reduction (2015-2030)*, auspiced by the United Nations Office for Disaster Risk Reduction, was developed through inter-governmental negotiations (UNISDR 2015). It provides a framework or guide for countries to plan the reduction of risks around 'natural' and man-made disasters, with an emphasis on disaster 'risk' management as opposed to disaster management. It is said to guide the prevention of new risk, reduce existing risk and strengthen resilience. The document sets out a framework for goals, guiding principles, priorities for action and the roles for different stakeholders. It itemises the drivers of risk: poverty and inequality, climate change, rapid urbanisation, poor land management, weak institutional arrangements, policies that are not risk-informed, and a lack of investment incentives. The report talks about the need to improve preparedness, response, rehabilitation and reconstruction, but says little about prevention in general, including the prevention of ignition of wildfires.

The document repeatedly emphasises the need for very broad engagement. This encompasses partnerships, coordination, coherence, and shared responsibilities, at the international, national, state government, local authority, local community levels, and business, indeed, an all-of-society approach. The document emphasises that risk reduction needs to be mainstreamed across all sectors. This requires a number of facilitators, such as access to "resources, incentives and decision-making responsibilities" (UNISDR 2015, p. 13). It nominates a few specific tasks, such as the articulation of responsibilities, the establishment of mechanisms for cooperation, development of public policies, legislation and new building codes and standards, and strengthening health care services. The approach is one of shared responsibility for reducing disaster risk, as well as an inclusive approach, seen as: "the open exchange and dissemination of disaggregated data... as well as on easy accessible up to-date comprehensible, science-based non sensitive risk information, complemented by traditional knowledge" (UNISDR 2015, p.13).

The report suggests that information be location-based, providing risk maps for decision-makers and access to real-time information. Models need to be developed, all widely disseminated to build knowledge and to improve dialogue. The priorities for action are set out as follows:

Priority 1: Understanding disaster risk

Priority 2: Strengthening disaster risk governance to manage disaster risk

Priority 3: Investing in disaster risk reduction for resilience

Priority 4: Enhancing disaster preparedness for effective response and to "Build Back Better" in recovery rehabilitation and reconstruction (p.14).

These priorities should be based on the understanding of disaster risk in all its dimensions of vulnerability, capacity, exposure of persons and assets, hazard characteristics, and the environment. Importantly it has outcome measures of success based on a substantial reduction of disaster risk, including loss of lives, livelihoods and health, and in economic, physical, social, cultural, and environmental assets. This is said to need the strong commitment and involvement of political leadership. The document outlines seven specific, measurable targets, such as numbers of affected people per 100,000 populations, within a set period of time.

This document has many valuable components, especially around shared responsibilities, coordination and inclusion. The undertaking it recommends is highly complex, advocating major change in approach across multiple sectors and in wide-ranging areas. However, little guidance is given about how such change can be undertaken; the structures needed to bring about change; and how to transition to achieve this, given multiple path dependencies and competing goals in many government policy areas, in business and within the community. It also says little about the responsibility of decision-making, and where and how this is undertaken. In most countries, decision-making and management is not well integrated but sectoralised, one-dimensional, and uncoordinated. As such, it does not handle complex problems well, as reported in many studies in the literature, in a range of subject areas (Howlett, Vince & del Rio 2017). Howlett, Vince and del Rio (2017) also point out that little research has been undertaken about how this should be done, noting that such complex integration carries substantial risks of failure. Yet, they argue the importance of such an integrative approach to particularly meet the challenges around broad areas such as sustainability, to avoid duplication, redundancies, contradictory approaches, and gaps in existing policy mixes, all of which are likely to have developed over a lengthy period of time. Often, single-issue approaches, fail to account for and measure externalities, the impact of their approaches on other people and the environment. Thus, goal conflicts are common where multiple parties are involved. The Sendai Framework appears to not consider how to overcome these management complexities.

Unfortunately, an emphasis on 'risk' in this report appears to replace 'prevention'. This appears to arise from the idea of 'natural' extreme events (see chapter one) yet fails to acknowledge the association of these events with anthropogenic climate change. Wildfire is perhaps a disaster that is somewhat different from other so-called 'natural' disasters. Wildfire problems arise from a combination of GHG emissions, creating climate changes that exacerbate 'natural' disasters, but wildfire also has direct human input that triggers or ignites many wildfires. Thus, actions to prevent this dangerous human intervention, as well as address climate change, should both be part of the prevention approach, as well as actions to mitigate the severity and spread of wildfire and exposure of people to the risk.

The approach taken by Europe

The European Union has powers in relation to both the prevention and suppression of wildfire through environmental and civil protection authorities (Ponce et al. 2015). These powers have been used to co-finance forest fire prevention by the member states. As noted above, a recent wildfire EU policy document recognises that considerable changes in approach are needed in order to provide an adequate response to changed fire circumstances (Faivie 2018). As with the Sendai framework, there is a strong emphasis on an integrative approach and a risk management type of approach. There is a call for "...more effective science-based forest fire management and risk informed decision-making which account for the socioeconomic, climate and environmental roots of wildfires" (p.12).

The report notes that there should be a shifting of the focus from suppression to prevention, that needs to be integrated with climate adaption, education, preparedness, suppression and restoration aspects. However, the prevention aspect again appears to be narrowly viewed, what this book would describe as mitigation. There is a strong emphasis on policy based on science-based findings, on considering ecological issues and being future-orientated. There is no mention about the issue that different branches of science may give conflicting findings, as well as the place of local and cultural preferences, hence the role for consideration of competing positions and value judgements.

Ponce and colleagues (2015) describe the need for a much higher level of mutual obligation between European governments and citizens than is perhaps suggested in the EU report. He believes there is an obligation to protect, including a duty to prevent and mitigate risks of disasters, including wildfires. However, whether, and how, this is applied in practice, could be debated, although some steps have been taken in Spain. Spain has enacted laws on wildfire risks that may produce serious or catastrophic threats to the environment, as well as people, property and the public service (Ponce et al. 2015). In Spain, this entails the prevention of dangerous activities related to fire. Permits for some activities will not be available at certain times of the year. These activities include fireworks, lighting a fire, logging, camping, and pedestrian and vehicle traffic in some vulnerable areas (Ponce et al. 2015). Such laws also include fire-related building regulations about construction and maintenance. Lack of coordination between the fire agencies themselves and with planning authorities are said to be a significant problem in Greece and Italy. These oversights are said to be connected with undervaluing the role of human activities in fires and thus a lack of attention to prevention. Prevention is described as "totally ineffective" and "an invisible objective" (Sapountzaki et al. 2011, p.1471).

United Kingdom

The authors could find limited information on integrated approaches to wildfire in terms of prevention, planning, response and recovery, in literature originating from the UK, yet this has been called for, for at least a decade now. The ANSFR Project (Accidental, Natural and Social Fire Risk Project), co-financed by the European Union, was undertaken over two years, 2009 and 2010, in collaboration between the Northumberland Fire and Rescue Service (UK) and similar organisations in Denmark, Italy and Finland (Stacey et al. 2010). An important conclusion in the project report was that fire services needed to work in close partnership with a range of organisations, including the police and local authorities, in order to comprehensively and successfully assess and manage fire risk. The report notes the importance of an even broader approach to encompassing international collaborative partnerships.

It recommends the establishment of a national risk prediction system, which calculates and categorises risk of wildfire on any given day.

Since 2008, Fire Authorities in the UK have been required to develop an Integrated Risk Management Plan to consider prevention, protection and response for wildfire, with a requirement to include communities and a wide range of other partners (Gazzard, McMorrow & Aylen 2016). However, some sectors and government departments were found to be poorly engaged in wildfire risk management. Those mentioned were the Department of Energy and Climate Change, the insurance industry and, especially residential development planners, who had little awareness of wildfire risk in the UK rural/urban interface.

The UK does not have a specific national wildfire agency or strategy. The statutory duty to extinguish structural and wildfires rests with 46 regional Fire and Rescue Services. Management of wildfire is divided between government departments. Prevention of ignition, in the form of managing public access to public land, and management of fuels, rests largely with the Department for Environment, Food and Rural Affairs (DEFRA). The Department for Communities and Local Government, Resilience and Emergency Planning manages the preparedness and emergency response responsibilities.

Community-based cross-sector networks emerged in the 1990s to redress this disconnect, as have cross-agency working groups, with collaborations between local land-owners, environmental groups and water authorities. Changes in fire management approaches in the UK were said to be led by local fire services, particularly the Northumberland Fire and Rescue Service. This has led to amendments in emergency planning, as well as recognition of the need to respond to climate change (Gazzard, McMorrow & Aylen 2016). However, the response to wildfire in the UK remains varied, fragmented and incomplete at the local level (Gazzard, McMorrow & Aylen 2016). The grass-roots responses to local issues give few considerations to the prevention of ignition, and conflicts exist in relation to prescribed burning.

The current national policy paradigm is said to still be one of fire suppression (Gazzard, McMorrow & Aylen 2016). Policy instruments, therefore, do not specifically identify wildfire (as distinct from structural fires), and suitable tools to quantify wildfire risk are not yet widely available. This is despite the National Planning Policy Framework for England and Wales, that considers both climate change and natural hazards in planning policy and decisions, suggesting that planning should take account of vulnerability to 'natural hazards', although wildfire is not specifically mentioned. Gazzard, McMorrow and Aylen (2016) believe that successful wildfire management requires the adoption of a cross-sector approach at the national scale, not just, as now, for the emergency response phase of large incidents but also at the prevention phase. They believe that progress is being made between the integration of fire and land management, especially at the prevention stage, although a coordinated and funded approach to understanding the socio-ecological systems is needed.

USA

In the USA, in 2001, Hann and Bunnell noted that natural resource and fire planning for the management of Federal public lands, and for State and private lands, developed differently and had independent planning. They believed that in order to achieve policy, budget and restoration planning for fire and land management, linkages are needed across national, regional, local and project scales. However, Gazzard, McMorrow & Aylen 2016) note that local responses have recently emerged to bring in adaptive governance within the social and ecological components of a system. They argue that the USA needs to move towards collaboration between communities, planners, architects and land managers. Such an approach is currently being researched in Australia, between fire services and urban planning (March et al. 2018a, b). Reflecting the notion of 'shared responsibility' used in Australia, the USA has the concept of 'reciprocal obligation', which covers the state responsibilities to protect the wellbeing of citizens, and the citizens' responsibility to the State and other community members (Ponce et al. 2015).

An extensive review on the prevention of wildfire ignitions was undertaken in 2013 by Prestemon and colleagues. The Report placed Land Management agencies as the organization responsible for the prevention of wildfire. It suggested the possible options for prevention are education, fuels management and law enforcement. The report notes that social drivers of fire, said to be income, development, demographics and culture, are not included as processes and patterns are largely beyond the control of land managers. The authors believe that the primary land management action that directly affects ignition occurrence is prescribed fire, although they note later that the evidence for this is not yet available.

Australia

Australia has three levels of government, all having some responsibilities around wildfire management. The Australian (Federal) Government is responsible for coordinating a national approach to both the environmental and international policy-related issues. State and Territory Governments (of which there are eight) have primary responsibility for land and fire management. Most states have up to three fire services responsible for urban fires, country fires and firefighting on public land such as state and national parks. Volunteers largely staff rural fire brigades. Local governments have responsibilities for enacting land-use planning under state legislation.

National approach

Building on The Sendai Framework for Disaster Risk Reduction, the Council of Australian Governments (COAG) developed a series of reports centring on a National Strategy for Disaster Resilience. The strategy document was first published in 2009 and updated in 2011, with an implementation review in 2015 (National Emergency Management Committee 2011). The reports call for the need to build a response to disasters, based on the ideas of shared responsibility and the development of resilient communities. The disaster resilience of people and households is said to be significantly increased by active planning and preparation for protecting life and property. A resilient community is reported as being one where the community understands the risks, prepares for a disaster event, works with local leaders and in partnership with emergency services to build resilience over time, supported by land-use planning and building controls. It also is one that recovers from a disaster quickly.

McLennan, Reid and Beilin (2019) say that the strategy gave impetus to fire and land management agencies in all states and territories to establish programs to enhance levels of natural hazard mitigation in the form of safety-related preparatory activities. However, the Strategy mentions prevention only in the list of prevention, preparedness, response and recovery. Resilience is largely defined by process outcomes, not what resilience looks like, nor the objectives being sought. Thus, it is hard to understand program success or failures. Information is described as a one-way street – from the top down. Translating the expressed vision of community resilience and shared responsibility in the context of climate change requires significantly more detail about how the policy will be enacted and how it will be recognised when, and if, it is achieved (Eburn 2015; Stanley 2015a).

The Federal Attorney-General's Department held a forum in 2009, with the aim of better responding to wildfire arson (Attorney-General's Department 2009). The subsequent report noted the need for an integrated approach, saying: "successfully addressing bushfire arson is beyond the capacity of any one agency or area of specialisation. An overriding message is that greater national collaboration is required across portfolios at all levels of government. This includes ensuring better coordination between police, fire and emergency services to engage in targeted prevention programs and share information in investigating crimes" (McClelland 2010, p.3).

Importantly, the forum agreed on actions to be taken. It is worth listing these as they represent a fairly comprehensive prevention program:

- Utilise fuel reduction and community education programs in high-risk fire and malicious lighting areas at the urban/rural interface, consistent with land management objectives

- Conduct removal programs of abandoned vehicles

- Ensure nationally consistent wildfire offences with a review of current legislation, including overseas models, noting that these actions recognise that many deliberately lit wildfires may be preventable utilising crime prevention techniques.

- Investigate best practice malicious lighting prevention measures

- Develop programs targeting known and recidivist malicious firelighters

- Investigate the development of a national malicious wildfire database

- Develop national strategies to raise community awareness of malicious fire lighting and incorporate prevention messages into existing community awareness programs

- Develop targeted awareness and prevention programs to malicious wildfire lighting-prone communities, including greater collaboration with education and welfare agencies

- Investigate the viability of a nationally consistent framework for data collection on malicious wildfires

- Develop spatial analysis tools to identify malicious wildfire hot spots

- Research socio-economic and demographic factors indicating a propensity to malicious wildfire lighting

- Develop evaluation tools for prevention program impacts

- Training of fire investigators

Unfortunately, much of this never went any further than a wish list. Indeed, malicious wildfire appears to have remained outside the major thinking on wildfire.

The Forest Fire Management Group (2014) produced a wildfire policy document with the involvement of all Australian State and Territory Governments. Unusually, the document provides a vision, strategic objectives, national goals and guiding principles. The Vision is stated as: "(F)ire regimes are effectively managed to maintain and enhance the protection of human life and property, and the health, biodiversity, tourism, recreation and production benefits derived from Australia's forests and rangelands" (Forest Fire Management Group 2014, p. 9). However, despite the promise, the document remains fairly general with high-level objectives, within a risk management approach. The document notes that greater investment in prevention and preparedness is essential. However, this again appears to be understood as increased and "smarter" planned burning, linked to reduced wildfire risk and better ecological outcomes as "(P)lanned fires are fundamental to this strategy" (Forest Fire Management Group 2014 p.8, 20).

A national symposium, Advancing Bushfire Arson Prevention in Australia, was held in March 2010, attended by the Australian Federal Attorney-General. The Symposium produced some key recommendations, including the need for a wide range of prevention strategies (Stanley & Kestin 2010). It was recognised that prevention is likely to cost a lot less than suppression and recovery from wildfire. There was a strong view about the need to improve the quality of data, and that there should be a national data system and national standards of interoperability in recording malicious wildfire ignitions. The symposium called for a multi-agency and multi-discipline approach that includes other agencies and the community, to address and prevent malicious lighting. However, the report concludes that more investment is required in impact evaluation to ensure that the efficacy of discrete programs is better understood. The symposium concluded that although there is interest in maliciously lit wildfire from all levels of government in Australia, there does not yet appear to be any cohesive whole-of-government approach to its prevention. Unfortunately, this remains largely true, a decade later.

Victorian Government

As the states in Australia are responsible for wildfire policy and implementation, there is variation in approaches between states with a complex system of various state government departments and organisations (Buergelt & Smith 2015). In Victoria, the Department of Environment, Land, Water and Planning has overall responsibility for emergency management. This department has the portfolios of energy, environment, climate change, water, planning and local government, and is responsible for managing 8.05 million hectares of public land. Emergency Management Victoria is tasked with implementing the emergency management agenda, leading and coordinating emergency preparedness, response and recovery with the emergency management sector and community (Parliament of Victoria 2017). Its roles include: liaison with the Federal Government; leading and facilitating key initiatives focused on system-wide reform with integrated policy, strategy, planning, investment and procurement; and, ensuring a stronger emphasis on shared responsibility, community resilience, and is community-focused.

In the state government's submission to the Parliamentary Inquiry into Fire Season Preparedness, undertaken by the state opposition party, it was said that: "all agencies, departments, industry, business, all levels of government and community need to work together to achieve a sustainable and efficient emergency management system that reduces the likelihood, effect and consequences of emergencies: 'we work as one'" (Parliament of Victoria 2017, p.75). Underpinning the current approach to emergency management in Victoria is the concept of shared responsibility. The document Safer Together: A new approach to reducing the risk of bushfire in Victoria, emphases the need for land and fire managers to work together in close partnership with Victorian communities and move to an evidence-based approach on fuel-reduction (DELWP 2015). The document embeds a fuel reduction target, with involvement with communities about where the planned burning should take place. Thus again, there is recognition of the need for an integrated approach to wildfire, but it would seem that there is a need for further action in this direction.

Local government

State, Regional and Municipal (local government) Strategic Fire Management Planning Committees were instigated following recommendations from the 2003 and 2009 Victorian Bushfire Inquiries (CFA 2015). Membership comes from representatives of organisations responsible for fire prevention, preparedness, response, recovery, and environmental and cultural uses of fire. The tasks of these groups are to develop regional strategic fire management plans and integrated fire management planning. The aim is "to provide a municipal-level forum to build and sustain organisational partnerships, generate a common understanding and shared purpose with regard to fire management and ensure that the plans of individual agencies are linked and complement each other" (Emergency Management Victoria 2015, p. 2).

Specifically, the fire management planning committees seek to work cooperatively and collaboratively on the development and implementation of plans through:

- implementing common planning models and methodologies
- allocating resources and responsibilities
- participating in common decision-making through the committee process

- collaboratively delivering fire management activities

- engaging cooperatively (Emergency Management Victoria 2015, p. 4)

Broader, Emergency Management Planning Committees have been established in each municipality in Victoria with membership comprising local government members and response and recovery agencies.

A place-based initiative

An important collaborative initiative, The Gippsland Arson Prevention Program (GAPP), is a place-based initiative, which has been operating for a number of years in the Gippsland region in Eastern Victoria. Local stakeholders, such as police, fire-brigades, local government, regional state departments and businesses, meet regularly to share local knowledge and activities around the prevention of wildfire arson (Stanley, Read & Willis 2016). Activities include: establishing areas of wildfire concern, educating the public of the dangers of maliciously lit wildfire and the need to report suspicious fire-related behaviour; and, coordinating prevention responses, such as patrolling. This initiative is unique to Gippsland; however, the state government has some interest in replicating the model in other Victorian regions. This was also recommended by the Parliamentary Inquiry into Fire Season Preparedness (Parliament of Victoria 2017). An evaluation of GAPP recommended that the program would be improved if wildfire data could also be improved. This data could include information about 'Persons of Interest' (people being investigated by the police), their characteristics, where suspects are operating and the target of ignition, together with locational vulnerabilities and fire risk.

Thus, it would appear that the management model, outlined above, is operating best in Victoria at the local government level. The GAPP model presents as the more comprehensive approach at the operational level, although there are many missing gaps in representation, such as the community, urban planners, schools and welfare representatives. While there appears to be recognition that an improved management approach, in general, is required around prevention, and at the national level there was an attempt to initiate a range of prevention initiatives, this has largely failed to occur.

Prevention programs

Drawing on the field of public health, prevention programs are commonly categorised into three types (Goldston 1987):

- Primary Prevention promotes a wellness approach, which gives positive messages about health and wellbeing or advises against certain behaviours, such as smoking

- Secondary Prevention targets specific groups at risk of acquiring a particular disease

- Tertiary Prevention **is** directed towards reducing the harm of symptoms.

This framework has been adapted for use in the field of criminology and could be used to structure the prevention of wildfires (Brantingham & Faust 1976; Stanley & Kestin 2010; Stanley & Read 2016). Primary prevention targets the whole population, such as media advertising about how to reduce fire risk around your home, or educational messages about the dangers of leaving camp-fires unattended. Secondary prevention is directed towards specific sub-groups in the population who may light a wildfire, such as police undertaking surveillance of youths who are suspected of lighting fires. Tertiary prevention is aimed at reducing the opportunities and desires for those known to light fires, such as through incarceration, treatment intervention, or removal from a risky environment.

However, there remains considerable confusion about prevention and wildfire, an issue referred to throughout this book and reiterated here. As noted in the earlier discussion, the term 'prevention' is used in wildfire management in some situations, but not in others. The initials used by many in risk management are PPRR. However, this often refers to 'Plan', Preparation, Response and Recovery, rather than 'Prevention', Preparation, Response and Recovery (Alexander 2015). An alternative approach used in an article examining hazard risk management in Europe is RPPR, where prevention is associated with planning (Sapountzaki et al. 2011). This is understood as:

- Recovery and reconstruction

- Pre-disaster or preventative planning, viewed widely, from defensive works to land-use planning, to evacuation plans

- Preparedness – alertness immediately prior to the onset of the hazard

- Response referring to reaction activities immediately before and after, such as emergency relief

In some contexts where prevention is mentioned, the text refers to adapting to, rather than stopping the problem. For example, a recent report, auspiced by the Queensland Fire and Emergency Services, was introduced by the Queensland Minister and Commissioner for Fire and Emergency Services. He stated: "Within the past decade we have experienced natural disasters of a size and scale that are almost unprecedented in our nation's modern history. The extreme heatwave and associated wildfires in late 2018 are a clear indication that we face new, unparalleled challenges in understanding and responding to the impacts of climate change on natural hazards which even now pose a significant risk to Queensland" (Chesnais et al. 2019, p.4). Yet, the report gave no suggestions about preventing climate change and the suggested 'prevention' responses related to how to adapt to the changing conditions, emphasising urban design and regional planning. Indeed, the Queensland government has paved the way for the Adani coal mine (with approval to extract 60 million tonnes a year). In June 2019 it approved the environmental report on the mine's impact, believing the mine to be important because it creates local jobs. Similarly, a report by the Victorian Government on reducing wildfire risk, offers, what it says is a 'new approach' but does not mention prevention (Victorian Government 2015). Australia does not have this issue on its own. An internet search of wildfire prevention across many countries reveals few programs on the prevention of ignition.

It could be argued that frameworks, such as those referred to, above, add to the confusion around what exactly prevention entails. The discussion is usually nestled within a planning framework, also a vital part of hazard and wildfire responses. Prevention carries the idea of stopping something from happening or stopping someone from doing something, but it also can include the notion of reducing harm. Indeed, mitigation is often used in place of prevention when talking about wildfire, and commonly refers to behaviour that seeks to minimise harm. The overwhelming form of wildfire mitigation/prevention undertaken in Australia is fuel reduction in the environment. In Victoria, this tends to be a 'one size fits all' approach almost exclusively on public land. This should be viewed as a Primary Prevention approach. There is presently a growing interest in Indigenous burning, where smaller and less intense fires are managed. This approach is used to a small extent in the Australian Capital Territory. The following sections examine some snapshots of types of prevention approaches undertaken internationally. Chapter 11 offers a more comprehensive range of prevention programs that could be undertaken.

Primary prevention

The most common form of primary prevention relating to wildfire is messaging and/or education that raises awareness about fire hazards and safety. This is usually done through the media, such as alerting the public of dangerous fire conditions and use of emergency service websites to guide behaviour in relation to fire. In Australia, education programs tend to concentrate on safety once a fire has occurred, such as smoke alarms, as well as how to prepare and defend properties (Muller 2009a). The police in Western Australia have engaged in a range of public education and fire awareness programs targeted at the whole community, with an emphasis on children and parents (Plucinski 2014). Unusually, the program has been reviewed and appears to show some success in outcomes around prevention of malicious fires. Examination of fire trends from 1 July 2004 to 30 June 2012 showed a decline in malicious and suspicious fires, which are independent of variations of fire danger and fuel availability. In addition, publicity around fire prevention that was associated with a major fire event also showed a reduction in subsequent malicious wildfires and those caused by cutting and welding equipment (measured over 1½ years).

Educational programs targeting the prevention of wildfire had a very early start in the USA. The program entitled Smokey Bear was initiated by the U.S. Forest Service in 1944, with the message, 'Only You Can Prevent Forest Fires,' later changed to 'Wildfires'. The campaign was widened, with bear toys, a book and songs and association with celebrities. A website with tips about fire prevention and a section for children is still available[1] The USA offers a range of educational approaches using websites, which give advice about equipment use, debris burning and campfire safety. For example, One Less Spark – One Less Wildfire toolkit is produced by the California Wildland Fire Coordinating Group[2]. This dedicated site offers a range of good quality approaches about fire prevention, targeting various groups of people, such as for children who may be inclined to play with matches. It also offers fire safety education through school programs, fair exhibits, posters and flyers, spread through radio and television, community meetings and the internet.

Another common approach is the restriction of times when people can burn-off debris and light fires in the open, such as BBQs and campfires, now a common approach used in many countries. Total Fire Ban days are decreed in Australia and also used in California when fire danger conditions arise. At other times Fire Permits need to be acquired on private property and parks.

---

[1] https://www.smokeybear.com/en
[2] www.preventwildfireca.org

Secondary prevention

Community reporting

Crime Stoppers is a program operating in about 20 countries, including Australia. Crime Stoppers offers the public with a means to report either suspicion of crimes or a belief that a crime may occur, in contrast to reporting once a crime has taken place. The reports may include malicious fire lighting. Anonymity for the reporter and offers of reward on capture vary between program locations. The reporting can relate to the risk of both reckless and malicious wildfires, thus caters for both civic and criminal causes of wildfire. However, the use of Crime Stoppers information in different states of Australia (and also probably internationally) appears to be quite variable, some states tending not to use the data, and some filtering the information according to the perception of usefulness by the police.

Situational crime prevention

Situational crime prevention is based on the idea that altering the environment will make it less attractive to a malicious fire lighter by reducing opportunities, rewards and motivation, and increase the effort and risks involved in committing an offence. As bushfire ignitions tend to follow patterns in time and place (see chapter 4) understanding, this is likely to facilitate ways to deter people from lighting fires. An exception is the rapid removing rubbish and dumped cars, a practice that has been shown to reduce ignitions (Cozens 2010). Such initiatives could be used a lot more.

Surveillance

Surveillance programs are commonly undertaken by police and fire agencies and include activities such as patrolling of high wildfire risk areas on days of high fire danger and monitoring the location of suspected arsonists. Operation Nomad began in South Australia in 1992. Under this program, known arsonists are visited on extreme wildfire risk days, and a highly visible policing presence is provided for high-risk wildfire areas. Other states have emulated versions of this program. Operation Firesetter, in Victoria, was established in 2010, following a recommendation of the Victorian Bushfire Royal Commission. This program supplies extra resources to the most severe fire risk regions on high fire risk days. This commonly comprises two or more extra staff who coordinate with, and support, local patrolling, with some regions also using the extra staff to visit 'Persons of Interest' in relation to their identified risk of fire lighting. Western Australia has also complemented a similar program with the establishment of a database of trend locations for malicious fire lighting. The effectiveness of these programs in preventing the malicious lighting of wildfires is unclear.

While there is national provision for a 'warning flag' for arson placed against records of convicted criminals in Australia, the Government of Ohio in the United States has gone a step further, introducing a register and database of convicted arsonists, available to law enforcement and fire investigation officials (deWine 2013). This approach has been recommended in Australia (see Stanley & Kestin 2010). In 2014 the Victorian Government introduced a $A12 million electronic monitoring program for a number of serious offenders, including convicted arsonists. However, this has been rarely used and would appear to be not very effective given the small number of arsonists apprehended and the often under-age status of firelighters.

There is some limited use of cameras as a fire prevention method. These are largely used in Australia by industry where wildfire will have a severe consequence on business. Cameras are fixed in places vulnerable to fire lighting and on patrol vehicles to record illegal activities.

Other programs

Education campaigns about the discarding of cigarettes have been undertaken in Australia, but their effectiveness is unknown (Muller 2009a). 'Fire-safe' cigarettes have been developed and are legally required in all 50 states in the USA, as well as in Europe and the UK and a number of other countries. However, again effectiveness is unclear. The 2009 Victorian Bushfire Royal Commission recommended a retreat and resettlement strategy where there is an unacceptably high wildfire risk, including the non-compulsory acquisition of the land by the state. However, 'unacceptably high risk' was not defined, nor was it established who should define it. The (then) Victorian Premier stated that people had a right to live where they pleased, a perspective reflected in Australian common law (Eburn 2015). Clearing vegetation from around electricity cables is undertaken in some locations, to prevent branches and trees connecting with cables, thus risking ignition. Effectiveness is unclear.

Screening tools may be used as a way of minimising the risk of firefighter arson. In Australia and New Zealand, a number of fire services have tested two screening instruments which target potential firelighters during the recruitment of volunteer firefighters. Many Australian fire services have introduced criminal records checks for new members. However, given that so few malicious firelighters are convicted, this is not likely to be a sufficient response. Psychological screening of fire service personnel is a far preferable option, although it is likely to be an expensive process.

Tertiary prevention

Tertiary prevention deterrents to malicious fire lighting come in the form of punishment and treatment. It is common for the media to publish calls to give tougher penalties for young people who light wildfires (Findlay 2002). The former Premier of NSW, Bob Carr, is reported as saying that young offenders needed to be "taught a lesson" and the NSW Government would "force juvenile arsonists to tour fire-ravaged areas and make them face fire victims in hospital burns wards" (Ellicott & Stock 2002, p.2). However, a blaming response is not necessarily going to lead to prevention.

Corrective approach

The Crimes Act 1958 (Victoria) outlines the offences of arson and wildfire arson. The conviction of intent to destroy or damage property, or where the person knows or believes that his conduct is more likely than not to result in destruction or damage to property by fire, is liable for up to 10 years imprisonment. The sentence could extend to 15 years if the defendant is found to have intended to endanger the life of another. This legislation encompasses recklessly lit fires as being satisfactory to prosecute as criminal intent. However, a person is not considered to be reckless in behaviour if he/she was carrying out fire prevention, fire suppression and other land management activity (Willis 2004). Also excluded are those too young to be criminally responsible and those who do not fully understand the potential damage they might cause, thus considered mentally unfit to stand trial (Muller 2009a).

Approaches to the investigation and apprehension of malicious firelighters vary between states in Australia. For example, New South Wales and South Australia investigate arson through the major crime squad, rather than using specialist arson investigators. Victoria has a small specialised service, but in 2012–13, the Victorian Government introduced a program that utilised 150 Bushfire, Arson and Explosives Liaison Officers for the fire season to assist local police with the prevention, intelligence and enforcement in relation to arson (Partington 2012). While the effectiveness of this scheme in Victoria is unknown, a similar scheme in New South Wales is reported by the New South Wales Police Force as contributing to a significant drop in arson events (New South Wales Rural Fire Service 2013).

In Victoria, there were 2,818 arson events recorded during the 2013-14 financial year. 549 offences in that period and a further 179 offences from previous years were 'cleared'. This term is defined as referring to a person processed in relation to an offence, removed from the list due to no offence having had occurred, or a person who could not be charged. Thus, a clearance rate of 19.5% was achieved for the year, or 25.8% if a carry-over from the previous year is included. From this group, 22 people went to trial and were sentenced for the principal offence of arson (of all types, including non-vegetation fires). This rate of conviction reflects a similar trend over the previous five-year period (Sentencing Advisory Council 2015). Thus, arson appears to be a very difficult crime to prosecute.

Of these convictions, 13 people were given an immediate custodial sentence, such as imprisonment, partially suspended sentence, youth justice centre order, hospital order, or a mix of imprisonment and community correction order. One person received aggregate imprisonment for all offences, not only arson. The average length of prison sentences imposed between 2009–10 and 2013–14 was just under two years and eight months (Sentencing Advisory Council 2015). Tomison (2010) places the conviction rate for arson at around four in every 1000 incidents (0.4%), although it has risen slightly in recent years. The Sentencing Advisory Council in Tasmania (2012) notes that the percentage of criminals convicted for that crime compared with the total number of crimes reported is the lowest rate of any crime in Australia.

Youth Justice Conferencing

Restorative Justice Conferencing has been used in NSW since 1997. It involves bringing a young offender and their family face-to-face with the victim and their support group (Pooley 2018). This approach aims to instil a sense of responsibility and remorse within the young offender, to produce reparation for the harm caused, empower victims and families of young offenders, and reintegrate the offender back into the community (Pooley 2018). Since 2006, young people who commit fire-related offences (aged 10 to 18) have been included in the program, with the added inclusion of firefighters used to educate the youth on the dangers of fire (see education section below).

Pooley (2018) undertook an evaluation of this program. Recidivism analysis revealed that 67.4% of young people who participated in conferencing between 1 July 2006 and 30 June 2016 subsequently re-offended within the follow-up period. The majority (38.7%) of young people re-offended within the first 12 months post-conferencing and a further 15.9% re-offended within the second-year post-conferencing, while about 5% re-offended within the third and subsequent further four years post conferencing. These trends are typical of young offenders and of those who participate in Youth Justice Conferencing more broadly. However, retrospective analysis of recidivism data revealed that most young people who re-offended did not commit a fire-related re-offence. This fits with existing literature that suggests that fire-specific recidivism is low compared to general recidivism (Ducat, McEwan &

Ogloff 2015; Lambie et al. 2009). In Lambie and colleague's (2009) 10-year follow-up of 200 young people referred to the NZ Fire Awareness and Intervention Program, fire-specific recidivism was low (2.0%). Similarly, in Ducat and colleague's (2015) 2.5 to 11-year follow-up of 1,052 persons over the age of 18 years convicted of arson in Victoria, fire-specific recidivism was 5.3%. Kolko & Kazdin (1990) have shown that children (with a sample of children aged 6 to 13 years) who light fires experience limited supervision, parental pathology and greater disturbances in individual psychopathology, parent-child relationships and stressful life events. Thus 'education' may not resolve the offender's developmental issues.

Counselling and treatment

Treatment of malicious firelighters

Specialised treatment for arson offenders is rare, with the development of specialised, evidence-based interventions only an emerging field (Doley, Dickens & Gannon 2016). A small number of behavioural treatment programs in New Zealand, Canada, the USA and South America, designed for generic offending, did not appear to reduce repeat fire lighting behaviour (Haines, Lambie & Seymour 2006, reported in Doley, Dickens & Gannon 2016). Two other small and largely unevaluated treatment programs in the UK, are reported by Doley, Dickens & Gannon (2016). Chaplin & Henry (2016) report that some success has been shown in a treatment program developed by Taylor (2013) for those with an intellectual disability and an interest in fire lighting, but again this has not been fully evaluated. In 2012, the Australian Centre for Arson Research and Treatment at Bond University developed and practised a treatment program for adult firelighters in Australia, although it does not appear to be now operating.

Gannon and colleagues at the University in Kent developed a comprehensive treatment program for malicious firelighters who are institutionalised in prison or in a mental health setting (Gannon et al. 2012). This program was based on extensive research, evaluated and supported by training manuals for practitioners. The researchers found that firelighters have unique psychological characteristics and particularly experience more angry thoughts than other offenders. They also have lower self-esteem and sense of control (Gannon et al. 2013). This program is discussed in greater detail in chapter 3.

Comprehensive training has been facilitated by Gannon in the UK. In incarceration settings using this assessment treatment approach, trained practitioners are playing a key role in sentence planning and parole board hearings for fire lighting prisoners. This is currently meeting a need that is not being met by existing treatment programs within the British Prison Service (The

British Psychological Society 2016). The use of the program in Australia is unclear. The Victorian Institute of Forensic Mental Health, Forensicare, offers an assessment and a broad intervention program, not specifically targeting firelighters (Muller 2009a). This paucity of treatment programs in Australia may be due to the low numbers of offenders who are convicted being exclusively firelighters and the criminal justice system's general preference for general offender programs such as the Problem Behaviour Program (Muller 2009a).

Targeted education programs

Since 1989, most Australian states have conducted fire education programs. However, these are predominately education-based interventions with linkages and referral systems to mental health or behavioural treatment services (Muller & Stebbins 2007). The UK, some European countries (particularly Denmark and Finland) and, to varying extent, the USA, run fire education services for children (Kolko 2002; Stacey et al. 2010; Willis 2004). The programs commonly target children and youth who show an interest in fire lighting (Muller & Stebbins 2007). While there are minor variations in the programs, they are usually conducted by firefighters and offer fire safety messages.

The Fight Fire Fascination is undertaken by the Queensland Fire and Emergency Services for children 3 to 17 years of age who have been involved in at least one inappropriate fire incident. The program is designed to support parents and guardians with their efforts to educate their children about fire. The program is based on the belief that children and young people can learn skills to remain safe from fire. It delivers three home visits, plus an event celebrating course completion. The program works in partnership with schools, mental health services and other community agencies.

Another program, the Juvenile Arson Offenders Program (JAOP), was a group-based program for convicted arsonists, also auspiced by the Queensland Fire and Emergency Services. The JAOP provides simulated fire activities and personal skills training over a three-day course in a non-clinical context to help reduce recidivism. According to one evaluation, JAOP appears '...promising because it is jointly organised between fire services and allied health services and appears to be effective in reducing recidivism and increasing other skills' (McDonald et al. 2012, p. 319). However, this program had funding withdrawn in late 2012 and no longer exists (Taylor 2013).

Juvenile Justice NSW, in partnership with Fire and Rescue NSW, provides problem fire lighting awareness and education to youth and their parents participating in Youth Justice Conferencing (Pooley 2018) (see above). A firefighter attends the conference to provide the educational aspect along with suggestions for the youth's outcome plan. This education, delivered within the conference and/or as a component of the outcome plan, aims to advance the young person's fire knowledge and improve their fire safety skills. Underpinning this is the assumption that the youth is not aware of the consequences of lighting fires. An evaluation of this program using content analysis found that 16 of the 23 youths who had participated in a conference attributed their problem fire lighting behaviours to a lack of understanding regarding the consequences of fires (Pooley 2018). Pooley suggests that fire education would best be combined with other interventions given the complexity of fire lighting behaviours.

The Juvenile Fire Awareness and Intervention Program (JFAIP) has been jointly run in Victoria by the Metropolitan Fire Brigade and the Country Fire Brigade for 25 years (Metropolitan Fire Brigade 2019)[3] A similar program is run in Western Australia (Department of Fire and Emergency Services[4] The Victorian program is voluntary and free. Children aged between 6 and 17 years who may engage in the following behaviours are eligible:

- fascination with, or curiosity about fire

- fire lighting behaviour due to:

  o   their family situation or pressures resulting from learning or social difficulties

  o   peer pressure generally associated with low self-esteem

  o   anger and revenge associated with family or friendship problems

  o   fires resulting from malicious or mischievous behaviour

The program is undertaken during home visits by two trained firefighters who seek to raise awareness of fire hazards and establish responsible fire-safe behaviour at home and in the community. The exact content of the program depends on local issues, such as geography, demography, emergency service structure and resources. A planned addition to the program is a preliminary screening questionnaire, the Behaviour Risk Tool, administered by the visiting firefighter. This tool identifies young people with psychosocial disturbance predictive of ongoing fire lighting behaviour, in order to recommend

---

[3] http://www.mfb.vic.gov.au/Media/docs/JFAIP%20Brochure%202012-329b56ee-2308-4b4a-87e2-ac02c9b8ee440.pdf).

[4] https://www.dfes.wa.gov.au/schooleducation/childrenandfamilies/Pages/jaffaprogram.aspx

supplementary mental health intervention, as the JFAIP program is not designed for children with mental health problems. Testing of the questionnaire found that 80% of the repeat firelighters and 70% of the non-repeat firelighters were correctly identified.

The program managers state that a key strength of the JFAIP program is that it is delivered by operational firefighters who can draw on their knowledge, experience and credibility that assists in building rapport with the young person and family (Muller & Stebbins 2007). While this initiative has been taken by fire services, there must be some concerns about the ability and appropriateness of some firefighters to act as councillors to children and youth, as well as their ability to administer the questionnaire. Some of the criteria for inclusion, shown above, suggest there may be some disturbances in the family. It is unclear what happens to young people not accepted into the JFAIP program. A preadolescent or adolescent who is continuing to engage in dangerous fire activities is likely to have considerable difficulties, and therefore needs expert counselling. It would be hoped that those firefighters who themselves engage in fire lighting (acknowledging it is likely to be a very small proportion of total firefighters, although the numbers are unknown) would be excluded from the JFAIP program.

Targeted education type programs are commonly small in scale and are vulnerable to funding cuts. Evaluation of the effectiveness of Australian juvenile crime prevention programs, encompassing the prevention of fire lighting, is limited to a few small projects and the effectiveness of these programs is yet to be proven on a larger scale (Morgan & Homel 2013). An independent review of the JFAIP found that nine from a sample of 29 boys referred to the program for fire lighting reoffended within a 12-month follow-up (McDonald 2010). Additional follow-up and comparison data would be needed to know if this was indicative of program effectiveness or, as tends to be a common pattern, children cease fire lighting as they age.

Children who commonly light fires have a range of problem or antisocial behaviours, and it is unlikely that education would address all motivations for fire lighting. The Northumberland Fire and Rescue Service, auspiced by the Northumberland County Council in the UK, run one-to-one education programs for children and young people who have demonstrated a concerning interest in playing with fire. The programs offer fire safety education and advice for children and young people, as well as their parents. The Accidental, Natural and Social Fire Risk project in Europe found that there is only limited evidence that education programs aimed at children and youth are successful (Stacey et al. 2010). This is of considerable concern, as the time resources of firefighters are limited, and these programs may be at the cost of mainstream firefighting preparation activities. McDonald (2010) is of the opinion that evaluations have revealed that youth intervention programs are central to changing fire-specific behaviours in young people and their parents/guardians, but only for low risk, non-pathological misusers of fire (McDonald 2010).

Overview of the effectiveness of prevention programs

Evaluation of the effectiveness of prevention programs is vital, although rarely done. An important exception is the high-quality work being undertaken in the UK on improving understanding and treatment of fire offenders (Gannon et al. 2012). Only a few crime prevention programs internationally have been subject to robust evaluation (Morgan & Homel 2013). The little research that has been undertaken to date offers mixed results (Prestemon et al. 2013). The complexity of measuring the effectiveness of the prevention of ignition appears to confound the few evaluations that have been undertaken. Evaluation of these programs is not an easy task, as something that did not occur is usually what is being measured.

The problems are illustrated with an example in three continents. Abt and colleagues (2015) examined the effectiveness of fire prevention projects on 17 US Bureau of Indian Affairs tribal units. The projects, which were assessed as a bundle, included projects dealing with law enforcement, targeting campfires, work with juveniles, fire activities such as burning debris, and equipment-caused wildfires. Weather and available fuel details were included. Thus, in effect, the model measured the probability that ignition would become established and be reported, rather than the prevention of ignitions as such, the authors acknowledging this complication. The length of time the program had operated and the number of law enforcement officers were found to reduce wildfires by 32% in the areas of malicious fires and equipment-caused wildfires. The evaluators made the tentative conclusion that the benefits of active prevention programs can exceed the costs of such programs. However, the measured benefits only related to the costs of suppression.

The Accidental, Natural and Social Fire Risk project in Europe found only limited evidence that education programs aimed at children and youth are successful (Stacey et al. 2010), while in contrast, some education programs in the USA have shown a deterrent effect (Kolko 2002). A collaborative approach in Western Australia, between the Fire and Emergency Service Authority, Western Australia Police, local shopping centre owners, and the Department of Education and Training, has been reported as being successful in reducing fires (Smith 2004 as cited in Beale & Jones 2011). The approach provided information about fire danger and encouraged reporting to Crime Stoppers through talks, door knocking and leaving flyers, fridge magnets, and branded shopping bags. This approach has similarities with the awareness-raising, and the promotional aspects of the Gippsland Arson Prevention Program discussed earlier in this chapter.

Conclusions

This chapter offers only a minimal overview of prevention programs undertaken internationally. Part of the reason for this is that it would seem there are few such programs written up and reviewed in the literature, suggesting a scarcity of such programs. A few, largely educational type programs for children and youth, can be found on web pages. Thus, a major conclusion that can be drawn from this chapter is that not a lot is done about the prevention of wildfire ignition. Indeed, the prevention of ignition is largely overlooked at the strategic level, in the framework on disaster risk response, auspiced by the United Nations, to national approaches in many countries. As noted previously, this oversight may be in part due to the linking of wildfire with 'natural' disasters, that are assumed to not be preventable. It is also likely to be due to historical attention to response and recovery, generally a much smaller task without the influence of climate change. Indeed, the Sendai Framework for Disaster Risk Reduction gives no attention to the need to reduce GHGs as a major tool to prevent catastrophic fires. Rather, it is more an adaptation document that offers best-practice adjustment to what is implied to be a situation that can't be prevented. Prevention should be an important part of the wildfire management approach, with improved integration into the prevention, preparedness, response and recovery process framework. Prevention is either not included in this framework or included and usually viewed very narrowly or confused with planning or preparation.

Despite this oversight, at the program and operational levels, there are a few good programs that target the prevention approach. These are the most common educational programs, although a few treatment programs are now being offered. Unfortunately, the evaluation of the effectiveness of some prevention programs being offered is rare. Evidence for effectiveness, associated with cost/effectiveness evaluation, may lead to greater resources being available for prevention programs.

However, the Sendai Framework document and most of the national strategic fire management reports, do recognise the importance of broad engagement and coordination with all levels of government, business and community. The report notes that: "Disaster risk reduction requires that responsibilities be shared by central Governments and relevant national authorities, sectors and stakeholders" (UNISDR 2015, p.13). It recognises the need for the inclusion of local communities and cultural or traditional knowledge. What is again absent is a model of how this could be achieved. Some levels of government are better placed to take the lead in particular areas. For example, the Federal Government has a responsibility to lead on responding to climate change and the reduction of GHGs, as well as the provision of resources to facilitate the best approach to other aspects of the response. This would particularly be in relation to the adequate funding of wildfire suppression. Local Government is best placed to understand local responses in relation to planning decisions and participation in local decision-making with the local residents. This whole-of-society inclusive approach to wildfire management is discussed further in chapter 10 of this book.

Chapter 6

Local government and bushfire prevention: The case of Victoria, Australia

Introduction

Local government is the primary mode of delivery for many of the services, regulations and governance arrangements affecting the quality of life for Victorians, including many relating to wildfire management. The state of Victoria in Australia is acknowledged as an extreme risk wildfire region due to the characteristics of its topography, high levels of flammable vegetation, high frequency of dry, hot fire weather, sometimes coinciding with long term drought. Wildfires themselves are "unplanned vegetation fires…, [it is] a generic term which includes grass fires, forest fires and scrub fires both with and without a suppression objective" (Australian Institute for Disaster Resilience 2019).

In this chapter, the main factors relating to wildfire risks are set out that relate to the role and capabilities of local government in Victoria. This serves as an illustration of the role in relation to wildfire prevention that local government is given authority under legislation to play and how this could be broadened and improved integration with other agencies responsible for risk management, especially fire services. Even while Victoria has one of the most advanced physically oriented treatments of wildfire internationally, there are many areas where improvements could be made. The chapter also illustrates how urban planning in Victoria has the authority to act on an important area of the prevention of ignition, where there is a risk in relation to a chain of ignitions within an existing wildfire.

The majority of Victoria's 79 local government areas include wildfire-prone land, meaning that this responsibility is ongoing and significant. The chapter argues that local government is bound by multiple requirements established at the state level, with three aspects being of particular significance, despite any shortcomings: urban planning; fire protection responsibilities and, the production of Municipal Emergency Management Plans (MEMPS). We suggest that the fire protection role and MEMPS are important but limited in their facilitation of proactive risk reduction. Further, while urban planning plays an important role, it is suggested that this leaves untreated many potential areas where risk management could be more effective, particularly in terms of forward strategic planning and reduction of social factors leading to fire risks. The next sections set out a brief description of wildfire and some of the contextual elements of relevance to local government action, before going on to describe the legislative basis for local planning action to reduce wildfire risks. The chapter concludes that while Victorian local government is highly advanced in its ability to act on certain physical aspects of wildfire risk, there are many areas of socio-economic and environmental concern that remain poorly dealt with.

Wildfire risks

The role of local government is directly linked with managing and responding to many of the fundamental processes of wildfire itself. While the propensity for a fire to burn is fundamentally a function of its supply of oxygen, fuels and heat (Mell et al. 2010), key wildfire likelihood and behaviour factors include weather conditions, sources of ignition, terrain, specific wind conditions, fuel amount, arrangement and size, moisture levels and energy content of fuels (Cheney 1981). Slope angle impacts upon fire progression (speed), the pattern of spread patterns and the length (and sometimes angle) of flame (Linn et al. 2010). As fires move uphill, they tend to heat and dry the fuels they are advancing towards, causing them to ignite more readily and with greater intensity (Linn et al. 2010). Windy conditions have a number of impacts on the behaviour of a fire in terms of heat levels, the speed and general spread of fires, including ember attack impacts, depending on the nature of source fuels of embers (Sharples et al. 2016). Changes to the direction in which fires are travelling are usually caused by wind shifts and interactions with topographical features, sometimes creating even more dangerous, unpredictable and larger fire fronts (Sharples et al. 2016).

As a general term, 'risk' can be understood as the probability that an unwanted outcome will occur – as a function of likelihood by consequence. A common description of risk is the result of interactions between the hazard itself (wildfire) exposure (proximity), and vulnerability (humans and structures that can be impacted on) (Crichton 1999). In this sense, the main risks defined as associated with wildfires are primarily based on their potential to interact with human settlements, where the potential for disastrous consequences are significant (Blanchi, Leonard & Leicester 2014). In Victoria, extensive areas are fire-prone based on being vegetated, and many ecosystems in these areas are reliant on fire. In this context, wildfire disasters occur when residential or other forms of development, including key infrastructure, is exposed to extreme fire conditions. This results in the ignition of multiple homes, properties or other structures whereby the fire cannot be contained by emergency response systems (Cohen 2000). While wildfire impacts are more likely in rural and peri-urban areas, it is also significant that low-density settlement patterns in urban/rural interfaces can affect the frequency and intensity of catastrophic wildfires, increasing risks (Butt et al. 2009) due to the proximity of vegetation to extensive numbers of structures in low-density development areas.

There is a significant history of high consequence destructive wildfires in Australia since European settlement (Williams 2011). In order of highest fatalities in descending order these are:

1. Black Saturday (VIC), 7-8 Feb 2009 - 173 fatalities and the destruction of more than 2000 homes.

2. Ash Wednesday (VIC, SA), 16-18 Feb 1983 - 75 people and the destruction of 1900 homes.

3. Black Friday (VIC), 13-20 Jan 1939 - 71 people were killed, and 650 houses were destroyed.

4. Black Tuesday (TAS), 7 Feb 1967 - killed 62 people and razed almost 1300 homes.

5. Gippsland fires and Black Sunday (VIC), 1 Feb-10 Mar 1926 - a total of 60 people were killed.

The Black Saturday 2019 wildfires mark a key point in time where widespread recognition that purposive, integrated and interdisciplinary action addressing wildfire risks is needed (Teague, McLeod & Pascoe 2010). In particular, the Victoria 2009 fires made it doubly clear that humans pose a key wildfire risk with their structures being proximate to vegetation, leading to extensive mapping of fire risk areas. The number of fires attended by fire response services during this 2009 fire season was 16,103, with the most devastating occurring on 7th February 2009 - 'Black Saturday' (Victorian Bushfires Royal Commission Interim Report 2009). The Victorian Bushfire Royal Commission (VBRC) was established to determine the causes, impacts and response to the fires and avenues for reducing wildfire risk so that such an event would not occur again. At the completion of its proceedings, the VBRC handed down 67 recommendations. Of these nine had direct mention of local councils and municipalities, with many more also having direct or implicit implications for local government (Teague, McLeod & Pascoe 2010). In addition, 11 other recommendations related in some way to urban planning and building regulations, most of which had direct implications for local government.

Key risk factors for the built environment and human settlement are multiple and synergistic; derived from the interaction between wildfires themselves, the characteristics of human structures, gardens or managed landscapes in which structures are located and related issues such as human response and management, maintenance, and a range of site-specific factors (Blanchi et al. 2014). In general terms, structures burn when sufficient fuel, heat and oxygen is available to initiate and maintain a fire if a structure is receptive to ignition in some way (Cohen 2008). If so, the fire's radiation and convection heating preheat the house for ignition, creating conditions for radiant heat, embers or sometimes direct flame contact, leading to ignition of the structure (Mikkola 2008). It has become apparent after careful research in recent years that ember attack is a prevalent cause of property loss in wildfires (Blanchi, Leonard & Leicester 2006; Cohen 2008). Windborne embers can be carried short distances or multiple kilometres, and ember attack also raises the risk of pre-ignition prior to the arrival of the main fire front (Mikkola 2008). Accordingly, building materials, structural design, site location and vegetation management can make a building more resilient or vulnerable to ignition during a wildfire (Blanchi, Leonard & Leicester 2006; Price & Bradstock 2013). Buildings need to be capable of withstanding a range of wildfire attack mechanisms.

While direct causality is difficult to establish in this complex area, the main inter-related factors that research suggests are most influential in the destruction of structures and related injury and death of humans are as follows (although many exceptions to this exist):

- Challenging and undulating topography, extreme fire weather, heavy fuel loads and long fire runs.

- The proximity of humans and structures to forests and vegetation, combined with intensity and direct delivery mechanism of fire impacts (heat, embers, flame contact, wind effects, tree or debris strike, explosions of flammables) to structures. This can also be related to remoteness and difficulty of access for active response and escape (Blanchi et al. 2014).

- Detailed design of structures – particularly flaws or weak points – that allow impacts described above to penetrate of igniting structures. Examples include low quality windows at ground level adjacent to fuels, openings that allow ember attack in walls and roofs, underfloor areas that allow flames and embers under structures, flammables in proximity to structures that fail in heat contexts, e.g. with PVC fittings.

- Age and poor maintenance of structures that contribute to the above risk factors.

- Garden and landscape design that contribute to the above risk factors being transferred to humans and structures.

- The proximity of adjacent structures that might provide heat, explosive force, and flame risk factors.

- The time of day, gender and roles (resulting from traditional roles in child-care, citizen fire services), and diurnal wind change effects typically in the late afternoon (Blanchi et al. 2014).

- Human decisions before and during events, including late escape, vehicular movements and active defence (Emergency Management Victoria 2018a).

Capacities and limits to local resilience using state-level regulation

With consideration for the factors outlined above, to understand how local government plays a role in wildfire risk management one must first understand that Australian local municipalities are a creation of state governments. Australia was established in 1901 as a federated commonwealth of 6 states and 2 self-governing territories. Bicameral parliaments exist at national and state level. Limitations to national powers were established, and these continue to have force according to section 106 and 107 of the Constitution. The Constitution facilitates a federated state system that favours states' powers being exercised according to their own interests and matters of concern, as "under the constitutions of each of the States, a State Parliament can make laws on any subject of relevance to that particular State. Subject to a few exceptions, the Australian Constitution does not confine the matters about which the States may make laws" (Parliamentary Education Office and Australian Government Solicitor 2010).

It is noteworthy, as a point of difference from many other nations, that local government in Australia does not have its own nationally recognised constitutionally established powers and responsibilities. As a result, powers and associated responsibilities related to urban planning, natural resource management, building regulation and emergency management are derived from state-based legislation. At the state level, local government does have recognition in the Victorian Constitution Act 1975. The Victorian Constitution recognises local councils as "a distinct and essential tier of government" (s 74). Democratically elected councils must ensure "the peace, order and good government of each municipal district" (s 74). Local governments are constituted and operated under the auspices of the Local Government Act (1989) as amended (2019). The Act is complex and extensive, being 514 pages at the time of writing. Overall, the local government has an extensive range of roles and responsibilities oriented to the following main areas:

- Resident entitlements and ratepayers voting rights in council elections local council election conduct

- Electoral commission independent electoral representation reviews

- Requirements for council governance

- Decision-making and meeting records, confidentiality and limits on decisions during elections

- Levying and payment of council rates and charges

- Preparation of council plans, budgets and annual reports

- Councils' powers to make and enforce local laws

In terms of emergency management and the wider roles of Disaster Risk Reduction, it is primarily the domain of local and state government in Australia. The National Australian Government provides funding support for specific emergency management purposes, but service delivery is the responsibility of states and councils. "Local government plays an important role in emergency management, both in partnership with other agencies, and through its own legislated emergency management obligations. Councils are not emergency response agencies but do have a long-established role in providing support to response agencies as well as coordinating relief and recovery support for the community" (Municipal Association of Victoria 2015).

At the state level, the two main Victorian Acts dealing with emergency management are the *Emergency Management Act 1986* and the *Emergency Management Act 2013*. The *Emergency Management Act 2013* deals essentially with Class 1 Emergencies. These include major fires, any other major emergency for which the Metropolitan Fire Brigade, Country Fire Authority or Victorian State Emergency Service is the control agency under the state emergency response plan; and, Class 2 Emergencies that are "other emergencies not falling into Category 1." Importantly, the *Emergency Management Act* 1986, is oriented towards "organisation and management that deals with the entirety of emergencies" (Section 3 of the Act), and oriented to three 'phases' of emergency:

1. Prevention – elimination or reduction of the incidence or severity of emergencies and the mitigation of their effects

2. Response – the combating of emergencies and the provision of rescue services

3. Recovery – the assisting of persons and communities affected by emergencies to achieve a proper and effective level of functioning (Municipal Association of Victoria 2015, p. 9).

The Local Government Act interacts with other legislation that relates to risk management. Of particular relevance to this chapter are the Planning and Environment Act (1989) and the Building Act (1989), as the governing mechanisms for building activity in Victoria. The latter is based upon regulation of construction, standards and the maintenance of specific building safety features. It is oriented to protection of the safety and health of building users while enhancing buildings' amenity.

Emphasising response and recovery: local government risk management

A primary mechanism for the management of risks at the local government level is the requirement for local Councils to prepare and maintain a Municipal Emergency Management Plan (MEMP) according to the requirements set out at s21 of the Emergency Management Act, 1986 (EM Act 1986). In parallel with the MEMP, there is a requirement to:

- Establish a municipal emergency management planning committee (MEMPC) (EM Act 1986 s21(3) that is responsible for development and maintenance of the MEMP, and its ongoing periodic consideration and adoption by the council (EM Act 1986 s21(4))

- Audits of the MEMP (EM Act 1986 s21A)

- Appointment of a municipal emergency resource officer (MERO) with the task of coordinating the use of local government resources for emergency response and recovery (EM Act 1986 s21 (1)).

A MEMP contains the following key elements based on a risk management process template (EMMV: Part 6.5):

1. Establishment of context and risk criteria

2. Hazard identification

3. Risk analysis

4. Evaluation and prioritisation of risks and possible treatments or responses

5. Acting in its own right and making recommendations to responsible bodies as regards risk treatments

6. Monitoring and review

This approach confirms with long-established risk assessment, and treatment 'processes' considered best practice in Australia, based on key publications such as the National Emergency Risk Assessment Guidelines (NERAG) Handbook (Australian Institute for Disaster Resilience 2015). However, actual 'content' analysis of local government MEMPs quickly reveals vast differences in emphasis, approach and access to resources available in both the production of the document itself and the ability to comprehensively treat risks. While the MEMPS are an important and powerful tool, compared with a wider, comprehensive and integrated view of risk reduction (March et al. 2018a), they include the following characteristics that limit their effectiveness:

1. A strong emphasis on response, combined with little to no attention to prevention

2. Risk assessment being undertaken as if settlements are static

3. Limited to no forward risk reduction action dealing with land use and development including growth and change

4. Limited integration of urban planning and building processes and personnel

5. Little to no inclusion of comprehensive programs to improve community members' resilience, despite the identification of at-risk groups being a common feature of MEMPS

6. Limited appreciation of recovery as a mechanism for risk reduction

Of course, the criticisms levelled above must be considered in the context of understanding that emergencies in Victoria are dealt with via an integrated response framework, referred to previously above, established under the Emergency Management Act (2013). Accordingly, local government is generally seen as a locally knowledgeable complement to the resources and activities of state-level fire services, State Emergency Services or the Victorian Police.

Local government: management of wildfire risks via urban planning and enforcement

We argue that a key disconnect exists between the activities of urban planning processes, particularly at the local government level, and wider risk management processes. Urban planning is increasingly understood as a key mechanism for the prevention and treatment of wildfire risks. Urban planning is potentially capable of managing (albeit within regulatory and socio-political limits) the location and arrangement of land use, clearing and development and protection of environmental values. Accordingly, this next section critically examines the main aspects of wildfire risk dealt with via urban planning at local government level.

Urban planning in Victoria operates according to the powers and responsibilities allocated via the Planning and Environment Act 1987 (P&E Act). In effect, the Local Government Act and the Planning and Environment Act inter-relate in a multiple ways, whereby day to day responsibilities of urban planning are allocated to local government via key sections of the P&E Act, particularly in plan-making processes (section 12) and plan administration oriented mainly to permit processes (section 13). Local governments' planning scheme, however, consists mainly of state-developed elements adapted from a set of standardised state-wide planning provisions called the Victorian Planning Provisions (VPP). In constructing their planning schemes, each municipality must include certain VPPs – the Planning Policy Framework (PPF), general and particular provisions, and definitions. Only the state-developed zones and overlays relevant to a municipality are used in a local planning scheme.

This means that across the entire state local planning schemes manage wildfire risk using state-wide policy in the Planning Policy Framework, application of a state standard mapping overlay known as the Bushfire Management Overlay (BMO), and use decision criteria for permit applications provided in the VPPs. The BMO is a state-standard overlay that is applied to land deemed to be at risk of wildfires, based on a state-government map of wildfire hazard areas. This triggers the need for a planning permit assessing bushfire risk for most developments in these areas. Any developments proposal in the BMO must satisfy relevant planning controls and building controls. The *Australian Standard AS3959-2009 – Construction of Buildings in Bushfire-Prone Areas* (Standards Australia 2009) sets the construction standards for building in wildfire-prone areas.

Overall, the provisions referred to above are effective as risk management approaches within the limitations of their application, and operate as a combination of building and planning provisions as needed:

1. New construction is designed and sited to respond to the likely fire intensity relevant to the location using a standard methodology. This is achieved through a combination of construction standards that align with estimated Bushfire Attack Levels (BAL) representing Kw/h heat flux loading on structures from 12kw/h to 40Kw/h and Flame Zone.

2. BAL ratings are applied in an interactive manner with setback distances from the highest assessed risk vegetation.

3. Highest risk vegetation is assessed according to categories of fuel loads and the slope of the land to provide an estimation of probable heat outputs and flame lengths that inform the BAL needed for a structure.

4. The AS3959 building code includes standards for construction (i.e. wall, roof and window systems, etc.) that prescribe heat and ignition properties of materials according to the likely BAL.

5. Standards are included to prevent the ingress of embers into structures' wall and roofs.

6. Firefighting response vehicle access, water supplies and signage are required.

7. Controls over vegetation are set as 'defendable space' to ensure setbacks to vegetation are maintained according to the relevant BAL.

8. Exemptions to normal native vegetation retention controls have been imposed so that application of bushfire provisions are not impeded.

With some variation, the application of these controls occurs at the multi-lot subdivision and individual permit application processes, administered by local government planners. The application and interpretation of these controls are guided by clauses in the VPP planning schemes that is remarkable insofar as it over-rides others in a way that may sometimes be counter-intuitive on deeper reflection, considering the many other goals sought by urban planning.

Wildfire planning Policy application

The policies and regulations listed above must be applied to all planning and decision making under the Planning and Environment Act 1987 relating to land that is:

- Within a designated wildfire-prone area

- Subject to a Bushfire Management Overlay

- Proposed to be used or developed in a way that may create a wildfire hazard

Strategies

- Give priority to the protection of human life by: Prioritising the protection of human life over all other policy considerations.

(Victoria Planning Provisions Clause 13.02-1S, authors' own emphasis)

Local volunteerism and wildfire management

Volunteer firefighting has a long history in Australia's history since colonial settlement, and from 1890 a Country Fire Brigades Board has existed in Victoria under the Fire Brigade Act (1890). In the aftermath of the devastating January 1939 fires in Victoria, steps were taken to more formally establish volunteer-based fire brigades across Victoria. The Royal Commission investigating the 1939 Black Friday fires included a recommendation to establish a single authority for firefighting in country Victoria. This integrated the various fire brigades, country fire brigades and the Forest Commission. Formal commencement of the Country Fire Authority (CFA) occurred on 2 April 1945. Over time basic equipment, facilities and training for brigades were provided, along with limited funding.

Today, the CFA is one of the largest volunteer organisations in the world, with approximately 60,000 volunteers, 1,800 career firefighters, community educators and support personnel. It includes 1,220 separates brigades across the state divided into 20 districts and eight regions (Country Fire Authority 2019). In addition, Parks Victoria and Forest Fire Management Victoria employ full-time professional fire officers in addition to training and facilitating significant numbers of volunteer fire volunteers and seasonal workers.

The long-term value of volunteer and professional firefighting in Victoria is considerable. The 2015 Fire Services Review undertaken as a Parliamentary Enquiry estimated the value of volunteers annually to be in the order of $A1 billion per annum (Country Fire Authority 2015). Key value-added by CFA and their volunteers include dissemination of wildfire knowledge and capability among the community, leveraging and multiplying government and paid staff investment, and wider community resilience, cohesion and benefits associated with volunteerism.

Local Fire Prevention Officers

Local governments in fire-prone areas are required to appoint Fire Prevention Officers as a statutory requirement to carry out municipal fire prevention. Any local government municipality within country areas of Victoria has responsibility under the Country Fire Authority Act (1958) to manage wildfire risks under Section 43 "duties and powers of councils and public authorities in relation to fire". "It is the duty of every municipal council and public authority to take all practical steps (including burning) to prevent the occurrence of fires on, and minimise the danger of the spread of fires on and from – any land vested in it or under its control or management: and any road under its care and management…".

The main mechanisms used to undertake this is via the appointment of a Municipal Fire Prevention Officer (MFPO). This is an executive officer role of the Municipal Fire Prevention Committee (MFPC), who is required to pursue the objectives stated in Section 43 above. This typically extends to issuing fire prevention notices for hazard removal to private landowners in their municipality if deemed necessary. The MFPO also has responsibility for the issuing (where appropriate) of permits to burn during fire danger periods.

Local government municipalities have prosecution powers under the CFA Act in terms of taking action regarding any failure to comply with Fire Prevention Notices and breaches of the conditions of Permits to Burn. Using this and associated powers provided under the Local Government Act Council officers may enter private land and property to treat fire hazards if notices for fire prevention are not complied with. Police powers may be used in parallel if necessary.

Vegetation management

In practice, there is considerable variation in the exercise of these powers and the resources provided to MFPOs across the state. For example, if significant amounts of land under Municipal control in a large remote local government represent a fire risk, it is typically impractical to seek to prevent or even reduce the risks of fires on this land in any meaningful way. On the other hand, where towns and settlements are in proximity to dangerous vegetation, the importance of taking practical steps to minimise danger becomes clearer, such as via the removal or modification of vegetation. Proactive local governments employ multiple officers to carry out fuel reduction activities along roadways, in reserves and in some instances on private land in instances where landowners are not complying with Fire Prevention Notices. Fuel reduction may be carried out in the form of prescribed burns or as slashing of grasses, trimming or cutting of trees and shrubs, and so forth. A number of exemptions from the controls preventing or regulating vegetation removal are allowed to public authorities if they are seeking to reduce wildfire risks. For example, under Clause 42.01-3 of the Victoria Planning Provisions firebreaks may be made and land along roadsides may be cleared as seen fit, and land around existing and new buildings may be cleared to facilitate necessary separation distances (Clause 52.12). The next section considers local governments' overall approaches to wildfire, including relationships with wider agencies and stakeholders.

Key capabilities and challenges for local wildfire risk management

The approaches used to deal with wildfire risk at local government level in Victoria are closely inter-related with a range of wider processes and stakeholder groups. Using six issues as organising principles, we discuss the lessons and issues associated with local government actions below.

Between shared responsibility and priority of human life

Shared responsibility (also discussed in chapter 7) is a key principle set out in a number of state-level documents and publications as a key principle underpinning emergency management in Victoria. It is described as follows, recognising that overall resilience must draw on all capabilities across the entire community. "Bushfire safety is a shared responsibility between the government and a range of stakeholders. Individuals are ultimately responsible for making their own decisions about how to respond to the bushfire risk" (Emergency Management Victoria 2018b, p.5). When combined with prioritising human life, also as a key principle, it strongly encourages a high standard of risk management, based upon widespread maximisation of all parties' capabilities "the protection of human life is paramount" (Emergency Management Victoria, 2018b, p.5).

These policies may also be somewhat cynically read to mean that while best efforts will be made to prioritise life, there is a limit to the resources and impacts on other goals such as economic growth and expenditure that government is prepared to make. When this state-level policy framework is contrasted with the powers and responsibilities of local government, the ability of municipalities to actively achieve wildfire risk management at this level is less clear. However, a number of recent policy changes suggest that improvement is being made. As previously indicated, state-imposed policy in local government planning schemes reiterates the priority of human life (Victoria Planning Provisions Clause 13.02-1S), suggesting that decision making should err on the side of caution. However, the principle of shared responsibility is not similarly translated to planning schemes in terms of providing for active development of resilience. This reinforces the position that the planning scheme as it stands is a representation of intended policy regarding roles and responsibilities, and that compliance with relevant wildfire regulation is sufficient. There is silence with regard to a range of pertinent issues (mentioned below) relating to actual regulatory mechanisms, despite the higher-order policy stating that strategy should: "Ensure planning controls allow for risk mitigation or risk adaptation strategies to be implemented" (VPP 2019: 13.01-1S).

It is noted, however, that at a strategic planning level, policy states that human life should be prioritised by "directing population growth and development to low risk locations and ensuring the availability of, and safe access to, areas where human life can be better protected from the effects of wildfire. Reducing the vulnerability of communities to bushfire through the consideration of bushfire risk in decision making at all stages of the planning process" (VPP: 13.02-1S). These high-level considerations can be discerned in strategic planning processes as set out in the following section.

Strategic level planning, local interests and actual action

Strategy can be understood as "a set of decisions that forms a contingent path through a decision tree" (Hopkins 2001, p.41). In simpler terms, it is the ongoing application of higher-order direction to lower-tier more detailed actions to achieve overarching goals that are dependent on coordination, consideration of changed circumstance, opportunity, avoidance of new threats, or acknowledgement of new expectations. Accordingly, strategic planning and action typically occur at higher levels of government or corporations.

The inclusion of new clauses in the VPP planning schemes that encourage new development to be directed away from areas of high fire risk (as in previous sections) is certainly in keeping with good strategic practice. However, it is noted that at the local government level, no formal inclusion of urban planners and indeed of forward planning is included in the production of MEMPS, indicating a considerable strategic coordination disconnect. While actual practice includes exceptions, it is significant that there is no formalised coordination of process for coordination between emergency services, local and state planners and other relevant parties in the release, design and development of land, between the range of parties involved, including the Victorian Planning Authority, Department of Environment, Land, Water and Planning (DELWP), Country Fire Authority, relevant local governments and other relevant parties.

Further, strategic planning relating to wildfire risk management as considered in VPP planning is oriented to new developments only, rather than the extensive low-density settlements that characterise peri-urban regions of

Victoria extending considerable distances beyond the boundaries of major settlements (Buxton et al. 2011). It is noted, however, that recent inclusion of the VPP policies mentioned above, seeking to direct development away from high-risk areas, will trigger the need to assess development proposals against these criteria, including providing opportunities for submissions from various interested agencies during scheme amendment processes (P&E Act: s17 & 21).

Referral processes set out the P&E Act (1987) do achieve, to some extent, the coordination purposes necessary for strategic planning. These are set out at Section 55 of the P&E Act (1987) as well as specific inclusions in VPP planning schemes at Clause 66. Accordingly, the Metropolitan Fire Brigade and Country Fire Authority are able to comment on and impose mandatory conditions upon applications for subdivision and development so as to ensure the interests of wildfire risk management are included in ongoing permit decisions.

The location of fire refuges (otherwise known as places of last resort) in existing vulnerable communities is seen as an important role that requires integrated action between local government, fire response agencies and Emergency Management Victoria (Emergency Management Victoria, 2018b). However, this level of attention is not typically extended to assessment and treatment of the range of other factors that drive local risks such as road systems, lot arrangements, fuel reduction programs, maintenance of vegetation on abandoned or poorly maintained land or other risk drivers.

Fuel reduction seeks to reduce the number of available fuels that support fires in strategically important locations, such as near to key assets or dwellings. The Victorian Bushfires Royal Commission found that fuel reduction burning could offer benefits in terms of modifying the intensity and progress of fires, ember production, and overall manageability of impacts (Teague, McLeod & Pascoe 2010). However, it was also noted that large areas need to be consistently burnt (amounting to a staggering goal of 5% of the state per annum, while some research suggests significantly more than this, see chapter 8) and that specific strategic sites near settlements also need to be burnt to have significant beneficial impacts. Some ten years after Black Saturday it is clear that this goal was unsustainable, has had significant impacts on native flora and fauna, and that there are many issues with fuel reduction including impacts on tourism, farming, viticulture, consumption of public resources and risks of loss of control of fires (Duff, Cawson & Penman 2019).

Local government, in seeking to manage land and vegetation in and around settlements is met with a challenging array of ownership and responsibility between public and privately owned land and responsibilities stretching across the Department of Environment Land, Water and Planning; Country Fire Authority; Parks Victoria; Vic Forests; Melbourne Water (and other private utilities); and, Forest Fire Management Victoria.

Between technical skills, expertise and roles

At the local government level, few personnel members have specific expertise in wildfire risk reduction or the prevention of ignition. The Country Fire Authority and staff from Parks Victoria and DELWP play advisory and statutory referral roles as described above. However, despite the MEMPS requirement to allocate a range of roles as part of the required Emergency Plan, few local government officers have qualifications and expertise in wildfire risk management. Further, specific expertise in the use of "Method 2" approaches are necessary to the use of AS3959 Building in Bushfire Prone Areas. Some limited numbers of practitioners have graduated from Bushfire Planning and design qualifications established after the 2009 fires, but many more will need to complete the qualification to have a significant impact (March 2017).

Recent policy changes to the VPP (2018) include the requirement that growth is assessed according to:

- Assessing and addressing the wildfire hazard posed to the settlement and the likely wildfire behaviour it will produce at a landscape, settlement, local, neighbourhood and site scale, including the potential for neighbourhood-scale destruction.

- Assessing alternative low-risk locations for settlement growth on a regional, municipal, settlement, local and neighbourhood basis.

- Not approving any strategic planning document, local planning policy, or planning scheme amendment that will result in the introduction or intensification of development in an area that has, or will on completion have, more than a BAL-12.5 rating under AS 3959-2009 Construction of Buildings in Bushfire-prone Areas (Standards Australia 2009) (VPP Clause 13.02-1S).

Accordingly, actual decision making by local government will continue to be challenged by the ongoing need for expertise.

Human factors: spatialising vulnerability, resilience and legacy risks

Policy such as that issued by Emergency Management Victoria state that wildfire resilience requires: "A community capacity building approach to bushfire safety focuses on approaches aimed at skill and network building to enhance communities' abilities to develop, plan for and execute their own bushfire safety options" (Emergency Management Victoria 2018b, p. 15).

However, local government agencies face considerable legacy risks that are beyond their abilities to modify. This is both in terms of vast numbers of structures and spatial layouts of settlements that were not designed and approved under wildfire regulations, and the vastly different capabilities and vulnerabilities of the population in wildfire-prone settlements. Few mechanisms exist to act on these vulnerabilities in a proactive manner to improve community resilience. The MEMPS encourages some mapping and data collection to assist preparation and response activities prior to events, but no powers exist to improve existing homes, and many local authorities struggle to monitor and act upon illegal structures being built to sub-standard levels. Areas that are clearly struggling in terms of socio-economic disadvantage are well known to have lower levels of resilience to hazards such as wildfires, yet local governments have limited capacity to address these areas of vulnerability.

The recent development of policy in the *Community Fire Refuges Policy* (2015) does offer some proactive options for local government in partnership with state emergency agencies establish and manage refuges in high fire-prone areas (Emergency Management Victoria, 2015). While currently limited in its application, the policy allows the identification of locations for, and construction of, Places of Last Resort in high-risk areas. These Community Fire Refuges and Neighbourhood Safer Places are intended as fall-back options that support communities if other risk management options have failed and require considerable ongoing education as to their use.

Planning and building code limitations

While we argue that the use of urban planning and building codes provide many benefits, it is important to understand their limitations and impacts on wider goals. Local government is charged with applying these regulations and is generally unable to impose more onerous or alternative approaches due to the widespread application of 'ultra vires' legal principles that limit the scope of regulation to that expressed in state-managed regulation. Accordingly, while wider state policy state encourages careful trade-offs between the loss of biodiversity and management of wildfire risks (VPP: 13.02-1S), in practice exemption clauses, particularly those at 52.12-1 provide for considerable exemptions without permits to create defendable space around buildings used for accommodation. This means that considerable ongoing loss of vegetation is likely to continue.

A number of significant limitations and omissions exist in AS3959 Building in Bushfire Prone areas exist. The first is that it is silent regarding the prevention of fire and ember ingress into underfloor areas, even while this is a well-known risk factor amongst practitioners. Further, the standard is not intended for application on slopes above 20 degrees, even while many wildfire-prone communities contain slopes in excess of this. In terms of the identification and treatment of high-risk settlements the Victorian Bushfire Royal Commission identified that special attention to these communities is needed.

Recommendation 46

The State develop and implement a retreat and resettlement strategy for existing developments in areas of unacceptably high bushfire risk, including a scheme for non-compulsory acquisition by the State of land in these areas (Teague, McLeod & Pascoe 2010, p. 33).

No standards or specific approaches have been developed at the time of writing, although it is noted that sporadic 'buy-back' schemes were utilised in a limited way.

Conclusions

In this chapter the main risk factors relating to wildfire risks were set out, including proximity of humans and structures to vegetation, hilly terrain, characteristics of structures and the vulnerability of humans – related to their particular vulnerabilities and decisions prior to and during wildfire events. The majority of local governments in Victoria include areas that are wildfire-prone, even while mapping and establishment of regulatory regimes are largely undertaken at state government level. The roles and responsibilities of local government were examined in regard to wildfire risk management in the state of Victoria, Australia. It was demonstrated that due to the federal and state-oriented legislated system used in Australia, that most powers and frameworks are set out at state government level, even while local government via the Local Government Act (1989) is tasked with a range of responsibilities oriented to the wellbeing of local residents.

Of the roles required of local government, the preparation and maintenance of local MEMPS were highlighted. These plans are important and play an important role in the management of wildfire risks. They are important as a link between a highly integrated system of state established actors, particularly fire response agencies and emergency controllers, as well as providing for collaboration between municipalities and other relevant parties. However, it was also shown that the MEMPS are oriented strongly to response activities, rather than to improving community resilience and proactive development of capabilities.

The comprehensive nature of urban planning and building controls was considered – mainly a task required of local government to administer via its responsibilities as Planning Authority and Responsible Authority as set out in the Planning and Environment Act (1987). These planning and building controls are effective in significantly reducing the wildfire risks associated with new development, achieved via a combination of separation, vegetation clearing, the resistance of structures to wildfire attack modes, and facilitation of firefighting. However, while recent policy changes suggest improvement, the focus of current controls on local development control is not matched by abilities to take wider strategic action in overall settlement patterns and the improvement of community resilience overall – particularly in improving the resilience of identified vulnerable people in the community.

Chapter 7

Empowering people and communities to address wildfire prevention

Introduction

This chapter explores the place of people and community in relation to the prevention of wildfire. It argues that, while there is a desire by fire authorities to include citizens in responsibilities associated with wildfire, the realisation of this practice appears to be rare. In Australia, engagement with the prevention of wildfire largely centres around requirements for the individual householder living in a fire-prone area to remove fire hazards and clear vegetation close to their house. It is argued in this chapter that, due to the potentially severe impact of wildfire, and the complexity, choices and value judgements associated with decision-making, it is very important for people to be engaged in discussions around prevention and in decision-making as part of their local community. To achieve active participation, the engagement process needs to establish governance arrangements, transparency, and easy information exchange. The community's views and decisions need to be incorporated into a wider prevention framework.

The concept of 'shared responsibility' between the government and community, a theme that is expressed in a number of policy fields, including with wildfire, is in part a recognition of the complexity and size of many issues faced by society today that governments are now expected to manage. This recognition includes the scale of resources needed to adequately respond to wildfire if entirely left to the government. Thus, the requirement for greater involvement of the community can be supported on many grounds. These grounds include: cost-sharing; ideas of inclusion and democratic participation; the notion that communities are best placed to support their more vulnerable members; recognition that local people know local conditions best; and ideas that there is not only one solution for all people, as a widespread of views is a good thing. The latter point recognises that in relation to the prevention of wildfire, there may not necessarily be 'the right' answer. Many decisions will actually be based on value judgements about risk, what people value and the priorities they hold.

This chapter offers a discussion on the community as an important base to build on governance and management arrangements around prevention.

While the need to involve the community in decision-making is often stated, true consultation rarely happens. Most decisions are either top-down or the decision-choice offered is very limited. This is reflected in the current community consultations around fire mitigation in Victoria. The option about fire management given to communities in a pilot program is along the lines of, 'in which areas of land do you want prescribed burning to occur?' Other options appear to be not offered.

The impact of wildfire on people and communities

While chapter one gives an overview of the impact and cost of wildfire, this chapter expands on this issue a little further. Wildfire prevention and suppression in the USA gives priority to the protection of resources (defined as homes and structures) and forests grown for timber (Scott et al. 2014). The protection of human life, then properties, is emphasised in many Australian documents. The environment is occasionally mentioned. For example, the (past) Department of Sustainability and the Environment (2012) in Victoria referred to maintaining the resilience of natural ecosystems to deliver services such as biodiversity, water, carbon storage and forest products.

There are two areas relating to social issues and the prevention of wildfire that are not commonly part of conversations. The first is how wildfire may impact, both directly and indirectly, on those who are already disadvantaged or vulnerable and may be least able to cope with the reverberating and often long-term impacts of a wildfire. Attention to how wildfire can adversely affect this group of people, and how the impact on them risks extending to other community members, is both an issue of equity and an issue of the need to account for these costs to society more broadly. The second area often overlooked refers to the psychological impact and potential trauma of fire. This includes how people relate to environmental damage that is associated with fire, as well as the lasting trauma that may impact wildfire victims. This trauma is likely to also extend to firefighters and other emergency response groups faced with wildfire. As will be discussed further in chapter 8, the environment is often minimised or excluded from many political and policy decisions in many countries.

The impact and flow-on costs of wildfire on vulnerable people

While the 'average' person in industrialised countries usually has fairly good levels of wellbeing, there are also a significant number of people who will be 'doing it hard' and a smaller sub-group 'doing it very hard'. It is common for people to rate their wellbeing close to 7.5 on a scale from 0 to 10 (International Wellbeing Group 2013). Although Australia has a welfare system that is better than found in many other countries, it still leaves 3 million people (13% of the population) living below the poverty line (Davidson et al. 2018). The official poverty rate in the USA is deemed to be 12.3% (Semega, Fontenot & Kollar 2018). However, this depends on where the poverty or social exclusion threshold is placed. In both Australia and the USA, research places the levels of poverty much higher, at just over one-third of the population, about 36% in Victoria and 37% in the USA (Stanley, Stanley & Hansen 2017; Stiglitz 2012).

Poverty increases vulnerability to adverse circumstances, including extreme events, such as wildfire. Those experiencing poverty or disadvantage are not likely to have the resources to enable them to better prepare for, and manage, a stressful time, or assist in recovery post-event. Indeed, receipt of a low income is likely to have increased vulnerability by dictating their living location. Reduced house prices are often associated with a poor location, such as on the edge of a city or settlement, offering lower levels of infrastructure and accessibility, but in a higher fire risk zone. Vulnerability is likely to increase where challenging or traumatic conditions have been experienced for a prolonged period of time. This issue is well documented in relation to long-term unemployed people and in households with a family member who has a severe disability, as with those who may suffer from mental illness. The costs associated with wildfire (prevention and preparation, and/or reparation and recovery) may shift people who are presently just managing, to a point where they begin to struggle. They may risk moving further into poverty where the ability to maintain adequate housing, quality food and meeting other physiological and psychological needs becomes more difficult for some people who were previously coping.

Little is known about the resilience of particular groups of people in terms of whether they have the ability to withstand various types of setbacks, such as short sharp adverse events and/or longer but less severe adverse conditions. An exception to this is work done on entrenched and transitory poverty in children (Ridge 2002). It was found that, while transitory poverty may have a severe impact on a child, entrenched or chronic poverty leads to extended periods of disadvantage and therefore needs the greatest attention. If this finding can be generalised to other circumstances, then those already experiencing longer-term hardships are most likely to experience higher adverse impacts when subject to a wildfire.

The sort of difficulties that may be experienced by those with few spare resources could encompass an inability to improve the capacity of a house to withstand wildfire, nor take out sufficient (or any) insurance. The 2009 wildfires in Victoria resulted in 8,150 insurance claims, costing $A1.2 billion. However, up to 30% of damaged homes had no insurance. In addition, $A160 million in emergency payments was made to policyholders. Transport to evacuate prior to wildfire may be difficult for those who are elderly or have a severe disability. As seen in the New Orleans Hurricane disaster in 2005, poorer people did not have the transport to evacuate the city and many were stranded in a stadium. In the 1983 wildfires in Victoria, of the seven people who died in the Mt Macedon fire, most died waiting for evacuation transport.

Lessons can be learned from other extreme events, commonly associated with climate change. Following the floods in Queensland in 2010-11, the Queensland Council of Social Services (2011) found that those already experiencing disadvantage were disproportionately adversely impacted. Particular areas of impact include:

- Lack of, or under insurance, and the rejection of flood insurance claims, that left most homeowners unable to live in or repair their homes

- Loss of employment through disruptions to, and closure, of local businesses

- Loss of rental tenancies and inability to meet higher bond payments and rents

- Increased pressure on public housing waiting lists

- Increased living costs (reported in ACOSS 2013)

Most people and organisations are not prepared for frequent occurrences of extreme events, as evidenced in the findings of people who are homeless (Pendrey, Carey & Stanley 2012). In a small exploratory study, it was found that extreme events tend to magnify pre-existing disadvantages and health issues for homeless people. Problems around access to safe shelter, food and water, as well as issues of mental illness, chronic disease, substance abuse and post-traumatic stress are exacerbated. The lack of stable accommodation again raises the transport problem. Those not owning cars, or not well involved with the local community, may find it difficult to receive help to move away from an emergency.

An extreme event also adversely impacts on the ability of an agency to provide services, due to the increase in demand, and the diversion of resources away from usual clients in order to assist people who would not be a client except for the emergency (ACOSS 2013; Pendrey, Carey & Stanley 2012). The Pendrey Carey and Stanley study also found welfare agencies to be under-insured, thus struggling themselves with a disaster, and without the resources to build community emergency responses. This is despite the fact that these agencies were often called on by the government to both build resilience and assist in the recovery from an extreme event.

Wildfire will impact on different people differently. The nature of the impact will depend on personal factors as well as factors external to the person. External factors include: the predictability, nature and severity of the wildfire; the person's living location and the location of the fire; federal, state and local government policy; planning which has been undertaken by business, government and communities; and, resources put in place to enable responses to emergencies and address longer-term impacts. Personal factors include knowledge and available information, and the resources and capacity to adapt. The impact can be lessened through family and community support, social capital and community connections available. Resources are not spread evenly throughout communities, so the task of adjusting to the impact will be much easier for some people than others.

Figure 7.1: Second and third order impacts of wildfire.

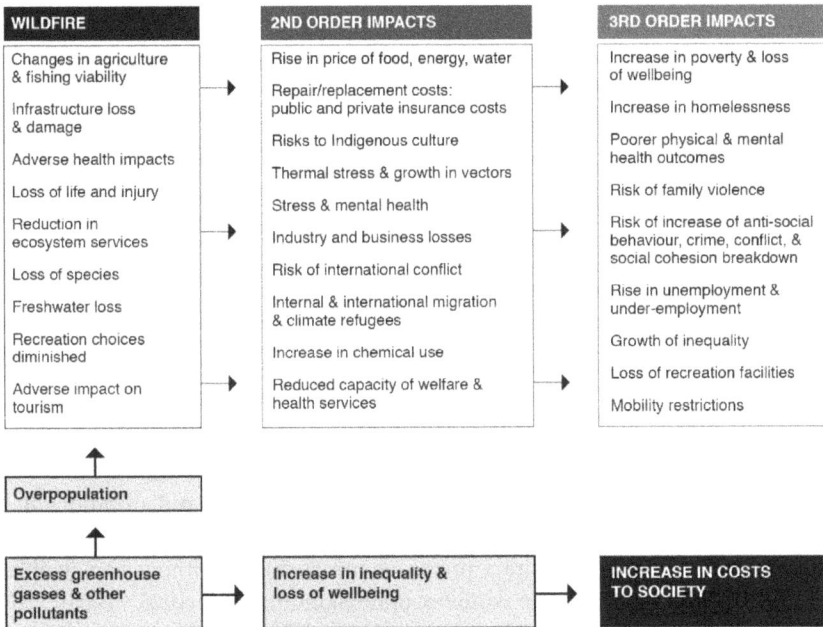

WILDFIRE	2ND ORDER IMPACTS	3RD ORDER IMPACTS
Changes in agriculture & fishing viability	Rise in price of food, energy, water	Increase in poverty & loss of wellbeing
Infrastructure loss & damage	Repair/replacement costs: public and private insurance costs	Increase in homelessness
Adverse health impacts	Risks to Indigenous culture	Poorer physical & mental health outcomes
Loss of life and injury	Thermal stress & growth in vectors	Risk of family violence
Reduction in ecosystem services	Stress & mental health	Risk of increase of anti-social behaviour, crime, conflict, & social cohesion breakdown
Loss of species	Industry and business losses	
Freshwater loss	Risk of international conflict	Rise in unemployment & under-employment
Recreation choices diminished	Internal & international migration & climate refugees	Growth of inequality
	Increase in chemical use	Loss of recreation facilities
Adverse impact on tourism	Reduced capacity of welfare & health services	Mobility restrictions

Overpopulation

| Excess greenhouse gasses & other pollutants | → | Increase in inequality & loss of wellbeing | → | INCREASE IN COSTS TO SOCIETY |

The impacts of wildfire are linked and interact in complex ways. Figure 7.1 provides some examples of the range of system impacts on people, and how this, in turn, progressively leads to second and third-order impacts. For example, wildfire may adversely impact agriculture, destroying crops and farm animals, adversely affecting the soil structure and destroying farm infrastructure. This may result in a rise in the cost of the impacted food groups, which in turn may affect the most vulnerable groups in society who may not now be able to afford to purchase that food. Figure 7.1 is stylized and illustrative and does not show the many complex interconnections; rather, it gives an impression of reverberations and chain-reactions that may arise from a wildfire. There will be a network of non-linear impacts that will vary according to many specific factors listed above. Independent to this, the costs to society will increase as the impacts increase and deepen and the occurrence of wildfires increases.

This offers a strong argument for why the community needs to be strongly involved in all phases of wildfire: the prevention of wildfire, the protection of people during a fire and the recovery phase. It particularly reveals the importance of wildfire prevention. While all people are likely to experience many adverse impacts, there will be a more severe and probably longer-lasting impact on certain groups of society, some of whom may never fully recover.

A well-functioning local community knows who is vulnerable to the impact of fire, has strong social supports established and good community connections. The community is also likely to be well aware of the local areas most vulnerable to wildfire, thus the locations that require the highest priority for protection and prevention measures to be put in place (Alcock 2004). This may also include knowledge about the locations where fires are more commonly lit, the times they might be lit and who it is who has been undertaking the lighting of fires. Measures such as blocking off roads and surveillance may be recommended by the local community, as well as support and intervention for those community members likely to engage in fire lighting. Unfortunately, as discussed in chapters 3 and 4, there is a strong link between social exclusion and isolation from the community and the behaviour of fire lighting.

The environment as a sense of place

The authors of this book conclude that, while the size and duration of a wildfire will have an important influence on how people experience the fire, it should not be seen as a direct proxy for measuring the impact on people. Rather, a broader and more complex understanding is needed. Research by Paveglio and colleagues (2016) suggests that it is important to better determine how residents come to understand and interact with the landscapes they live in, and how they understand wildfire risk in their living location (Paveglio et al. 2016).

Paveglio and colleagues (2016) explored how wildfire affected personal wellbeing. The research examined the impact of 25 large wildfires in Washington, Oregon, Idaho, and Montana, USA. They included people up to 15 kilometres away from the fire, in order to capture the situation of residents who may have been impacted by smoke or experienced economic impacts in terms of business closures. A purpose-built wellbeing questionnaire was used to examine self-reported psychological conditions. The questionnaire included questions on health, sleep disturbance, anxiety and feelings of helplessness. Additional questions were asked in relation to: perceptions of unusual wildfire characteristics; personal impacts, including events such as loss of income, injury, and a need to evacuate; perceived impacts to others; loss of landscape attachment; attitudes about fire management; and acres burned, as well as duration and distance of their property from the fire. From this wide selection of possible impacts, the most statistically significant associations with reduced wellbeing were a loss of connection to the landscape post-fire, personal impacts such as damage to property, residents' expectations about wildfire impact in their locality, and disruption of resident routines.

Reid and Beilin (2015) undertook related research in Australia to better understand why some people showed a reluctance to evacuate as a fire approached, despite the policy message in Victoria, since 2009, being to leave early. They also wished to explore what motivates people to undertake activities in relation to the risk of wildfire. They investigated the meaning of home, place identity and attachment in places where living with wildfire risk is part of their reality. The study was undertaken in the Adelaide Hills, a peri-urban landscape on the fringe of the city of Adelaide, South Australia. It was also undertaken in small settlements near a range of mountains called The Grampians, located in western Victoria, approximately 290 km from the city of Melbourne. Both areas have a long history of serious wildfires. The findings suggested that 'home' was regarded as something beyond the physical house boundary. 'Home' embodied the whole of the landscape, where boundaries blurred between domestic spaces and the non-human world. This was reflected in activities undertaken by the residents, such as gardening, re-vegetation, walking in the landscape, learning the names of flora and fauna, and viewing the mountains and locally significant species of trees. These activities defined the place they call 'home', as well as at times a long-term attachment with the place. This is likely to describe the 'lifestyle' group of people who have moved into the rural/urban interface, a group discussed in chapter 4. It is also likely to represent some of the more traditional farming families in Australia, who live in more isolated areas and develop a strong attachment and conservation perspective towards their property.

Paton and colleagues (2015) remind us that such an environmental perspective is not new. People have utilised forests for agriculture, livelihoods and hunting over history, and still do in some locations today, such as in Indonesia and parts of South America. Indeed, fire was commonly used as a tool for promoting livelihood from the forest, such as flushing out animals for food. Thus, living in, or close to a forest has, especially in the past, been a balance between risk and hazard, perhaps a choice people still are making in association with a love of nature held by many people.

Reid and Beilin (2015) argue that these findings have significant implications for understanding community responses to wildfire, and for communication between fire management agencies and residents who live in fire-prone places. The dominant focus on the house, by most fire management agencies, may fail to connect with people's broader sense of home within the landscape. Burton (2016) talks of the opposition to tree clearing with many 'hill dwellers' in the USA who would prefer to take fire risk, noting that "...at the heart of the debate over appropriate precautions in the face of foreseeable disaster, are questions about values and how different individuals, communities, nations, and governments prioritize and harmonize these arguably conflicting values and moral commitments" (Burton & Sun 2015, p.8).

However, there is a risk that emotional attachment to a property may lead the person to take high risks with wildfire (Pidot 2015). Emotional attachment may also help explain the tensions between fire management's community education focus on individual responsibility for control of wildfire mitigation prior to a fire, while also instigating the withdrawal of personal control by strongly encouraging people (or in some locations compulsorily requiring people) to evacuate during a wildfire. Reid and Beilin argue that, when people stay at home or return to their home during a wildfire, it may be to protect values that extend beyond the house. These perspectives may also be behind some public dissatisfaction with prescribed burning as a tool for wildfire mitigation. Thus, "management actions such as prescribed burning on public land are in effect, analogous to the burning of people's homes" (Reid & Beilin 2015, p. 102).

The impact described above could be viewed as a form of vicarious traumatization. The effect of wildfire does not begin and end with those directly victimized or distressed by the result of the fire to others and the environment. There are likely to be other forms of vicarious trauma that may impact those fighting the fires and other emergency service personnel, as well as other support people, volunteers and witnesses (Stanley 2002).

As discussed in chapter one, wildfires can cause indirect physical injury. For example, smoke can include thousands of individual compounds in the categories of particulate matter, hydrocarbons, other organic chemicals, and other components such as carbon monoxide. There has been little research on the adverse health effects of wildfire, prescribed burns and agricultural burns. It is only comparatively recently that the extent of the adverse impact on people is being revealed, especially for vulnerable groups of people (Weinhold

2011). This includes children, older people, pregnant women, smokers and those with chronic respiratory problems, but may also include those with conditions like asthma and chronic pulmonary disease and stress. Indigenous Australians are more vulnerable and had more hospital admissions for ischemic heart disease than other Australians, three days after exposure to smoke (Weinhold 2011).

Shared responsibility

The term, 'shared responsibility', is often used in the context of emergency management in Australia. This idea originated from the 2009 Victorian Bushfires Royal Commission. It was reinforced by the Council of Australian Government's National Strategy for Disaster Resilience, where shared responsibility was defined as a "whole-of-nation, resilience-based approach to disaster management" (COAG 2011, p. ii, reported in McLennan & Handmer 2014). The Victorian Bushfires Royal Commission noted that the term is variously interpreted. However, the report arising from this Inquiry states that "the state, municipal councils, individuals, household members and the broader community" must all accept increased responsibility for community safety from wildfire. As McLennan and Handmer noted in 2014, what shared responsibility actually entails, has never been clearly defined, a situation that continues to the present. Eburn (2015) believes that the ambiguity over who has responsibility for what in relation to bushfire management, is exacerbated by a lack of political consensus about the management of the Australian landscape in general. Eburn notes that, as is the case in the USA, most land-use policies and decisions are made at low levels of government. There is a lack of land-use planning and strategic planning that sets the framework for much lower-level planning (Stanley, Stanley & Hansen 2017). However, Eburn notes that there is a more recent movement towards a model that believes individuals and the community should be more 'resilient' as the community's part of shared responsibility – again variously, and rather circuitously defined and thus a concept with little meaning.

In practice, the term 'shared responsibility' in Victoria is largely interpreted as each specific agency or department having an allocated task, rather than an integrated or shared approach with the community that offers two-way communication. For example, individuals are said to have a responsibility to attend community education meetings. State agencies and Municipal Councils to have a responsibility to implement vegetation and roadside management programs and ensure compliance with building and land-use planning provisions. McLennan and Handmer (2014) point out that the concept implies a social contract, that is, a balance of rights and responsibilities between the government and communities. However, half of the contract is missing, the part about the rights and benefits that citizens would receive. They say there is a need to develop a more inclusive governance framework that comprises a broader social participation throughout, from agenda-setting through to implementation and evaluation. Relating to the subject of this book, this would need to be pursued inter alia through the agenda of the prevention of wildfire.

While not necessarily using the same words, the idea of sharing responsibility is present in a wide range of policy settings, as well as disaster management, across a number of countries, including Europe, the UK and the USA. This idea has arisen due to the complexity of problems found today in many countries, such as social insecurity, climate change and a growing mistrust of democratic institutions (McLennan & Handmer 2014). The idea includes the sharing of risks, decision-making and responsibilities. McLennan & Handmer (2014, p.22) believe that: "We want to challenge the easy assumption that governments can and should manage all risks. We want to see a new understanding between government, regulators, the media and the public that we all share a responsibility for managing risk and that, within the right circumstances, risk can be beneficial and should be encouraged" (Better Regulation Commission 2006, p.5).

A largely unsuccessful attempt to establish such an arrangement was initiated under the Cameron government in the UK, under the label of the 'Big Society'. The stated purpose of this movement was to give communities more power by transferring power from the central government. People were encouraged to take an active role in their communities and facilitate local organisational development, while government information was to be made more open and transparent. However, at the same time, the British Government undertook large cuts in public expenditure programs, leading to criticism that the purpose of the scheme was more a cost-shifting exercise (Sullivan 2012). The rhetoric about shared responsibility was not seen in practice, and government regulation and intervention remained, with the impact of limiting the role of local decision-making.

Community participation in the prevention of wildfire

Community participation and involvement around the prevention of wildfire is likely to guide policy and programs that can deliver preferences for local citizens and their communities and give better substance to the idea of shared responsibility (Alcock 2004). Although referring to the provision of social services, Alcock says that "…policy makers (and policy practitioners) do not know best what the priorities… should be. It is local people who know what they need, and hence they should be involved in the process of determining priorities and developing and delivering service provision" (Alcock 2004, p.91). These points are illustrated with the two groups of people referred to above, whose perspective does not usually get included in wildfire policy and management. These are those who will experience the greatest vulnerabilities to wildfire and those who express values important to them in relation to the environment. Both views are legitimate; both need a voice in decisions around the prevention of wildfire.

It could be argued that civil society is already functioning well in Australia. Although dated, the latest figures from the Productivity Commission (2010) state that the number of Australian community sector organisations was estimated at around 600,000, with 4.6 million volunteers with a wage equivalent value of $A15 billion. These figures represent the structured part of civil society. While the community sector and interest groups can assist people in having a voice, it is the community of people referred to in the idea of shared responsibility. It is argued in this book that it is a community, that should be resourced and more formally linked to decision-making around wildfire, and particularly the prevention of wildfire.

As numerous studies have suggested, for adaptation to any form of change to be successful, individuals and communities need to be actively involved in decision-making processes (King, Feltey & Susel 1998; Nelson & Wright 1995; Putnam 1995). Governance structures that emerge out of community decision-making result in a more democratic and therefore, more effective response, as individuals and communities take responsibility for the resolution of problems. This is especially important in the case of wildfire since the prevention of wildfire is not a 'once-off' event but one that is an on-going development and change process.

Drawing from a similar issue in local government, Leitch and Inman (2012) report barriers that may also hamper community participation, namely:

- A lack of local information sufficient for decision making - an absence of locally relevant, accessible and useful information to guide action

- A lack of financial and human resources

- Complex competing issues and responsibilities around complex issues

- A lack of progress or support from tiers of governance. Leadership, collaboration and consistency from all tiers of government is needed

- A lack of community concern or backlash from the community

Such issues may be barriers to shared responsibility by the community in relation to the prevention of wildfire. These issues, with a few additions, are discussed further below. The discussion also draws on community and local government consultations that were undertaken in three Australian states by one of the authors of this book, and colleagues, about participation in local decisions about adaptation to climate change, findings that are likely to relate well with issues around the prevention of wildfire (Stanley et al. 2013). Reference to findings from these community consultations is discussed in the next few sections.

A lack of local information

The community needs to be well informed about all aspects of wildfire, and the full range of prevention choices. Quality and useful information is dependent on the accurate collection of information and reporting about the causes of wildfire, a repeated theme of this book.

A lack of financial and human resources

A lack of resources for the community, particularly a dedicated budget, was viewed as a barrier to participation (Stanley et al. 2013). This included time, as community action was largely voluntary. The community spent considerable time applying for small grants. This issue was referred to repeatedly in all consultations and workshops, an issue also reported elsewhere (Gurran, Norman & Haminc 2012). Uncertainty around legal and insurance implications also proved to be a barrier to participation.

Of particular concern in relation to wildfire is that people who light local wildfires (accidentally or maliciously) tend to come from the local community (see chapters 3, 4 and 11). Thus, there is an element of risk in relation to discussion with the community about wildfire vulnerability. It is argued in this book that transparency is likely to offer a solution to this serious problem. Discussion with communities suggests that local people usually have a good idea about who is at risk of lighting a fire. Thus, identification, intervention and prevention approaches, such as surveillance, should assist in the protection of the community from wildfire. Keeping the issue 'underground' is not likely to be helpful in prevention, and places barriers around positive approaches to protect the community and assist the offending person to deter from further lighting. Of course, resources are needed for such an approach, but probably far less than the costs associated with wildfire, if such protective approaches are not taken.

Complex issues and responsibilities

Arnstein's ladder of participation outlines eight types of participation, ranging from non-participation, through various forms of token participation, to gradations of citizen power (Arnstein 1969). Ison and Schlindwein (2006) point out that the variations in these eight steps essentially relate to the extent of power given to a citizen, an issue also noted by other researchers (Reddel 2004). Ison and Schlindwein say that in fact, participation is more complex than Arnstein's ladder of participation suggests, as most problems are not clearly defined nor have straightforward solutions. The boundary around problems is not always clear, especially where there are many interdependencies. Situations are usually complex and therefore, difficult to describe and explain comprehensively and accurately. There is often uncertainty about social values and wants, and the assessment of future developments and impacts. There may be controversy about the nature of the issues and what to do about them.

However, on the positive side, social learning, or the collective process of people who are given resources, support and a conducive policy environment, may lead to a convergence of goals and expectations (Collins & Ison 2006). Agreement may be established on changed behaviour and concerted action, through the co-creation of knowledge. Thus, a means is provided for addressing complex problems through active social learning and participation. The authors probably recognize that this process presupposes goodwill and the absence of a hidden agenda, as well as a willingness (and capability) by some individuals to relinquish their power over decision-making. There is also an assumption that people will participate in this process, a choice that some community members will not always take. Additionally, some people will need help or support to participate.

Problems in governance: linking top-down and bottom-up decisions

The relationship between government, community, and individual responsibility for disaster prevention, is "fraught with pitfalls" (Burton & Sun 2015, p.7). The local consultations in Victoria, referred to above, reported that a lack of clarity about who made decisions, and how they were made, was a barrier to community participation. There was a lack of a structure within which the community could express their views. There was also a perception by many that their views are not necessarily acted upon anyway.

Researching from the UK, Jordon (2010) writes of the lack of integration between top-down policies and bottom-up choices and decisions, with an absence of governance structures to link these two processes and achieve an integrated framework that works in a seamless way. This lack of integration can result in some serious downsides in the context of public participation and the idea of shared responsibility. Without integration, the ideas arising from community participation have nowhere to go. This leaves a space for those in the community with power and with vested interests to lobby and push through their personal interests. The community can be left to fight against decisions they do not like, and the situation can become adversarial, with little opportunity to solve problems (Berke 2002). Such an outcome will leave citizens disenchanted and disempowered, as found in recent work in a regional area in Victorian (Stanley et al. 2013). Community members will be more reluctant to engage in decision-making on the next occasion. Worse, there is a risk that this experience of lack of control may lead to a lack of engagement in wildfire prevention, planning and preparation.

On the other side, the Government in large part sees its role as overseeing contracts and social programs by setting and monitoring standards, reporting requirements, outcomes against targets, publishing league tables and producing descriptive statistics (Jordon 2010). In the context of wildfire, the emergency services tend to offer top-down advice, some education, and orders/requirements, with little opportunity for upward feedback or input of local knowledge and values. This one-way conversation tends to leave out aspects of quality, flexibility, relationships, trust, inclusion and empowerment. Jordon (2010) believes that the emphasis in the wider policy setting, on contractual arrangements, self-reliance and consumption, has led to an impoverishment of support, respect, belonging, community and solidarity among populations. This leaves people less able to cope with adverse circumstances, as well as a government with fewer processes on which to build social policy.

Where does local responsibility begin and end?

The boundaries of a shared relationship would seem to be an important question that has not received much consideration. In the consultations referred to above, people were looking for leadership and helpful guidance in decision-making. At the same time, government representatives wished the community would express their views more clearly. The communities' views about powerlessness and of not being heard by authorities are also expressed in the literature. For example, Paschen and Ison (2011) drawing on Australian research, found a growing sense of frustration in the community. They believe that: "...locals do not feel listened to by the different levels of government nor do they feel that their own agency to act is facilitated by current practices and arrangements" (Paschen & Ison 2011, p. 4).

Leitch and Inman (2012) note that governments generally assume that residents will consider and inform themselves about the risk to their own properties, but personal responsibility is not generally broadened to a responsibility to the wider community, an issue discussed further in chapter 7. Many fire-prone areas are also places of tourist attractions; the natural environment being an important component of the economic base (tourism) and as a lifestyle attraction for retirees. Thus, ethical responsibilities may also extend to the responsibility of the permanent locals for the interests of short-term residents and day-trippers (March, Nogueira de Moraes & Stanley 2020).

A lack of community concern or backlash from the community

The Australian consultations noted that barriers were established by some sectors in the community due to a lack of urgency, interest or priority, and in other cases by fear (Stanley et al. 2013). Indeed, concern as to whether people would be able to cope with the gravity of the 'truth' (especially around climate change) led some people to believe that clear information was sometimes not given to the community. The issue of an adverse impact on property prices was expressed in the consultations, as well as discussed in the literature (Macintosh 2012). Similarly, it was perceived that there might be a risk of exposing governments to a political backlash from landholders and legal ramifications. Communities felt that they should set priorities for their attention. For example, some community members felt that a lack of local transport was a matter of greater concern, especially in the context of wildfire. On a positive note, many of those consulted viewed most communities as strong and resourceful.

The ideas around shared responsibility at times carry baggage around notions of laziness and bludging. This can be seen particularly in relation to unemployment benefits in Australia. The view by some is that, as government benefits and services encourage dependence, people have a 'responsibility' to accept low paid work when available, as a condition of receipt of unemployment benefits. This ideology has coincided with a reduction in self-organised associations such as trade unions, churches and activist organisations (Blond 2010). There is also a diminution in 'neighbourly' type behaviour and volunteers, which traditionally provided supportive structures for people. Women largely undertook these roles, but these activities were credited with little value in the rush to return women to the workforce, ironically, to be 'productive'. Additionally, those experiencing disadvantage may remain invisible, and their invisibility may be re-enforced by their lack of involvement in consultations (Cuthill 2004). Thus, while it is desirable to have a wide range of community representation, this may be difficult in practice, as active participation often only involves a minority of people (Connors &

McDonald 2010; Cuthill 2004). Providing resources to an informal group would assist participation.

A narrow view

There is a risk that considerations around community participation will be treated as short term and incremental, dealing with issues as they are presented rather than moving towards a longer-term vision, again a perspective found in the literature (Trutnevyte, Stauffacher & Scholz 2012). Thus, the actions become largely responsive rather than proactive. There is also a need to think beyond physical structures and consider how disadvantaged individuals will cope and how people deal with psychological impacts. The consultations (referred to above) also drew attention to the lack of consideration of the bigger environmental picture. This included issues such as natural capital, ecosystem services, habitat and biodiversity loss, and intrinsic rights of other species (see chapter 8) (Stanley et al. 2013). This suggests there is a need for information for communities about links between ecosystem services and wellbeing and other related issues and the building of community capacity in this area. Thus, the process of the prevention of wildfire should not be seen as a single event, but as part of a process of social learning and step-wise decision-making for an adapting community (Macintosh 2012; Yuen, Jovicich & Preston 2013).

Building a community

The process of local, community-based decision-making assumes a place-based approach. However, the boundary of what is defined as a local place is often variable. In Victoria, the regional boundaries for police and emergency services do not overlap. However, strong identification of place would be likely to assist decision-making. Participants in the Australian consultations felt very strongly about local issues. While there was not always cohesion, the establishment of good governance arrangements would assist in the expression of desired outcomes. A strong sense of place should facilitate the engagement of people to draw on their local knowledge, support structures and social capital, to assist in the management of uncertainty and risk.

Apart from the many other arguments as to why communities should be involved in the task of wildfire prevention, as indeed with other aspects of fire, dealing with wildfire is too large for the government to undertake alone, without a large contribution by other sectors and the community. Some communities will be able to take on this participatory role. Other communities will need support to enable inclusive consultations, particularly in those communities already struggling with disadvantage, as referred to above. Thus, the first (and on-going) task may be to build and support the capacities of communities to enable them to participate and be, as far as possible, responsible for their own welfare. There are also practical benefits with this participatory approach that were found in other fields. For example, a meta-analysis of environmental monitoring found that decisions arising from this monitoring typically took between three and nine years to be implemented (Danielsen et al. 2010). However, the time was considerably shortened, taking up to 12 months only, when local people were involved in the monitoring process. Thus, participation by the community may lead to time efficiency.

The need to re-build community also comes from a range of eminent voices. Eckersley notes that as a society we have lost sight of any collective belief that society could be different – instead of a better society, we seek to better our own position in society (Eckersley 2004). There has been a loss of community, tradition and shared meaning, creating an empty self, which needs to be 'filled' (Cushman 1990, quoted in Eckersley 2004). Hamilton and Denniss express similar views about a hollow consumer society (Denniss 2017; Hamilton & Denniss 2005). Rifkin (2011, p. 541) believes there is a need to move from "belongings to belonging", all changes that are likely to build personal wellbeing and community strength. There is perceived to be a need to rebuild social structures and community support as a means to promote relationships, trust and reciprocity, all components of social capital. These interactions can be developed through the establishment of horizontal social safety nets for vulnerable community members to enable the community to respond to challenges, such as wildfires, rather than a reliance on vertical and hierarchical government provisions, as is the present situation. As Blond says: "…perhaps the greatest challenge facing the modern state is how to ensure adequate support for its citizens… by cultivating and harnessing horizontal social bonds and self-regulating communities" (2010, p.77). A decade earlier, Giddens (1998) made similar arguments about the need for building support networks, self-help and the cultivation of social capital. Re-building social structures may take time in disadvantaged locations with poor levels of infrastructure. However, many rural communities already have strong community connections and social capital networks.

Adger (2003) found human capital and social capital to be key determinants of adaptive capacity. Similar findings were revealed in empirical work that measured the drivers of social inclusion and wellbeing (Stanley et al. 2011). Modelling revealed the importance of:

- having sufficient income (by implication, education and work)
- having accessibility (transport)

- having personal relationships and connections (social capital – networks, trust)

- feeling good about yourself (such as self-esteem, confidence)

- having control over your personal environment (such as capabilities to make choices, problem solve) (Brain, Stanley, Stanley 2019, p.11)

Also found to be important were beliefs about whether or not a person could control outcomes in their life (Stanley et al. 2011). Those with a high belief in external control (being controlled) were more likely to be at risk of social exclusion (1% significance). There was also a strong association (1% significance) between firm internal beliefs of control (able to control their own life) and satisfaction with life. These findings suggest that individuals with high wellbeing will have a much greater capacity to effectively respond to issues around wildfire. Those people who believe that they were not able to control what happened in their life were more likely to suffer from negative affect, less likely to have good bridging networks and less likely to have a strong sense of community.

A strong community is also likely to improve the inclusion and opportunities for vulnerable members who have a propensity to light fires, as it may be the social exclusion and lack of embeddedness in the community that promotes such behaviour. The local community is usually able to identify where this type of assistance is needed and, given resources, a strong, cohesive community can provide much-needed information, support and connections for firelighters. Under such conditions, collective efficacy develops, a linkage of mutual trust and willingness to intervene for the common good.

An illustration of the value of community involvement

This section illustrates one form of shared responsibility that is available in 26 countries, with varying degrees of activity. Crime Stoppers (see also chapter 5), is a not-for-profit organisation, which enables the community to report a suspicion that crime has occurred or may occur. The report is passed onto the police who review its veracity and investigate where warranted. A longitudinal study (2010 to 2017) examined the factors that impacted on community reporting suspicions in relation to malicious fire lighting to Crime Stoppers Victoria. The final wave of 630 survey respondents was completed in six rural local government areas deemed to be at high risk of wildfire, plus a largely urban control suburb (Read & Stanley 2018). The survey sought information on the reasons why people did, or did not, report their suspicions to authority: the police, emergency hotline (000) or to Crime Stoppers.

Survey respondents were asked what they would do when faced with 19 scenarios in relation to a fire situation. The action choices were 'do nothing', 'handle the situation themselves', 'call the emergency services number', or 'call Crime Stoppers Victoria'. The scenarios were presented in three categories of event severity. The findings suggest that the potential actions taken by survey respondents vary greatly, depending on circumstances associated with the fire. People are less likely to report when the person under suspicion is a child, and when the person is close to or known to the witness, anonymity in reporting is important. Certain beliefs about the fire lighting or the perpetrator are likely to increase the chance of it being reported: where there is a belief that the fire was deliberately lit; where the perpetrator is viewed as a 'difficult youth'; and where there are beliefs that the fire could become a fatal wildfire.

Given a choice of responses to a suspected fire event, there was a range of views about what was appropriate, and a surprising number of people would either 'do nothing' or 'handle the situation themselves'. For example, on a Total Fire Ban Day, if they were the only witness to people leaving an unattended campfire burning, 66% of people would 'handle the situation themselves', presumably by extinguishing the fire. If they were witness to a lit cigarette being thrown out of a car on a Total Fire Ban Day, 26% of people said they would 'handle it themselves', and 29% of people would 'do nothing'. Again, on a Total Fire Ban Day, in response to the scenarios: 'if someone you know starts a small growing fire', 24% said they would 'handle it themselves'. Where a wildfire with fatalities occurred, and the respondent saw the same car in areas where other fires had occurred, surprisingly, 7% would 'do nothing'. Again, with a fatal wildfire and the respondent found out it was their own child who had lit the fire, 2% of people would 'do nothing', and 24% would 'handle it themselves'.

The group that would not make an official report tended to have been more victimised by crime and have a belief that the police did not help them. They consistently would not report across all scenarios, were fearful of revenge, tended to have a personal association with the suspect, and reported less attachment to the community. The pattern of reporting malicious fire lighting was reflected in reporting other crimes. Of those who had been subject to a crime (property or personal crime), only 44% said they had reported this crime. Property crimes were 1.6 times more likely to be reported (61%) compared to personal crimes (39%). Those residents with higher levels of wellbeing were more likely to report illegal fire lighting. The findings from this survey reflect the few studies that have been reported in the literature on crime reporting (Goudriaan, Wittebrood & Nieuwbeerta 2006; MacDonald et al. 2012).

This study illustrates one example of how the community can assist with the prevention of dangerous fires being lit. The program could be enhanced a number of ways. These include by further encouragement of reporting; improvements in knowledge about what to report and what constitutes suspicious behaviour around fire lighting; feedback to the reporter about the usefulness of the report; improved relations between the community and the police; and the provision of counselling and support services for the reported person and their family, the lack of such services found to be a deterrent to reporting true.

Conclusions

This chapter emphasises the importance of a genuine system of shared responsibility in relation to wildfire and especially the prevention of wildfire. A well-developed model of shared governance is likely to lead to better outcomes in terms of reduced fire lighting and thus, a reduction in the number of fires that need to be suppressed. While the rhetoric is in many official documents, implementation of this approach is largely lacking, at least in Victoria and probably internationally. There is an absence of a governance structure that is able to integrate community wishes into policy and program design about wildfire prevention. The community perspective tends to be diminished in importance. While technical knowledge about fire services is unlikely to be available in a community context, other forms of knowledge are important to utilise. This includes knowledge about areas where the community has concerns about fire vulnerability, areas where environmental conservation is seen as important as well as information about members of the community who may be at risk of lighting fires. It may also include drawing on the leadership abilities of community members to strengthen cohesion, teach children about fire risk and offering support activities for struggling youth. Such shared responsibilities are likely to lead to improved communication, shared learning and shared support, ideas and values between emergency services and the community, thus an improved approach to wildfire prevention. The approach to shared responsibility will need to include resources to support some community members to enable them to participate. Shared responsibility also implies responsibilities on the part of emergency services, such as a willingness to share power and decision-making, even where values between emergency services and the community may not always be in alignment. It also includes financial resources and a willingness to share knowledge and data with community members.

Chapter 8

Prevention of wildfire at the expense

of the environment

Introduction

This chapter argues the case against the narrow, one-sided approach to the 'prevention' of wildfires that is predominately in use in Australia and many other countries. Even although some form of human activity starts nearly all fires, either directly or indirectly, the predominate approach to addressing the 'prevention' of wildfire is to modify, change or destroy the natural environment as it currently stands. As discussed in chapters one and 5, while a few programs directly address the prevention of ignition, most are targeted towards the reduction of the size and intensity of a wildfire, once it is ignited. The authors argue that this dominating approach is undertaken to the exclusion of many other possible prevention activities. It is argued that the way prescribed burning is currently undertaken is at a high cost to the natural environment, other species, people and the economy. It offers a short-term, limited approach, which, in some situations, is generating long-term costs, when there are other choices available that may offer a more effective and sustainable outcome in many, but not all, situations.

This is not to argue that there is not a place for modification of the environment, such as prescribed burning. All effective measures are needed to prevent and reduce the impact of the severe wildfires that many countries are now experiencing. However, it is argued that a very different approach to much of the current prescribed burning should be taken. This involves careful management of fire, including clarity about why the prescribed burn is being undertaken, for ecological purposes or wildfire mitigation purposes. The effectiveness of prescribed burning on future wildfires in different ecological systems and individual species, as well as the introduction of non-native species, needs to be understood, as is the impact on the ecology. The extent and heat of the prescribed burn, as well as the ecological level of the burn (ground cover, middle storey, treetops), the frequency of the burn, and the need for gaps in the area burnt to provide ecological retreats, all need broad interdisciplinary knowledge and careful management.

This approach is modelled on practices adopted by Australian Indigenous people and by some American Indian tribes, prior to European settlement.

There were rules for fire use, dependent on detailed knowledge and a spiritual connection. "An Arnhem[1] man explained, 'you sing the country before you burn it. In your mind you see the fire, you know where it is, and you know where it is going, and you know where it will stop. Only then do you light the fire'" (Gammage 2011, p.161). However, factors such as climate change, population growth, the packing of soils due to introduced European farm animals that cause a reduction in soil moisture, and the extinction of species, have created a more complex task around prescribed burning. Importantly, an improved approach to prevention of wildfire should reduce the need for prescribed burning.

The state of the environment

Planetary boundaries

Planetary Boundaries, as shown in Figure 8.1, define the environmental limits in which humans can safely operate (Steffen et al. 2015). Disturbance beyond these boundaries creates risk uncertainties that may substantially alter earth systems creating a world that is far less habitable. Of the nine fields shown in Figure 8.1, two, biosphere integrity and biogeochemical flows, have already reached the top edge of the high-risk outer circle zone. Biosphere integrity, which has a strong association with wildfire, is measured with two components: the global extinction rate of well-studied organisms, and the Biodiversity Intactness Index. The latter measures changes in population abundance as a result of human impacts at a biome or ecosystem level, using the preindustrial era as a reference point. These measures are said to be incomplete and imperfect but the best available, given that many species are not yet adequately scientifically documented.

Land-system change and climate change are also of particular relevance to wildfire, both of which are operating outside the safe operating space. Land-system change has been re-defined since the first iteration of the Planetary Boundaries model in 2009, now measuring the size of the three major forest biomes remaining: tropical, temperate and boreal. These forests have a stronger association with climate change than other biomes. Steffen and colleagues (2015) suggest that climate change and biosphere integrity are the core planetary boundaries, through which other boundaries operate, as they function at the level of the whole earth system and have coevolved for nearly

---

[1] Arnhem Land is a large tract of country in northern Australia, in what is now Northern Territory. Indigenous people have occupied the land for tens of thousands of years.

four billion years. Crossing one or more of the boundaries may adversely impact on the core boundaries and seriously impact human wellbeing.

Figure 8.1: Planetary Boundaries.

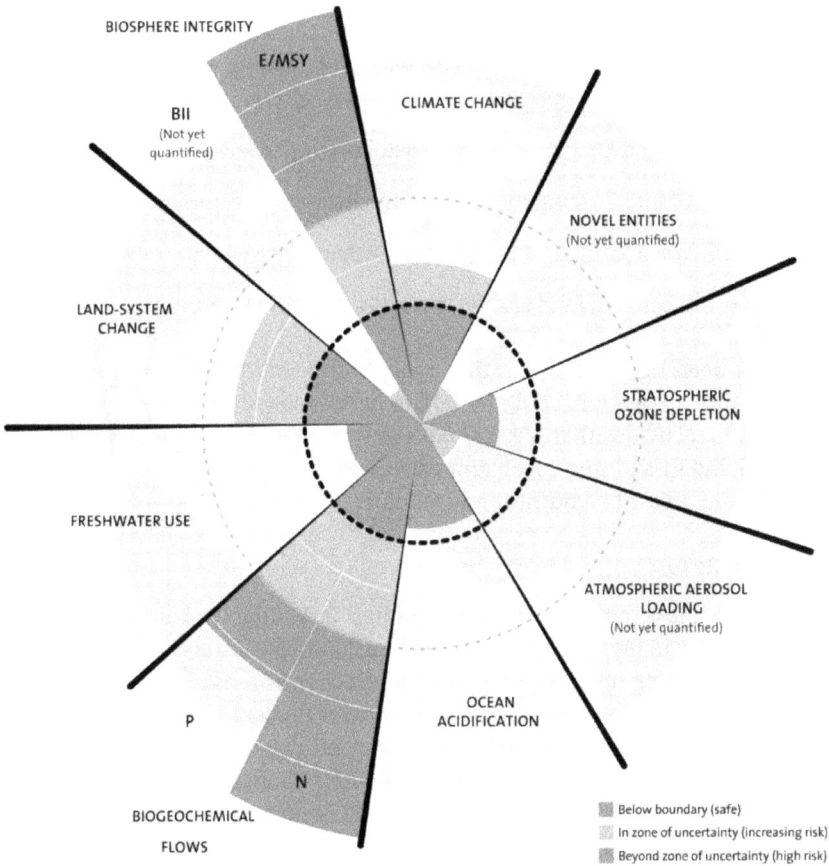

Source: J. Lokrantz/Azote based on Steffen et al. 2015.

Thus, the loss of forests from wildfire and through land-clearing is of serious concern. As of September 2019 three extensive forest fires are burning: the Amazon rainforest that is said to provide 20% of the earth's oxygen, the Congo Basin forest in Africa, the second-largest tropical rainforest to the Amazon, and extensive fires in the Indonesian forests (Pérez-Peña & Stevis-Gridneff 2019; Rayda 2019; Turkewitz 2019). Environmental modification, such as forest thinning and prescribed burning is unlikely to be the answer to fire prevention in these locations.

The scientists outline many reasons why the nine planetary boundaries have become unbalanced, including:

- The burning of fossil fuels

- Land clearing and loss of tree cover (leading to problems such as erosion, dust, growth in deserts)

- Land degradation (such as salt build-up in soil due to irrigation)

- Chemical contamination of freshwater, land and oceans

- Waste contamination (by rubbish and sewerage)

- Weed and feral animal spread (native and non-native)

As has been noted earlier in this book, both wildfire, and many measures aimed at fire mitigation, could be said to be associated with three of these six concerning activities that risk human safety: the burning of fossil fuels, land clearing and loss of tree cover, and weed and feral animal spread, a risk that occurs after prescribed burning and wildfire.

Biodiversity loss

Biodiversity loss presents a grim picture. Very little is known about an estimated 8.7 million species, with 86% of land species and 91% of marine species remaining undiscovered (Sweetlove 2011). The risk is that species are being lost before they are even really known. Current losses are occurring almost as fast as when the Earth suffered a catastrophe 65 million years ago and half of all species on earth, including dinosaurs, became extinct (Bernstein 2010). The current extinction rate is up to 1000 times faster than the natural or background loss rate, and increasing, with threshold levels for survival little understood (Berger 2004). As well as the loss of species, the abundance of species is down by 60% since 1970 (World Economic Forum 2019). Due to climate change alone, about one-third of species will be lost by mid-century, if extinctions continue at the same pace (IPCC 2007).

Australia's biodiversity is declining, with some of the highest extinction rates of plants and animals of any country. More than 1,700 species and ecological communities are known to be threatened and at risk of extinction (Van Dijk 2019). Many of Australia's iconic animals are under severe threat. The koala's home territory coincides with urban development in Australia, leading to a 'threatened' extinction rating in Queensland and 'vulnerable' rating Australia-wide. The population is now estimated to be less than 1% of the numbers at the time of European settlement of Australia in 1770 (Jones 2012).

The key threats to biodiversity are said to be loss, degradation and fragmentation of habitat, invasive species, and altered fire regimes (Steffen et al. 2015). As noted above, much of this is due to land-use change, such as due to population growth, land clearing for agriculture and forestry, and changes in ecosystems arising from wildfires and the management of wildfire. Eastern Australia ranks in the top 10 of the world's major deforestation fronts, and the only industrialised nation in this group (Preece & Oosterzee 2017). 395,000 hectares of land was cleared in Australia in 2015-16, this rate is increasing annually. Most of the clearing is happening in Queensland, where 80% of Queensland's threatened species live in forest and woodlands. Land clearing and fire threatens species by removing their habitat; restricting the movement of bird, animals and insects to enable them to adjust to climate change; changes ecosystems, thus changing food supply and shelter; and facilitates the introduction of pests, including predators, and weeds (Morton, Sheppard & Lonsdale 2012; Zukerman 2011).

This loss of biodiversity is rarely drawn to people's attention. However, when asked, people oppose extinction (Garnett 2012). In a survey, 75% of people said they would become upset if a bird became extinct (only 7% disagreed) and 74% said there was a moral obligation to protect threatened birds (5% disagreed). In Australia, people may feel secure in a belief that the national parks, covering 13% of the country, are providing the protection. However, Flannery reports that the rate of loss of wildlife in these parks is also occurring at much the same rate as outside the parks (Flannery 2012). What Flannery describes as "Australia's first extinction wave" began when the First Fleet landed in Australia and by the 1940s, 10% of mammal species were extinct (2012, p.7). The second extinction wave is underway in Australia and is now reaching areas in the north of Australia that missed the first wave.

The environment as a strategic goal for society

The environment is overlooked

At this point, the reader is asked to bear with an apparent diversion, a discussion on the value of the environment. This discussion is offered as background to wildfire policies around mitigation, presently adopted in many countries. The United Nations Environment Program stated that the vision created at the Rio de Janeiro, Conference of the Parties, on climate change, in June 2012, will only be possible "if the environmental and social pillars of sustainable development, from forests to freshwaters, are also given equal if not greater weight in development and economic planning" (UNEP 2011 Foreword by Steiner).

Pearce and Turner (1990) describe a closed circular system where natural resources are input to the economic system and waste products from production are put back into the environment, onto the land, in the air and in water. However, this circular system has two flaws that are creating unsustainability in the environment. The first problem is that natural resources are being used at an ever-increasing rate. Some resources are being rapidly eradicated, such as forests, many animal species, and clean water. The nature of non-renewable resources is that once they are used, they are irreplaceable. These resources will not be available for future generations. The second problem is that waste is being generated at a rate that is beyond the ability of the environment to detox and absorb it into natural systems. Hence there is a build-up of GHGs and other pollutants beyond the environmental absorption rate. Natural land and ocean sinks removed 56% of all carbon emissions emitted from human activities during 1958-2010, each sink in roughly equal proportion, the emissions now exceeding the natural capacities.

The authors argue that the recognition of the life support functions of natural systems, and therefore the value of the environment, tends to be poorly understood. In the human food chain, biodiversity loss is said to be affecting health and socioeconomic development, with implications for wellbeing, productivity, and even regional security (World Economic Forum 2019). Economics often places equilibriums as a central concept, but one that rarely includes consideration of the environment. However, Pearce and Turner believe that "if we are interested in sustaining an economy, it becomes important to establish some conditions for the compatibility of economies and their environments" (1990, p.42).

Economics has not developed an existence theorem that makes provision for environmental sustainability, whatever economic systems or policies are pursued (Pearce & Turner 1990). With a few exceptions, particularly around environmental regulation and other environmental legislation, individuals generally operate according to their own needs or preferences within physical limitations and social norms. Thus, the common good, in terms of social justice, environmental sustainability and rights, do not have a strong voice. It is often left to an advocacy campaign to raise concerns and represent such interests.

There is an assumption that people have full knowledge of the possible choices and their impacts and what value should be placed on them. Yet it is not possible to obtain full knowledge about the role of the natural environment because we do not understand very much about these natural systems as yet, nor their interface with humans.

If global life support systems become further seriously impaired, future generations may have little opportunity to ameliorate the damage or adapt. There is a requirement for a generalised obligations approach. Obligations of the present generation are required to maintain a stable flow of resources into the future in order to ensure on-going human life, rather than just meeting individual requirements. Inter-generational equity can be described as each generation leaving 'enough' and 'as good' for future generations. This is achieved by providing a constant natural capital stock supported by policies directed towards renewable resources, enhanced technology and recycling. Future generations should be offered compensation for loss of productive potential.

Neo-liberal economics overlooks the critical interdependence between economic, social and environmental factors. Economics has been ground in the idea that natural resources are free and benefits in the present are worth more than benefits in the future. Keynes, writing in the 1930s, thought economics would solve the problem of scarcity through economic growth, a prediction that has not proved to be correct given the diminution of the natural environment (Common 1995). He argued in the 1930s that one day, not that far away, we will all be rich, and to achieve this outcome we need to not restrict the means of achieving this (Schumacher 1973). Schumacher (1973, p.20) notes Keynes words, that "avarice and usury" will be necessary to reach this desired outcome.

Economic practice and policy have not treated the environment as a capital resource but as a free, indefinitely renewable asset (Pearce et al. 1991; Sukhdev 2012). The profits of many large corporations would not exist if the true cost of the environmental resources used in production were included in the accounts. For example, externalities arising from extraction and production in mining activities, are underwritten by the public (Sukhdev 2012). Rifkin (2011) describes how economic activity leads to a temporary value at the expense of resource use, environmental loss and the build-up of waste.

In 1990, Pearce and Turner undertook extensive analysis on the fundamental connection between the environment and the economy. Pearce and Turner note that "economic systems are dependent on ecological foundations and ultimately on the maintenance of the global life-support system" (1990, p. 226). Almost a decade after this work, Giddens also refers to the impact of the environment on social outcomes, saying that "ecological issues... must at this point be brought into the core of the theory and practice of social welfare. The rights and obligations of citizenship can no longer attach only to the classical framework of the welfare state, in which the environment is an externality" (Giddens 1997, p.195).

Pearce was one of the first authors to query the Gross National Product (GNP) as a measure of economic progress. He believed that GNP failed to measure the 'true standard of living' as it largely ignores environmental assets and treats them as if they have a zero or near-zero price. Thus, conventional measures of wealth are incorrect and lead to incorrect policy actions (Ash et al. 2010). The outcome of this pricing is that if something is under-priced, too much of it will be consumed (Pearce 1991). The extent and form of integration between economic, social and environmental issues vary greatly between theorists and policymakers, commonly depending on ideology and political persuasion.

Valuing the environment

Common (1995) offers a holistic perspective on a life support system for humans. This appears to be related to the idea of Gaia popularized by Lovelock (2006), where there is a belief that the earth functions as a self-regulating living being. Common notes that the extinction of any species will alter the way that the biosphere functions, although he notes that little is understood about this. Species extinction reduces the species that may be useful to humans in the future. Loss of genetic diversity will impact on evolution. It is the loss of these life support services that are viewed by many as the most worrying (Common 1995). The Millennium Ecosystem Assessment report (2005) popularised the concept of ecosystem services, although the idea had been used for some time.

As with the general public, the extent and value of the environment are still little understood by the research and scientific community, and even less information is available about the economic value of non-marketed services (Millennium Ecosystem Assessment 2019). The costs of the depletion of these services are rarely tracked in national economic accounts. Accompanying this is also a loss of local knowledge about the operation and use of ecosystem services, as economic growth in developing countries leads to urbanisation, forest loss, and loss of small landholdings. There has been little work undertaken on understanding the optimal level of environmental assets. While criticised for some methodological shortcomings, an article in *Nature* reported the value of natural capital and ecosystem services (over 10 years ago) as US$33 trillion, global GDP being US$30 trillion (Constanza et al. 1997).

Pearce[2], Markandya and Barbier (1989) argued that the total economic value of the environment is:

---

[2] Much of the views expressed in this chapter are drawn from the work of David Pearce, an early champion for addressing climate change and the environment.

Actual Use Value + Option value + Existence value

Pearce and Turner (1990) identify 'use' values of the environment:

- As a stock for providing resources for production – timber, water, food, medicines, raw materials

- As a system which provides regulation services for humans, such as climate and air quality, carbon sequestration and storage and receptor of other waste from production and wastewater treatment, pollination, the maintenance of biogeochemical cycles in the environment, soil formation, erosion control and nutrient cycling and a moderator of extreme events

- As a place for recreation, cultural services, educational services, tourism, sense of place and the provision of value to humans (aesthetic enjoyment and spiritual comfort)

Use value

With a growing interest in research about wellbeing and green spaces, there is now evidence that green spaces may be health-enhancing and contribute significantly to the quality of life (Ward Thompson et al. 2011). Rook (2013) reports that green space has been found to reduce overall mortality and cardiovascular disease. People in an urban environment have higher levels of inflammatory diseases such as allergies, inflammatory bowel disease, and other autoimmune diseases such as multiple sclerosis, than those living in a rural environment. This is said to be due to reduced exposure to organisms such as microbiota found in natural environments, which have a role in immunoregulation in humans. Natural areas also improve wellbeing, facilitating the enjoyment of fresh air, quiet and places to meet friends. Those living in an urban area with more, and better-quality green space, were found to have lower levels of stress and improved mental health, than those with less or poorer green space areas (Ward Thompson et al. 2011).

The natural environment has been found to be especially important for child development in the areas of physical and mental health (Gill 2011). Being in nature allowed "unstructured play, generating a sense of freedom, independence and inner strength" (Watson & Albon 2011, p. 82). Interaction with nature was found to positively impact on the mood of children who have behavioural problems. Outdoor play, especially in more natural environments, gives children a sense of freedom, healthier personal development, increased cognitive functioning and emotional resilience, as well as opportunities for self-discovery (Pretty et al. 2009).

The loss and alteration of ecosystems impact human health in other ways. Over half of the 100 most prescribed drugs in the USA have been in some way designed by nature (Bernstein 2011). Loss of habitat has moved species closer to humans, risking the transfer of diseases. There is greater use of bush food with inherent disease risks in some industrialising countries. SARS virus has the flying fox as a reservoir species. Deforestation is forcing them to move out of forests for food, concentrating them around remaining food sources, risking the concentration of the infection in the population.

Environmental services that are directly used in production are the easiest to value and can be assessed with economic valuation methods. These include 'willingness to pay', or willingness to accept compensation for changes in the levels of goods, or the trading price where there are choices of goods (Ash et al. 2010). Indirect uses of the environment, such as cultural services, enjoyment and recreation, can be economically valued. However, this is moving further into the area of intangibles, where the services become important to issues like social wellbeing and personal identity. Environmental regulation services can be valued through a change in the flow of these services through a management change (Ash et al. 2010). If there is a complete loss of an ecosystem service, then the loss of option values need to be also added. Regulation ecosystem services are still not easy to measure due to both our poor knowledge of them still, and the complexity of the services.

Options value

'Option' value can be described as where, although the service is not currently being used, it still has value because it can be used in the future by the existing or following generations. There are three important features that need to be taken into consideration when valuing the environment: irreversibility, uncertainty and uniqueness. The loss of species and ecosystems has the element of irreversibility. If a mistake is made, it very often cannot be corrected afterwards. When irreversibility is placed with uncertainty, then this should lead to even more caution about how the environment is treated. A person should be willing to pay more if the risk is uncertain. Similarly, given the lack of knowledge of many aspects of the environment, there is a recognition that knowledge will increase over time, and therefore the environment should be preserved in the expectation that knowledge will increase. All add up to the need to err on the side of caution. The rational economist has problems accounting for existence value as actions may be motivated by factors other than maximising utility. If this is what people want, then policy needs to take existence value into account. There is an argument for maintaining optimal natural resources rather than existing natural capital, those that are present now. Optimal stocks may be above existing stocks and certainly will be in the future as the natural environment is destroyed.

Common (1995) offers another insight suggesting that economics approaches sustainability from the point of view of humans. Sustainability is the ability to have constant consumption by humans and human interests. Humans are commonly viewed as feeding off the environment, not part of it. Values are apportioned according to individual human preferences. Many of the definitions used for sustainability leave out particular components. Brundtland's definition is person-centric. "Sustainable development is development that meets the needs of the present without compromising the ability of future generations to meet their own needs" (World Commission on Environment and Development 1987, p. 8). It fails to consider whether the life of other species is important for humans and if other species have intrinsic rights of their own to existence (Common 1995).

This view is taken to the extreme by many in business today who rationalise that they have a 'legitimate' occupation which maximises output and growth, and thereby the welfare of all people. Their reward is a high level of recompense as they are undertaking a public good. Thus, the need to maintain growth is used as the rhetoric to maintain their privileged position of access to, for example, minerals and other mining products. The value of the proposed Adani coal mine in Queensland, Australia, is that it provides (an uncertain number) of jobs, although the cost is likely to be pollution of a massive underground water storage used by towns and farmers, the inevitable extinction of a bird species, inevitable damage to the Great Barrier Reef, and extensive GHG pollution over a long time.

In contrast to many economists who start with human interests, ecologists start with humans as part of a wider system, not just involved with consumption (Commons 1995). Resilience is viewed as the ability of the system to go back to normal functioning after a shock. "Tropical ecosystems experience low variability in temperature and precipitation and are characterized by stable population sizes but low resilience. They are vulnerable in the face of large disturbances, (such as forest clearing, whereas)…temperate ecosystems have evolved in the face of larger climatic variability and exhibit less stability in population sizes but greater resilience and are more robust in the face of large-scale human disturbance" (Common 1995, p.51). Although resilience is now increasingly being used in both environmental and social issues, in most cases the ecosystem, or indeed people, will not be able to return to prior or 'normal' functioning, as with climate change and the new experience of wildfire risk, prior conditions now no longer exist, or will not do so in the future.

Intrinsic value

Intrinsic rights are the rights of all living things to exist; this not being dependent on how humans view them or value them from their perspective. Like humans yet to be born, other species depend on living humans to create the conditions in which they may flourish (Jordon 2010). The boundaries of these rights vary between religions and philosophies. While intrinsic rights is not a common view of Western cultures, it is a perspective that is often found in other cultures and religions, such as Hindu, American Indians, Indigenous Australians and Taoism (Ash et al. 2010). Ash gives the example of Indigenous Australians where landscape-level features have intrinsic value while individual plants and animals usually don't, except where they are a personal totem.

While there is an increasing (but slow) recognition by some companies of the need to place a value on the use of the environment, there is still almost no recognition of values relating to option or intrinsic values of the environment. In part, this is because the intrinsic value cannot be translated into income. There is a current debate, largely in academic circles, in relation to, choice and value. The cost of saving a single species is high, such that there is a belief by some that particular species need to be sacrificed to allow resources to be given to important ecological systems. The alternative view is that all species are important, and none should be lost. As noted above, both these measures are used in relation to the biosphere integrity category in the Planetary Boundaries work, a field that is, as noted, of direct relevance to the issues of fire.

Failing to, and incorrectly valuing the environment

Australia's National Strategy for Ecologically Sustainable Development (Department of the Environment and Energy 1992) defines ecologically sustainable development as "using, conserving and enhancing the community's resources so that ecological processes, on which life depends, are maintained, and the total quality of life, now and in the future, can be increased". Intergenerational equity, the precautionary approach and biodiversity conservation are three essential components relevant to sustainable development. The Strategy states that knowledge about wildfire and its effects on ecological processes, "is far from complete"; thus, the guiding principle needs to be the precautionary one.

Decisions about the use of many resources are being made by a fairly small group of people in society, commonly those with wealth who are part of major companies. The average person is not a part of these decisions, even although these resources may be on public land and may have an adverse impact on common land, and human and ecological or environmental welfare. Even if land is privately owned, the stewardship value, or the need to look after the land, is usually not part of the consideration made by the company. Government represents an interpretation of the public good, so may influence the decision depending on political judgements. With the siloed, single-issue approach based on functional government departments and the dominance of economic growth ideology, possible value judgements other than economic growth, tend to be overlooked by many national governments today.

Although not normally viewed in this way, it could be said that inequity occurs when those who don't value the environment impose their values (which is commonly personal gain) on other people and other species. For example, a timber company cutting down a forest for personal gain is imposing a cost on the person who places a high intrinsic value on the forest. The problem is that it may not just be a matter of financial compensation when the forest cannot be replaced in its original form.

Decisions about investments are made by the company according to the present and future monetary value of the product and the opportunities for company profit. The present is valued more highly because of time preferences in economics – the traditional belief being that a person would prefer to have something now rather than later. The assumption behind this is that people will be wealthier in the future; therefore, the project is likely to have more value now than in the future. The future is discounted, the higher the discount rate, the higher the value of the current capital stock. In reality, the higher the discount rate, the greater the discrimination against future generations.

Decisions about resource use are not necessarily consistent with optimising the lifetime welfare maximisation of the resource, favouring present capital stock depletion and unsustainability (Pearce & Turner 1990). It could be questioned as to whether there is a rational way to measure the marginal utility of consumption, that is the value of consumption for the same person over time and between different people. Secondly, there is an assumption that real consumption will increase over time. The irony is, as Pearce and Turner note, high discount rates can lead to environmental degradation, which in turn will diminish real consumption in the future. This problem is far more salient than when Pearce wrote this commentary over 20 years ago. It is clear that unless environmental degradation ceases, the future welfare of many people will be greatly diminished. This is especially so for those with lower financial resources who are not in a position to purchase scarce resources. The current wave of refugees is in large part due to climate change impacts and competition for resources, as well as the conflict generated by this competition (Klein 2019).

Connecting the threads

The chapter to date has discussed the critical importance of the environment. To summarise, lead scientists have identified major interacting trends of environmental degradation that are likely to both threaten and diminish human life for current generations and may risk on-going human existence, unless these trends are halted. Damage to the environment is present with human activities associated with wildfire and wildfire mitigation activities, including GHGs; land clearing and loss of tree cover; land degradation; species loss; and, weed and feral animal spread. In NSW, one-third of threatened wildlife species and one-half of threatened plants are at risk from frequent fires (New South Wales Office of Environment and Heritage 2017, reported in Zylstra 2017). The current wave of species extinction, and subsequent loss of ecosystem services, also overlooks both option and existence rights of other species, a situation many people would not support.

A major driver of this destruction is due to a failure to put a market value on the environment, thus allowing it to be overlooked or excluded, as well as the treatment of the environment as a renewable resource in economic business decisions. There appears to be little evidence that international policies around environmental modification as a means of preventing or controlling wildfire include a review of trade-offs. Nor is there evidence around the respective costs and benefits of these measures, as well as where, and how, they are effective in relation to the prevention of wildfire. While there is some discussion on the ecological benefits of wildfire, this discussion appears to merge issues and outcomes, and at times used to justify wildfire mitigation activities. Of course, the problem is that wildfire itself results in many severe environmental concerns, thus increasing the importance of evaluating likely outcomes as well as the range of available options around fire prevention. The next section further examines the use of fire and other environmental disturbances to prevent fire.

A new wave of environmental destruction

Use of environmental modification

Earlier chapters in this book have briefly discussed fuel reduction or environmental modification approaches in the name of wildfire prevention. However, many such measures are also said to be used for invasive species control, wildlife habitat improvement, and ecosystem restoration (Hahn et al. 2019). This activity is dominated by prescribed burning in many countries (Kelly, Giljohann & McCarthy 2015). It is also supported by the clearing of undergrowth in smaller areas closer to an urban setting by slashing or mowing, by forest thinning approaches in some countries, through manual or mechanical means, livestock grazing, and use of herbicides. Prescribed burning is defined as "the controlled application of fire under specified environmental conditions to a predetermined area and at the time, intensity, and rate of spread required to attain planned resource management objectives" (AFAC 2017).

Controversy over fuel reduction

Fuel reduction strategies are a contested method of wildfire prevention (Altangerel & Kull 2013; Bond & Mercer 2014; Buxton et al. 2011; Holland et al. 2013). A Victorian Parliamentary Inquiry (held by the opposition) into fire season preparedness (2017) produced 22 findings and 12 recommendations. Recommendation 5 stated that in conjunction with a risk-based approach, a minimum of 5% annual burning target be reinstated. Not having a designated figure may result in lower levels of prescribed burning, resulting in a build-up of fuel, risking mega-fires and more prescribed burning in the future (Parliament of Victoria 2017). This issue divided the Parliamentary Inquiry, as a minority report did not support this recommendation. The state government did not adopt this recommendation.

The issue is rarely discussed in a public venue in Australia, decisions largely resting with fire authorities. A powerful and emotive lobby group in Victoria advocates for extensive prescribed burning, with a few forceful proponents advocating for higher levels of prescribed burning, up to 20% of the state annually (Parliament of Victoria 2017). In contrast, 300 Australian scientists have signed a petition asking for a tightening of regulations that allow land clearing, noting that "Australia's high rates of forest loss and weakening land clearing laws are increasing bushfire risk, and undermining our ability to meet national targets aimed at curbing climate change" (Maron et al. 2019). They note that tree clearing impacts the regional climate, increasing local summer temperatures and depleting soil moisture, it removes the windbreak value of trees that can slow the spread of fire, and contributes to climate change.

The USA appears to reveal similar wide perspectives on fuel reduction (McCaffey et al. 2014). A review of the literature found that there was a (qualified and unqualified) acceptance of prescribed burning, although the level of support varied between studies, with varied views about the ecological value. Some studies found support for forest thinning. Lower levels of support were present for livestock grazing as a means of fuel reduction, and few supported the use of herbicides. Forest health was seen to be a parallel, and sometimes more dominate consideration, than reducing fire risk.

However, Dupéy and Smith (2018) note that most studies (86%) that examined how effective response, exposure, individual knowledge, and perceived risk, influenced public support for prescribed burning and mechanical thinning, did not provide participants with information related to the forest ecosystem in question. They found only two studies that specifically addressed homeowner perceptions of the influence of climate change and climate variability on wildfire risk and the need for prescribed burning (Ojerio et al. 2011; Schulte & Miller 2010). They argue that this information is necessary to provide an accurate frame of reference from which to answer risk perception, decision making, and other related questions.

Victoria

The use of environmental modification activities, particularly prescribed burns, have been widely used in Australia since the 1970s, with increased use in recent years, as has the prevalence of wildfire. Zylstra (2017) reported on a limited 1966 study on burning, using low to moderate intensity fires alight for up to one hour in leaf litter and low shrubs in a West Australian Jarrah forest (McCaw 2013). The researcher, McArthur, warned that his observations were tentative and may subsequently be proved wrong. In subsequent experiments in a Jarrah forest, fuel load was found to have no effect on the rate of spread of the fire and only a very minor effect on flame height. Despite this inconclusive finding, fuel-reduction burning has underpinned Australian fire management for more than 50 years, being the most widely used mitigation technique (McCaw 2013; Parliament of Victoria 2017; Zylstra 2017). Tellingly, as noted by Zylstra (2017), forests are spoken of as a source of fuel, rather than a natural asset.

In Victoria, prescribed burns by authorities mainly take place on public or common land, including national parks, state forests and reserves, totalling approximately 7.7 million hectares in Victoria. Prior to the 2009 wildfires in Victoria, the Victorian Bushfire Royal Commission (2009) stated that about 1.7% of public land was subject to prescribed burning (about 130,000 hectares). Following the severe wildfires in Victoria, in February 2009, the subsequent Royal Commission recommended that 5% of public land be subject to a prescribed burn annually. This was revoked in 2015. It was said that a hectare target was not the most cost-efficient way of reducing risk to people and property and that such an approach can have negative impacts on biodiversity (Penman 2015). The policy was changed to one where prescribed burning can be undertaken on public and private land where there is deemed to be a high fire risk and in areas close to dwellings (Commissioner for Environmental Sustainability 2018). The aim is to reduce the risk to a 70% chance of a wildfire impacting people and property.

While it is hard to know how this target can be measured, it is said to equate to burning between 225,000 and 275,000 hectares (Parliament of Victoria 2017). This land area roughly equates to the 5% target, with 275,000 hectares planned under this target in 2015-16. This is a process target, rather than an impact target that takes account of the effectiveness of the approach. An update of the prescribed burning report (AFAC & FFMG 2017) offers a much more comprehensive approach to prescribed burning, in which maintaining or improving biodiversity and the resilience of natural ecosystems is viewed as an important objective of prescribed burning. However, this perspective is yet to be transferred into practice in the field. Ward estimates that close to 100% of activities to reduce fuel risk in Victoria is prescribed burning, undertaken on a landscape scale including the burning of wet forests and the sides of streams, turning them into dry areas (reported in Parliament of Victoria 2017).

This controversy is in part due to the failure to factor the ecological values held by some community members into fire management decisions, as discussed in chapter 7. It is due to the lack of research on the size and distribution of many species and on ecological systems. It is also due to the lack of transparency and public debate, hindered by historical approaches continuing a narrow perspective. The Victorian Flora and Fauna Guarantee Act 1988 lists 517 land vertebrates as endangered and about 1800 plants. There is also an Advisory List of 284 vertebrates and 177 invertebrates that are considered endangered, but little is known about them, as they have not been scientifically investigated (DELWP 2019; Victorian Department of Sustainability and Environment 2009).

The failure to provide evidence around prescribed burning has been repeatedly recognised in the literature. In 2003, it was said that by "the early 1980s, and despite almost two decades of ecological research spanning the 1960s and 1970s, no significant advance had been made in understanding the effects of repeated fuel reduction burning on the forests and heathlands of Victoria. The principal reason for this was a lack of statistically sound fire experiments" (Department of Sustainability and Environment 2003, p.vi). More recently, it is noted that "in many jurisdictions, prescribed burning has never been reviewed in a systematic way" (AFAC & FFMG 2016, p. 8).

A recent Victorian State of the Environment report (Commissioner for Environmental Sustainability 2018) revealed that no specific data was available for the report on the environmental effects of wildfire, the only information available held by emergency management agencies was property loss from wildfires over the past three years. The report noted that there is an incomplete record of an assessment of Tolerable Fire Intervals for flora and fauna, although it would appear that a higher number of ecological burns are needed to enable seed setting.

USA

In the USA, prescribed burning has been used as a land management tool in the timber industry, for land clearing, agriculture, ecological purposes and for wildfire prevention, since the 1930s (Leopold 1987, reported in Huang et al. 2018). However, Martin (2016) notes that a total fire suppression policy continued into the 1950s and 1960s. The author argues that this led to increased fire risk by suppressing all fires, thus leaving high levels of fuels in the forests. Biswell, from Berkeley School of Forestry, California University, believes that prescribed burning is needed to control large fires. He heavily influenced policy supporting prescribed burning and even grazing in forests, in the 1950s to 1980s, arguing that suppressing all fire was doing more harm than good and fire was essential for fire-dependent ecosystems. The dominant policy of managing forests only as fire-free wood factories was questioned. In 1964, Congress passed The Wilderness Act to define areas where no further resource-extractive industries could take place, although Martin (2016) notes that "thoughtful, deliberative, science-based" approaches to these issues are lacking.

In 2017, 4.6 million hectares were subject to a prescribed burn, 80% to meet forestry objectives and 20% associated with agriculture (Melvin 2018). As a definition of forestry objectives is not given, it is unclear what this encompasses. States in the USA work independently in relation to permits to undertake prescribed burns; thus, differences in approach exist at national, regional and state levels. The greatest numbers of prescribed burns occur in the South West of the USA, particularly in Florida and Kansas. Thus, it is said to be difficult to obtain a definitive perspective of the extent of the practice.

While the size of the prescribed burn areas appears to be also increasing for the USA as a whole, the increase in these burns is largely occurring in the West of the USA. Melvin (2018) notes that prescribed burning is not undertaken as much as is desired. The three major impediments are unsuitable weather, capacity to undertake the burning, with air quality/smoke management concerns, accounting for 74% of all concerns. Liability and insurance concerns accounted for 18%, air quality and smoke management 4%, while environmental concerns were not offered as a choice in the survey. According to the 2014 National Emissions Inventory, nearly 50% of all fire-related PM2.5 emissions in the USA are from prescribed fires, with over 75% of these emissions coming from prescribed fires in the south-eastern states. This includes all purposes, such as sugarcane burning in Florida, not just prescribed burns to reduce fuel loads.

The current practice is increasingly part suppression, part prescribed burn, suppression being undertaken on sites of major assets and communities at risk, and 'burning out' viewed as 'a prescribed fire conducted under urgent, but not emergency, conditions' (Melvin 2018, p. iv). An occasional practice noted in the USA, and reported anecdotally in Victoria, is to let large wildfires burn out without active suppression if property and people are considered to be safe (Hann & Bunnell 2001; Yocom et al. 2019). Such a response acts as a prescribed burn. Yocom and colleagues (2019) report that wildfires may even be allowed to grow larger.

Fuel reduction through by slashing vegetation

In Victoria, fuel reduction in the rural/urban interface areas is often undertaken by slashing the sides of roads and at times in forested areas. This approach necessitates repeated slashing, as the native ground covers often become replaced by non-native grasses and weeds that can grow rapidly. The heavy machinery undertaking the slashing that disturbs the soil and uproots the new native plants increases this transition to weeds, as well as rising weed spread by using the machinery across the environment (McLaren et al. 2016). Similarly, larger plants comprising the middle story, are removed to allow access to the machinery. The introduced weeds are often less fire-resistant than the native ground cover, as they tend to dry off in summer, and particular weeds, such as serrated tussock and gorse present a significant fire risk (McLaren et al. 2016). The weed competition can have negative consequences on native plants, altering natural ecosystem fire regimes and other aspects of hydrology (McLaren et al. 2016).

The effectiveness of environmental modification

The effectiveness of environmental modification for fuel reduction is unclear (Ellis, Kanowski, & Whelan 2004). The benefit over cost has not yet been demonstrated (Parliament of Victoria 2017). However, the few studies that have been undertaken suggest that prescribed burning is a very blunt instrument, with variable outcomes in relation to fire. Zylstra (2017) has undertaken the only model for south-east Australian forests that examines the mechanisms by which species-level plants influence fire behaviour, looking at the flammability of plants, the gap between plants, and the sheltering effect of plants from wind flaming the flames. There are also unintended adverse consequences that may arise with prescribed burning: concerns that a prescribed burn will turn into an uncontrolled wildfire, that the prescribed burning is not effective in reducing wildfire risk, and the harm it may cause to humans, business and ecological systems. In addition, there is growing evidence of the low feasibility and high cost of prescribed burning (Furlaud & Bowman 2017; Parliament of Victoria 2017). Particularly concerning is some evidence that the burning may be increasing the fire risk (Penman, Bradstock

& Price 2013, personal communication 1998; Zylstra 2017, 2018). This is reported in some other countries, for example, in Indonesia, repeated fires have led to the formation of fire climax grasslands that have low productivity and subject to frequent fires (Ekayani 2011).

Kirkpatrick (2013) writes of the difference in outcome between February 7, 1967, and January 4, 2013 wildfires in Tasmania, where fire risk ratings were comparable, yet the outcome was far more tragic in 1967, as 100 people lost their lives, and none did in 2013. In 1967, the practice was for farmers to light fires in the bush near their properties, with the belief that this would protect their place from fire. According to Kirkpatrick, the main reason for the different outcomes was the change of approach of the emergency response agencies. By 2013 the agencies had developed integrated emergency response plans and informed the local population about how to prepare for fires and what to do when a fire occurs. Kirkpatrick notes that "fuel levels in the bush are very much a minor issue in mitigating property damage and human mortality from vegetation fires" (Kirkpatrick 2013).

This result was found after the severe 2009 wildfires in Victoria, where no difference was found in terms of property loss in terms of being adjacent to a state forest (land subject to higher fuel control levels) than being adjacent to a national park, with lower reduction of fuel levels prior to the fire (Kirkpatrick 2013). Prescribed burning in remote areas was found to have little impact on risk for humans, while prescribed burns next to properties were found to be five times as effective in terms of reducing risk (Kelly, Giljohann & McCarthy 2015), a view supported by other researchers (for example, Ingamells 2016b). The greater reduction in building loss occurred where there was reduced ground fuel close to the building. Prescribed burns were said to be useful for controlling moderate fires but less effective for containing fires during severe fire weather conditions (Ingabmells 2016b). Kirkpatrick (2013) notes that fuel-reduction burning will not reduce a wildfire on extreme and catastrophic fire days in the south-eastern Tasmanian wet eucalypt forests. Here, the fire can leap bare paddocks, water and fire breaks, and can create spot fires up to 20 kilometres ahead of the main fire (Kirkpatrick 2013).

Furlaud, Williamson & Bowman (2017) modelled the effectiveness of prescribed burns in Tasmania, simulating more than 11,000 fires on a typically dangerous fire-weather day. The researchers found that prescribed burning had little impact on reducing the extent and intensity of wildfires and that about one-third of the state (not 5%) would need to be burnt annually, to make an impact on reducing wildfire. Ellis, Kanowski and Whelan (2004) say that an estimated 25% to 50% of the fire-prone landscape would need to be burnt annually in NSW to achieve fuel loads of less than 8 tonnes a hectare. This represents 15 million hectares of forest, woodland, shrubland and heathland a year in New South Wales. The magnitude of this task makes it unachievable, even if there were no detrimental consequences for the environment. More realistic smaller-scale burn-offs, however, had almost no effect on the extent and intensity of a wildfire. In a review of the scientific literature, Ingamells (2016b) reports that fuel reduction in undergrowth would need to be burnt every three years to be effective, a task not feasible with current climatic conditions and would have significant negative impacts on Victoria's plants and animals. Ingamells (2016b) also reports that there is no obvious correlation between the extent of fuel reduction burns and the extent of wildfires in any year in Victoria, from 1933/34 to 2012/13.

Zylstra (2017) tested a flammability model, finding that the model used only surface fuels; it was only able to explain 11% of the burning variability. When it included plants and their species-specific traits, it explained 80%, a seven-fold improvement. He concluded that flammability is not driven by fuel loads, but by the species of plants present. More frequent fire, therefore, creates more flammable forests and increases the spread of fire in the landscape, while causing localised extinctions (Gill, Stephens & Cary 2013). Re-growing Ash forests are temporarily more flammable but still have the capacity to develop into mature, fire-resistant forests. If they are re-burnt too soon, however, loss of the dominant canopy tree can convert near-pure stands into much more flammable heathland formations. Loss of tall wet forests leads to the ecosystem losing its capacity to form a fire-resistant mature forest, risking the perverse outcome of greater flammability. There is an urgent need to research forest types and fire impact, leading to an understanding of complexity, rather than one approach fits all.

Associated problems with fighting fire with fire

Chapter one in this book overviews a range of adverse impacts associated with wildfire, although considerably more research is needed around these issues to both better understand the need for improved prevention of wildfire and to be able to target resources to address the most serious impacts. Even less is known about the impact of environmental modification as a tool to reduce the impact of wildfire. The Victorian government "has no procedures in its planned burning management process that ensure that the requirements of threatened species are accommodated" (Parliament of Victoria 2017, p.62). The lack of understanding and monitoring of prescribed burns on flora and fauna was an issue noted by the Victorian Bushfire Royal Commission (2010). It would seem that this situation has not changed much. Questions on prescribed burning, such as its effectiveness, how often should it be undertaken and in what sort of natural environments, the value choices that need to be made, how prescribed burning impacts on flora and fauna, the relative impact of wildfire versus prescribed burning on ecosystems... all need to be answered.

There is growing evidence of the air pollution problems associated with wildfire, but the health impacts of prescribed burning have not been adequately assessed (Parliament of Victoria 2017). Liu and colleagues (2017) quantified the emissions of a range of both gaseous and particulate pollutions from fires in the USA, using measurements obtained from on research aircraft. They found that wildfires are a large source of particulate pollution in the western states of the USA, currently under-estimated by more than a factor of three in emissions inventories. Comparison of these results to those obtained from prescribed burning indicates that wildfires are a larger source of pollution; however, wildfires consume more fuel than prescribed burning. They note that a definitive assessment of the trade-offs between wildfires and prescribed fires is needed to confirm that wildfire events can be reduced significantly by prescribed burning. Other research has found that prescribed burning is one of the most prominent sources of PM2.5 (very small particulate matter that can harm health) in the south-eastern USA (Huang et al. 2018). The issue of type and timing of prescribed burns is a problem for grape-growers and winemakers in Australia, as even half an hour of exposure to smoke can damage grape flavour (Parliament of Victoria 2017).

However, it is the impact on the environment that is of relevance in this chapter. The impact of prescribed burning on biodiversity, particularly fauna species, is not currently monitored. However, isolated data exists from small scale studies of individual species and on inferences drawn from life-history characteristics (for plants) and habitat associations (for animals), rather than on empirical studies of biodiversity at a landscape scale (Commissioner for Environmental Sustainability 2018).

The Commissioner for Environmental Sustainability (2018) notes that biodiversity in the Mallee in north-western Victoria are particularly at risk. One-quarter of hollow-bearing trees are destroyed during fuel reduction burns (Bluff 2016). The Gippsland Environment Group reported they had investigated the outcome of prescribed burns on biodiversity within the Gippsland Lakes Coastal Park in Victoria, an area with 59 threatened species. It was noted that one of the identified reasons that 18 small mammals are lost, rare, or are in severe decline, has been what they describe as inappropriately prescribed burning and the intensity of burns (Parliament of Victoria 2017). The group also reported that prescribed burns are destroying large numbers of hollow-bearing trees that provide nesting sites and shelter for 13% of all terrestrial species.

Mountain and Alpine Ash are species of trees that can live for 200 years but can only reproduce after 20 years; thus, they are particularly vulnerable to fire frequency (Bowman & Murphy 2015). This vulnerability can be seen in major fires that occurred in the alpine areas. Young trees regenerated after the first fire; however, 97% of these young trees (covering 5,537 hectares) were lost after a second major fire in 2013. Some areas were subject to 3 burns in 10 years (Ellis, Kanowski & Whelan 2004). Currently, fuel reduction burns occur every 4 to 10 years, and more often in some places. These timeframes shorter than natural fire regimes for many ecosystems and said to be a major threat to biodiversity, risking extinction of a range of native species (Giljohann et al. 2015; Lindenmayer 2007). The viability of this alpine ash ecosystem is further threatened by fire frequency, as when the old trees die, the altered understory of regenerating trees are more flammable than mature trees and the Mountain Ash is replaced by other species (Zylstra 2017). Species like the greater glider (an iconic Australian animal) are impacted by planned burns due to loss of tree hollows in the Ash forests (Ellis, Kanowski & Whelan 2004). Thus, prevention measures other than prescribed burning should be used to protect Mountain and Alpine Ash ecosystems, such as closer monitoring and facilities for immediate suppression responses.

Research on the impact of prescribed fire and wildfires on the environment appears to be more common in the USA. For example, Masters and Waymire (2012) examined the impact of fire frequency and forest thinning practices on the Pushmataha Wildlife Management Area in southeast Oklahoma over a 28-year period. They report that woodland-grassland and forest-shrub birds have steeply declined across the southeast USA because of fire exclusion and densification of forests. They found that Woodland-grassland and forest-shrub obligate songbirds, white-tailed deer, and Rocky Mountain elk have responded favourably to restoration thinning and a more focused burn regime on a one, and three, year cycle. However, the purpose of this experiment was to move the forest type from forest to woodlands. Indeed, restoring, enhancing, or maintaining ecosystem health appears to have been of primary importance in much of the research over the last decade (Fryar 2012). Many research articles express concern about not knowing the impacts of prescribed burning on plants and animals. Rebbeck (2012) found that while prescribed fire can favour Oak regeneration, little is known about the effects of fire on invasive plants in eastern. Oak forests. Similarly, Perry (2012) notes that the interactions between fire, bats, and bat habitat are not yet fully understood.

Prescribed burn and wildfire risks

Prescribed burning also has the effect of reducing the effectiveness of natural biodiversity fire protections. For example, lyrebirds[3] rake the forest floor, a practice that reduces both fire risk and fire intensity (Nugent et al. 2014). On average, lyrebird foraging was found to reduce litter fuel loads by 25%, slightly lower than the acceptable risk level of 30% designated as acceptable in Victoria, but much higher than the risk levels actually achieved in Victoria in 2018. This, of course, is only relevant where the lyrebirds exist, current fire practices being likely to reduce the abundance and influence the distribution of lyrebirds.

For some types of ecosystems, prescribed burning of under-storey results in rapid growth and fuel loads at the ground and at the small tree level that may return higher than pre-burning (McMurray, reported in Parliament of Victoria 2017). This regrowth may also take the form of a secondary growth native plant, such as bracken, which is highly inflammable (Wannon Conservation Society reported in Parliament of Victoria 2017). It may also encourage the growth of other more flammable native plants due to drying of the forest and changes in soil structure due to fire (Wombat Forestcare reported in Parliament of Victoria 2017). Prescribed burning also encourages the growth of non-native grasses that dry off in summer, replacing the summer green native grasses (Parliament of Victoria 2017). While some environmental burning in Australia is important for ecological reasons such as the release of seeds, some forests, such as temperate forests, are not designed to be burnt, and burning may dry the forest, increasing the risk of wildfire. Responding to considerable controversy, research on cattle grazing in the high country found that this had no impact on the reduction of wildfire and an adverse impact on the spread of shrubs, which proved to be more flammable (Ingamells 2007). Prescribed burning can kill many animal and insects, both directly, and by removing their food supply, especially when the prescribed burn increases in intensity. Ward believes that the fuel reduction program represents a bigger threat to native wildlife than wildfires (reported in Parliament of Victoria 2017).

Back-burning

Some concerns are also present with the practice of back-burning. Back-burning describes the lighting of a fire to reduce the spread and intensity of an existing wildfire. However, it also blocks escape routes for animals, reptiles and small mammals travelling from the main wildfire. Moving from outside in

---

[3] Lyrebirds are an Australian bird that is ground dwelling in forests and builds large mounds of leaf litter.

is also a practice used in prescribed burning as a means of controlling the fire spread. Barraclough, in evidence to the Parliamentary Inquiry, said the practice of lighting the entire perimeter of a prescribed burn area, and then dropping aerial incendiaries, creates a very hot fire due to heat updrafts (reported in Parliament of Victoria 2017). Thus, while some animals may manage to escape a wildfire, a prescribed burn may destroy more.

Animal rescue

The RSPCA notes that while there is an overarching emergency animal welfare plan for Victoria in emergency wildfire situations, there is not one for prescribed burning (Roberts reported in Parliament of Victoria 2017). The Parliamentary Inquiry recommended (Recommendation 9) that animal welfare be given a higher practical priority in the planned burning process including consultation with veterinarians and wildlife volunteers and that they are given access to the area as soon as it is safe to assist injured animals (Victorian Government 2017). However, they also note that animal welfare should not be a reason to not undertake 'necessary planned burns' (Parliament of Victoria 2017, p.62). Hylands (2019) has investigated the post-fire management of injured animals, finding that the great majority of these animals are killed, rather than being rescued.

Fire services and their role in prevention: the pressure – to do something!

There is anecdotal evidence that large prescribed burns were undertaken in order to meet the 5% target in Victoria, regardless of the effectiveness of burns. Meeting the target also resulted in repeated burning of some land in the Mallee region, as this proved to be an easier task than burning other areas (Parliament of Victoria 2017; personal communication). While the Mallee area in North Western Victoria represents 2-3% of the state's risk to life and property, 17% to 20% occurred in this region in the years 2012-2014.

While the most risk to lives and property in Victoria lies in an arc surrounding the Greater Melbourne and Geelong region, the rural/urban interface areas, the majority of prescribed burns from 2012 to 2014 occurred outside this area. This is due to the risks to people if a prescribed burn turns into an uncontrolled fire (Penman 2015). Such a disaster happened in Lancefield, a peri-urban area outside Melbourne, in 2015, when a prescribed burn destroyed five houses and other buildings and burnt 2,700 hectares (Milman 2015). More recently, prescribed burns in WA resulted in 50 on-going wildfires (Office of Bushfire Risk Management 2018). In 1995, fire-related costs were 16% of the U.S. Forest Service budget, but by 2015, half of the budget was devoted to fire (Atleework 2018).

In the absence of other programs, Kirkpatrick records a desire for more fuel reduction burning (2013). He believes that this is, in part, a desire for people to cope emotionally with their powerlessness in the event of extreme natural events (Parliament of Victoria 2017). Such a perspective may also apply to firefighters in the new world of extreme wildfires. McMurray (reported in Parliament of Victoria 2017) argues that there is a cultural interest in fire and burning. It may also in part be due to a male-dominated culture that emphasises physical activity.

In broad terms, mandate-establishing or enabling legislation relevant to prescribed burning establishes a requirement for prescribed burning. At the same time, legislation providing for the protection of native flora and fauna and/or threatened species is typically directed to conserving flora and fauna and managing threatening processes. Some legislation makes it an offence to harm or kill certain flora and fauna species (in many cases an unavoidable outcome in prescribed burning) and can apply to threatened species populations or ecological communities. They can also mandate the preparation of threatened species recovery plans that can specify constraints or compliance requirements for prescribed burning. Thus, there is a clear, unacknowledged conflict, that is largely undiscussed and unresolved.

Selected patch fuel reduction

The use of a mosaic form of prescribed burning was recommended over 15 years ago in a report for the Bushfire Research Unit, in the NSW National Parks and Wildlife Service (Kenny et al. 2003). This method of prescribed burning takes account of the small-scale ecological responses of plants and animals to fire regimes (Gill & Bradstock 2003: Gill, Allan & Yates 2003). It is commonly a lower-heat fire that burns in patches, allowing for escape routes for animals. Such a response requires detailed mapping of the ecological responses of plants and animals at landscape scales. Gammage (2012) reports that about 70% of Australia's plants need or tolerate fire, but it is critical to differentiate between these plants, knowing when they should be burnt and how much. While there is a current growing interest in the method, again it is not widely apparent in operations. The approach also requires good knowledge of the landscape ecology, knowledge that is currently largely unavailable.

There is a long history of mosaic type burning being practised by Indigenous populations in the USA, Canada, Europe, Australia and India, knowledge and skills being built up over thousands of years (Paton, Buergelt & Flannigan 2015). Indigenous people often employed fire management to achieve a range of purposes, including the health and wellbeing of the country. For example, First Nations, Métis, and Inuit used fire to simulate particular plant species, reduce pests and disease and to aid hunting game (Paton et al. 2015). Indigenous burning was not a haphazard mosaic. It was a "planned, precise, fine-grained local caring...effective burning (that) must be predictable" (Gammage 2012, p.2). It was undertaken on a small area basis with an ordered network of fire regimes (Flannery 2012). "Detailed knowledge was crucial and each family cared for its own ground, and knew not merely which species fire or no fire might affect, but which individual plant and animal....they first managed country for plants...then they managed for animals" (Gammage 2012, p.3).

Fires lit by Indigenous Australians rarely extended over large areas, most patches being less than 5 hectares, but could be up to 30 hectares. The time between fires varied according to the dominant species: northern grasslands annually, lit about 10am in the morning, and it would be out by mid-afternoon; Kangaroo Grass every 2 to 3 years; Mulga once a decade; dry ridges every 15 to 25 years; Mountain Ash every 400 years. Similarly, fauna needs a varied regime of burning to maintain food and shelter. Gliders and possums need frequent fires; rat kangaroos need casuarinas burnt about every 7 years; a native mouse needs heath burnt 8 to 10 years apart; tammar wallabies need melaleuca burnt with a gap of 25 to 30 years. Indigenous Australians took account of wind, humidity, aspect, target plants and animals, fuel loads and rain forecasts, in the decision about what day and what hour to burn (Gammage 2012). Gammage goes on to say that three rules applied: ensure all life flourishes, make plants and animals abundant, convenient and predictable, think universally, act locally.

New settlers and colonisers in Australia, Northern America and India sought to suppress fires as permanent settlements became established, thus breaking the pattern that shaped the ecology and landscape. As a result, wildfires were more severe when they occurred. Steffenson (reported in Parliament of Victoria 2017) argued that the Australian landscape just could not handle hot and extensive prescribed burns. The complexities in relation to wildfire are much greater than when Indigenous people were managing fire. People have spread over the landscape. The soft soils that were present over much of Australia let the water soak in rather than run off; however, they have largely gone as farm stock spread. This resulted in dryer land and loss of springs and soaks, which has led to a loss of grasslands, such as kangaroo grass and other herbs, orchids, lilies and winter annuals have been lost due to both inept burning and compacted, overgrazed soils (Gammage 2012). The dryer environment due to the alteration of landscape and climate change is increasing vulnerability to wildfire.

It would seem that there is a strong ecological argument for low heat patchwork burns done on a cycle that maintains undergrowth vegetation. While prescribed burning can work in key locations to reduce fire spread rate and intensity, at present it needs to be used more effectively and where it is most needed, to protect people and wildlife (Kelly, Giljohann & McCarthy 2015). At the same time, there is a need to control feral predators, such as foxes and cats (Rijksen & Dickman 2014). Small mammals are vulnerable to a loss of vegetation cover and loss of vegetation structural complexity after severe wildfire. This results in both a loss of food source and exposure to predators, which may also move into an area opportunistically to gain easier food sources (Gill, Stephens & Cary 2013).

What conclusions can be reached?

It would seem that some broad conclusions can be reached from the discussion in this chapter. The process of environmental modification as the major form of prevention of wildfire needs considerable research and reflection. This is especially so when many other opportunities to reduce the wildfire risk, are being overlooked. The issue has now become urgent, with the natural environment now at great risk internationally, such that the long-term future of humanity is at risk (Flannery 2019; Steffen et al. 2015).

Thus, urgent steps need to be taken to move prescribed burning to a mosaic model, to build the evidence on the value (or otherwise) of prescribed burning; and, build the knowledge on the various impacts of fire on fine-scale ecology and landscapes. This knowledge needs to be disseminated widely. It is clear that choices will need greater nuances about the wider outcomes and value choices. It was interesting to the authors of this book that a great deal of local knowledge about ecology and the impact of prescribed burning was revealed in the submissions to the Parliamentary Inquiry into Fire Season Preparedness (Parliament of Victoria 2017). However, it would seem that this knowledge is not collated or documented. In particular, the adoption of a wider approach to the prevention of ignition is critical – it is rare that a one-horse race meets all needs.

Chapter 9

Fires amid a flood of data

Introduction

Contemporary scientific enquiry is currently being re-shaped by trends that are also re-defining the conduct of our everyday lives. The availability of increased computing power, data, and storage are changing the capacity of governments, companies, and individuals to filter, process and gain insight from the vast quantities of data we generate in our on and off-line lives. In particular, the use of linked 'big data' to predict individual people's interests or behaviours (such as purchases or movements) is being pursued at pace.

The new world of 'big data' creates challenges for behavioural and social scientists that have been trained to approach the world from their given epistemological perspective. Where previously, power calculations were used to determine participant sample sizes; today, the entire population is the sample. Where theory drove the careful crafting of questions and collection of data, in the new era, we collect everything – mostly because we are no longer restricted by storage constraints. In the old world, our statistical methods provided confidence intervals and insight into 'why' results were as they appeared; in the new, we just know that something works and care less about why. If we can predict that 'someone will do something' and we are correct 99.9% of the time, do we really care if the algorithm is a 'black box', or that the results fit with theory? Probably not. All that matters is that our prediction is correct.

The application of these principles to the understanding of serious crime is beguiling for law enforcement authorities. Rather than relying on theories, nous, experts, and experience, if the likely perpetrators of crime can be identified with big data and machine learning methods, it could save valuable police time and resources while simultaneously improving the effectiveness of enforcement activity. Not only is this scenario attractive, but given the right combination of datasets, it is also entirely possible. But do we have the right data or at least know what data to collect?

Although the length of the fire season is growing, arson-related[1] crime is a particular concern in the warmer, drier months of the Australian Summer and

---

[1] The term 'arson' is used in this chapter to connote a maliciously lit wildfire.

Autumn. As described at length elsewhere in this book, Australian wildfires are increasing in their frequency and intensity due to a combination of climate change, urban encroachment and population growth. In a single act, a person, whose activities commonly go either unnoticed or unchecked, can ignite a wildfire, creating widespread, lasting devastation of lives, communities, wildlife, and the broader environment; requiring the mobilisation of emergency services (police and fire) in the acute phases of the fire, and long-term economic, health, and environmental rehabilitation in the longer term. Predicting and preventing these acts of wilful disaster is, therefore, a priority.

In Victoria, we consequently have a set three elements that should combine to enable the prediction and prevention of arson to occur. Firstly, we have a set of social and community desires that arson should be prevented. Secondly, we have a motivated police force, fire authorities, environmental management protection authorities and health services, who wish to prevent fire. Lastly, each of these authorities has datasets related to either at-risk or known-risk individuals, criminal records, fire locations, fire histories, and fire characteristics. Can we bring these things together? Theoretically yes. But practically?

The following analysis describes the challenges that Victoria currently faces in constructing a comprehensive dataset, and therefore understanding of, the who, where and when of arson-prediction. We identify strengths in the datasets, weaknesses, gaps, present preliminary analyses based on available (and excluding mystifyingly unavailable) data sources and suggest a pathway forward for better coordination of data, and therefore prediction between agencies for the future. We divide the discussion of data into that associated with 1) people, and 2) places. While drawn from examples in a single state, Victoria, we have framed this discussion in a manner also relevant to other jurisdictions, as similar issues can be found in many fire management systems and countries.

This chapter also visits issues raised in other parts of the book. It offers empirical findings to complement chapter 3, illustrates some of the difficulties that will be faced in following the coordination of approaches to prevention of wildfire, as discussed in chapter 10. This is particularly so in relation to the integration of data on wildfires, discussed in chapter 2, and arguably a critical component of the task of improving the response of prevention of wildfire ignition.

Data related to people

The primary official dataset available that relates to people considered 'at risk' of lighting malicious fires (both urban and rural) in Victoria comes from the

LEAP (Law Enforcement Assistance Program) database. The LEAP database is primarily designed for operational policing purposes and provides a chronological history of all recorded contacts between Victoria Police and people at an identifiable individual record level.

One of LEAP's strengths is that it is vast. It contains millions of entries for hundreds of thousands of people, covering many crimes, and dating back decades. However, while this lends itself to investigation and interrogation using 'big data' techniques, it was not expressly designed for this purpose and therefore (like most administrative datasets) contains weaknesses. Most of these stem from the fact that humans are still the intermediary between incidents and the recording of those incidents, leading to individual and systemic variation in reporting standards and practices over time.

Similarly, there is an acknowledged and necessary lag in reporting crimes and contacts within the LEAP dataset due to the ordinary process of policing, itself. For example, previously unsolved offences may be backdated in time and only later updated in the record. Practically, this means that an arson (or other) conviction may not be included in LEAP statistics produced at the end of (for example) the month of March because no suspect has yet been processed. However, if an offender was eventually processed in October for this crime, statistics reproduced in October for the month of March would differ to those produced earlier in the year. Though investigators do not rely on LEAP for investigations, the practical issue with this for identification of at-risk individuals in real-time or at critical times for wildfire arson (e.g. at the start of the fire season) is that the dataset is not accurate in real-time due to these time lags.

Finally, the dataset also only contains information known to the police. It is well understood that the clear majority of incidents and offences committed go unreported or unrecorded. This means that regardless of its size, the LEAP dataset likely only considers the 'tip of the iceberg' with relation to total fire-related criminal activity.

How big is too big?

Despite its described shortcomings, LEAP is currently the primary dataset used to identify particular Persons of Interest (POIs) who are judged to be at risk of wildfire arson reoffending. This means that the size of the LEAP dataset has continued to grow to the extent that there are now too many POIs than can be reasonably monitored or managed by operational forces. It is simply impossible for officers to keep track of every person on the LEAP POI list.

In 2017/18, the authors of this book attempted to assist Victoria Police with this issue by identifying patterns in the data from POIs in the LEAP dataset and identify whether this list could be reduced for the purposes of more efficient and targeted list management. Two separate efforts were made to understand the dataset. Firstly, descriptive analyses were undertaken to check for irregularities and outliers, but also to describe the basics of cases included in the LEAP dataset. Secondly, a series of predictive analyses were undertaken to determine whether characteristics of the dataset and criminal case histories could be used to predict whether the next recorded incident in a person's file was likely to be arson-related. The impetus behind this approach was to enable a better focus of police monitoring resources toward 'high risk' POIs. The success to which this was achieved is described below.

Dataset characteristics

The dataset examined contained a sample with a total of 258,707 individual rows, representing the time-ordered criminal case histories of 3,692 persons' criminal records. 2,692 records were cases (related to arson), and 1,000 were controls with no records relating to arson. The following descriptive analysis concerns cases, only.

Each individual case had multiple rows, representing chronologically recorded individual incidents, interviews or convictions associated with the person at the time of data extraction. This meant that many people were potentially still criminally 'active' and at different stages of their ultimate criminal record history at the time of data extraction. Descriptive statistics should, therefore, be read with this in mind and not as a complete history of individuals. The dates of recorded incidents spanned the years 1951 to mid-2017.

Further, some variables were supplied to the research team in an abridged manner in order to protect individual confidentiality. For example, the year of birth rather than the date of birth was recorded for each person. Therefore, the estimated age in years for each case was calculated as the date of recorded incident or offence, minus the 1st of January of their recorded birth year. On average, this produced a 6-month error in estimated age for any person at the recorded date of any incident.

Several variables used in the analysis were calculated or derived, based on the originally supplied dataset. The purpose of these new variables was to prepare the dataset for analysis in a manner that facilitated prediction of future arson-related events. In addition to the calculation of the 'age at the date of incident' variable described above, this involved the preparation of the following:

1. Calculation of a unique incident number for each person, enabling estimation of the rank order of any incident in the person's recorded history.

2. Calculation of the time gap between recorded incidents in days

3. A series of dummy variables recording (1 = Yes, 0 = No) capturing text from the incident reporting details whether the incident involved:

    a. Firearms

    b. Arson (coded as 'criminal damage by fire')

    c. An 'incident' rather than an arrest, warrant, interview, or was a recording of a 'flag' against the person for a possible previous arson-related event

4. Calculation of cumulative counts of incidents as above

5. Estimation of whether there were future arson-related incidents in the person's criminal record that had not yet occurred

6. Derivation of whether recorded potential arson-related incidents involved burning grass, trees, vehicles, occupied or unoccupied buildings, and whether an accelerant was used in the ignition

7. The individual's criminal history as either a victim or perpetrator of a variety of non-arson related incidents including individual incidents and cumulative counts of:

    a. Family violence

    b. Assault

    c. Intervention orders (IVOs) as a complainant or subject

    d. Violence of any description

8. The residential postcode of the perpetrator at the time of the incident and postcode (where available) of the incident

Descriptive statistics

Gender

The dataset contained 322 females (12%) and 2,369 males (88%). One case had no gender recorded.

Age at time of the incident

Figure 9.1 shows the mean male, female, and overall ages for all arson-related events involving the categories of materials and assets burned as recorded in the LEAP dataset. Both vehicle and grass/tree fires tended to be lit by younger age-suspects than building fires and younger males than females in general. Occupied building fires were lit by the older-aged people, potentially representing a more utilitarian (i.e. for insurance or other purposes) rather than expressive motive.

Figure 9.1: Mean age of potential arson-related records for males, females and overall, combined groups.

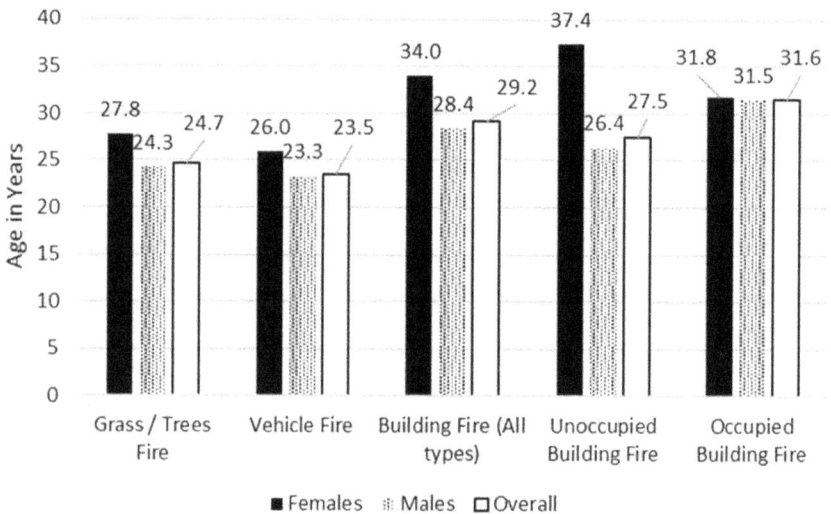

The distribution of age-ranges for both grass/tree (Figure 9.2a-d), vehicle, occupied, and unoccupied building fires shows these trends in greater detail. Of note is the 'spike' in fire incidents among people at or around age 40, for all fire types with the exception of vehicles.

Figures 9.2a-d: Distribution of age of arson-related offences for across fire types for all arson-related records.

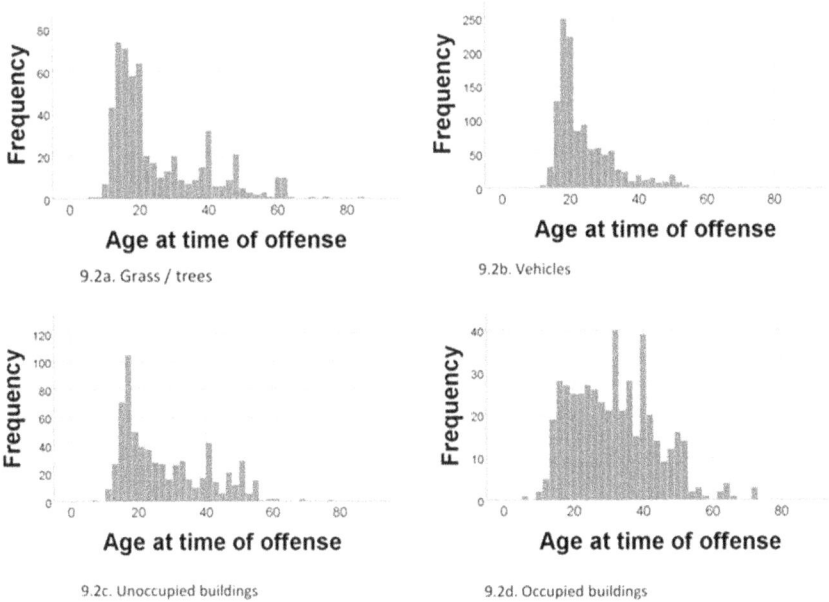

9.2a. Grass / trees

9.2b. Vehicles

9.2c. Unoccupied buildings

9.2d. Occupied buildings

Chronology of incidents

In comparison to other incidents recorded in each person's record, arson-related incidents occurred much earlier in both age, and the chronology (e.g. rank-ordered incidents) of people's recorded police contact history. Figure 9.3 shows the mean incident number associated with each category of the arson-related incident for males and females in comparison to non-arson-related (other). For clarity, incident number 1 would represent the first recorded criminal act or contact with police in the LEAP dataset, while incident number 100 would represent the 100th.

The evidence shows that for males, grass / tree fires appeared earlier in criminal records, alongside unoccupied buildings and other building fires. Although executed at young ages, vehicle fires tended to fall later in criminal careers alongside occupied building fires. For females, the patterns were slightly different, with occupied building fires appearing earliest, followed by trees / grass, and vehicle fires. Building fires in these charts represent combined occupied and unoccupied fire incidents. When compared to the recorded mean chronological incident number of all other non-arson related records within each person's history, it is evident that arson-related incidents tended to appear relatively early within criminal careers.

Figure 9.3: Mean incident numbers for males and females related to fire types, with lower incident numbers indicating incidents earlier in a total criminal history.

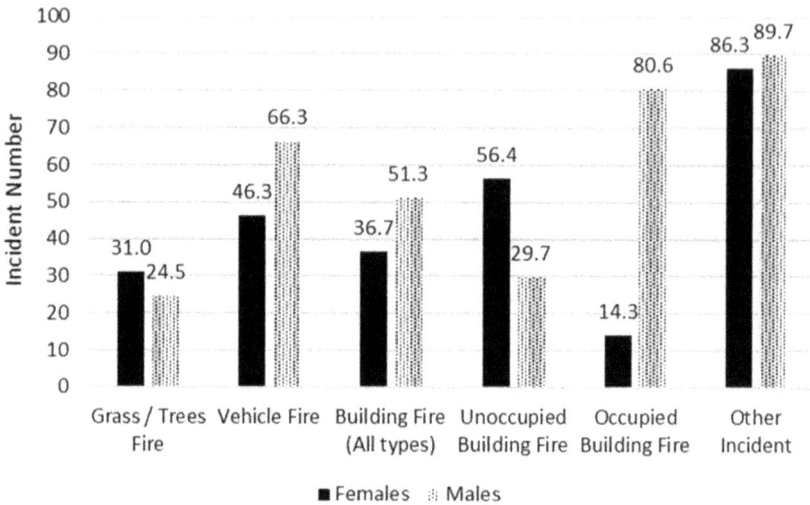

Number of arson-related incidents

The mean number of arson-related incidents recorded for each person at the most recent available date of their criminal record was 2.84 (sd = 3.98). Again, this was a heavily skewed distribution. The median count of arson-related offence for both males and females was 2.

Predictive analytics

Though describing patterns of suspicious fire activity and criminal behaviour provides insight into the characteristics and patterns of behaviour of those who light fires, of more practical use, would be the ability to predict whether individuals were likely to light fires into the future. This would provide enforcement agencies with an ability to more closely target their monitoring activities toward high-risk individuals rather than spread across a larger population, thus prioritizing the more determined offenders while at the same time assisting fire prevention.

Therefore, a series of event classification experiments were conducted using the modified LEAP dataset to predict whether an arson-related incident was likely in the person's future after their initial potential arson-related event, which placed them into the LEAP dataset, to begin with. That is, we asked the question, "Is this person likely to light a fire in the future?". Two approaches were undertaken. The first was a logistic regression; the second was a multilayer perceptron neural network. The results of both approaches are described below.

Logistic Regression

To estimate the likelihood of an individual within the LEAP dataset committing a further arson-related incident after the initial event (future arson-related charge vs no future arson-related charge) a direct logistic regression was performed that included predictive factors of:

- Gender (male, female)

- Time gap (time gap in days between recorded events in the person's criminal record)

- Multiple Arson (whether the person had multiple previous arson-related incidents recorded against them)

- Arson Count (cumulative number of arson-related events made against the person)

- Age of Offense (age at the time of the recorded incident)

- Victim (cumulative number of incidents in the person's record related to being a victim of crime)

- Offender (cumulative number of incidents in the person's record related to being a potential perpetrator of crime)

- Assault (cumulative number of incidents in the person's record related to potential assault as either a victim or perpetrator)

- IVO (cumulative number of incidents in the person's record related to intervention orders made on their behalf or against them)

- Family (cumulative number of incidents in the person's record related to family violence)

- Incident number (cumulative number of incidents, interviews and all other recorded events in the person's record)

Results of the overall model showed that the set of included variables significantly contributed to the prediction of further arson-related incidents after the initial arson-related incident (X^2(10, N=169454) = 43088.36, p <.001). Further, Table 9.1 shows that, with the exception of gender, all included variables significantly contributed to the prediction of future arson-related incidents. However, it should be noted that because of the large size of the LEAP dataset, the test is overpowered and therefore overstates the contribution of many variables to the outcome.

Table 9.1: Results of individual predictor variables included in the logistic regression equation.

Variables	B^*	Wald test	Odds ratio*	95% confidence interval for odds ratio*	
				Lower	Variables
Gender	-.002	.01	1.002	.962	Gender
Time gap	-.001	778.04	.999	.999	Time gap
Multiple arson	-2.208	25594.04	.110	.107	Multiple arson
Age of offense	-.019	687.33	.981	.980	Age of offense
Victim	.030	219.12	1.031	1.027	Victim
Assault	-.001	7.71	1.004	1.001	Assault
Offender	-.004	405.20	1.007	1.006	Offender
IVO	-.003	4.01	1.003	1.000	IVO
Family	-.037	421.34	.964	.960	Family
Arson count	.052	404.94	1.053	1.048	Arson count
Incident number	-.007	932.78	.993	.992	Incident number

*Decimals shown to 3 decimal places for accuracy.

Observation of individual variables in the analysis indicates that the 'multiple arson' indicator was the most influential variable among the observed set. This variable indicated whether a person had recorded at least 2 previous arson-related incidents. Importantly, this variable was not available to the model at the time of the person's 2nd event, but only the incident number *after* it was recorded. The direction of the beta coefficient indicates that the risk of future fires diminishes after the 2nd recorded arson-related incident.

Other patterns observable in the beta coefficients are that, generally, the cumulative count of offences tends to reduce the risk of future fires, with the exception of being a victim of crime, and arson counts themselves. This, potentially counter-intuitive result can be interpreted in line with the general trends observed in the descriptive analyses that arson tends to be an early career crime, performed at younger ages and chronologically earlier in a person's history of incidents and police contacts. Conversely, the likelihood that someone will be involved in a future fire decreases dramatically after the initial 2 to 3 fire incidents but gradually increases again with further arson-related crime.

Table 9.2: Observed vs predicted future arson events after an initial charge based on each incident row for each person in the LEAP dataset using the logistic regression analysis.

		Predicted future arson		Percentage Correct
		No	Yes	
Observed future arson	No	97154	14625	86.9%
	Yes	24783	32892	57.0%
				76.7%

Table 9.2 shows the observed and predicted classification results from the model. The overall correct classification was 76.7%. 86.9% of rows were correctly classified as not committing a future arson-related offence, and 57% of rows were correctly classified as committing a future arson-related offence or incident. For the purposes of effectively and efficiently managing a database of people who were considered to be 'at risk' of committing arson in the future, these results hold promise that some included people on the list can be reliably removed without undue concern they will be 'missed'. This would allow Police effort to be better focused on those who remain at risk of committing another arson-related incident.

Multilayer perceptron network

The second analysis undertaken was for the same predictive purposes as the logistic regression; however, a machine learning algorithm was applied known as a multi-layer perceptron network (MLPN). This network also used identical input variables from the manipulated LEAP dataset described above to differentiate between people's records that indicated their likely future involvement in a fire or not. However, unlike the logistic regression, the MLPN allows a more flexible approach where input variables are not required to consist of linear combinations of one another. While this can lead to improved predictive results, interpretation of the results can be more challenging because the model contains 'hidden' layers made up of multiple combinations of variable properties. Hence, the model creates a training dataset (75%) of available data, that it then tests on a validation dataset (25%)

to determine whether the model has been trained correctly and can be reliably used on new, unseen data.

Table 9.3a-b: Observed vs predicted future arson events after an initial charge based on each incident row for each person in the LEAP dataset using the MLP network analysis for both the training (a) and validation (b) dataset.

Table 9.3a		Predicted future arson		Percentage Correct
		No	Yes	
Observed future arson	No	69445	9030	88.5%
(training dataset)	Yes	17695	22686	56.2%
		73.3%	26.7%	77.5%

Table 9.3b		Predicted future arson		Percentage Correct
		No	Yes	
Observed future arson	No	29334	3970	88.1%
(validation dataset)	Yes	7486	9808	56.7%
		72.8%	27.2%	77.4%

Table 9.3 shows the classification results produced by the MLPN, which are comparable to those produced by the logistic regression. It is important to note that because the MLP network randomly assigns individual cases to either the training or validation dataset prior to analysis, results can vary marginally between runs.

The calculations that underlie the MLP network do not produce a succinct set of beta weights that can be used for estimating risk for new cases. However, the output produces a standardised table of influence for each variable that can be used to understand which input variables are / were most important in the analysis.

In order of importance, this indicated that the 'incident number', 'time gap', 'offender', 'multiple arson', 'victim', and 'arson count' variables were most important. Unlike the logistic regression, however, the direction of effect for these variables is not interpretable from the output and may not be linear. It does indicate, however, that maintaining a collection of these variables is important for future analytical or predictive work.

Conclusions

The analysis of person-level data within the LEAP dataset demonstrates that, even with imperfect administrative datasets such as LEAP, significant improvements to the efficiency of POI lists can be made through person-level data analysis. Trimming the dataset to only include those individuals predicted at a point in time, to be likely to engage in a future arson-related crime, could significantly reduce the volume of POIs under observation without compromising the likelihood of correctly identifying at-risk individuals.

Data related to places

Despite the comprehensive list of factors included in the LEAP dataset, one variable not included related to where the POI lived and/or the location of the fire associated with the POI. This is because, unfortunately, this data is either not available through LEAP, or is only available at a low-level of accuracy (e.g. the post-code level). This presents an obvious gap in the data available for predicting arson-related crime and the likely location of fires.

While police data is reasonably comprehensive at the person-level, the recorded location of fires was not linked with the LEAP database. However, it is located elsewhere in the emergency services and public asset management system. For example, in Victoria, the Department of Environment, Water and Land-use Planning (DELWP) has recorded the location of nearly 29,000 fires in Victoria for the past 50+ years, alongside each fire's cause, including categories for 'malicious' fires (i.e. arson). Figures 9.4a-c, below, shows the a) location of all recorded fires recorded by DELWP, b) the location of all fires reported to have been ignited by lightning, and c) and d) the location of reported 'malicious fires' for the entire state and surrounding the Melbourne metropolitan area. Much of this information is publicly available through the Victorian Government's Open Data Portal[2].

---

[2] (www.data.vic.gov.au).

Figure 9.4a: Heatmap of the location of all recorded fires in the DELWP dataset across all categories.

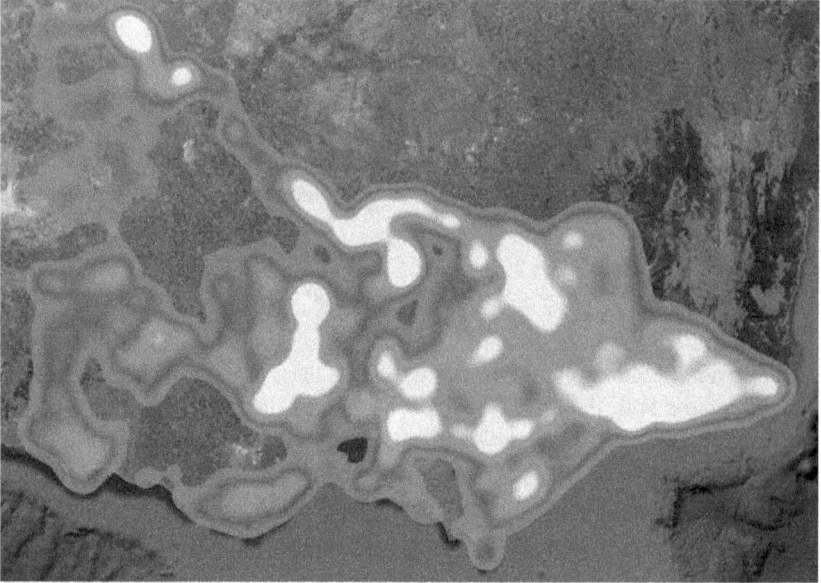

Figure 9.4b: Estimated location of all fires recorded as ignited by lightning strikes in the DELWP dataset.

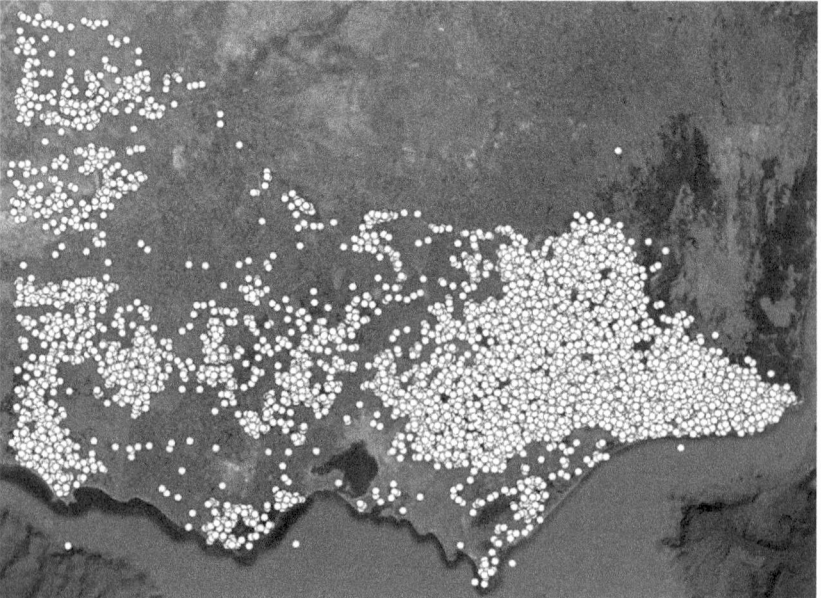

Figure 9.4c-d: Estimated location of all malicious fires lit in Victoria as recorded within the DELWP dataset, with close-up (inset, top right) of the area surrounding Melbourne.

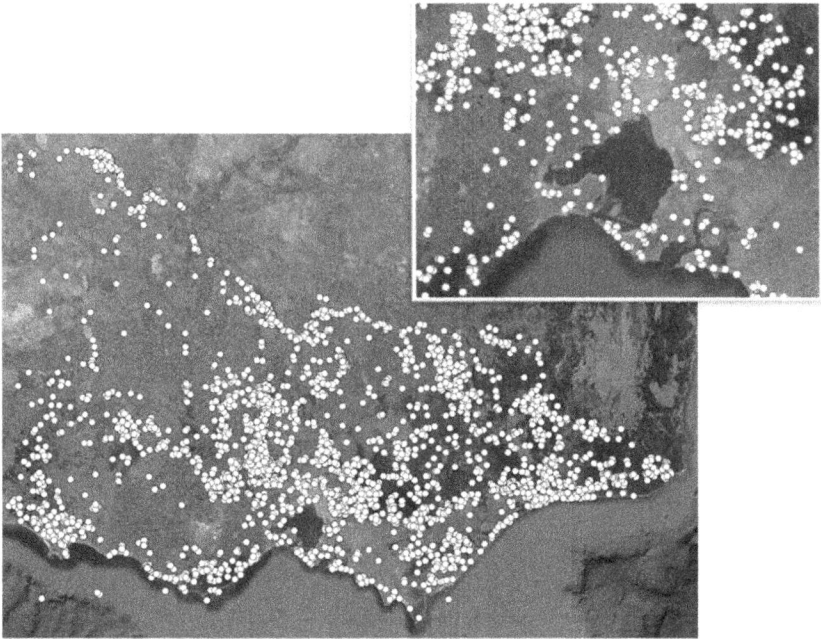

The location information contained within these datasets is reasonably detailed (although detail is not provided here), providing insight into the nature of various fire categorisations in Victoria. For example, clear differences can be observed between the location of fires categorised as malicious and those classed as caused by lightning. Malicious fires appear more often at the interface between urban or residential areas and bushland, where access roads also appear. Conversely, lightning fires appear heavily concentrated in the North-Eastern highlands and occur throughout inaccessible terrain in areas with no obvious access.

Despite the observed detail, however, there are again gaps and uncertainties in the data. For example, a few reported points are located outside the coastline in the ocean, highlighting that accuracy of some of the location data is potentially questionable. Further, there is little information available as to how agreement on the categorisation of ignition causes associated with each point has been reached and how this classification regime may have changed over time; is this by committee, consensus, on-ground reports, educated guess, or otherwise? While distinction might more easily be made between fires started maliciously and those started by lightning, distinction between those considered deliberately malicious or started by 'campfires', 'pipes, cigarettes or matches', 'burning off', or simply 'unknown' (which constitutes over 2,500 fires, alone), is less clear (see Figure 9.5 and also chapter 2).

Figure 9.5: Estimated location of all categories of fires recorded within the Victorian DELWP dataset.

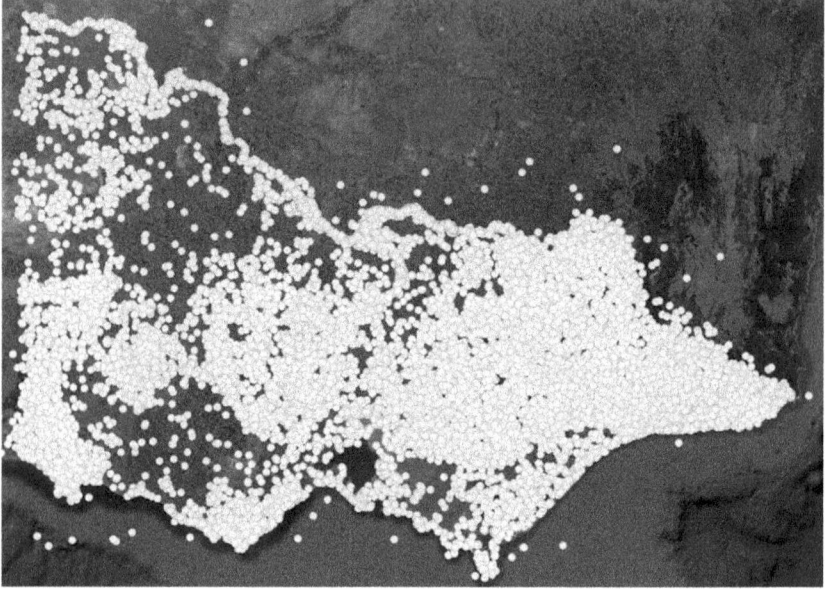

While DELWP data appears comprehensive in both its volume and nature, it is possible that further inconsistencies will occur when it is compared to data collected from the Country Fire Authority (CFA). This may in part be due to a record being kept of only those fires attended by each fire service organisation; thus, it is unclear what level of 'double-counting' may be present in the data. However, clarity is needed around this issue to enable data sets to be amalgamated and the causes of fire in Victoria to be better understood, as this is important information for priority setting for prevention responses. Given the likely disparities, it is uncertain whether, or how, these datasets could be merged or understood in a cohesive manner. This again clouds potential understanding of the nature and characteristics of fire in Victoria. Further, while we know that comparable CFA datasets exist, the process of gaining access to them for the purposes of comparison and interrogation is difficult and contrasts markedly with the open data policy of DELWP, above, leaving residents and communities who could benefit all the poorer.

Summary - bringing data related to people and places together

This information and maps provide an intriguing taste of what should be possible in the nascent age of big data and analytics. However, the collection and organisation of the data into useful structures is the key. A lack of data transparency, availability, consistency in approaches and data content in emergency services datasets is common internationally. It is not an exaggeration to say that the current state of data related to fire and firelighters (e.g. suspected or confirmed arsonists) contains sufficient gaps to make it virtually unusable as a resource for predicting or preventing fire in the future.

The lack of continuity present between data sources (Victoria Police, DELWP, CFA) and the different emphasis that each agency gives the data it holds - whether focused on people or places - significantly reduces the value of each data set. A fire data management strategy in Victoria for the future should seek to alleviate these issues. A dataset arbiter, overseeing the collection and linking of data collection and analysis between agencies could bring great value to any high fire-risk area, including Victoria, assisting to better target scarce resources, and identify and prevent the proliferation of firelighters and fire events that have scarred so much of the history of Victoria and the lives of Victorians. Such an effort is well within the grasp of current technology, data management, governance, and analytic means. At little cost it could be implemented almost immediately should inter-departmental will exist.

Our recommendations are, therefore, as follows:

1. A central fire data office should be established with a sole purpose of linking and coordinating the people and place data currently captured by each of the named agencies, and other organisations as appropriate (e.g., Metropolitan Fire Brigade, Department of Health and Human Services). This issue is discussed further in chapter 10.

2. The office should have the mandate to enforce the collection of fire-related data in a format that allows the linking of all incidents with police records and other person and incident-related data.

3. The place-based CFA and DELWP datasets should be merged and all collected data standardised in relation to the coding of ignition sources, heat sources, GIS location standards and all other fields.

4. The current LEAP dataset should be culled to reduce the presence of persons of interest, to those flagged from the dataset as having investigative priority.

Section 3:
The way forward

The last two chapters offer an overview of ideas about the place of prevention and governance arrangements and ideas about potential prevention programs. Chapter 10 sets out a broad overview of the position and role of prevention, while chapter 11 offers suggestions about prevention programs.

Chapter 10

A new approach to the prevention of wildfires

The severity of the wildfire problem

The severity of the wildfire problem is in large part about climate change. The World Economic Forum produces an annual *Global Risks Report* where it rates the economic, societal, geopolitical, technological and environmental threats according to the likelihood of occurrence and impact. The 2019 report has environmental risks dominant for the third year in a row. The top three risks that are thought most likely to happen are: 'extreme weather events', 'failure of climate change mitigation and adaptation', and 'major natural disasters'. The 'impact' risk-rated 'extreme weather events' as the second-highest risk, 'major natural disasters' as the fourth-highest risk and 'failure of climate change mitigation and adaptation' as fifth. The Intergovernmental Panel on Climate Change (IPCC) bluntly said in October 2018 that we have at most 12 years to make the drastic and unprecedented changes needed to prevent average global temperatures from rising beyond the Paris Agreement's 1.5°C target. The eminent climate scientist, Hansen (2018), writes that, with 2018 being another year of storms, fires and floods, the world is most clearly sleepwalking into catastrophe.

Jones (2010) documents the beginning of a scientific understanding of climate change. Back in 1824, Fourier said that the atmosphere maintained surface heat on Earth. By1896, the Swedish chemist, Arrhenius, had coined the name, 'the Greenhouse effect' and calculated the relationship between changes in carbon dioxide levels and atmospheric temperature. The issues about environmental problems were discussed beyond the scientific community, even early in the Industrial Revolution. Malthus (1766-1834) spoke about the limits to land supply and the reduction in food per capita as the population grew. Marx (1818-1883) wrote about the failure of modern capitalist economic systems due to their unsustainability, particularly in relation to environmental destruction (Pearce & Turner 1990). Early economic thought considered the role of the market, growth and resources, and many of these ideas have been re-introduced into contemporary environmental debates (Pearce & Turner 1990). However, mainstream economists held, and many still hold the view that unlimited growth is possible, given an efficiently functioning price system and free markets supported by technological change.

Bryson (2010) tells the story of the start of the oil rush. The drilling was undertaken as part of a search for a better illuminate than whale oil and kerosene squeezed from coal. Bissell formed the Pennsylvania Rock Oil Company and sent Drake out to search for oil. On 27 August 1859, one and a half years later, Drake and his men hit oil. Bryson goes on to say that "the first problem for the company was where to store all the oil they were producing. ...for the first few weeks they stored oil in bathtubs, washbasins, buckets and whatever else they could find. ...although no one appreciated it at the time, they had just changed the world completely and forever" (Bryson 2010, p.131). Similarly, electricity came into practical commission in September 1882 when Edison, who had laid fifteen miles of cable, switched on the lights in a whole street in New York (Bryson 2010). By 1900, electricity in cities in Westernised countries was increasingly the norm.

Towards the end of the 20th Century, a little more than 100 years later, in addition to improved living conditions for many, particularly in the Western world, severe adverse consequences of these discoveries had begun to be revealed and experienced. This is not an unusual pattern when new technologies are introduced. Many of these adverse consequences are associated with the rapid rise in GHGs. This problem is recognised only after many countries, and economic and societal structures and patterns of living had been locked into a dependency on non-renewable energy. But not all countries. Many people in non-industrialised[1] countries have not yet established a comprehensive dependency on fossil fuels. However, these countries are speeding rapidly towards this outcome. Ideological beliefs about 'progress' and a way of living in a 'developed economy' have become major blocks to actions to solve the problem of greenhouse gas emissions.

Overcoming path dependencies

Easter Island is famous for almost 900 giant stone figures, averaging 4 meters high and 13 tons weight, built by people who were master craftsmen and engineers. However, to achieve this, they totally denuded the island of trees, the native palm being used for constructing agricultural tools and aiding in

---

[1] This book refers to 'industrialised' and 'non-industrialised' rather than the more common terms, 'developed' and 'developing' and countries. This is to avoid the implicit value judgement that only countries that have adopted a Western style economy are 'developed'. In reality, a country may have a well-developed more traditional form of economy.

the transport of the Island's statues, leading to the downfall and collapse of the Easter Island society (de la Croix & Dottori 2008). It is worth quoting Wright's conclusion to his book on the historical loss of civilizations: "We are now at the stage when the Easter Islanders could still have halted the senseless cutting and carving, could have gathered the last trees' seeds to plant out of reach of the rats. We have the tools and the means to share resources, clean up pollution, dispense basic health care and birth control, set economic limits in line with natural ones. If we don't do these things now, while we prosper, we will never be able to do them when times get hard. Our fate will twist out of our hands. And this new century will not grow very old before we enter an age of chaos and collapse that will dwarf all the dark ages in our past" (Wright 2004 p. 132).

While there is still much to understand about both climate change and wildfires, fundamental knowledge is there, sufficient to understand the need for change. While additional knowledge will improve the nature and effectiveness of responses, the need for urgent responses is absolutely clear. Yet, like the Easter Islanders, insufficient action is being taken. Democratic systems tend to not be set up for the decisive and quick responses that are needed. Humans tend to interpret information within the context of their personal ideology, choosing and distorting the information so that it fits their belief systems and self-interest. Decisions are rarely made in a logical and reasoned way, there being multiple and complex factors which have created the failure to appropriately respond to date. These include issues such as political expediency, self-interest, partial knowledge, muddled thinking, fear of change and sectoral pressures, as well as highly resourced campaigns designed to misrepresent factual information.

Rifkin (2011) argues that much of our thinking is based on a historical paradigm. This served developed nations well in moving people to, and through the industrial revolution and the basis of energy that marked this change, coal-generated electricity. However, this thinking, which still pervades our dominant economic, business and management models, is now based on self-interest, competitiveness and power, fear of change, and in recent decades, rampant consumerism. Sukhdev (2012) talks about corporation 1920, which is still commonly operating today, where profits for shareholders and financial sustainability of the corporation are the business objectives.

Industrialisation, and the neo-liberal approach as an organisational framework, has been shown to be inadequate as a tool for the future (Alexander 2015). It is unclear how society is going to move to a different regime. Change will require an understanding that many of the issues that need to be resolved are systemic on an international scale and need to be solved by nations each playing their part. It will also require an awareness of value judgments or choices, with a recognition that there will be gains and losses in these choices. People in a privileged position need to share resources for the common good. Extensive change involves upheaval in existing systems to install new governance arrangements. However, solutions to these issues will need to be found if the threat of wildfires is to be reduced.

Pearce, an early pioneer in environmental economics, expressed the following view nearly three decades ago: "Maintaining temperatures to 2.5C above pre-industrial levels by 2030 would contain temperature increases to below the maximum temperature experienced during the last several million years in which human beings have been on the earth. To allow temperatures to rise above this level would, therefore, be to enter into a 'zone of ignorance' which lies outside human history" (Pearce et al. 1991, p.16). Such warnings are still being given: "Despite warnings over the last 30 years, we are still developing global infrastructures to extract every economically accessible ton of coal, barrel of conventional or shale/sand oil and cubic meter of natural gas and coal-seam gas" (UNEP 2011).

However, a turning point for the coal industry may be on the horizon. Quiggin (2019) (optimistically) believes that: "By 2030... most developed countries will have stopped using coal-fired power. The others will be moving fast in that direction. So far under President Trump, the United States has closed 50 coal-fired power stations and will almost certainly never build another". Unfortunately, this turning point may be slower in Australia. The Federal and Queensland governments are, in 2019, supporting the opening up of a major area in Queensland to coal mining. Unfortunately, Quiggin offers support to the nuclear industry as an alternative to fossil fuel. Moving from one environmental disaster to the potential occurrence of another is not the answer.

Without an urgent response to climate change, the conditions that exacerbate wildfires will only worsen, making a broader response to the prevention of wildfires, as propounded in this book, more critical. Reducing emissions is harder in the context of catastrophic fires. Climate change and wildfire interact and compound the problems in feedback loops (Meadows 1997). This can be seen in the permanent loss of permafrost in western Canadian permafrost peatlands over the past 30 years (Gibson et al. 2018). Rising temperatures melt the permafrost and wildfires have expanded this loss by 25%. The impact of permafrost thaw is one of the potentially most important biogeochemical feedbacks to anthropogenic climate change, through increasing the soil carbon dioxide respiration rate. Today, many of those seemingly far off concerns are becoming a reality, with sobering implications for the world population of nine billion by 2050 (UNEP 2011).

Thus, the need for action on climate change is both clear and urgent. Although the destructive impact of GHGs has been widely recognised for at least 40 years, the trend in growth in world GHG continues. The reasons for this are, as noted above, the difficulties in changing embedded behaviour. Also, many and complex reasons for inaction are bound up with ideology, value judgements, cultural practices, politics, past ways of thinking, habits, beliefs, competing agendas and ignorance. People are not necessarily always aware of the motivations behind their thinking and actions (Ison 2010). Beliefs, habits and ways of thinking have been formed over a lifetime and have become embedded in language, culture, society's structures and governance arrangements. Climate change, Klein argues, "is a civilizational wake-up call, a powerful message delivered in the language of fires, floods, storms, and droughts. Confronting it is no longer about changing the light bulbs. It's about changing the world—before the world changes so drastically that no one is safe. Either we leap—or we sink" (Klein 2014).

A new framework for the management of wildfire

Major change is needed

There is increasing recognition of the convergence of many serious challenges, including how to prevent wildfire, that requires new thinking and new solutions that will arise not from adjustments to business as usual, but from completely new approaches to the problem. The present commonly used approach to hazard management, with risk reduction being central to a chain of activity based on preparedness, response, rehabilitation and reconstruction, is discussed in chapter 5. This book argues for a modified approach but is not alone in this call. Sapountzaki and colleagues (2011, p.1447) describe the risk management chain as fragmented, "where information, knowledge, and policy actions run in parallel without any linkages, feedback, and mutual interactions", along with funding for the tasks. The lack of integration with spatial and land-use planning is said to be particularly concerning, as "in most hazard cases, inappropriate, absent, inadequate or poorly implemented spatial planning is related to the hazard causes (for instance arson and negligence as causes of forest fires are strongly related to urban sprawl and the uncontrolled development of WUI)" (Wildland-Urban Interface) (Sapountzaki et al. 2011, p.1447-8). This is not to say that single organisations responsible for a specific task, such as fire suppression, are not effective and responsive to new developments in their field of expertise.

Greece, Italy and Germany come in for criticism for fragmentation in the risk management chain (Sapountzaki et al. 2011). The countries are said to have top-down patterns of policymaking and implementation, with segregation of responsibilities and an administrative culture that impedes coordination, resulting in a culture of blaming (Sapountzaki et al. 2011). The

Lazio region in Italy is said to suffer from a separation between policy fields in terms of funding, legal aspects, and spatial planning. As a result, there risks the occurrence of double funding, under-funding and ineffectiveness, as well a lack of accountability.

Integration requires a response that understands the problem from a systems approach that cannot be provided by any single entity or sector operating on its own (Butcher et al. 2019). This is not likely to be a simple modification of the present approach to problem-solving, which is usually linear, deconstructionist, single discipline, risk-averse and has short term horizons. The approach needs to be strategic, long-term, seek solutions on multiple fronts, recognise the complexity and establish a planning framework of principles that define and structure the approach. The Victorian Bushfire Royal Commission Implementation Monitor (2012) also notes how large this task is. To share responsibility requires altering institutions, such as laws, regulations, workplace cultures or social expectations. Boundaries need to be broken down between agency-directed and community-based initiatives (McLennan & Handmer 2014, p.9). Management of this type of intervention also involves linking policies and programs between functional government departments, a task that has been found to be very difficult to achieve. Without a major change to intra-departmental processes, inter-government integration is not possible.

Butcher and colleagues (2019) believe that the traditional bureaucratic model of public administration is not up to the task of addressing complex social problems, as collaboration: needs time, effort, emotional energy and dedicated commitment and resourcing; can be unpredictable; requires a capacity to tolerate a lack of certainty; external legitimacy with stakeholders; and sustained confidence and goodwill with the executive and board. Finally, nimbleness and adaptability are needed to cope with on-going change. Buxton and colleagues (2011), in the context of wildfire, refer to Complex Systems Theory that is present in an environment of continuous change, uncertainty and non-linear associations (Folke et al. 2002). Ison (2010) believes that policymakers have not been able to rise to the challenge to date, despite 'wicked' problems being defined about 40 years ago.

While there are guides available about how to approach these issues, little is said about how and where to develop skills to undertake this approach and if current structures are in a form to enable such an approach to take place. System thinking requires reflective thinking. This entails a querying of assumptions and 'truths', holistic thinking about issues, understanding what can best be done about a situation, defining boundaries within which action can be undertaken, and understanding the trigger points and the positive and negative feedback loops. Because of the complex and interconnected nature of human, economic and natural systems, one particular impact or decision can lead to a chain of impacts, affecting several different sectors of society. Negative feedback loops provide an alert that something needs adjustment. A positive feedback loop expands the condition: growth, population, erosion, epidemics. Missing this feedback is a common source of system malfunction (Meadows 1997). Where there is a lack of transparency or information and public input about government decisions, this diminishes feedback about impact. As a particular change in circumstance can have a very different effect on different people and places, local knowledge and local planning is also very important to complement and enhance regional, state and national issues, thus combining high-level strategic perspectives and local interests.

Such major change is often described in the context of a transformative approach, rather than an ameliorative approach (Prilleltensky & Prilleltensky 2006). Transformational change is a growing field of work in academia that is more advanced in the European context. Prilleltensky & Prilleltensky understand a transitional approach to be ground in:

- Framing issues and problems around issues of power and problem solving

- Values placed in the foreground

- Multiple levels of analysis with collective wellbeing in the foreground

- A prevention focus

- The outcome aimed at enhanced wellbeing with power-sharing and equity in the foreground

- Intervention shares power and participation rather than being "expert-driven"

- Professional expertise provides empowerment, program development and evaluation, rather than seeing issues as technical matters.

To put this another way, transition can be viewed as changes in markets, user practices, policy, cultural discourses, and governance arrangements that support multiple actor interactions between firms, user groups, scientific communities, policymakers, social movements and special interest groups (Geels & Schot 2010, reported in Coenen, Benneworth & Trufferd 2012). As called for in many documents, such outcomes require a collaborative approach to wildfire management.

In talking about social innovation in general, Parés, Ospina and Subirats (2017) describe this as cooperative processes and practices that are based on citizen involvement, to improve existing solutions to social demands. As illustrated in Figure 10.1, this involves blurring boundaries between government, business and not-for-profits as well as civil society organizations. The process is disruptive in nature as it affects power, routine and beliefs embodied in basic routines, resources and authority flow of the existing management process (Ospina & Subirats 2017; Pelling 2010; Westley & Antadze 2010, referred to in Parés). Thus, transformation is a "confronting and challenging process" (O'Neill & Handmer 2010). Skinner (2010) talks of the need for the creation of an appropriate culture within organisations, particularly government, to enable innovation to facilitate complex processes around wicked problems. A collaborative environment offers people both the encouragement to take risks and support if the risks they took do not prove to be successful.

Figure 10.1: An integrated model for wildfire management.

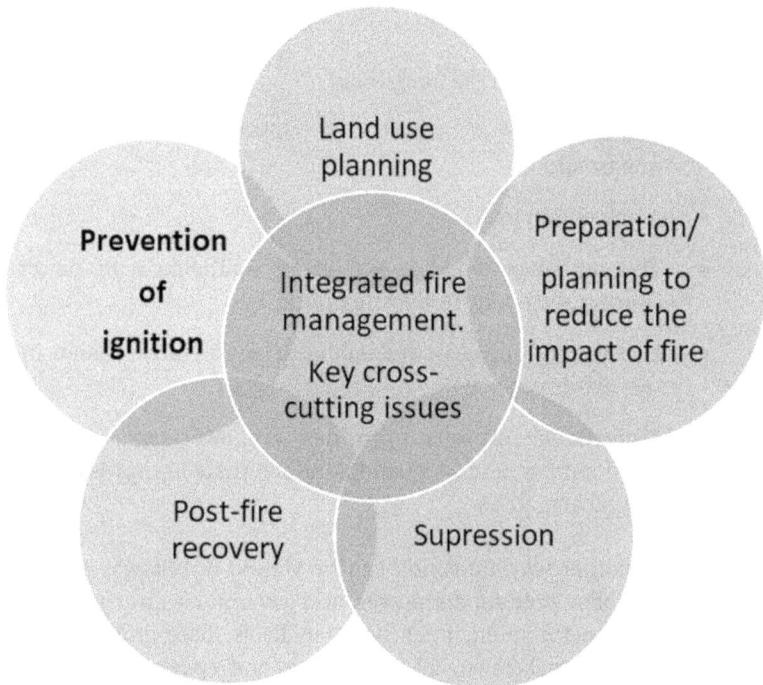

A new model

An integrated framework is suggested in Figure 10.1. It shows the range of activities that need to be undertaken to manage wildfire. These activities largely reflect those widely documented in the Sendai Framework and other major reports (see chapter 5). These are land-use planning; preparation and planning to reduce the impact of fire, including fuel reduction; fire suppression; post-fire recovery, and prevention of ignition. It is an integrated systems-based approach that brings together the five major work areas. This involves both vertical and horizontal connections that bring together multi-stakeholder engagement. However, what is commonly left out in this system of 5 groups of activities, is the prevention of wildfire, the authors of this book see prevention as a critical component.

The central area in Figure 10.1 deals with cross-cutting issues, central to all activities. It includes climate change mitigation; elucidation of the Strategic goals and outcomes, Tactical approaches or programs and the Operational sides of activities (STO) (discussed further below). It also addresses stakeholder role definitions and a new focus on the regions.

While each of these 5 activity areas is a system themselves, the rest of this chapter largely addresses this central integrating area that unites the activities and the prevention component of this model.

Cross-cutting issues for an integrated approach to wildfire management

Management integration

Complex systems are managed in many fields of business and sometimes in government by applying vertical and horizontal integration of governance. Vertical integration seeks to link decision-making through the hierarchical management levels, while horizontal integration links strategies and programs across departments, organisations and groups.

The vertical decision-making direction encompasses strategic, tactical, and operational processes, following the model referred to above, that was developed by Van de Velde (1999) in the transport field. However, this structure is now used in many settings. The decisions about strategic directions, including policy, cover the overall vision (such as, where do we want to be in five years' time?), and outcomes and values being sought in the line of work. The tactical level addresses the programs or services that will be needed in order to achieve the vision and policy goals, and the mix and coordination of programs. This task usually sits with middle management. The third component in the framework is the operational level, where the specific projects are managed, often at a local level, as actions arising from the strategic and tactical decisions. The timespan of decisions made becomes shorter as this moves from strategic, through tactical, to operational levels. The Moran Review (Commonwealth of Australia 2010) states that strategy requires having a vision over a decade or more, especially beyond the next election cycle, while operational planning is much more short-term.

In terms of the horizontal dimension, responsibilities, in relation to aspects of wildfire, fall within the jurisdiction of a variety of national, state, and local agencies. Multiple agencies are responsible for components of activity around wildfire, with malicious fires even more broadly. The breadth of those implicated (but rarely formally integrated in a governance structure) in wildfire issues can be seen in the following partial list: rural and metropolitan fire services, police services, law courts, correctional services, parole and rehabilitation services, forensic mental health services, schools, federal, state and local functional government departments, insurance companies, academic researchers and community members.

A properly integrated vertical and horizontal decision-making tree should result in the coordination of goals, leading to improvements in outcomes and efficiencies in the use of resources, as well as handling multiple objectives, trade-offs and uncertainty (Misni & Lee 2017). Organisational structures also appear to be not well integrated into strategic and tactical approaches; thus, there are difficulties in establishing desired outcomes, long-term plans, effective and efficient organisational structures to establish comprehensive and effective actions on the ground, including those targeting prevention (Buergelt & Smith 2015). The authors of this book believe that the wellbeing of society and the environment should not be viewed as trade-offs, but as fundamental outcomes being sought in any field of work.

Important, although rarely mentioned in the literature, is the reverse communication flows, where consideration is given to the effectiveness of the work program (Smith 2001). A review or evaluation should be undertaken in order to understand whether the operational projects are achieving the desired outcomes; whether the programs are successful and whether the program mix comprises the best options to achieve the strategic goals. This review should also consider whether the strategic goals are what is desired, or have circumstances changed since they were established, and the goals need to be modified (Misni & Lee 2017). Of course, financial flows will need to also be adjusted to reflect the respective successes of achieving the outcomes being sought. Such feedback should also result in adjustments to the system, where needed, to improve inclusion and decision-making across the stakeholders.

Vision, goals that form the strategic direction

A clear sense of direction, vision and goals, or the 'common good' for citizens, is a fundamental starting point to effectively tailor a comprehensive response to the activities illustrated in Figure 10.1, including the prevention of wildfire. Issues relating to sustainability and equity for subsequent generations means that considerable choices need to be made about the desired outcome goals. At present, in Australia, these strategic discussions are rare, especially with politicians and policymakers. Discussion is needed about the sort of life people would like; about the ideological basis and value judgments which form the basis of these choices; about the implications of these choices for individuals and society; and about what is possible given the present environmental and social global trends. The future can be shaped in particular directions if the types of choices and outcomes that are possible are made explicit, if people are given the opportunity to make choices, and if they believe that their choice will count. Prilleltensky & Prilleltensky (2006) state that value choices in politics and programs should be around self-determination, participation, responsiveness to the common good, support for community and social justice. Jackson (2009), along with many others, expresses a vision where the economy is not separated from society and the environment.

A strategic vision of a sustainable environmental, social and economic future is expressed in progressive cities like London, Vancouver and Freiburg (Stanley, Stanley & Hansen 2017). This vision is likely to have broad application to other fields, like wildfire management. The vision takes into consideration a balance between a healthy society, the environment and the economy, and provides guidance for future planning and action (Cuthill 2004). The outcomes include:

- increasing economic productivity, i.e. value from economic activity, rather than economic growth

- reducing the environmental footprint made by humans, and protect the natural environment and the rights of other species

- increasing social inclusion and wellbeing and reduce inequality

- improving health and safety outcomes

- promotion of intergenerational equity

- engaging the community widely as an essential ingredient in social sustainability and a matter of basic human rights

- implementing integrated governance arrangements

The last two points relate to processing goals. Setting clear objectives and time-bound achievements enables targets and associated costs to become transparent (Gough 2018).

In order to be successful, local communities need to participate in establishing a community vision and desired outcomes relevant to local stakeholder groups, as discussed in more detail in chapter 7. This might include the balance between the risk of fire and fuel reduction in the natural environment, the protection of highly valued areas of land, or how local decisions are made. Such an approach is advantageous as it can provide "a degree of mutual understanding and even ownership among the stakeholders" (Healey 1998, p. 14). Successful visioning can also help to develop shared leadership between elected officials and community members, and collaborative and consensus-building processes that actively engage citizens (Ayres et al. 1990; Ayres 2012; Cuthill 2004). The visioning exercise empowers the community in a bottom-up exercise; however, success will also be dependent on factors such as abilities, issues, time and resources available (Morse 1996). The exercise must find a balance between personal and common interests.

The inclusion of prevention in the wildfire management model

The barriers to wildfire prevention action

The barriers to action on the prevention of ignition of wildfires have been discussed throughout this book but are worth reiterating here. Despite the potential severity of the outcome of wildfires and the increasing risks they will pose to many people, societal structures, the environment and other species, there has been little coordinated strategic reflection of how best to prevent wildfires. As noted above, the Victorian Bushfire Royal Commission Implementation Monitor (2012) notes that the barriers to an improved approach to wildfire centre around problems in organisational culture, communication, coordination, interoperability, information collation and sharing. Issues that also relate to prevention approaches. Decision-making on wildfires tends to be often politically and ideologically framed. Within some organisations, the approach to fire management is based within a traditional male cultured hierarchical organisational structure. What is needed is an adaptive, flexible and inclusive organisation, which is also responsible for organisational tasks and decision-making beyond the emergency response (Australian Associated Press 2017; Blond 2010).

The present approach to the prevention of wildfire ignition has been summarised in this book as being small in scale, uncoordinated, lacking a comprehensive approach and rarely evaluated (Stanley & Read 2016). Despite the noted long-standing lack of attention on wildfire ignition (for example, Catry et al. 2009), the field remains hindered by a small and narrow approach to research. An exception to this has been a specialised body of research within the field of psychology over the past decade or so, which examines the characteristics and treatment of arsonists. More recent research on wildfire is heavily weighted towards fire suppression, particularly modelling fire movement, also a critical area where research is needed. Research on the prevention of wildfires has been greatly lacking in interest in the topic, including from academic journals, and research funders.

The field of prevention is severely hampered by poor data, as discussed in chapter 9. This is in part due to issues relating to data collection methods and the lack of inter-readability of data, but also due to a lack of accountability and transparency in some fire service agencies. While some data about fires is being collected by emergency response agencies, such as fire locations and the ignition target, some agencies share this information, while others choose not to make it available to the public or academics for research. It is argued that this information should be available as an integrated and shared data source across all agencies and stakeholders who have an interest in fire. In short, human started wildfires are poorly understood (Balch et al. 2017).

Learnings from the crime prevention sector

An important part of the prevention of ignition is the prevention of crime. The National Crime Prevention Framework was developed by the Australian Institute of Criminology (AIC), gathered from international standards, including the United Nations, as a resource which outlines the most effective approaches to the prevention of crime (undated). Effective crime prevention involves:

- strong and committed leadership at all levels
- collaboration between multiple stakeholders to address the wide-ranging causes of crime
- the application of research and evaluation findings targeted to areas of the greatest need and adapted to suit local conditions
- a focus on outcomes and measurable results
- implementing effective crime prevention policies and interventions
- promoting an active and engaged community, and being responsive to the diversity and changing nature of communities

- long-term commitment to achieving sustainable reductions in crime

- coordination across sectors to embed crime prevention into relevant social and economic policies, including education, employment, health, and housing policies, particularly those directed towards at-risk communities, children, families and youth

Such a framework around crime prevention needs to be embedded in governance and decision-making around the prevention of ignition of wildfires.

A prevention of wildfire model

While strong connections need to be made between the components or each of the activities in Figure 10.1, they also need to be viewed as separate systems, each with its own governance structure. Figure 10.2 offers a structure for the management and governance process that is specific to addressing the prevention of ignition. Such a step introduces a new approach commensurate with the importance of the issue. Innovation that is both disruptive and prompts a shift in public institutions and power relationships (Martínez 2011, reported in Parés, Ospina & Subirats 2017) is of particular importance to build and develop the field of prevention of wildfire. At times the problem needs to be solved, not by more or better governance, but with new forms and systems of governance. Such governance needs to examine issues from the present, to how to vision and plan for the future (European Union 2011). O'Neill & Handmer (2010, p.2) say that: "transformation calls for a re-evaluation of how people conceive of themselves and others in both their relationship with the environment, but also within wider political processes." The structure outline in 10.2 does not conform with existing administrative structures, such as local government; rather, it allows the many issues which cross boundaries to be addressed more easily.

The model in Figure 10.2 offers a means of joining up community decision-making and actions with higher policy initiatives and strategies. Such a system can emerge while the older systems are being adapted (Gualini, Mourato & Allegra 2016). While such a new system is likely to emerge through a place-based approach at the local level, it needs to be scaled-up and scaled-out. The placed-based organisation, Gippsland Arson Prevention Program (GAPP), referred to a number of times in this book, is probably a good example of a new model of operation piloted and proven in Victoria. It is one that is likely to be rolled out to other locations in Victoria, hopefully with a few adjustments. The model presented in Figure 10.2 is a possible framework for management and decision-making – one that could be modified according to local need and preference. Importantly, the model shifts much of the activities around prevention more to the local level. This is where the risk of ignition happens and needs to be addressed.

This approach to the prevention of ignition should be resourced by the Federal and State Governments. It would take the form of a public good, essential for societal wellbeing, where all people can gain access to the benefits arising from the activity.

Figure 10.2: New model tasked with the prevention of ignition of wildfire.

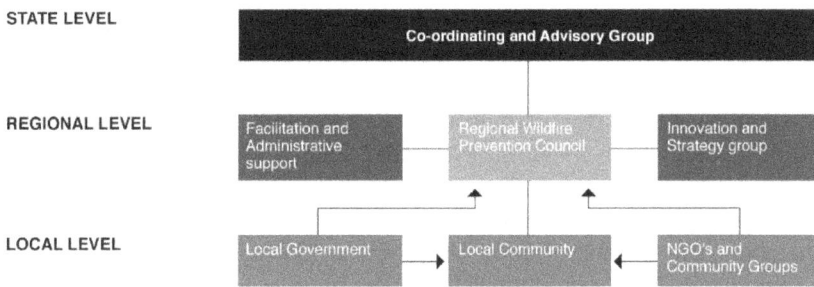

STATE LEVEL	Co-ordinating and Advisory Group		
REGIONAL LEVEL	Facilitation and Administrative support	Regional Wildfire Prevention Council	Innovation and Strategy group
LOCAL LEVEL	Local Government	Local Community	NGO's and Community Groups

Regional Wildfire Prevention Council

As can be seen in Figure 10.2, the coordinating body in each region is the Regional Wildfire Prevention Council, supported by an administrative support group and an innovation and research support group. The Regional Council would be comprised of representatives from each of the sectors. This Council would set priorities, co-ordinate approaches, secure resources and oversee progress at a regional level, working closely with state and local levels. The Council would have the role of facilitating public forums to discuss broad issues and principles around wildfire decisions. This would include issues such as the boundaries between personal freedoms and community protection, how we understand an 'acceptable' degree of risk, how do we know when a community is sufficiently 'resilient' to wildfires, should people be forced to move house if they are in a highly vulnerable area to wildfire, and who should pay the cost and/or compensation? As discussed by Eburn (2015), these decisions are political, and many of them are grounded in values. Informed decisions made through such discussion need to be accepted by all involved, even if they conflict with how the government would prioritise public safety (Eburn 2015). However, some decisions may need changes in government policy and Emergency Services and Local Government Legislation, changes that would need to be coordinated at the regional level by the state government, and perhaps the federal government, as discussed below.

A support Facilitation and Administration Group would act as a Secretariat for the Councils. This group would offer administration support, manage a website and communication strategy, and facilitate communication at state and local levels. An Innovation and Strategy Group, comprised of those with specialised knowledge, and researchers would bring forward new knowledge, technologies and developments, which will impact on, and facilitate the process.

Co-ordinating and Advisory Group

A state-based Co-ordinating and Advisory Group would assist the Regional Wildfire Prevention Council. Such a body would be independent of the government but have government representation in its membership. It would comprise representation from state government departments, business and the research sector. The Group would collect key learnings from the Regional Councils and feed these back to the State and Federal Government departments to allow for the adoption of this knowledge in policy and government programs. Such a group would offer information, coordination, direction, and targets for Local Government. The Group could also play a strong role in the review of the Planning Act in order to update the capacities of planning in the light of climate change. It could make representation and suggestions in relation to other legal agencies that will be involved with adaptation, such as the Victorian Civil and Administrative Appeals Tribunal. Other tasks would include clarifying and facilitating best practice on wildfire prevention and be a conduit of up-dated information. It would review and provide feedback to improve operational effectiveness and co-ordinate learning from other regional adaptation structures.

An important role of this state-level coordinating group would be to address issues beyond the local level, issues of state or national importance. This could be, for example, locations of high heritage value or of high conservation value, where the impact of decision-making has significance to many Australians. Local decisions would be coordinated with regional and national issues. It also may be that such an overarching body should set standards and targets to achieve in broad areas, such as levels of GHGs from fire. Such information should be fed up to the Federal Government.

Local Community level

Local responses would be coordinated and facilitated by a Local Community Group led by the community sector. These Groups would provide information, resources and a central organising and coordinating point for the community.

They would have an office and resourced administrative support as well as a secure operational budget. They would initiate and support projects responding to wildfire prevention and provide input into other points of decision-making. This would be a point of community capacity building, a knowledge centre and provide a means of addressing specific vulnerabilities.

It could be possible that the model for these Local Community Groups is a social enterprise. A social enterprise is a business with mainly social objectives whose surpluses are primarily re-invested in the business or community. The social enterprise will require management and administrative functions to perform its roles, perhaps through an arrangement with a suitably skilled local entity. Shareholders who are members of the local community and local community organisations own the social enterprise. The shareholders would select the Board, which should include a balance of people with requisite directorial skills and representation of key stakeholder groups.

The Local Community Group offers a centrally coordinated community hub, which will:

- coordinate a wildfire prevention plan and program

- raise, distribute and coordinate resources.

- provide an information service to advise regional residents/visitors of wildfire prevention needs and options

- provide assistance around prevention programs and activities

- monitor progress in the local community

- represent the community in other sector decision-making on wildfire prevention and other issues, such as emergency responses to extreme events

- understand particular vulnerabilities to wildfire and coordinate an approach to address these vulnerabilities

- provide leadership and volunteering opportunities

- possibly also provide job training

The Group brings together people who have the expertise with those who have the resources, time and desire to work towards change. It would assist those who have additional barriers to responding to wildfire prevention, such as unable to clear around their house due to disability. These centres are a point of coalescence for those who might otherwise be excluded. The community centre can receive financial resources to be spent through the members' democratic decisions, thus encouraging other community organisations to emerge resulting in "collective investment in chosen projects, through the exercise of community self-rule" (Jordon 2010, p.173). A successful trial of this type of community organisation is being undertaken in rural Victoria to coordinate and provide community transport (Wines et al. 2014).

Innovation and Strategy Group

Research and evaluation are fundamental to the successful application of prevention of wildfire processes and programs. While there has been little research undertaken on wildfire in general, there has been even less research on the role of humans in relation to wildfire (Muller 2009a). Ten years later, the lack of research was still identified in a recent Roundtable (Huhes 2019), particularly in areas such as different risks at different locations and local impacts; how prescribed burns can be undertaken in a way that protects ecological systems; and how to more effectively use resources, based on a broad perception of costs and benefits. The Innovation and Strategy Group would oversee and guide research and evaluation and recommend policy and programs to the prevention of ignition system.

An improved knowledge base is needed to enable better-targeted prevention responses. Assessment and referral pathways for youth firelighters have been developed in the UK, in the areas of health and education. Data sharing systems within fire services and to a lesser extent across country borders have been set up between some European countries. Arson prevention programs in Australia tend to draw material from the USA, a very different ecology and culture. Prevention should be built on a structured, evidence-based approach with clearly defined outcomes leading the development of a shared knowledge base, improved and uniform data collection, multi-disciplinary and cross-sector approaches and consideration of all parts of the system.

In addition, research has greatly fallen short in providing policymakers with knowledge on which to base good policy. Often policy has to be made on limited knowledge, not helped by the development of policy practice that now all too often assumes that, even where research is available, a theoretical and empirical basis for action is not necessary. Research and information are key elements of any decision-making process, especially when decisions are to be made under uncertainty. The failure to differentiate between areas requiring evidence and those requiring a value position, has been a major hurdle in the establishment of indicators and thresholds. The absence of research evidence on many areas has not helped this distinction, often resulting in ideological led action.

Resources to support the Innovation and Strategy Group would mainly come from the Federal and State Government, supported by business and philanthropic organisations. The benefit of good public service is traditionally difficult to measure, as there are incentives for people not to reveal the true value of the good to them (Stopher & Stanley 2014). The difficulties measuring prevention activities makes understanding benefit/cost even more difficult. However, the recent catastrophic wildfires in Australia should provide some level of benchmark of costs, if such measurement is undertaken comprehensively and over time.

Overview and conclusions

This book argues that the move to a risk management approach to wildfire, has led to a very narrow view, and it is argued, has led to a neglect of the prevention of ignition, by-passing this step and starting with the idea of how to reduce the intensity of wildfire, called mitigation. This book argues for a total re-thinking as to how wildfire is addressed. The task requires a whole of society response to wildfire prevention, one that joins in with fire services to better address the growing concerns about wildfire. As expounded in chapter 5, it is argued that integration of existing functional areas in government is needed, such as between land-use planning and emergency services, two of the authors currently researching the challenges around this for Australia. The effectiveness and impact of fire management need to be better understood, with the choices and trade-offs transparent and wide input into nuanced and localised decisions about this practice. There is a wide choice of opportunities that could, and should be, undertaken around prevention, especially in the context that the overwhelming proportion of fires that are started by people. There are a few small positive signs of change, with some evidence of a shift away from transactional governance (simply buying services) towards relational governance (participating more holistically and strategically in the solution of wicked problems) (Butcher et al. 2019).

Quay (2010, p.498) suggests that an anticipatory governance approach is needed for decision-making, particularly in a context of high uncertainty, such as with wildfire, where the current model of 'predict and plan' is only viable under stable and predictable futures. Anticipatory governance is described as a way to use foresight to reduce risk, using anticipation of the future through a wide range of scenarios based on risk assessments, creation of flexible adaptation strategies and monitoring and action. "Yet, for all that governments speak of partnership, networks, co-design, and collaboration in their formal communications and policy statements, there remains a palpable gap between the rhetoric and the reality" (Butcher et al. 2019, p. 76, referring to Butcher & Gilchrist 2016).

However, this approach is difficult to achieve, in a context of the many influences of how and why certain decisions are made, such as political expediency, and fails to discuss the externalities associated with decisions. Such an approach will mean changes at the personal, group, community, regional, national and international levels to achieve vertical integration (Ison 2017). This will also require a coordinated response at the strategic, tactical and operational levels, across functional areas and stakeholders to achieve horizontal integration. While this will also change practice across the response continuum of prevention, planning, emergency response and recovery, this book concentrates on the prevention of ignition dimension of wildfires. Developing better cooperation between stakeholder agencies will also not be easy. Agencies have their own particular responsibilities and organisational culture and priorities, making coordination of activities difficult.

Part of this is task is to be much clearer about terms and concepts, such as 'resilience', 'mitigation', 'natural hazards', 'fire suppression'. Clarification is needed as to whether a 'controlled' wildfire is being sustained as a 'prescribed burn' or is extinguishment the outcome being sought, and also whether the purpose of the fire is 'ecological' or to reduce fuel. Behind all this, there is an urgent need to improve data recording for consistency, transparency and to enable a broad understanding of fire metrics across sectors. Chapter 12 offers suggestions about the bundle of prevention tactics that could/should be undertaken to prevent wildfires.

Chapter 11

Prevention programs

Introduction

Chapter 10 gave an overview of a new governance model that could be used to understand, instigate and coordinate policies and programs to prevent wildfire ignition. This book has argued that the prevention of ignition has been largely overlooked internationally. Rather, there is a reliance on preventing the spread and intensity of a wildfire, and on the ability to suppress the fire, once ignited. It has argued that missing the first step, the prevention of ignition, results in higher costs, as the fire needs to be extinguished and the damage repaired. The costs are in terms of resources and outcome impacts on people, infrastructure, business and the environment. This is not to say that reducing the severity of a fire and being able to quickly put the wildfire out is not highly important, but these activities also have associated costs, which, it is argued, could be reduced if there was more focus on preventing ignition. As with much in life, decisions need to be made on both knowledge and value judgments. There is an urgent need for both these components in our approach to wildfire.

Internationally, there appears to be only a small proportion of possible prevention programs being utilised. This is likely to be due to a number of reasons outlined in this book and summarised here. Firstly, the impacts of climate change have occurred much faster than anticipated, resulting in a rapid increase in the frequency and severity of wildfires, compared to what was, until recently, 'normal'. Secondly, there is a lack of recognition of the human role in wildfire ignition, in part due to a very narrow disciplinary approach taken in relation to wildfire. This narrow view has been exacerbated by path dependency, where 'solutions' to wildfire were mainly seen as about controlling the fire (mitigation and suppression), tasks undertaken by the services within a country that specialise in suppressing fire.

Thirdly, other sectors, such as academia, government departments, business, non-government organisations and the community, have largely not engaged in issues around wildfire, although this currently seems to be slowly changing as the wildfire situation worsens. This narrow approach may be partly due to a reluctance by fire services to engage more widely. There tends to be a dominant culture associated with fire services, based on a hierarchical command structure, with a largely traditional male culture predominating.

While such a structure is likely to be important for firefighting activities, it also acts as a barrier to other increasingly important ways of operating, such as involving the community in decision-making. Fourthly, there are strong re-enforcements that act against change in ways of operating. Path dependency is discussed in chapter 10. There may be many benefits to an individual that arise from local fire-brigade membership. There are few opportunities that society offers for men to belong to a community organisation, with accompanying social capital and friendships. However, additional complications may arise when such an organisation also has to deal with authority issues, emergencies, trauma and associated high feelings from the community, at times leading to hero status.

Fifthly, dealing with wildfire, and especially prevention, is a highly complex process. Often it is easier to simplify the process by narrowing the aspects to a manageable level. This is especially so when the input and support from a range of organisations are not embedded in the governance and decision-making process. Success in fire prevention needs to involve multiple approaches, arising from wide-ranging participation, implying the need to have good governance, resources and knowledge, as well as open discussion about choices of actions and value judgements. While the need for this approach is largely acknowledged in some countries, it is difficult to put in place in practice, requiring the willingness to undergo considerable changes. Sixth, messages to the public tend to be through the media, often with a common portrayal of crisis, heightened emotions and tragedy, rather than in the form of constructive advice about prevention. Finally, the fire services respond in the way they know how and where their expertise lies – in a fire, rather than broadening their approach to respond to the many complexities of the prevention of wildfire.

A comprehensive approach

This chapter provides suggestions about prevention policies and programs that could be utilised in relation to wildfire. It is organised around the causes of wildfire ignition, and how these causes can be targeted as a means of reducing the likelihood of ignition. It is important to note that this overview is only the beginning of a journey that needs to be based on considerably more research and evaluation of the effectiveness of particular projects, and the best combination of projects to achieve the best possible outcomes. As Doley and colleagues (2011) state, identification of risk factors for fire lighting is in its infancy. Similarly, it could be added, is the approach to the prevention of recklessly lit and accidental fires.

The nature of the prevention approaches suggests there will be wide variation in how quickly impacts will take effect, as a mix of long, medium and shorter-term approaches are required. Similarly, projects need to be at vastly different scales and initiated by a wide range of agencies and people, from international, to local small site approaches. There is a need for proximate and distal approaches (Weatherburn 2001). Distal causes may reflect background pre-dispositions, such as the person experienced child abuse and neglect, while proximate causes may be the immediate encouragement of a peer group to commit the crime. Similarly, some approaches will address factors that increase the risk that a crime of wildfire ignition will occur, such as removing a dumped car, while other approaches will directly target those who have shown a propensity to light fires, in order to deter them from repeating this crime (Weatherburn 2001). However, even this is complicated further, due to the range of typologies of people who have a propensity to light wildfires, as illustrated in chapter 3 of this book. Not all people will respond to a prevention program in the same way (Andresen 2014). For example, surveillance based on personal contact and reminding a potential firelighter that they are being watched may actually increase the chance of fire lighting. The person may be reminded of their behaviour and perhaps pick up a tacit message that they are defined as a firelighter, so fulfil expectations.

The authors suggest that the process and governance arrangements outlined in chapter 10 are critical for understanding the total picture, in terms of the ability to undertake a wide approach to prevention policies and programs and evaluate what works best, why, and where. Disciplines covering the reasons for fire lighting cover the fields of psychology, criminology and sociology, all with strong implications for integrative disciplines, such as planning, social work, economics and geography. Psychology seeks to understand personal behaviour; criminology often considers the opportunity for crime; sociology considers societal structures. All of these issues could be said to be part of the causes of ignition. Thus, a network of programs will be needed, that cover the range of prevention approaches, primary, secondary and tertiary.

The Australian Institute of Criminology, in the National Crime Prevention Framework, developed for the Australian and New Zealand Crime Prevention Senior Officers' Group, calls for an integrative approach. It states that: "programs that have been shown to be effective in reducing recidivism depend upon the close cooperation between agencies within the criminal justice system and those agencies outside it, including a range of government agencies responsible for housing, health and education, non-government service providers, local industry and the community" (Australian Institute of Criminology undated, p. 8).

The Prevention Framework nominates the requirements for effective crime prevention and the establishment of protective factors through:

1. Addressing the environmental conditions that promote and sustain crime. This includes both situational approaches and broader planning initiatives by designing and modifying the physical environment to reduce the opportunities for crime to occur.

2. Eliminating risk factors and enhancing protective factors to reduce the likelihood that individuals will engage in offending behaviour. This includes intervening early in critical transition points in a person's development to address those factors that may lead them on a pathway to future involvement in crime.

3. Strengthening communities by addressing social exclusion and promoting community cohesiveness. Aspects of social exclusion, including neighbourhood disadvantage, unemployment, intergenerational disadvantage, limited education prospects, poor child health and wellbeing and homelessness, are important to understand.

4. Enhancing the capacity of criminal justice agencies to prevent crime and reoffending.

However, this framework fails to look at the personal reasons for committing the crime that may be instrumental or expressive. Thus, a person who illegally lights a wildfire may do so to achieve a purpose, such as destroying evidence of another crime. Alternatively, they may be responding to an emotional need, that is created by mental illness, or a desire to belong to a group with high esteem, or some other personal reason. Wildfire prevention programs can also be targeted to improve the expression of these personal causes of ignition.

Prevention of wildfire ignition

As discussed in this book, the causes of wildfire ignition can broadly be classified into three categories: natural, accidental and malicious, although as already noted, there is an overlap between these areas. This section gives an indication of some possible prevention of ignition responses that could be utilised. Here again, local knowledge is vital. The full range of possible prevention actions, their respective cost, viability and potential effectiveness, need to be workshopped at the local level. This should lead to the establishment of priorities, and the introduction of an associated implementation, monitoring and evaluation plan. This process does not require re-inventing the wheel as a substantial number of ignitions are criminal events, and many of these may be preventable using the knowledge that has traditionally been applied to other crime (Muller 2009a). Again, although straying into mitigation, the risk of wildfire has been exacerbated in many countries (Spain, China, Brazil, etc.) through the planting of Australian eucalypts, a species that is highly fire-prone. Removal of these plantations, replacing them with the indigenous slower-growing species that are more fire-adapted, would reduce fire risk.

Natural ignition

Following the discussion in this book, natural causes of ignition largely refer to lightning, but could also refer to less common causes, such as a volcanic eruption and ignition in rubbish dumps etc. While prevention does not appear to be an option for volcanic events, research suggests that some lightning events may be related to climate change, with lightning predicted to increase with temperature increases. This is especially so where lightning and a dry storm is involved, also likely to be linked with climate change due to changes in rainfall patterns. Clearly, policy to reduce GHG emissions is a vital prevention policy to reduce the increase in lightning strikes and thus potential wildfire ignitions. Humans are also involved in the association between lightning and wildfire. Repeated prescribed burning is changing the make-up of some ecological systems, changing the dominant vegetation, such as mountain ash forests in Australia, to smaller scrub vegetation which has greater flammability. Thus, in some situations, the forest is more likely to ignite following a lightning strike.

While this strays from the causes of ignition towards a risk reduction approach, the policy adopted in the USA and Russia of extinguishing lightning or human wildfire ignition in a remote area by immediate suppression from the air could be a more effective approach than exclusively relying on environmental modification. Those that undertake this work are called 'rappelers' (Fowlkes 2019). There are 13 rappel crews in the USA, particularly concentrated in the Pacific Northwest. They respond quickly, being able to be in the air within 10 minutes of a call, seeking to extinguish the fire before it spreads. The firefighters rappel about 200 to 300 feet from a helicopter to extinguish the fire. They may be supported by ground crews. Crews in the USA also undertake routine smoke searches over forests. Alternatively, some firefighters are parachuted into a forest fire, then supplied by parachute with food, water, and firefighting tools, allowing self-sufficiency for 48 hours. This response to suppression is more widely used in Russia, with 4,000 'smoke jumpers' from 340 bases. This may be the only form of firefighting over 800 million hectares (2 billion acres) of forests (Hodges 2019). They may be supported by local firefighters in more populated areas and also rappelers from helicopters. Improved surveillance in general, such as fire towers and cameras, would facilitate a quicker response to fires in forested areas.

Maliciously lit wildfires

As discussed in chapter 2, there is no agreed international perspective on the extent of malicious fire lighting. This is in large part due to the inconsistent and incomplete data collections by fire and other emergency services agencies. This has exacerbated the problem of the low number of malicious wildfire lighters apprehended. In turn, this has narrowed the present knowledge base of criminal firelighters, with a reliance on the characteristics of institutionalised offenders (Ellis, Kanowski & Whelan 2004; Muller 2009a). Improved knowledge and processes are vital to the success of prevention of malicious fire lighting. Until this happens, prevention-based on situational and community crime prevention approaches in local areas are likely to be more successful. This should also include process improvements, all linked to coordination in approach, as discussed in chapters 4 and 10, such as the provision of information to other services when known arsonists or suspected firelighters travel or move interstate (Ellis, Kanowski & Whelan 2004).

Gannon and colleagues (2012) have developed a Multi-Trajectory Theory of Adult Firesetting[1] that examines why an adult with associated mental health problems may wish to light a fire. The theory is largely targeted towards treatment once the person is apprehended (see chapter 3). While it is noted that there are many types of behaviours that may lead to fire lighting, Gannon and colleagues offer four key overarching psychological vulnerabilities likely to be associated with what they call firesetting:

- Inappropriate fire interest/scripts

- Offence-supportive cognition or general criminal sentiments that may support fire lighting, self/emotional regulation issues or poor coping or emotional responses, problem-solving or impulsivity

- Communication problems, such as social skills issues, emotional loneliness, and low assertiveness

These psychological vulnerabilities arise from the person's aetiology or up-bringing. The propensity to light a fire is influenced by proximal and triggering factors, such as life events, contextual factors, internal affect/cognition, biology

---

[1] Firesetting refers to "any problematic act of setting fire to property, including the natural environment, outside accepted social and cultural boundaries" (Doley, Dickens & Gannon (2016, p.1). This definition does not include 'accidental' fires.

and culture, as well as being influenced by any moderating factors, particularly mental health and self-esteem.

This theory is a major contribution towards understanding the psychological predisposition and circumstances relating to an adult who has a propensity to light fires. It is important for understanding an effective treatment approach that may be offered to an apprehended or self-referred firelighter. However, the purpose is a little different to what is being sought in this book, which endeavours to understand how to prevent fires being lit. Thus, the model needs to be broadened to enable a full suite of activities/programs that may deter/prevent the person lighting a wildfire. This model would also include issues external to the person. These include environmental/spatial or local influences that may make it easier or more difficult to light the fire, triggering factors external to the person, such as group influences and other protective factors, such as a source of support. It is the contextual interaction with a person's vulnerabilities that risks leading to fire lighting, or not. However, when the central concern is the prevention of fire lighting, then if the context or environment can reduce the fire lighting risks, then these issues are important when addressing issues from a wildfire, rather than a person perspective. Prevention approaches may address more than one of the dimensions discussed here, so may not sit neatly into one of the risk categories. This is especially so when the local community becomes more deeply involved in prevention.

Primary prevention

Brantingham and Faust (1976) list the following as general primary crime prevention approaches:

- General social and physical wellbeing programs
- Environmental design
- Crime prevention education

The authors of this book are of the view that prevention programs that address disadvantage need to be much broader than just targeting individuals, as implied in the first dot point, above. As noted in chapter 4, research has shown that on the fringe of major cities in Australia and around rural settlements it is the lag in infrastructure services that are contributing to reduced opportunities to earn income and secure social inclusion. Other primary prevention programs should centre on child development, and the prevention of child abuse and neglect, support structures for struggling families, and building community supports to achieve healthy, inclusive, vibrant communities. The initiation of a broad change in communities and the subsequent impacts on people are likely to have a long timeline, thus needing a long-term plan. Community change is closely associated with an urban and spatial planning approach. The following discusses some of these in more detail. Building infrastructure and other environmental changes, as well as support and welfare programs in disadvantaged neighbourhoods, should assist in improving opportunities and wellbeing for residents. This is likely to reduce the risk of anti-social behaviour, including wildfire lighting. Australia has a large population of youth who are unemployed, under-employed and disengaged from education and employment (see chapter 4). The most common age-group for fire lighting is youth. Many youths live in the outer suburbs of large cities and rural settlements where there are fewer job opportunities, very poor public transport and fewer services, as well as being close to bush and grasslands. Reducing the risk of such 'forgotten' youth engaging in troublesome behaviours, including a chance some will engage in fire lighting, needs to be urgently addressed.

Early intervention and prevention of child abuse and neglect

A common finding in research looking at the characteristics of youth who engage in malicious fire lighting is a background of child abuse and neglect and an associated tendency towards engagement in fire lighting activities (Stanley 2002). In many countries, the services to address this are insufficient, and many children are left experiencing an abusive environment, which may lead to consequent disturbed behaviour (Stanley & Goddard 2002). It is vital, for many reasons, that services that prevent child abuse and neglect are widely spread and shown to be effective.

Improving infrastructure, services and transport

The risk of becoming involved in crime, or being victimised, is greater in those communities that experience high levels of social exclusion or a lack of social cohesion. There is also growing recognition of the importance of addressing social exclusion (deprivation, disadvantage and limited access to services) and assisting disadvantaged groups to reduce their risk of involvement in crime (Andresen 2014; Brain, Stanley & Stanley 2018; Nicolopoulos 1997; Prestemon & Butry 2005). Aspects of social exclusion, including neighbourhood disadvantage, unemployment, intergenerational disadvantage, limited education prospects, poor child health and wellbeing, and homelessness, are said to be among the strongest predictors of adolescent aggression, delinquent behaviour and a range of negative long-term outcomes (Andresen 2014).

Further research into the effectiveness of community-based primary prevention programs in achieving long-term reductions in crime, is required. However, Andresen (2014) notes that programs that aim to address social exclusion and cohesion are likely to be more successful when they:

- identify communities in need, based on evidence and community consultation, and analysis of factors that may contribute to social disadvantage or exclusion

- increase opportunities to participate and promote community involvement and consultation in program design and decision-making

- encourage representation from diverse groups, particularly those community members most at risk of being marginalised

- coordinate efforts between agencies across government and non-government sectors to target multiple areas of disadvantage, supported by neighbourhood regeneration

- are provided with ongoing human, financial and physical resources and

- regularly review progress to ensure that initiatives remain on track

The research reported in chapter 4 found that accessibility to meet major needs, such as education and work, is very important for good outcomes, an emphasis on facilitating public and active transport, aligned with good spatial planning and density to support the financial viability to build infrastructure, is very important. Thus, spatial planning needs to play a far more important role than it does now in many countries. As an aside, it is interesting to note the association between fire lighting and a shortage of affordable housing and homelessness in California. One of the recent fires in California was ignited from an open fire in a homeless camp in a forest.

Crime prevention through environmental design

Newman (1972) wrote of how crime could be prevented by reducing the opportunities for crime through the design of the built, street layout, and landscaped environment. He believed that site design could facilitate natural surveillance. Design can facilitate the presence of people who can watch what is happening, especially where there are open spaces and good street lighting. Thus, the potential offender is likely to be aware that people feel a sense of belonging to their community and could be watching their activity. This gives cues to the potential offender that the area is not conducive to criminal behaviour (Newman 1972). Much of this thinking is based on the work of Jacobs (1961), who was critical of urban planning that leads to the decline of neighbourhoods which then leads to barriers in human interaction. This approach is linked to work done on situational crime prevention, and also where a strong sense of community is present, both discussed further, below. It is more likely to be effective where malicious fires are lit in a more urban setting or on the fringe of settlements.

Strengthen the opportunities for informal networks, social capital and support structures

Community development programs that focus on strengthening informal networks and enhancing community structures have the potential to build community capacity, which can, in turn, provide opportunities to mobilise communities to address local crime problems. This was discussed in chapter 7. The imperative task of preventing wildfires can only be effectively achieved if the community plays a far more central role in many activities on the ground (Carpenter et al. 2012; Stanley & Read 2016). Carpenter and colleagues (2012) note that people in isolation have their limits in bringing about change, while collectively a lot more can be achieved, especially where there is an inspirational leader. This is especially so when the firelighter comes from the same community. The international organisation, Crime Stoppers, uses the understanding that a community, especially one in a rural setting, is likely to know who is at risk of fire lighting. There needs to be opportunities to draw on local knowledge and increase the involvement of communities in prevention programs that are based on strong two-way communication (Howes et al. 2013). A more distributed and participatory approach to normative decision-making would also assist in the implementation and adoption of local decisions because of local buy-in and commitment.

Success has been reported with community reporting of suspected malicious or unlawful fire lighting in Western Australia (Plucinski 2014). The strategy involves informing the community of the level of malicious fire lighting in their area and encouraging reporting of suspicious behaviour to Crime Stoppers. There is widespread involvement of the messaging about this, with door knocks, shopping centre displays and school visits. The program appears to have been successful. The number of wildfires dropped from 45 to 4 in the same period in successive years in one area. In another area, the number of deliberately lit fires dropped from 123 in December 2001 to 49 in December 2002. This approach was particularly effective with malicious and suspicious wildfires, use of cutting and welding machines, and use of matches or lighters.

Unfortunately, the loss of the idea of a neighbourhood, through car travel and structures such as large shopping developments, has reduced the protective qualities of the community (Andresen 2014). Thus, the watchful eye over the activities of local youth, by neighbours and community members may have broken down in some locations. However, policies that keep the prevention of fire lighting in mind can use design, as discussed above, to build spaces and structures that attract youth, keep them busy, take advantage of community surveillance and offer non-criminal activities as the optimum choice.

Urban planning to reduce the risk of ignition in the rural/urban interface areas

Much of the discussion of possible prevention of fire lighting approaches have good spatial and land planning as a fundamental structure. Chapter 6 discusses the role of local government, pointing out the siloed approaches between emergency services and urban and land-use planning. This has occurred despite the spatial patterns that can be found internationally in wildfire ignitions, discussed in chapter 5. It is clear that a major danger area for ignition can be found in the rural/urban interface, where housing spreads into new urban developments in what was often farming areas, or where people build close to a forest setting for lifestyle reasons.

The risk of wildfire now suggests that urban planning needs to give much stronger attention to the positioning of land releases and how these are established. Improving opportunities for 'a good life' in outer fringe suburbs, discouraging peri-urban development, establishing both a hard urban boundary, as well as densification policies to absorb extra population, are important ways to reduce the risk of wildfire ignition. This is a planning issue, one that is not being adequately addressed in Australia and in other areas experiencing severe fires, such as Southern Europe and the USA.

Llausàs, Buxton and Bellin (2016) point out that there is no current planning that encompasses a clear, unified and strategic vision about how to address future challenges, an issue also pointed out by a number of authors (see Buxton et al. 2006; McKenzie 1997; Millar 2010). Instead of a collective approach that plans a spatial area and coordinates this planning with bordering spatial areas, there is an individual approach to permit applications that results in ad hoc outcomes and land use. Such an approach is less able to anticipate and cater for long-term needs and the improvement of adaptive capacity for a changing environment (Llausàs, Buxton & Bellin 2016). Stronger planning legislation is needed to restrict new buildings in high fire danger locations. However, difficulties are created by the complexity of the planning system together with data limitations and availability, that can complicate decision-making and increases the risk of litigation. Planners need to give stronger adherence to planning overlays, such as wildfire and vegetation overlays in Victoria. A recent example in Victoria, where the wildfire overlay rated an area as at extreme risk of a catastrophic wildfire that is almost certain to occur, was apparently ignored. A major tourist development was built, that has resulted in a large increase in numbers of people in the area, with associated fire risk (Stanley 2015b).

Information about dangers

While information about potentially risky behaviour in relation to the ignition of wildfires is largely relevant to accidental or reckless fires, some information-based programs may lead to a reduction in the risk of malicious fire lighting. However, such communication would need to be undertaken carefully, so as to not encourage the reverse effect, that increases the person's excitement about fire and desire to light a fire. Knowledge about the risk of fire could be embedded in school subjects, such as in science classes. Such content could include information about the consequences of wildfire, and a safe and confidential way concerns could be reported to the school. Of course, such messaging is not likely to be successful unless pathways to address the identified concerns accompany the program. This particularly relates to intervention options for people with a desire to light fires. Such options are limited in Victoria, and their absence can deter people from reporting such behaviour, especially where they personally know the offender (Read & Stanley 2017).

Secondary prevention

Secondary prevention measures target specific situations and people where there is believed to be some element of risk. Brantingham and Faust (1976) note that secondary prevention approaches generally have a short to medium time span to take effect, but there may be blurring between the form of primary and secondary prevention approaches.

Situational crime prevention

Situational crime prevention involves altering the circumstances which are more conducive to a crime being committed in a particular location. Such approaches are commonly undertaken in a crime hot spot area. Thus, situational crime prevention seeks to reduce repeat episodes of crime where crime has already occurred. Cornish and Clark (2003, p.90) give a useful summary of actions that can be taken. Addressing each of these components should reduce the incidence of fire lighting, as malicious fire lighting is often patterned in terms of geography and time (see chapter 4). A summary of possible ways to increase the 'guardianship' is to:

- Increase the effort for the firelighter, e.g. preventing easy access to a vulnerable site, forested areas behind a school or in national parks on high fire danger days

- Increase the risk they will be caught, e.g. increasing surveillance through the obvious use of cameras and increase lighting on the site, as well as car patrols

- Reduce the rewards for undertaking the fire lighting, e.g. reduce the presentation of 'hero status' for firefighting

- Reduce provocations that may lead to criminal behaviour, e.g. facilitate education and employment for unemployed youth, as well as pro-social recreational options

- Remove excuses, e.g. reduce rubbish piles and dumped cars, widely advertise fire bans and in multiple languages

In some areas, it may be difficult to undertake situational crime prevention, especially in more isolated locations. There needs to be careful examination of situational crime prevention; that it is actually preventing crime, rather than just moving it elsewhere. Roads allow access to potential firelighters who commonly undertake their activity away from visibility and/or seek a place where they believe the fire is more likely to ignite and perhaps the fire may not be discovered immediately. However, roads are a conundrum, as they are necessary to provide access to fire trucks to allow suppression of fires but may also allow access to a firelighter. Christensen (2008) suggests that there are options to reduce the risk of access points. This includes the use of locked gates, establishing areas that can be used for recreational purposes, and removing sharp curves in tracks, thus increasing long-distance visibility. There is an increasing range of emerging crime and safety surveillance methods available (e.g. number plate recognition software), which may assist in deterring and apprehending offenders. Patrolling may be undertaken from cars and also from aircraft and drones, as is the policy with some forestry companies. Police resources employed in areas at greatest risk of malicious fire lighting, even when not targeting particular persons, have been shown to be effective (Prestemon & Butry 2005). Muller (2009a) writes of 'the 4pm grassfire'. Local knowledge needs to be documented so it is not lost with personnel change.

A National Arson Prevention Symposium was held in Melbourne in 2010 (Stanley & Kestin 2010). One of the workshops, reported by Cozens and Christensen (2011), undertook a discussion on what might be the more successful situational strategies to reduce the occurrence of wildfire arson.

Many of the strategies listed above were discussed. The most commonly suggested approach was signage providing information about illegal behaviour, damage, risk and warnings, including notices in other languages for non-English speakers (Cozens & Christensen 2011). Additional suggestions by the workshop included:

- limiting access for children to fire lighting products, however, this may be difficult

- removing dumped cars and rubbish, as well as derelict structures, a common practice now

- increased use of fire hot spots by community groups

- partnership with Neighbourhood Watch or Forest Watch groups

- creating a feeling of community ownership of the area, perhaps naming the area after the community

Greater involvement of the community in prevention

The community is a large under-utilised resource. There has been talk since the 2009 Victorian Bushfires Royal Commission of 'shared responsibility' and 'community engagement', but this approach has rarely been put into practice (National Emergency Management Committee 2011; Teague, McLeod & Pascoe 2010). There are many opportunities for preventative action here, which need to be accompanied by the community gaining decision-making capacities, resources and power-sharing. Anonymous reporting of a suspicion of reckless or malicious fire lighting, available through Crime Stoppers, is a very powerful process. However, our research has shown that some members of the public are reluctant to report due to lack of knowledge of fire lighting behaviours, and risks and uncertainty of the reason for the suspect's behaviour (Read 2015). Increased education of the public around the arson event, about the reporting process and addressing other identified barriers to reporting, would increase the reporting response to Crime Stoppers.

An important way of granting more responsibility and decision-making to the community is through a program such as the Gippsland Arson Prevention Program (GAPP). In this place-based model, emergency services, local business, a large forestry company and local government collaboratively undertake measures to prevent malicious fires. This is done through information campaigns, managing hot spots for fires and organised car patrols on high fire danger days, as well as sharing resources and information between the organisations. The first recommendation in the report from the Parliament of Victoria (2017) on preparation for wildfire was to provide additional support to

GAPP and establish programs of this type in other wildfire-prone areas, that involved both the community and government agencies.

Dumped cars

As noted above, the rapid removal of dumped cars is an important prevention activity, due to the frequency of fires lit in these vehicles. This needs to be undertaken quickly, as most ignition of dumped cars occurs within 24 hours of their abandonment (Ransom 2007). Measures that reduce car theft, and reducing the likelihood of abandonment of cars, such as free car removals, are important ways to reduce malicious burning of vehicles (Muller 2009a).

Media and copycat fires

As with the paucity of research on malicious fire lighting in general, the impact of media on fire lighting remains a topic needing considerable work. Based on the media impact on other crimes, it is likely that aspects of the media encourage fire lighting for some people. The association between media reports of suicide and copycat attempts is well established, such that much of media now does not report suicides (Doley, Ferguson & Surette 2013; Surette 2011). The Royal Australian & New Zealand College of Psychiatrists (2019) alerts the media that: "certain ways of reporting and discussing suicide can alienate members of the community, sensationalise the issue or inadvertently glamorise suicide", a position that could well be taken in relation to wildfire ignition. Research has shown that children learn behaviours and values from the media (Surette 2002). The association between exposure to media crime content and criminal behaviour is often instructional, with the media functioning as crime catalysts (Doley, Ferguson & Surette 2013).

This influence comes from media generally, as well as news coverage, and films and videos. For example, a 20-year-old Rural Fire Service volunteer was described in a national Australian paper as "raised on a diet of action movies". He had a "longstanding desire to emulate the feats of firemen", which became "a lust after watching TV images of firefighters hauling people from the wreckage of the World Trade Centre". He wanted "the same accolades and recognition". He started fires using the same method as portrayed in the war file, "Stalag 17" (Chulov 2002, p.1 & 4). Indeed, the media reporting wildfire often uses language associated with the military and war, such as strong, courageous, well-trained and well-disciplined 'fighters' who use 'tactical field manoeuvres' (Burton 2016).

Surette (2002) believes that copycat crimes could occur for one in four crimes, although the rate is hard to determine as evidence is reliant on self-reports of criminals who have been apprehended, admit the crime, and correctly report why they lit the fire. The low apprehension and conviction rate associated with malicious wildfires, does not assist understanding of copycat arson (Muller 2008b; Tomison 2010). Those apprehended may also have lit fires prior to their arrest. So, while clustering of ignitions is sometimes present, it is not possible to determine accurately whether or not this is due to serial offending. Media content that portrays crime as rewarding, justified, and unchallenged, has been correlated with self-reported copycat criminality (Doley, Ferguson & Surette 2013). In relation to the crime of fire lighting, it is likely that copycat lighting is encouraged by firefighting hero representations in the media, as well as the excitement and adrenalin rush associated with fighting fires (Chulov 2002; Hinds-Aldrich undated). Malicious firelighters who have a disturbing interest in fires may associate themselves with fire services to serve their need to be associated with fire.

Doley, Ferguson & Surette (2013) offer recommendations to reduce the copycat impact of media. The fire, as such, should not be kept in the spotlight, with visual images kept to a minimum. The methods of ignition should not be reported, as well as detailed reports about the crime that may appear to glorify or justify the crime. Similar sensational and dramatic type characteristics about the fire event are thought to be features associated with copycat suicides (Siask & Värnik 2012). The media could report on the punishment for those convicted, and on the negative consequences of fire.

The associated connections between these behaviours and with fire lighting suggest vulnerability to media representation is an issue that needs more research in relation to the media more broadly and the form of media, including the internet and social and restricted media forms. Copycat fire lighting is likely to exist as a distinct sub-group, which potentially requires targeted prevention initiatives (Doley, Ferguson & Surette 2013).

Screening of firefighters

While it is now common to undertake criminal checks on volunteer firefighters, the effectiveness of this is likely to be low due to the small number of criminal convictions in relation to malicious fire lighting. Psychological screening of fire service personnel should also be mandatory, with associated treatment interventions once a person has been identified as at risk of lighting fires.

Tertiary prevention

Tertiary prevention aims at providing an appropriate response once a person has committed a malicious fire lighting offence or started a fire, whether it be criminal prosecution and punishment and/or appropriate treatment. Thus, it aims to prevent further fire lighting by a person who has already been identified as likely to commit a fire lighting offence or has already committed this offence.

Intervention and treatment

There are very few targeted treatment programs for firelighters, whether they are children, youth or adults. Despite the fact that there may be early signs of fire lighting and such children can often be identified in a school context, youth fire lighting is also under-reported. Research shows that by the time a child is caught playing with fire, there have been ten previous fire-starting events (Williams 2013). Children may be referred to general counselling, but often this is in the context of a broad spectrum of anti-social behaviour. A differential diagnosis is very important for treatment so that the cause of the fire lighting is understood, such as curiosity, crisis response, delinquent or pathological behaviour. There are distinct patterns of antisocial behaviour (Kolko & Kazdin 1990) and a strong predictive relationship between past and future fire lighting (Rice & Harris 1996), extending into adulthood (Putnam & Kirkpatrick 2005). This is discussed further in chapter 3. Directing resources to the high-risk group should assist in reducing fire lighting as well as reduce the incidence of other anti-social behaviours. The Youth Firesetting Support Guide (Stanley & Read 2016), a state-wide multi-agency resource and referral system across judicial, health and education systems, is a tool that can be used as a guide to the use of current general intervention opportunities in Victoria. Apart from the importance of having treatment options, additional reporting of suspicion will arise from the community perception that their reporting of suspicions to Crime Stoppers will be meaningful, as the person will be offered assistance to change their behaviour (Stanley & Read 2013).

Correctional

Arson is considered a serious offence, commonly tried in Victoria in the County Court (Sentencing Advisory Council 2015). The maximum penalty is 15 years imprisonment if the defendant is found to have intended to endanger the life of another through the destruction of property with fire. In Victoria, 22 people were sentenced for arson (of all types, including non-vegetation fires) in 2013–14 and 23 people in the previous year (Sentencing Advisory Council 2015). Of the 22 people in 2013–14, 13 were given a custodial sentence, defined as imprisonment, a partially suspended sentence, a youth justice centre order, a hospital order or a mix of these. Seven people were given a Community Correction Order. The average length of prison sentences imposed between 2009–10 and 2013–14 was just under two years and eight months (Sentencing Advisory Council 2015).

As there were 3,315 arson offences recorded by Victoria Police in 2012-13, the implicit imprisonment rate for arson in Victoria that year was less than 1%. It is not known how many fires were lit by each of these people. Also, some people suspected of arson are not able to proceed to a trial due to being under-age or having a mental illness. Despite this, it would seem that those who end up being charged are a very small number in comparison to the number of firelighters operating. The Sentencing Advisory Council (2012) in Tasmania notes that the percentage of criminals convicted for that crime, compared with the total number of crimes reported, is the lowest rate of any crime in Australia. Tomison (2010) places the conviction rate at around four in every 1000 incidents (0.4%), a figure based on recorded fires, not the number of fires ascertained by satellite imagery. Of those sentenced for an arson offence in Victoria from 2010 to 2015, just under one-quarter was female (Sentencing Advisory Council 2015). Of those sentenced for a principal offence of arson, the average number of offences for which they were charged was 4.7 (Sentencing Advisory Council 2015). A limitation of these sentencing statistics is that they do not distinguish wildfire arson from structural and other forms, recording only the broad category of arson. Given the issues noted above about low rates of detection and the proportion of arsonists who are not prosecuted due to mental health issues, those convicted of arson represent only a subset of arson offenders and may not be representative of all those who light wildfires.

NSW has experienced many severe fires in mid-2019, and as a result, legislation was changed to increase the non-parole period for a convicted malicious firelighter, from 5 to 9 years (NSW Government 2019a). There is a growing body of evidence that looks at the impact of imprisonment. This literature notes that imprisonment does not act as a strong deterrent, and neither does an increase in the length of imprisonment, given the complex nature of offending (Lansdell, Anderson & King 2011; Ritchie 2011). As only between 2% and 5% of criminals are in prison, this suggests that the threat of prison is very week as a crime deterrent (Andresen 2014). However, Prestemon and colleagues (2012) showed that arrests of arsonists could be highly effective at reducing this behaviour. This is also shown in research undertaken by Donoghue and Main (1985). They found that law enforcement in the USA, as measured by a state's annual number of law enforcement actions, was negatively related to the occurrence of wildfire arson, but not other forms of human-ignited wildfire.

Studies have also sought to understand how imprisonment impacts the recidivism rates of arsonists. For example, a New Zealand study found that, from a sample of 1,250 offenders who were imprisoned for an arson-related primary offence, only 6% had committed arson-related offences in a 10-year follow-up (Edwards & Grace 2014). However, the rates of recidivism for violent and other non-violent offences were much higher, with a reported 49% and 79% reoffending respectively. The low recidivism for malicious fire lighting may be associated with the lower levels of repeat arson in general and/or the low apprehension rate. No Australian state has a systematic program for treating arsonists in the jail system, during non-custodial sentences or combined with support for post-release for prisoners.

Similar trends were also found in an Australian study looking at the offending histories of charged arsonists (Muller 2008). Of the 133 wildfire arson defendants who came before an NSW court, only a small number had records of prior arson or wildfire arson-related offending. However, prior offences for other crime types were much higher, with over one-third of wildfire arsonists having a previous conviction for some other offence in the previous seven years (Muller 2008). This predominant non-specific reoffending trend has been observed in other studies (Doley et al. 2011; Ducat, McEwan & Ogloff 2015) and has been found in child and adolescent firelighters (Lambie et al. 2013). However, higher rates of arson recidivism have been found in studies that use clinical samples as opposed to criminal justice data (Ducat, McEwan & Ogloff 2015). Nevertheless, it is important to understand rates of arson recidivism, as those who engage in reoffending tend to have a prolonged interest in fire, suffer substance abuse and are of a younger age group (Doley et al. 2011).

Improving the apprehension rate

With only a small percentage of those who commit wildfire arson apprehended and convicted, the apprehension rate needs to be improved. Woods (2011) notes that there is a tendency that high priority is not given to the investigation of fires due to the police workload and that most fires have traditionally been put out quickly (Woods 2011). However, to gain a behaviour change in those arsonists who are caught, there must be a associated treatment program associated with apprehension. Depending on the place and crime, 50% to 75% of the prison population had been in prison before and will be in prison again.

Increasing the apprehension rate will require considerably more resources to investigate the cause of wildfire ignition and police staff to follow-up where a criminal intent was found. The numbers of people allocated to these specialist tasks are historically very low. The task of investigation and apprehension is very difficult. In the deliberately lit 2009 Marysville fire, 38 people died. 250 police investigators took over 4,000 statements in relation to this fire. As noted previously, the task would be considerably easier if there was more research undertaken on the potential firelighter, and data collection was greatly improved.

Training in the investigation of serial arson was initiated by the National Wildfire Coordinating Group in Australia and taken up in the USA and Canada. The course provided Police and Fire Service fire investigators with skills for these groups to improve their joint investigations, sharing information and identifying offenders (Woods 2011). In 2009, the ACT Rural Fire Service in Australia, adopted this course, offering training across Australia and New Zealand. It would appear that this course is not now available. Such a program would be highly valuable, Woods remarking that the course assists in making wildfire-prone communities safer from this crime. Lansdell, Anderson & King (2011) call for an integration of the arson legal framework across Australia but note that a broader integrated approach involving police, fire services and other correctional services is needed.

Grubb and Nobles (2016) and Braga (2011) report that hotspot policing, or police patrolling, has been shown to be effective in preventing crime generally. Also, nighttime patrols of areas where malicious fire lighting is occurring could assist in preventing repeat fire lighting events, especially in the first couple of weeks after the initial crime and up to about two blocks away from an initiating event. However, all this research has been undertaken in relation to urban crime. Research is needed as to whether such prevention approaches would prevent the lighting of wildfires.

A new category of prevention of malicious fires

Malicious lighting of wildfires associated with land clearing and/or illegal logging can also be associated with violence and intimidation. However, prosecutions are rare (Human Rights Watch 2019). More than 300 killings in the past decade have occurred over conflict around land clearing in the Amazon rainforest. However, only 14 of these deaths ultimately went to trial, said to be largely due to the failure by the police to conduct proper investigations. With wildfires raging in the Amazon rainforest, Brazil's President has banned the use of fire to clear land throughout the country for 60 days, although the President has repeatedly insisted the Amazon should be opened to development and has defunded the agencies responsible for reporting illegal activity (Darlington et al. 2019).

Wildfires rage yet again in Indonesia, the severity of the fires reflected those that occurred in 2015. Again, fire lighting is associated with land clearing, often associated with large agricultural companies. Researchers from Harvard and Columbia universities in the USA, examining particulate matter (PM 2.5), estimated that the 2015 Indonesian fires were associated with 91,600 deaths in

Indonesia, 6,500 in Malaysia and 2,200 in Singapore (France-Presse 2016). The 2019 fires have been estimated to place 10 million Indonesian children at risk (The Guardian 2019). Thousands of schools have been closed due to pollution. Greenpeace has accused the Indonesian government of not imposing any serious sanctions on the palm oil and pulpwood companies. Instead, the Indonesian government decided not to grant new licenses for oil palm plantations in 2018 and set up restoration in 336 villages. However, the program has some shortcomings in that it offers advice but fails to monitor progress (Normille 2019).

Meanwhile, multiple wildfires continue to burn in Africa, across Angola, Zambia and the Democratic Republic of the Congo. While many of these fires are a slash and burn approach associated with agriculture, some of these fires get out of control, and other fires are opening up new agricultural areas, both events exacerbated by climate change. While some fires may be small, the numbers are high, with over 6,900 fires recorded by NASA's satellite in Angola and 3,400 in Congo, in one week in 2019 (Cascais 2019). The forest in the Congo Basin has been described as the earth's "second green lung" after the Amazon region, as like the Amazon, the forest absorbs a large amount of carbon dioxide. Madagascar, once covered by forests, now has only about 10% of forest left with large areas being lost to forest fires each year. This is due to the practice of slash and burn operations which move farms to more fertile areas every few years.

The consequences of these fires for all of humanity are such that an international effort is needed to put preventative actions in place. These include heavy penalties for corporations who are responsible for lighting the fires. This suggests that the International Criminal Court should be taking action here. Where the fire lighting is associated with traditional agricultural practices, alternative approaches and knowledge development is needed to support these farmers, to be facilitated by the international community. Fire suppression must be supported where local services do not have the resources to undertake this work (Turkewitz 2019).

Reckless/accidental behaviour, leading to wildfire

Reckless and accidental wildfires encompass a wide range of events, although there is variation between countries about how these events are categorised. While prevention approaches are viewed separately in this section, as noted earlier, there is a scale of culpability in relation to reckless and accidentally caused fires. This is partly recognised in some countries, through the use of criminal charges, where if there is a conviction, could result in a fine (the amount often depends on the financial resources of the person), or a short or long jail sentence (Miller 2017). This approach appears to be case dependent, small in number and rather ad hoc (Saillant 2007). The punishment appears to be to recover some costs of a resultant wildfire and/or offer an example to the public about being careless with fire. This is yet another situation around wildfire that needs extensive review and public discussion to bring in a consistent approach that is couched in social justice.

Primary prevention

In the Western states in the USA, as in many other parts of the world, the most vulnerable wildfire areas have the fastest growing population (Burton 2016). Reconciling high fire danger zones with planning zones to limit subdivision in dangerous interface areas in new development areas should have high priority. Burton believes that people are not informed of the risks, and there is a patchwork response by the local government around mitigation approaches, such as building codes and defendable space. Indeed, a recent Roundtable on local government and fire identified that local Councils themselves, particularly Councillors, need to be better informed about climate change (Hughes 2019). It is common internationally for agencies with a fire interest to give educational type messages to the public. These messages range widely, from not parking a car on any type of dry vegetation and putting out campfires, to messages targeting children playing with fire.

Secondary prevention

The reinsurer, Munich Re, argues for improved management of overhead power lines. Trees should be cleared in forested areas around the lines. In high-hazard areas in the vicinity of populated land, the powerlines should be underground or technology that delivers greatly reduced wildfire risk be utilised. The Australian Greens political party calls for the mandatory placement of power lines underground in all new developments that have a high fire risk.

The Victorian Bushfire Royal Commission (2010) found that the need to replace ageing electricity infrastructure to protect human life "was imperative" (p.13). The Commission recommended:

- the progressive replacement of all single-wire earth return power lines in Victoria with aerial-bundled cable, underground cabling or other technology, to be completed in the areas of highest wildfire risk within 10 years

- the progressive replacement of all 22-kilovolt distribution feeders with aerial bundled cable, underground-cabling or other technology that delivers greatly reduced wildfire risk

- The State requires distribution businesses to change their asset inspection standards and procedures to require that all single-wire earth return power lines and all 22-kilovolt feeders in areas of high wildfire risk are inspected at least every three years

- The State requires distribution businesses to review and modify their current practices, standards and procedures for the training and auditing of asset inspectors

- The State amends the regulatory framework for electricity safety to require that distribution businesses adopt, as part of their management plans, measures to reduce the risks posed by hazard trees (p.12)

It is unclear whether these recommendations have been taken up.

The Office of the Auditor General Western Australia (2013) found similar issues in Western Australia, with a significant public safety risk that the electricity network will ignite a wildfire. The report noted that the wood pole network has suffered from decades of under-investment, requiring expenditure well above usual maintenance levels, needing $2 billion expenditure to 2022.

The Fire Services Commissioner (2012) in Victorian commissioned a report in response to the fire services responding to three significant landfill fires that occurred in January 2012. Importantly, the report states that "it appears that fire on landfill facilities is not a major concern of operators" (2012, p. 9), as none of the three landfill sites examined in the FSC report complied with all existing regulations to address fire in the site.

In Australia, the police can gain valuable information about suspicious fire lighting behaviour, that may be associated with malicious or reckless activities, from a local member of the community. This information can be reported directly to Crime Stoppers, where it is passed onto the police. Research has been undertaken on the factors that influence community reporting of suspicion of fire lighting to authorities, as there is wide variability with a person's propensity to report, this varying greatly depending on circumstances (Read & Stanley 2017, 2018). The 'success' of reports in leading to an arrest and conviction of a firelighter is unknown.

Tertiary prevention

As noted in chapter 2, civic fines are not sufficient to serve as a deterrent, not evenly applied, and are difficult to enforce in Victoria (Parliament of Victoria 2017). Increasing the consequences for illegal and reckless behaviour that could (or did) lead to wildfire may serve as a deterrent to fire lighting. The report,

Inquiry into Fire˘ Season Preparedness (Parliament of Victoria 2017), recommended that the penalties be increased, and enforcement strengthened for offences against Total Fire Ban requirements. A further possible amendment could be that those who caused a wildfire by burning rubbish should pay the full cost of putting the fire out and the damage caused to people, structures and the environment. New South Wales recently amended legislation so that a person who recklessly or deliberately lit a fire on a Total Fire Ban Day can receive a jail sentence of up to 14 years (NSW Government 2019b).

Research in Victoria reveals that, if a wildfire is judged to be large and dangerous, a person is more likely to report their suspicions to an authority. This is likely to occur whether their suspicions concern a stranger or a child, but not if the child is their own or the person is an intimate of the reporter. Where the person is well known, there is a 50% chance that the person will 'handle the situation themselves' rather than report their suspicions to an official. A youth who is described as 'difficult' is more likely to be reported to an official agency than a youth who is not viewed as such. The perceived intentions of the offender, whether the fire was viewed as accidental or intentional, can alter reporting to an authority by as much as 17%. Other factors that influence reporting includes the amount of crime in general in the reporter's living location (the more crime, the less likely to report a suspicion of fire lighting); and also the reporter's trust in police and other law authorities (the higher the trust, the more likely they are to report a suspicion of fire lighting).

Conclusions

This book opened with a recognition of wildfires burning around the world and will close with the same story. August and September 2019 sported media coverage of extensive wildfires in major forest systems, particularly in the Amazon rainforest and in Indonesian rainforests. Extensive rural/urban interface wildfires were occurring in the coastal areas of northern NSW and Queensland, extending north into the tropical area where fire has been largely an unknown issue. Media reports that in Indonesia, 40,000 people have been treated for acute respiratory infections, schools are shut, including 100s in Malaysia and airports closed (Massola & Rompies 2019). 99% of these fires were said to be caused by malicious lighting.

In Australia, reports suggest that there were probably two major causes of ignitions – land clearing in the forests and malicious lighting in Australia. Action to prevent these ignitions is urgently needed, involving political will, resources to identify, charge and prosecute offenders where they are an adult, and above all knowledge, education, and changing behaviour and circumstances leading to the ignition. Behind these direct responses, as argued in this book, there are major context adjustments to be made. These are in relation to reducing climate change, reducing population growth, spatial planning, and research and evaluation to build knowledge about effectiveness and costs and benefits of policies, programs and actions. In particular, a transition to a new approach to managing the prevention of wildfire is needed, that is inclusive, open, and based on empirical knowledge, wisdom and value stances. Yet, in Victoria meetings between "emergency services and government officials", a meeting held earlier this year due to the second warmest half-year on record across Australia, centred on suppression, with an announcement of a fleet of 100 helicopters and planes to support firefighters (Grieve & Preiss 2019, p.12). A wider perspective did not appear to be considered.

In looking for some inspiration for closing words in this book, we delved into a recent inspirational publication, Degrowth in the Suburbs: A Radical Urban Imaginary, by Alexander and Gleeson (2019). The book deals with a related topic, the damage being done by economic growth and the overuse of natural resources. However, there are words of wisdom there for the issues around wildfire. There is a need for a vision of alternative worlds, what they might look like, and how they might be realised. There is a need for a cultural change, where small actions and practices at the household and community scale mobilise change. This appears to be a recipe for change in relation to addressing climate change wherein the absence of political will, community response, where it is able, steps in. There is a need for a culture shaped by vision and values that lives on a 'fair' ecological footprint. Alexander and Gleeson (2019) express the view that efforts to producing a strong and progressive top-down policy change would be wasted. The authors of this book are not quite so pessimistic, as, in part, the issue of wildfire and its impacts have greater visibility than neo-liberal and market ideologies. Certainly, a desire to change is happening in Victoria, especially with the Victorian Police, but shortfalls in resources and short-term populist political directives are not helping.

Another very interesting body of work has come from the European Union (Mair et al. 2019). The report touches on some critical issues about decision-making. It notes that thinking collectively can overcome individual bias and significantly improve the quality of outcome but only if all critical information, unique knowledge and expertise, is shared. An environment of psychological safety needs to be established to enable the sharing of critical information, ideas, questions and dissenting opinions. This also needs to recognise the importance of emotions in decision-making, as sensing citizens' concerns, fears and hopes could provide important new information to guide policy choices. Science is not value-free; there is a need to be transparent about the values encompassed in decisions. Policymakers need to understand the values, as well as the interests and expectations of citizens.

This book only touches on some of the issues around wildfire. It hopefully opens up a field which demands connections, knowledge, communication, ideas, and significant and urgent change. However, as Flannery (2019) says in relation to climate change, which is also apt for the prevention of wildfires, "the gloves are off", business-as-usual, political agreements or technological innovations have not halted the upward trajectory of wildfire ignitions.

References

ABC News 2019, 'SKM charged with environmental offences over Coolaroo recycling plant fire, 8 Mar 2019', https://www.abc.net.au/news/2019-03-08/skm-charged-with-environmental-offences-over-coolaroo-fire/10883016

ABS (Australian Bureau of Statistics) 2013, 2011.0.55.001 *Census of Population and Housing 2011*, customised report, http://.abs.gov.au/ausstats/abs@.nsf/lookep/2011.0.55.001Main%20Features22011

Abt, K Butry, D Prestemon, J & Scranton, S 2015, 'Effect of fire prevention programs on accidental and incendiary wildfires on tribal lands in the United States', *International Journal of Wildland Fire*, vol. 24, pp. 749-762.

(ACOSS) Australian Council of Social Services 2013, *Extreme weather, climate change and the community sector: ACOSS submission to the Senate Inquiry into recent trends in and preparedness for extreme weather events*, https://www.acoss.org.au/images/uploads/ACOSS_submission_to_Senate_Inquiry_into_extreme_weather.pdf

Adger, W 2003, 'Social capital, collective action, and adaptation to climate change', *Economic Geography*, vol. 79, no. 4, pp. 387-404.

AFAC (Australasian Fire and Emergency Service Authorities Council) & FFMG (Forest Fire Management Group) 2016, *National guide for prescribed burning operations*, https://knowledge.aidr.org.au/media/4869/national-position-on-prescribed-burning.pdf

AFAC (Australian Fire and Emergency Services Authorities Council) & (FFMG) Forest Fire Management Group 2017, *National guidelines for prescribed burning strategic and program planning*, https://knowledge.aidr.org.au/media/4897/national-guidelines-for-prescribed-burning-strategic-and-program-planning.pdf

Ager, A Day, M Short, K & Evers, C 2016, 'Assessing the impacts of federal forest planning on wild re risk mitigation in the Pacific Northwest, USA', *Landscape and Urban Planning*, vol. 147, pp. 1–17.

Alcock, P 2004, 'Participation or pathology: contradictory tensions in area-based policy', *Social Policy & Society*, vol. 3, no. 2, pp. 87-96.

Alexander, D 2015, 'Disaster and emergency planning for preparedness, response, and recovery, Natural Hazard Science', *Oxford Research Encyclopedia*, https://oxfordre.com/naturalhazardscience/view/10.1093/acrefore/9780199389407.001.0001/acrefore-9780199389407-e-12

Alexander, S & Gleeson, B 2019, *Degrowth in the suburb: a radical urban imaginary*, Palgrave, Macmillan, Singapore.

Altangerel, K & Kull, C 2013, 'The prescribed burning debate in Australia: conflicts and compatibilities', *Journal of Environmental Planning and Management*, vol. 56, no. 1, pp.103-120.

American Psychiatric Association 2013, *Diagnostic and statistical manual of mental disorders: diagnostic and statistical manual of mental disorders*, (5th ed.), American Psychiatric Association, Arlington, VA.

Andresen, M 2014, *Environmental criminology: evolution, theory, and practice*, Routledge, London & N.Y.

Anwar, S Langstrom, N Grann, M & Fazel, S 2011, 'Is arson the crime most strongly associated with psychosis? - A national case-control study of arson risk in schizophrenia and other psychoses', *Schizophrenia Bulletin*, vol. 37, pp. 580-586.

Arango, T 2018, Behind most wildfires, a person and a spark: 'We bring fire with us', *New York Times*, August, 20, https://www.nytimes.com/2018/08/20/us/california-wildfires-human-causes-arson.html

Arnstein, S 1969, 'A latter of citizen participation', *Journal of the American Institute of Planners*, vol. 35, pp. 216-214.

Arson Control Forum 2004, *Implementing arson reduction programs: findings from the Arson Control Forum's new projects initiative*, Office of the Deputy Prime Minister, Research bulletin no. 2, http://www.stoparsonuk.org/arson/documents/Research_Doc_5_Arson_Terminology.pdf

Ash, N Blanco, H Brown, C Garcia, K Henrichs, T Lucas, N Ruadsepp-heane, C Simpson, R Scholes, R Tomich, T Vira, B & Zurek, M 2010, *Ecosystems and human well-being: a manual for assessment practitioners*, https://www.unep-wcmc.org/resources-and-data/ecosystems-and-human-wellbeing--a-manual-for-assessment-practitioners

Atleework, K 2018, 'Power lines are burning the West', *The Atlantic*, May 25, https://www.theatlantic.com/technology/archive/2018/05/power-lines-are-burning-the-west/561212/

Attorney-General's Department 2009, *Report on the National Forum to Reduce Deliberate Bushfires in Australia*, https://library.dbca.wa.gov.au/static/FullTextFiles/070276.pdf

Australian Associated Press 2017, 'Victorian Country Fire Authority investigator says she was harassed by managers', 18 Oct https://www.theguardian.com/australia-news/2017/oct/18/victorian-country-fire-authority-investigator-says-she-was-harassed-by-managers

Australian Institute for Disaster Resilience 2019, 'Bushfire: Australian Disaster Resilience Glossary', Australian Institute for Disaster Resilience, https://knowledge.aidr.org.au/glossary/?wordOfTheDayId=&keywords=Bushfire&alpha=&page=1&results=50&order=AZ

Australian Institute of Criminology 2006, *Bushfires lit deliberately during adverse bushfire weather*. Bushfire arson bulletin No. 39, Australian Institute of Criminology, Canberra. https://aic.gov.au/publications/bfab/bfab039

Australian Institute of Criminology 2017, *Proportion of deliberate bushfires in Australia*. Bushfire arson bulletin No. 51, Australian Institute of Criminology, Canberra, https://aic.gov.au/publications/bfab/bfab051

Australian Institute of Criminology (undated) *National crime prevention framework*, Australian Institute of Criminology, Canberra, https://www.police.qld.gov.au/sites/default/files/2018-10/NCP%20Framework.pdf

Ayres, J 2012, Essential ingredients in successful visioning community visioning programs processes and outcomes, in N Walzer & G Hamm (eds.), *Community visioning programs: processes and outcomes*, Routledge, New York, 16-32.

Ayres, J Hein, C & Cole, R 1990, *Take Charge: Economic Development in Small Communities - Empowering Rural Communities for the 1990's*, Ames, I.A., North Central Regional Center for Rural Development.

Badlan, R Sharples, J Evans, J & McRae, R 2017, 'The role of deep flaming in violent pyroconvection', paper presented at the *22nd International congress on modelling and simulation*, Hobart, Tasmania, Australia, 3 to 8 December, https://ozewex.org/event/the-22nd-international-congress-on-modelling-and-simulation-modsim2017/

Baird, R 2006, 'Pyro-terrorism: the threat of arson-induced forest fires as a future terrorist weapon of mass destruction', *Studies in Conflict & Terrorism*, vol. 29, no. 5, pp. 415-428.

Balch, J Bradley, B Abatzoglou, J Nagy, C Fusco, E & Mahood, A 2017, 'Human-started wildfires expand the fire niche across the United States', *Proceedings of the National Academy of Sciences*, vol. 114, no. 11, pp. 2946-2951.

Bandura, A 1976, 'Self-reinforcement: theoretical and methodological considerations', *Behaviorism*, vol.4, no. 2, pp. 135–155.

Barnett, W Richter, P & Renneberg, B 1999, 'Repeated arson: data from criminal records', F*orensic Science International*, vol. 101, pp. 49-54.

Barron, A 2018, Time to refine key climate policy model, *Nature Climate Change*, vol. 8, pp. 350–352, www.nature.com/natureclimatechange

Barrowcliffe, E & Gannon, TA 2015, 'The characteristics of un-apprehended firesetters living in the UK community', *Psychology, Crime and Law*, vol. 21, no. 9, pp. 836-853.

Bates, M 2004, *Managing landfill site fires in Northamptonshire*, Environment and Transport Scrutiny Committee, University College Northampton, http://www.scirp.org/(S(i43dyn45teexjx455qlt3d2q))/reference/ReferencesP apers.aspx?ReferenceID=128140

BBC News 2018a, 'Military called in to tackle fire near Saddleworth Moor', 27 June https://www.bbc.co.uk/news/uk-england-manchester-44634023

BBC News 2018b, 'Saddleworth Moor fire is out after more than three weeks', 18 July, https://www.bbc.co.uk/news/uk-england-manchester-44880331

BBC News 2018c, 'Winter Hill TV mast fire: Man arrested as blaze continues', 29 June, https://www.bbc.co.uk/news/uk-england-lancashire-44654410

Beale, J & Jones, W 2011, 'Preventing and reducing bushfire arson in Australia: a review of what is known', *Fire Technology*, vol. 47, pp. 507-518.

Beck, U 1992, *Risk society, towards a new modernity*, Sage Publications, London.

Bell, R Doley, R & Dawson, D 2018, 'Developmental characteristics of firesetters: are recidivist offenders distinctive? *Legal and Criminological Psychology*, vol. 23, pp. 163-175.

Berger, S 2004, 'Species dying 1000 times faster', *The Age*, November 18, p.12.

Berke, PR 2002, 'Does sustainable development offer a new direction for planning? Challenges for the twenty-first century, *Journal of Planning Literature*, vol. 17, no.1, pp. 21-36.

Bernstein, A 2010, 'Reduced biodiversity directly affects human health', Radio National, The Science Show, June 5, https://www.abc.net.au/radionational/programs/scienceshow/past-programs/index=2010

Bernstein, A 2011, 'Reduced biodiversity directly affects human health', *The Science Show, ABC Radio National,* 26 June.

Berwyn, B 2018, 'It's complicated: While CO2 causes long-term warming, aerosols can have both a warming and a temporary cooling effect', *Inside Climate News,* August 23, https://insideclimatenews.org/news/23082018/extreme-wildfires-climate-change-global-warming-air-pollution-fire-management-black-carbon-co2

Besenyö, J 2017, 'Inferno terror: forest fires as the new form of terrorism', *Terrorism and Political Violence,* July, https://doi.org/10.1080/09546553.2017.1341876

Better Regulation Commission, 2006, *Risk, responsibility and regulation – Whose risk is it anyway?* London, https://www.scie-socialcareonline.org.uk/risk-responsibility-and-regulation-whose-risk-is-it-anyway/r/a11G00000017tVBIAY

Biasia, R Colantonib, A Ferrarac, C Ranallid, F & Salvatid, L 2015, 'In-between sprawl and fires: long-term forest expansion and settlement dynamics at the wildland–urban interface in Rome, Italy', *International Journal of Sustainable Development & World Ecology,* vol. 22, no. 6, pp. 467–475.

Blanchi, R Leonard, J Haynes, K Opie, K James, M & Dimer de Oliveira, F 2014, 'Environmental circumstances surrounding bushfire fatalities in Australia 1901–2011' *Environmental Science & Policy, vol.* 37, pp. 192-203.

Blanchi, R Leonard, J & Leicester, R 2006, *Bushfire risk at the rural-urban interface.* Bushfire Cooperative Research Centre, Melbourne, http://bushfirecrc.com/sites/default/files/managed/resource/bushfire_risk_at_the_rural_urban_interface_-_brisbane_2006_0.pdf

Blanco, C Alegria, AA Petry, NM Grant, J Simpson, HB Liu, S Grant, B & Hasin, D 2010, 'Prevalence and correlates of firesetting in the US: results from the National Epidemiologic Survey on Alcohol and Related Conditions', *Journal of Clinical Psychiatry,* vol. 71, pp. 1218–1225.

Blond, P 2010, *Red Tory: How left and right have broken Britain and how we can fix it,* Faber and Faber Ltd, London.

Bluff, L 2016, *Reducing the effect of planned burns on hollow bearing trees - fire and Adaptive Management Report,* no.29, https://www.ffm.vic.gov.au/__data/assets/pdf_file/0006/21120/Report-95-Reducing-the-effect-of-planned-burns-on-hollow-bearing-trees-2016.pdf

Bond, T & Mercer, D 2014, 'Subdivision policy and planning for bushfire defence: a natural hazard mitigation strategy for residential peri-urban regions in Victoria, Australia', *Geographical Research,* vol. 52, pp. 6-22.

Brett, A 2004, '"Kindling theory" in arson: how dangerous are firesetters?' *Australian and New Zealand Journal of Psychiatry,* vol. 38, pp. 419-425.

Bowman, D & Murphy, B 2015, 'Ashes to ashes: Increased fire frequency threatens Alpine Ash forests', *National Environmental Research Program,* University of Tasmania, http://www.lifeatlarge.edu.au/__data/assets/pdf_file/0018/650007/Reshaping-alpine-landscapes-summary.pdf

Bowman, D Murphy, B Boer, MB Bradstock, RA Cary, GJ Cochrane, MA Fensham, RJ Krawchuk, MA Price, OF & Williams, RJ 2013, 'Forest fire management, climate change, and the risk of catastrophic carbon losses,' *Frontiers in Ecology and the Environment*, vol. 11, no. 2, pp. 66-68.

Bradstock, R Penman, T Boer, M Price, O & Clarke, H 2014, 'Divergent responses of fire to recent warming and drying across south-eastern Australia', *Global Change Biology*, vol. 20, pp.1412-1428.

Braga, A 2001, 'The effects of hot spots policing on crime', *The Annals of the American Academy of Political and Social Science*, vol. 578, no. 1, pp. 104-125.

Brain, P Stanley, J & Stanley, J 2018, *Making the most of opportunities*, report to the Municipal Association Victoria, unpublished report.

Brain, P Stanley, J & Stanley, J 2019, *Melbourne: how big, how fast and at what cost?* March, MSSI, University of Melbourne, Melbourne, https://sus tainable.unimelb.edu.au/__data/assets/pdf_file/0006/3065334/MSSI-Research-Paper-2019_Stanley_et_al.pdf

Brantingham, P & Brantingham, P 1981, *Environmental criminology*, Sage, Beverly Hills, CA.

Brantingham, P & Brantingham, P 1993, 'Environment, routine and situation: toward a pattern theory of crime', *Advances in Criminological Theory*, vol. 5, pp. 259-294.

Brantingham, P & Brantingham, P 1995, 'Criminality of place: crime generators and crime attractors', *European Journal of Criminal Policy and Research* vol. 3, pp. 5-26.

Brantingham, P & Faust, F 1976, 'A conceptual model of crime-prevention', *Crime and Delinquency*, vol. 22, no. 3, pp. 284-96.

Bryant, C 2008a, *Understanding bushfire: trends in deliberate vegetation fires in Australia.* Technical and Background paper no. 27, Australian Institute of Criminology, Canberra.

Bryant, C 2008b, *Weekly patterns in bush reignitions*, Bushfire Arson Bulletin No. 55, 28 October, Australian Institute of Criminology, ACT.

Bryson, B 2010, At *home: a short history of private life*, Random House, Australia.

Buergelt, P & Smith, R 2015, 'Wildfires: an Australian perspective', in D. Paton (ed) *Wildfire Hazards, Risks, and Disasters*, pp. 101-121, Elsevier, Oxford.

Bulwa, D 2008, 'Accidental fire-starter furious at punishment', *SFGATE*, August 10, https://www.sfgate.com/news/article/Accidental-fire-starter-furious-at-punishment-3200351.php

Bureau of Meteorology 2019, *2019 Australian Weather Calendar*, http://www.b om.gov.au/calendar/

Burton, L 2016, Problems in the wildland-urban interface, *The Denver Post*, June 2012, https://www.denverpost.com/2012/06/21/problems-in-the-wild land-urban-interface/

Burton, L & Sun, L 2015, (eds.), Cassandra's curse: law and foreseeable future disaster, *Cassandra's_ (Studies in Law, Politics and Society)*, Elsevier, https://www.emerald.com/insight/content/doi/10.1108/S1059-433720150000068011/full/html

Butcher, JR & Gilchrist, DJ 2016, *The three sector solution: delivering public policy in collaboration with Not-For-Profits and business*, ANU Press, Canberra.

Butcher, JR Gilchrist, DJ Phillimore, J & Wanna, J 2019, 'Attributes of effective collaboration: insights from five case studies in Australia and New Zealand', *Policy Design and Practice*, vol. 2, no.1, pp. 75-89.

Butt, A Buxton, M Haynes, R & Lechner, A 2009, 'Peri-urban growth, planning and bushfire in the Melbourne City Region', paper presented at the *State of Australian Cities*, National Conference, 24-27 November, Perth, Western Australia, http://researchbank.rmit.edu.au/view/rmit:13842

Buxton, M Haynes, R Mercer, D & Butt, A 2011, 'Vulnerability to bushfire risk at Melbourne's urban fringe: the failure of regulatory land use planning', *Geographical Research*, vol. 49, no. 1, pp. 1-12.

Buxton, M Tieman, S, Bekessy, T Budge, D Mercer, M Coote, M & Morcombe, J 2006, *Change and continuity in peri-urban Australia, state of the peri-urban regions: A Review of the literature*. RMIT University, Melbourne, http://researchbank.rmit.edu.au/view/rmit:160299

California Department of Forestry and Fire Protection 2015, *Incident information,* http://cdfdata.fire.ca.gov/incidents/incidents_stats

Cambridge Advanced Learner's Dictionary 2017, (3rd ed.), Cambridge University Press, UK, https://webforpc.com/software/dictionary/cambridge-advanced-learners-dictionary-download-free/

Canter, D & Fritzon, K 1998, 'Differentiating arsonists: a Model of firesetting actions and characteristics.' *Legal and Criminological Psychology*, vol. 3, pp. 73-96.

Cardille, J Ventura, S & Turner, M 2001, 'Environmental and social factors influencing wildfires in the upper Midwest, United States', *Ecological Applications*, vol. 11, no. 1, pp. 111-127.

Carpenter, S Arrow, K Barrett, S Biggs, R Brocks, W Crépin, A. ... DeZeeuw A 2012, 'General resilience to cope with extreme events', *Sustainability*, vol. 4, pp. 3248–3259.

Cascais, A 2019, 'Amazon versus Africa forest fires: is the world really ablaze?' *DW*, 30 August, https://www.dw.com/en/amazon-versus-africa-forest-fires-is-the-world-really-ablaze/a-50229553

Catry, F Damasceno, P Silva, J Miguel Galante, M & Moreira, F 2007, 'Spatial distribution patterns of wildfire ignitions in Portugal', paper presented at the *Wildfire* conference, January, Seville, Spain, https://www.academia.edu/1804467/Spatial_distribution_patterns_of_wildfire_ignitions_in_Portugal

Catry, F Rego, FC Bação, F & Moreira, F 2009, 'Modeling and mapping wildfire ignition risk in Portugal', *International Journal of Wildland Fire*, vol. 18, pp. 921-931.

CBC radio Canada 2018, 'How do CO2 emissions from forest fires compare to those from fossil fuels?' https://www.cbc.ca/radio/quirks/sept-15-2018-summer-science-camping-under-a-volcano-plastic-in-beluga-bellies-and-more-1.4821942/how-do-co2-emissions-from-forest-fires-compare-to-those-from-fossil-fuels-1.4821944

CFA (Country Fire Authority) 2015, *Working together: Integrated fire management planning*. CFA, Burwood East, Vic, http://www.cfa.vic.gov.au/about/working-together/

CFA (Country Fire Authority) 2017, *Annual Report 2016-17*, CFA, Victoria, https://www.cfa.vic.gov.au/documents/20143/203205/CFA-Annual-Report-2017.pdf/92403a6f-9799-84cc-cc13-e76bbdac43ff

Chaplin, E & Henry, J 2016, 'Assessment and treatment of deliberate firesetters with intellectual disability', in R Doley, G Dickens & T, Gannon (eds.) *The psychology of arson a practical guide to understanding and managing deliberate firesetters*, Psychology Press and Routledge Academic, NY, pp. 55-67.

Cheney, NP 1981, 'Fire Behaviour', in, A M Gill, RH Groves & lR Noble (eds.), *Fire and Australian Biota*, Australia Academy of Science, Canberra.

Chesnais, M Green, A Phillips, B Aitken, P Dyson, J Trancoso, R Rajan, J & Dunbar, C 2019, *Queensland: state heatwave risk assessment*, Queensland Fire and Emergency Services, 14 May.

Christensen, W 2008, 'The prevention of bushfire arson through target hardening', *Flinders Journal of Law Reform*, vol. 10, no. 3, pp. 693-713.

Chulov, M 2002, 'Arsonist burned with desire to be fire hero', *The Australian*, 4 June, pp. 1 & 4.

Clarke, R (ed) 1992, *Situational crime prevention: successful case studies*, (2nd ed.) Harrow and Heston, NY.

Climate Action Tracker 2018, April, https://climateactiontracker.org/countries/australia/

COAG 2011, *National strategy for disaster resilience: building our nation's resilience to disasters*, Council of Australian Governments, Canberra, ACT.

Coen, J Stavros, N & Fites-Kaufman J 2018, 'Deconstructing the King Megafire', *Ecological Applications*, vol. 6, pp. 1565-1580, https://www.ncbi.nlm.nih.gov/pubmed/29797684

Coenen, L Benneworth, P & Trufferd, B 2012, 'Toward a spatial perspective on sustainability transitions', *Research Policy*, vol. 41, pp. 968-979.

Cohen, J 2000, What is the wildfire threat to homes? Thompson Memorial Lecture, April 10, https://www.fs.fed.us/rm/pubs_other/rmrs_2000_cohen_j003.pdf

Cohen, JD 2008, The wildland-interface fire problem: a consequence of the fire exclusion paradigm. *Forest History Today*, vol. 20 pp. 20–26.

Cohen, LE & Felson, M 1979, 'Social change and crime rate trends: a routine activity approach', *American sociological review*, vol. 44, pp. 588–608.

Collins, K & Ison, R 2006, 'Dare we jump off Arnstein's ladder? Social learning as a new policy paradigm', paper presented at Participatory Approaches in Science & Technology conference, 4-7 June, Edinburgh, https://www.researchgate.net/publication/42793728_Dare_we_Jump_off_Arnstein%27s_Ladder_Social_Learning_as_a_New_Policy_Paradigm

Collins, K Owen, Price, F & Penman, T 2015, 'Spatial patterns of wildfire ignitions in south-eastern Australia', *International Journal of Wildland Fire*, vol. 24, pp. 1098–1108.

Commissioner for Environmental Sustainability 2018, *State of the environment report: Scientific Assessments*, Melbourne, Victoria State Government.

Common, M 1995, *Sustainability and Policy: Limits to Economics*, Cambridge University Press, Cambridge.

Commonwealth of Australia 2010, *Ahead of the game: blueprint for the reform of Australian Government Administration*, Department of Prime Minister and Cabinet, Canberra.

Connors, P & McDonald, P 2011, 'Transitioning communities: Community, participation and the Transition Town Movement', *Community Development Journal'*, vol. 46, no. 4, pp. 558-572.

Constanza, R et al. 2007, 'The value of the world's ecosystem services and natural capital', *Nature* vol. 387, no. 6630.

Constanza, R d'Arge, R de Groot, R Farberk, S Grasso, M Hannon, B Limburg, K Naeem, S O'Neill, RV Paruelo, J Raskin, RG Suttonkk, P & van den Belt, M 1997, 'The value of the world's ecosystem services and natural capital', *Nature*, vol. 387, no. 6630, pp. 254-260.

Cornish, D & Clarke, R 1986, *The reasoning criminal: rational choice perspectives on offending*, Springer-Verlag, NY.

Cornish, D & Clarke, R 2003, 'Opportunities, precipitators and criminal decisions: a reply to Wortley's critique of situational crime prevention', *Crime Prevention Studies*, vol. 16, pp. 41-96.

Coughlan, M & Petty, A 2012, 'Linking humans and fire: a proposal for a transdisciplinary fire ecology', *International Journal of Wildland Fire*, vol. 21, pp. 477-487.

Country Fire Authority 2015, *The value of CFA volunteers*, Parliamentary Enquiry: Fire Services Review, Melbourne, https://www.parliament.vic. gov.au/images/stories/committees/SCEP/Fire_Season_Prepardeness/Subm issions/Submission_39_-_Volunteer_Fire_Brigades_Victoria-Attachment_7.pdf

Cox, C 2018, 'Everything we know about the Saddleworth Moor fire so far', *Manchester Evening News*, 27 Jun, https://www.manchestereveningnews. co.uk/news/greater-manchester-news/saddleworth-moor-fire-carrbrook-army-14837737

Cozens, P 2010, 'Overview: environmental criminology and the potential for reducing opportunities for bushfire arson', in Stanley J & Kestin T (eds.), *Advancing bushfire arson prevention in Australia*, report from "Collaborating for Change: Symposium advancing bushfire arson prevention in Australia", Melbourne, 25–26 March, Monash Sustainability Institute, Melbourne, pp. 49–53, http://www.aic.gov.au/media_library/conferences/2010-bushfirearson/ad vancing_bushfire_arson_prevention.pdf

Cozens, P & Christensen, W 2011, 'Environmental criminology and the potential for reducing opportunities for bushfire arson', *Crime Prevention and Community Safety*, vol. 13, no. 2, pp. 119-133.

Crichton, D 1999, 'The risk triangle', in J Ingleton (ed), *Natural disaster management* pp. 102-103, Tudor Rose, London.

Crime Statistics Agency 2016, *Spotlight: arson offences,* https://www.crime statistics.vic.gov.au/crime-statisticshistorical-crime-datayear-ending-30-september-2016/spotlight-arson-offences

de la Croix, D & Dottori, D 2008, 'Easter Island's collapse: a tale of a population race, *Journal of Economic Growth,* vol. 13, no. 1, pp. 27-55.

Crutzen, P & Andreae, M 1990, 'Estimates of worldwide biomass burning: biomass burning in the tropics: impact on atmospheric chemistry and biochemical cycles', *Science,* vol. 250, no. 4988, https://www.ncbi. nlm.nih.gov/pubmed/17734705

Curman, AS 2004, *Spatial-statistical analysis of arson activity in the Greater Vancouver region of British Columbia,* M. A. Thesis, Arts and Social Sciences, School of Criminology, Simon Fraser University, Burnaby, Canada.

Cushman, P 1990, 'Why the self is empty: towards a historically situated psychology', *American Psychologist,* vol. 45, no. 5, pp. 599-611.

Cuthill, M 2004, 'Community visioning: facilitating informed citizen participation in local area planning on the Gold Coast, *Urban Policy and Research,* vol. 22, pp. 427–455.

Dalhuisen, L Koenraadt & Liem, M 2017, 'Subtypes of firesetters', *Criminal Behaviour and Mental Health,* vol. 27, pp. 59-75.

Danielsen, F Burgess, N Jensen, P Pirhofer-Walzl, K 2010, 'Environmental monitoring: the scale and speed of implementation varies according to the degree of people's involvement', *Journal of Applied Ecology,* vol. 47, pp. 1166-1168.

Darlington, S Trucco, F Garcia, J & Britton, B 2019, 'Bolsonaro bans land-clearing fires in Amazon for 60 days', *CNN,* August 29, https://edition.cnn. com/2019/08/29/americas/brazil-amazon-bolsonaro-fire-ban-intl/index.html

Davidson, AM 2006, *Key determinants of fire frequency in the Sydney basin,* Unpublished honours thesis, Australian National University, Canberra.

Davidson, P Saunders, P Bradbury, B & Wong, M 2018, *Poverty in Australia,* ACOSS/UNSW Poverty and Inequality Partnership Report No. 2, ACOSS, Sydney.

Davis, MR & Bennett, D 2016, 'Future directions for criminal behaviour analysis of deliberately set fire events', in RM Doley, GL Dickens & TA Gannon (eds.), *The psychology of arson: a practical guide to understanding and managing deliberate firesetters,* pp. 131-146, Routledge/Taylor & Francis Group, NY.

Deloitte Access Economics 2016, *The economic cost of the social impact of natural disasters,* March, http://australianbusinessroundtable.com.au/ assets/documents/Report%20-%20Social%20costs/Report%20-%20The%20economic%20cost%20of%20the%20social%20impact%20of%20 natural%20disasters.pdf

DELWP (Department of Environment, Land, Water and Planning) 2015, *Safer together: a new approach to reducing the risk of bushfire in Victoria,* Victorian Government. Melbourne.

DELWP (Department of Environment, Land, Water and Planning) 2019, 'Past bushfires', *Forest Fire Management,* https://www.ffm.vic.gov.au/history-and-incidents/past-bushfires

Department of Sustainability and Environment 2003, *Ecological effects of repeated low-intensity fire in a mixed eucalypt foothill forest in south-eastern Australia: summary report (1984–1999),* December, Victoria Government.

Denniss, R 2017, *Curing affluenza: How to buy less stuff and save the world,* Black Inc, Australia.

Department of Sustainability and Environment 2012, *Code of Practice for Bushfire Management on Public Land,* June, Victorian Government, Melbourne.

Department of the Environment and Energy 1992, *National strategy for ecologically sustainable development,* Australian Government, Canberra, https://www.environment.gov.au/about-us/esd/publications/national-esd-strategy

Dervis, Z & Qureshi, R 2016, *Trends in income inequality: global, inter-country, and within countries,* Brookings Institute, August, https://www.brookings.edu/wp-content/uploads/2016/08/income-inequality-within-countries_august-2016-003.pdf

Dickens, GL & Sugarman, P 2012 'Differentiating firesetters: lessons from the literature on motivation and dangerousness', in GL Dickens PA Sugarman & TA Gannon (eds.), *Firesetting and mental health: theory, research and practice,* pp. 48-67, RCPsych Publications.

Dickens, G Sugarman, Edgar, S, Hofberg, K Tewari, S & Ahmad, F 2009, 'Recidivism and dangerousness in arsonists', *Journal of Forensic Psychiatry & Psychology,* vol. 20, pp. 621-639.

Doherty, TJ & Clayton, S 2011, 'The psychological impacts of global climate change,' *American Psychologist,* vol. 66, no. 4, pp. 265-276.

Dolan, M & Stanley, J 2010, 'Risk factors for juvenile firesetting', in J Stanley & T Kestin, (eds.), *Collaborating for change: Symposium advancing bushfire arson prevention in Australia,* pp. 31-2, Monash Sustainable Institute, Melbourne.

Doley, R 2003, 'Making sense of arson through classification', *Psychiatry, Psychology and Law,* vol. 10, pp. 346-352.

Doley, R Dickens, G & Gannon, T 2016, 'Deliberate firesetting – an overview'. in R Doley, G Dickens & T Gannon (eds.) *The psychology of arson: a practical guide to understanding and managing deliberate firesetters,* pp. 1-7, Psychology Press and Routledge Academic, UK.

Doley, R Ferguson, C & Surette, R 2013, 'Copycat firesetting: Bridging two research areas', *Criminal Justice and Behavior,* vol. 40, no. 12, pp.1472-1491.

Doley, Fineman, K, Fritzon, D & McEwan, T 2011, 'Risk factors for recidivistic arson in adult offenders', *Psychiatry, Psychology and Law,* vol.18, pp. 409-423.

Donoghue, L & Main, W 1985, Some factors influencing wildfire occurrence and measurement of fire prevention effectiveness, *Journal of Environmental Management,* vol. 20, no.1, 87-96.

Doolittle, M & Lightsey, M 1979, 'Analysing wildfire occurrence data for prevention planning', *Fire Management Notes*, vol. 39, no. 2, 507.

Doyle, K 2018, 'Prescribed burning debate rages as Australia finds there's no time to burn going into peak fire season', *ABC News online*, http://www.abc.net.au/news/2018-09-13/is-the-prescribed-burn-window-closing-in-australia/10236048

Drake, DS & Block, CR 2003, 'An evaluation of arson-associated homicide in Chicago – 1965 to 1995', in CR Block & RL Block (eds.), *Public health and criminal justice approaches to homicide research*, Proceedings of the 2003 meeting of the Homicide Research Working Group, HRWG Publications, Chicago, IL.

Ducat L, McEwan T & Ogloff J 2015, 'An investigation of firesetting recidivism: factor related to repeat offending', *Legal and Criminological Psychology*, vol. 20, no. 1, pp. 1–18.

Ducat, L McEwan, T & Ogloff, JR 2017, 'A comparison of psychopathology and reoffending in female and male convicted firesetters', *Law and Human Behavior*, vol. 41, no. 6, 588-599.

Ducat, L & Ogloff JR 2011, 'Understanding and preventing bushfire-setting: a psychological perspective', *Psychiatry, Psychology and Law*, vol. 18, pp. 341-356.

Ducat, L Ogloff, JR & McEwan, TE 2013, 'Mental illness and psychiatric treatment amongst firesetters, other offenders, and the general community', *Australian and New Zealand Journal of Psychiatry*, vol. 47, no.10, pp. 945-53.

Duff, TJ Cawson, JG & Penman, TD 2019, 'Determining burnability: Predicting completion rates and coverage of prescribed burns for fuel management', *Forest Ecology and Management*, vol. 433, no. 15, pp. 431-440.

Dupéy, L & Smith, J 2018, 'An integrative review of empirical research on perceptions and behaviors related to prescribed burning and wildfire in the United States', *Environmental Management*, vol. 61, pp.1002–1018.

Dutta, R Das, A Aryal, J 2016, 'Big data integration shows Australian bush-fire frequency is increasing significantly', *Royal Society Open Science*, http://rsos.royalsocietypublishing.org

DW 2017, *How climate change is increasing forest fires around the world*, http://www.dw.com/en/how-climate-change-is-increasing-forest-fires-around-the-world/a-19465490

Eburn, M 2015, *Policies, institutions and governance of natural hazards: Annual project report 2014-2015*, Bushfire and Natural Hazard CRC, Melbourne.

Eckersley, R 2004, *Well & good: How we feel & why it matters*, The Text Publishing Company, Melbourne.

Edwards, J 2015, 'Lancefield bushfire: controlled burn that destroyed homes "poorly planned, under-staffed" *ABC News*, 19 November, https://www.abc.net.au/news/2015-11-19/lancefield-fire-poorly-planned-under-staffed-report-finds/6952528

Edwards M & Grace R 2014, 'The development of an actuarial model for arson recidivism', *Psychiatry, Psychology and Law*, vol. 21, no. 2, pp. 218–230.

Ekayani, M 2011, *Comparison of discourses in global & Indonesian media and stakeholders' perspectives on forest fire*, Cuvillier Verlag, Göttingen.

Ellicott, J & Stock, S 2002, Young firebugs to face their victims - bushfire crisis' *The Australian*, edition 1, 3rd January, P.2.

Ellis, S Kanowski, P & Whelan, R 2004, *National Inquiry on Bushfire Mitigation and Management*, 31 March, Commonwealth of Australia, https://www.dfes. wa.gov.au/publications/GeneralReports/FESA_Report-NationalInquiryon BushfireMitigationandManagement.pdf

Ellis-Smith, T Watt, BD & Doley, RM 2019, 'Australian arsonists: an analysis of trends between 1990 and 2015', *Psychiatry, Psychology and Law*, vol. 26, no. 4, pp. 593-613.

Emergency Management Victoria 2015a, *Emergency management manual Victoria*, Melbourne, Emergency Management Victoria, Melbourne, http://files.em.vic.gov.au/EMV-web/EMMV-Part-6A.pdf

Emergency Management Victoria 2018a, *Emergency management manual Victoria*, State of Victoria, Melbourne.

Emergency Management Victoria 2018b, *Bushfire safety policy framework*. Melbourne Emergency Management, Victoria.

Environment Policy 2003, 'Putting out the fire: Saving Greece's forests', *Environment Policy*, http://www.greece.gr/ENVIRONMENT/Environmental Policy/AttackingTheRoot.stm

Eriksen, C & Prior, T 2011, 'The art of learning: wild fire, amenity migration and local environmental knowledge', *International Journal of Wildland Fire*, vol. 20, no. 4, pp. 612-624.

European Union 2011, *Cities of Tomorrow: Challenges, Visions, Ways Forward*, European Union, Brussels.

Evans, S 2019, 'Uni team solves firestorm puzzle', *The Age*, January 9, p. 11.

Faidley, P 2015, *Correlation of risk factors and methodologies in juvenile fire setters: Literature review*, in part fulfilment of the Master of Emergency Management (Fire Investigation) Charles Sturt University, NSW.

Faivie, N 2018, *Forest fires: Sparking firesmart policies in the European Union*, November, European Commission, Brussels, Belgium.

Faivre, N Jin, Y Goulden, M & Randerson, J 2016, 'Spatial patterns and controls on burned area for two contrasting fire regimes in Southern California', *Ecosphere*, vol. 7, no. 5, pp. 1-24.

FAO (Food and Agricultural Organisation of the United Nations) 1999, *FAO meeting on public policies affecting forest fires*, FAO Forestry Paper 138, UN Food and Agriculture Organization, Rome, Italy.

Farmers for Climate Action 2016, 'Australian climate farmer survey', Farmers for Climate Action, https://d3n8a8pro7vhmx.cloudfront.net/farmersfor climateaction/pages/64/attachments/original/1480387204/FCA_survey_dig ital.pdf?1480387204

Farnsworth, S 2012, 'Black Saturday arsonist jailed for almost 18 years', *ABC News*, 27 April, http://www.abc.net.au/news/2012-04-27/black-saturday-arsonist-sentenced-to-28holdholdhold29/3976564

Fathi, D 2018, 'Prisoners are getting paid $1.45 a day to fight the California wildfires', November 15, American Civil Liberties Union, https://www.aclu.

org/blog/prisoners-rights/prisoners-are-getting-paid-145-day-fight-california-wildfires

Ferguson, C Doley, R Watt, B Lynehan, M & Payne, J 2015, *Arson-associated homicide in Australia: a five year follow-up*, Trends and issues in crime and criminal justice, 484. https://aic.gov.au/publications/tandi/tandi484

Findlay, M 2002, 'Search for the spark that animates the firebugs', *The Australian*, Edition1, 8th January, p.11.

Fineman, KR 1980, 'Firesetting in childhood and adolescence', *Psychiatric Clinics of North America*, vol. 3, pp. 483-499.

Fineman, KR 1995, 'A model for the qualitative analysis of child and adult fire deviant behavior', *American Journal of Forensic Psychology*, vol. 13, pp. 31-59.

Fire Services Commissioner Victoria 2012, *Towards improved fire management in landfill sites*, July, https://files-em.em.vic.gov.au/public/EMV-web/Fire_Management.pdf

Flannery, T 2012, 'After the future: Australia's new extinction crisis', *Quarterly Essay*, Issue 48, https://www.quarterlyessay.com.au/essay/2012/11/after-the-future

Flannery, T 2019, 'The gloves are off: 'predatory' climate deniers are a threat to our children', *The Conversation*, September 17, https://theconversation.com/the-gloves-are-off-predatory-climate-deniers-are-a-threat-to-our-children-123594?utm_medium=email&utm_campaign=Latest%20from%20The%20Conversation%20for%20

Folke, C Carpender, S Elmqvist, T Gunderson, L Holling, C & Walker, B 2002, 'Resilience and sustainable development: building adaptive capacity in a world of transformations', *Ambio*, vol. 31, no. 5, pp. 4370440.

Forest Fire Management Group 2014, *National bush fire management policy statement for forests, and rangelands*, The Council of Australian Governments, ACT.

Foss-Smith, P 2010, *Understanding landfill fires*, Waste Management World, https://waste-management-world.com/a/understanding-landfill-fires

Fowlkes, C 2019, 'Siskiyou Rappellers prepare for lightning strike', *Ashland Tidings*, August 9, https://ashlandtidings.com/top-videos/how-rappellers-prepare-for-wildfire-in-southern-oregon

France-Presse, A 2016, 'Haze from Indonesian fires may have killed more than 100,000 people – study', *The Guardian*, 19 September, https://www.theguardian.com/world/2016/sep/19/haze-indonesia-forest-fires-killed-100000-people-harvard-study.

Frankenberg, E McKee, D & Thomas, D 2005, 'Health Consequences of Forest Fires in Indonesia', *Demography*, vol. 42, no.1, pp. 109-129.

Fryar, R 2012, 'An overview of prescribed fire in Karkansas and Oklahoma over the last 40 years', paper presented at *Proceedings of the 4th fire in Eastern Oak Forests* conference, United States, Department of Agriculture & Forest Service, http://www.nrs.fs.fed.us/

Furlaud, J & Bowman, D 2017, 'To fight the catastrophic fires of the future, we need to look beyond prescribed burning', *The Conversation*, December 15, https://theconversation.com/to-fight-the-catastrophic-fires-of-the-future-we-need-to-look-beyond-prescribed-burning-89167

Furlaud, JM Williamson, GJ Bowman, D 2017, 'Simulating the effectiveness of prescribed burning at altering wildfire behaviour in Tasmania, Australia', *International Journal of Wildland Fire*, vol. 27, no.1, pp. 15-28.

Gammage, B 2011, *The biggest estate on earth: how Aborigines made Australia*, Allen & Unwin, NSW.

Gannon, TA & Barrowcliffe, E 2012, 'Firesetting in the general population: the development and validation of the firesetting and fire proclivity scales', *Legal and Criminological Psychology*, vol. 17, pp. 105-122.

Gannon, T Ó Ciardha, C Barnoux, N Tyler, N Mozova, K & Alleyne E 2013, 'Male imprisoned firesetters have different characteristics than other imprisoned offenders and require specialist treatment', *Psychiatry*, vol. 76, no. 4, pp. 349-364.

Gannon, T Ó Ciardha, C Doley, R & Alleyne, E 2012, 'The Multi-trajectory theory of adult firesetting (M-TTAF),' *Aggression and Violent Behavior*, vol. 17, no. 2, pp. 107-121.

Gannon, TA & Pina, A 2010, 'Firesetting: psychopathology, theory and treatment', *Aggression and violent behavior*, vol. 15, pp. 224-238.

Ganteaume, A Camia, A Jappiot, M San-Miguel-Ayanz, J Long, M Lampin, C 2013, 'A review of the main driving forces of forest fire ignition over Europe', *Environmental Management*, vol. 51, no. 3, pp. 651-662.

Garnett, S 2012, 'Saving Australian endangered species – a policy gap and political opportunity', *The Conversation*, 26 November, https://theconversation.com/saving-australian-endangered-species-a-policy-gap-and-political-opportunity-10914

Gazzard, R McMorrow, J Aylen, J 2016, 'Wildfire policy and management in England: an evolving response from Fire and Rescue Services, forestry and cross-sector groups', *Philosophical Transactions B*, Royal Society B, vol. 371, http://dx.doi.org/10.1098/rstb.2015.0341

Geels, FW & Schot, J 2010, 'The dynamics of socio-technical transitions: a socio- technical perspective', in Grin J Rotmans J Schot J (eds.), *Transitions to sustainable development: new directions in the study of long term transformative change*, Routledge, London.

Geller, JL Fisher, WH & Bertsch, G 1992, 'Who repeats? A follow-up study of state hospital patients' firesetting behavior', *Psychiatric Quarterly*, vol. 63, pp. 143-157.

Geller, JL Fisher, WH & Moynihan, K 1992, 'Adult lifetime prevalence of firesetting behaviors in a state hospital population', *Psychiatric Quarterly*, vol. 63, pp. 129-142.

Genton, M Butry, D Gumpertz, M & Prestemon, J 2006, 'Spatio-temporal analysis of wildfire ignitions in the St Johns River Water Management District, Florida', *International Journal of Wildland Fire*, vol. 15, pp. 87-97.

Gibson, C Chasmer, L Thompson, D Quinton, W Flannigan, M & Olefeldt, D 2018, 'Wildfire as a major driver of recent permafrost thaw in boreal peatlands', *Nature communications*, vol. 9, no. 3041, https://www.nature.com/articles/s41467-018-05457-1

Giddens, A 1997, *Sociology*, 3rd edition, Polity Press, UK.

Giddens, A 1998, *The Third Way: The Renewal of Social Democracy*, Cambridge, Polity Press.

Giljohann, K McCarthy, M Kelly, L & Regan, T 2015, 'Choice of biodiversity index drives optimal fire management decisions, *Ecological Applications*, vol. 25, no. 1, pp. 264–277.

Gill, MA 2005, 'Landscape Fires as Social Disasters: an overview of 'The Bushfire Problem',," *Global Environmental Change B: Environmental Hazards*, vol. 6, pp. 65–80.

Gill, T 2011, *Children and nature: a quasi-systematic review of the empirical evidence*, London: London Sustainable Development Commission, Greater London Authority.

Gill, AM Allan, G & Yates, C 2003, 'Fire created patchiness in Australian savannas', *International Journal of Wildland Fire*, vol. 12, pp. 323-331.

Gill, AM & Bradstock, RA 2003, 'Fire regimes and biodiversity: a set of postulates', paper presented at the *Proceedings of the Australian National University Fire Forum*, February 2002, CSIRO Publishing, Melbourne.

Gill, A Stephens, S & Cary, G 2013, 'The worldwide "wildfire" problem', *Ecological Applications*, vol. 23, no. 2, pp. 438-454.

Gippsland Arson Prevention Program 2017, *Fire Submission No. 85, Inquiry into bushfire preparedness,* https://www.parliament.vic.gov.au/images/stories/committees/SCEP/Fire_Season_Prepardeness/Submissions/Submission_85-GAPP.pdf

Givetash, L 2019, 'The Amazon is still on fire. Conservation groups blame illegal logging and criminal networks' *NBC News*, https://www.nbcnews.com/news/world/amazon-still-fire-conservation-groups-blame-illegal-logging-criminal-networks-n1056236

Global Forest Watch Fires 2018, 'Fire report for Indonesia', 5 Aug – 12 Aug, https://fires.globalforestwatch.org/report/index.html#aoitype=PROVINCE&dates=fYear-2018!fMonth-8!fDay-5!tYear-2018!tMonth-8!tDay-12&aois=Aceh!Bali!Bangka- …

Goldston, SE (ed), 1987, *Concepts of primary prevention: A framework for program development*. California Department of Mental Health, Sacramento.

Gonzalez-Mathiesen, C March, A & Stanley, J 2019, 'Challenges for wildfire-prone urban-rural interfaces: the case of Melbourne', *Urbano*, vol. 22, no. 39, 88-105.

Goodwill, A 2014, Where to next? Importance of directional considerations in offender geo-spatial sequential decision-making, *Legal and Criminological Psychology*, 19, 218-220.

Goodwill, A & Alison, L 2006, 'The development of a filter model for prioritizing suspects in burglary offences, *Psychology, Crime and Law*, vol.12, pp. 395-416.

Goudriaan, H Wittebrood, K & Nieuwbeerta, P 2006, 'Neighbourhood characteristics and reporting crime: effects of social cohesion, confidence in police effectiveness and socio-economic disadvantage', *British Journal of Criminology*, vol. 46, pp. 719–742.

Gough, M 2018, 'Prioritising natural disaster funding – mitigation vs recovery', *Aither: Think Piece* http://www.aither.com.au/wp-content/uploads/2017/03/Aither-Think-Piece-Prioritising-disaster-funding.pdf

Gralewicz, NJ Nelson, T & Wulder, MA 2012, 'Spatial and temporal patterns of wildfire ignitions in Canada from 1980 to 2006', *International Journal of Wildland Fire*, vol. 21, no. 3, pp. 230-242.

Green, SW 1931, 'The forest that fire made', *American Forests*, vol. 37, pp. 53-54.

Grieve, C & Preiss, B 2019, 'East Gippsland to bear brunt of fire season', *The Age*, 19 September, p. 12.

Grubb, J & Nobles, M 2016, 'A spatiotemporal analysis of arson', *Journal of Research in Crime and Delinquency*, vol. 53, no. 1, pp. 66-92.

Gualini, E Mourato, JM & Allegra, M 2016, *Conflict in the city: contested urban spaces and local democracy*, Jovis, Berlin.

Gurran, N, Norman, B & Haminc, E 2012, 'Climate change adaptation in coastal Australia: An audit of planning practice,' *Ocean and Coastal Management*, http://www.sciencedirect.com/science/article/pii/S09645691 12002955

Hann, W & Bunnell, D 2001, Fire and land management planning and implementation across multiple scales, *International Journal of Wildland Fire*, 2001, vol. 10, pp. 389–403.

Hahn, G Coates, A Latham, R & Mjidzadeh, H 2019, 'Prescribed fire effects on water quality and freshwater ecosystems in moist- temperate Eastern North America', *Natural Areas Journal*, vol. 39, no. 1, pp. 46-57.

Haines, S Lambie, I & Seymour, F 2006, *International approaches to reducing deliberately lit fire: Prevention Programs Final Report*, New Zealand Fire Services Commission Research Report no. 60, Uni Services Ltd., New Zealand.

Halton, M 2018, 'What the fire near Saddleworth Moor means for wildlife', *BBC News*, 28 June, https://www.bbc.com/news/science-environment-44643827

Hamers, L 2018, 'Wildfires are making extreme air pollution even worse in the northwest U.S.', *Science News*, vol. 194, no. 4, p. 9.

Hamilton, C & Denniss, R 2005, *Influenza: when too much is never enough*, Allen & Unwin, UK.

Hansen, J 2018, *Climate change in a nutshell: the gathering storm*, 18 December, http://www.columbia.edu/~jeh1/mailings/2018/20181206_Nutshell.pdf

Hartley, J 1982, *Understanding News*, Methuen, London.

Healey, P 1998, 'Collaborative planning in a stakeholder society', *Town Planning Review* vol. 69, no.1, pp. 1-21.

Heller, M & Polsky, S 1976, *Studies in violence and television.* American Broadcasting Company, NY.

Henkey, T 2018, *Urban emergency management: planning and response for the 21st Century*, Elsevier, UK.

Hinds-Aldrich, M undated, 'Firesetting firefighters: Reconsidering a persistent problem, *International Fire Services Journal of Leadership and Management*, vol. 533, https://www.academia.edu/1052901/Firesetting_Firefighters_Re considering_a_Persistent_Problem--Firefighter_Arson_Research

Hodges, G 2019, 'Russian smokejumpers', *National Geographic Magazine*, May, https://www.nationalgeographic.com/environment/natural-disasters/russian-smokejumpers/

Holland, M March, A Yu, J & Jenkins, A 2013, 'Land use planning and bushfire risk: VFA referrals and the February 2009 Victorian fire area', *Urban policy and Research*, vol. 31, no. 1, pp. 41-54.

Holpuch, A & Anguiano, D 2018, 'Trump blames forest management again on California fires visit', *The Observer, California*, 18 November, https://www.theguardian.com/us-news/2018/nov/17/donald-trump-visit-california-wildfires

Hopkins, LD 2001, *Urban Development: The logic of making plans*, Island Press, Washington.

Howden, M 2019, UN 'Climate change report: Land clearing and farming contribute a third of the world's greenhouse gases', *The Conversation*, August 8, https://theconversation.com/un-climate-change-report-land-clearing-and-farming-contribute-a-third-of-the-worlds-greenhouse-gases-121551

Howes, M Grant-Smith, D Reis, K Bosomworth, K Tangney, P Heazle, M McEvoy, D & Burton, P 2013, *Rethinking disaster risk management and climate change adaptation: Final report.* National Climate Change Adaptation Research Facility, Gold Coast, Australia.

Howlett, M Vince, J & del Rio, P 2017, 'Policy integration and multi-level governance: dealing with the vertical dimension of policy mix designs', *Politics and Governance*, vol. 5, no. 2, pp. 69-78.

Huang, R Zhang, X Chan, D Kondragunta, S Russell, AG & Odman, MT 2018, 'Burned area comparisons between prescribed burning permits in southeastern United States and two satellite-derived products', *Journal of Geophysical Research: Atmospheres*, vol. 123, pp. 4746–4757.

Hughes, L 2019, *Be prepared: climate change, bushfire and local governments'*, Expert Roundtable and Media Training 19th Feb, https://citiespower partnership.org.au/events/climate-change-bushfires-and-local-govern ment-roundtable/

Hughes L & Alexander, D 2017, *Climate change and the Victoria bushfire threat: update 2017*, Climate Council of Australia Ltd., Australia.

Hughes, L & Fenwick, J 2016, *The burning issue: climate change and the Australian bushfire threat*, Climate Council of Australia Ltd., Australia.

Human Rights Council 2018, *Report of the detailed findings of the Independent International Fact-Finding Mission on Myanmar*, 17 September, https://www.ohchr.org/en/hrbodies/hrc/myanmarffm/pages/index.aspx

Human Rights Watch 2019, *Rainforest mafias: how violence and impunity fuel deforestation in brazil's amazon*, September 17, https://www.hrw.org/report/2019/09/17/rainforest-mafias/how-violence-and-impunity-fuel-deforestation-brazils-amazon

Hylands, P 2019, Creative Cowboy Films, https://www.creativecowboyfilms.com

Icove, DJ & Estepp, M 1987, 'Motive-based offender profiles of arson and fire-related crimes', *FBI Law Enforcement Bulletin*, vol. 56, pp. 17-23.

Inciardi, J 1970, 'The adult firesetter' *Criminology*, vol. 8, pp. 145-155. https://doi.org/10.1111/j.1745-9125.1970.tb00736.x

Ingamells, P 2007, 'A blazing row over grazing', *HeraldSun,* January 24, https://www.heraldsun.com.au/news/opinion/a-blazing-row-over-grazing/news-story/92b6669a9c906802990887f0feadc6be?sv=7502a4ac589dba093c6c19d330e9690d

Ingamells, P 2016a, 'Appreciating limits of fuel reduction burns vital to effective fire management in Victoria', *The Sydney Morning Herald,* January 10, https://www.smh.com.au/opinion/appreciating-limits-of-fuel-reduction-burns-vital-to-effective-fire-management-in-victoria-20160110-gm2o3t.html

Ingamells, P 2016b, *Submission to Environment and Planning Committee: Inquiry into Fire Season Preparedness,* Victorian National Parks Association, Carlton, https://www.parliament.vic.gov.au/images/stories/committees/SCEP/Fire_Season_Preparedness/Submissions/Submission_32_-_Victorian_National_Parks_Association_VNPA.pdf

Insurance Information Institute 2019, *Facts + statistics: wildfires,* https://www.iii.org/fact-statistic/facts-statistics-wildfires

International Wellbeing Group 2013, *Personal Wellbeing Index,* 5th Ed., *Centre on Quality of Life,* author, Deakin University, Melbourne, Australia, http://www.deakin.edu.au/research/acqol/instruments/wellbeing-index/index.php

IPCC (Intergovernmental Panel on Climate Change) 2007, 'Summary for policymakers', In *Climate change 2007: impacts, adaptation and vulnerability,* Contribution of Working Group 11 to the Fourth Assessment Report of the Intergovernmental Panel on Climate Change, Cambridge University Press, Cambridge, UK.

IPCC (Intergovernmental Panel on Climate Change) 2019, *Climate change and land: IPPC Special Report on climate change, desertification, land degradation, sustainable land management, food security, and greenhouse gas fluxes in terrestrial ecosystems: summary for policymakers,* Draft 7 August, https://www.ipcc.ch/report/srccl/

Irfan, U 2018a, 'The West is on fire ... again', *Vox,* https://www.vox.com/2018/7/20/17582890/wildfires-2018-carr-fire-california-cranston-ferguson-colorado

Irfan, U 2018b, 'California's wildfires are hardly "natural" — humans made them worse at every step', *Vox,* August 9, https://www.vox.com/.../california-wildfires-2018-mendocino-carr-ferguson-climate

Ison, R 2010, Governance that works, *Ideas Australia needs now,* 25 July, Centre for Policy Development, p.81. https://onlinedocumentaryme lissakliese.files.wordpress.com/2010/08/morethanluckideasaustralianeedsnow4.pdf

Ison, R 2017, *Systems practice: how to act: in situations of uncertainty and complexity in a climate change world,* 2nd ed., Springer, Open University, Milton Keynes, UK,

Ison, R & Schlindwein, S 2006, 'History repeats itself: current traps in complexity practice from a systems perspective', paper presented at 12th Australia New Zealand Systems Society conference *Sustaining our Social and Natural Capital,* 3-6 December, Katoomba, NSW Australia.

Jackson, T 2009, *Prosperity without growth? The transition to a stable economy,* March, Sustainable Development Commission, UK.

Jackson, B & Frelinger, D 2007, *Rifling through the terrorists' arsenal Exploring groups' weapon choices and technology strategies,* October, RAND Corporation, https://www.rand.org/content/dam/rand/pubs/working_pa pers/2007/RAND_WR533.pdf

Jackson, HF Glass, C & Hope, S 1987, 'A functional analysis of recidivistic arson', *British Journal of Clinical Psychology,* vol. 26, pp. 175-185, https://doi.org/10.1111/j.2044-8260.1987.tb01345.x

Jacobs, J 1961, *The death and life of great American cities,* Random House, NY.

Jaffe, M 2019, 'Climate change is transforming Western forests and that could have big consequences far beyond wildfires', *The Colorado Sun,* July 25, https://coloradosun.com/2019/07/25/climate-change-reshaping-western-forests/

Jenner, L 2018, 'Agricultural fires seem to engulf Central Africa', *NASA,* June, https://www.nasa.gov/image-feature/goddard/2018/agricultural-fires-seem-to-engulf-central-africa

Jenner, L 2019, '2019 Huge forest fires in Venezuela create havoc', March 29, and, Wildfires in Far Eastern Russia have increased, March 20, *NASA,* https://www.nasa.gov/image-feature/goddard/2018/agricultural-fires-seem-to-engulf-central-africa

Jia, G Shevliakova, E Artaxo, P De Noblet-Ducoudré, N et al. 2019, 'Land-Climate Interactions', IPCC (Intergovernmental Panel on Climate Change) (ed), *Climate change and land: IPPC special report on climate change, desertification, land degradation, sustainable land management, food security, and greenhouse gas fluxes in terrestrial ecosystems: Summary for Policymakers,* Draft 7 August.

Johns, C 2014, 'Climate change, carbon and wildfires', *Future Directions International,* 7 October, http://futuredirections.org.au/wpcontent/uploa ds/2014/10/FDI_Strategic_Analysis_Paper_-_Climate_Change_Carbon_ and_Wildfires.pdf

Johnsen, T 2018, 'Forest fires in Sweden - huge areas burned in 2018', *Forestry.com,* August 6, https://www.forestry.com/editorial/forest-fires-sweden/

Johnson, S 2014, 'How do offenders choose where to offend? Perspectives from animal foraging, *Legal and Criminological Psychology,* vol. 19, pp. 193-210.

Johnson, S Summers, S & Pease, K 2009, 'Offender as forager? A direct test of the boost account of victimization, *Journal of Quantitative Criminology,* vol. 25, pp. 181-200.

Joint Counterterrorism Assessment Team 2019, 'Recognizing arson with a nexus to terrorism', *First Responder's Toolbox,* https://www.dni.gov/ files/NCTC/documents/jcat/firstresponderstoolbox/First_Responders_Tool box-Recognizing_Arson_With_a_Nexus_to_Terrorism_Originally_ Published-14_April_20171_May_2019-survey.pdf

Jones, B 2010, 'Democratic challenges in tackling climate change', *Perspectives,* Whitlam Institute, University of Western Sydney, December, https:// www.whitlam.org/publications/democratic-challenges-in-tackling-climate-change

Jones, D 2012, 'Koala Cul-de-sac? Development a dead end for wildlife' *The Conversation*, 27 August, https://theconversation.com/koala-cul-de-sac-development-a-dead-end-for-wildlife-9047

Jordon, B 2010, *What's wrong with social policy and how to fix it*, Polity Press, Cambridge, UK.

Judd, A 2018, 'B.C. wildfires map 2018: current location of wildfires around the province', *Global News*, 9 August, https://globalnews.ca/news/4232690/b-c-wildfires-map-2018/

Keeley, J & Syphard, A 2018, 'Historical patterns of wildfire ignition sources in California ecosystems', *International Journal of Wildland Fire*, vol. *27*, pp. 781–799.

Kelly, L Giljohann, K. & McCarthy, M 2015, 'Percentage targets for planned burning are blunt tools that don't work', *The Conversation*, 30 March, https://theconversation.com/percentage-targets-for-planned-burning-are-blunt-tools-that-dont-work-39254

Kennedy, PJ Vale, EL Khan, SJ & McAnaney, A 2006, 'Factors predicting recidivism in child and adolescent fire-setters: a systematic review of the literature', *Journal of Forensic Psychiatry and Psychology*, vol. 17, pp. 151-164.

Kenny, B Sutherland, E Tasker, E & Bradstock, R 2003, *Guidelines for Ecologically Sustainable Fire Management*, NSW Government, Sydney.

Ker, P 2009, 'Water harvest from dams may fall 30%', *The Age*, 18 February, http://www.theage.com.au/national/water-harvest-fromdams-may-fall-30-20090217-8aa4.html

Kilgore, B 1973, 'The ecological role of fire in Sierran conifer forests', *Quaternary Research*, vol. 3, pp. 496-513.

King, A 2017, 'Climate change to blame for Australia's July heat', *The Conversation,* August 4, https://theconversation.com/climate-change-to-blame-for-australias-july-heat-81953

King, C Feltey, K & Susel, B 1998, 'The question of participation: toward authentic public participation in public administration, *Public Administration Review*, vol. 58, pp. 317-326.

Kirkhim, R 2019, 'Soldiers Hill car fires, why arsonists burn', *The Courier*, March 21 https://www.thecourier.com.au › News › Latest News

Kirkpatrick, J 2013, 'Does fuel reduction burning help prevent damage from fires?' *The Conversation*, 21 January, https://theconversation.com/does-fuel-reduction-burning-help-prevent-damage-from-fires-11600

Kitzberger T, Falk, DA, Westerling, AL & Swetnam, TW 2017, 'Direct and indirect climate controls predict heterogeneous early-mid 21st century wildfire burned area across western and boreal North America', *PLoS ONE* vol. 12, no. 12, https://journals.plos.org/plosone/article/file?id=10.1371/journal.pone.0188486&type=printable

Klein, N 2014, *This changes everything: capitalism vs the climate,* Simon & Schuster, UK.

Klein, N 2019, *On fire: the burning case for a green new deal*, Allen Lane, UK.

Kocsis, RN & Itwin, H 1997, 'An analysis of spatial patterns in serial rape, arson, and burglary: the utility of the circle theory of environmental range for psychological profiling,' *Psychiatry, Psychology, and Law*, vol. 4, pp.195-206.

Kolden, C & Henson, C 2019, 'A Socio-ecological approach to mitigating wildfire vulnerability in the wildland urban interface: A case study from the 2017 Thomas Fire', *Fire*, vol. 2, no. 9.

Kolko, DJ 2002, *Handbook on firesetting in children and youth*, Academic Press, NY.

Kolko, DJ Day, BT Bridge, JA & Kazdin, AE 2001, 'Two-year prediction of children's firesetting in clinically referred and non-referred samples, *Journal of Child Psychology and Psychiatry*, vol. 42, pp. 371–380.

Kolko, DJ & Kazdin, AE 1986, 'A conceptualization of firesetting in children and adolescents', *Journal of Abnormal Child Psychology*, vol. 14, no.1, pp. 49–61.

Kolko, DJ & Kazdin, AE 1990, 'Matchplay and firesetting in children: relationship to parent, marital, and family dysfunction', *Journal of Clinical Child Psychology*, vol. 19, no. 3, pp. 229-238.

Kolko, DJ & Kazdin, AE 1992 'The emergence and recurrence of child firesetting: a one-year prospective study, *Journal of Abnormal Child Psychology*, vol. 20, pp.17–37.

Koson, DF & Dvoskin, J 1982, 'Arson: a diagnostic study', *Bulletin of the American Academy of Psychiatry and Law*, vol. 10, pp. 39-49.

Lambie, I Loane J, Randell, I & Seymour, F 2013, 'Offending behaviours of child and adolescent firesetters over a 10-year follow-up', *The Journal of Child Psychology and Psychiatry*, vol. 54, no. 12), pp. 1295–1307.

Lambie, I & Randell, I 2011, 'Creating a firestorm: a review of children who deliberately light fires', *Clinical Psychology Review*, vol. 31, no. 3, pp. 307-327.

Lambie, I Randell, I Ioane, J & Seymour, F 2009, *An outcome evaluation of New Zealand Fire Service Fire Awareness and Intervention Programme Final Report*, Wellington: NZ Fire Services Commission.

Lambie, I Seymour, F & Popaduk, T 2012, 'Young people and caregivers' perceptions of an intervention program for children who deliberately light fires', *Evaluation and Program Planning*, vol. 35, pp. 445-452.

Lansdell, G Anderson, J & King, M 2011, '"Terror among the gum trees" – is our criminal legal framework adequate to curb the peril of bushfire arson in Australia?' *Psychiatry, Psychology and Law*, vol. 18, no. 3, pp. 357-377.

Lawson, S 2019, 'Why aren't there many wildfires in China?' July, *Quora*, https://www.quora.com/Why-aren't-there-many-wildfires-in-China

Leitch, A & Inman, M 2012, *Supporting local government to communicate coastal inundation, resources kit prepared for the Sydney Coastal Councils Group Inc.*, CSIRO Climate Adaptation Flagship, Brisbane.

Leone, V Lovreglio, R Martin, M Martinez, J & Vilar, L 2009, Human factors of fire occurrence in the Mediterranean Ecosystems, in E. Chuvieco, (ed.) *Earth observation of wildland fires in Mediterranean ecosystems*, pp149-170, Springer-Verlag, Berlin.

Leopold, A 1987, *Game management*, University of Wisconsin Press, USA.

Lewis, C 2018, 'Arson attack blamed for field fire in Barnsley', *The Star*, 27 June, https://www.thestar.co.uk/news/arson-attack-blamed-for-field-fire-in-barnsley-1-9224141

Lewis, S & Perkins-Kirkpatrick, S 2018, 'Australia burns while politicians fiddle with the leadership', *The Conversation*, https://theconversation.com/australia-burns-while-politicians-fiddle-with-the-leadership-101905

Lewis, ND & Yarnell, H 1951, *Pathological fire setting (pyromania): nervous and mental disease*, monograph number 82, Coolidge Foundation, NY.

Lindell, J 2019, 'More than 50 cars burn near homes and bush across Canberra in December', *The Canberra Times*, January, https://www.canberratimes.com.au/story/5997440/more-than-50-cars-burn-near-homes-and-bush-across-canberra-in-december/

Lindenmayer, D 2007, 'Firestorm' *Four Corners*, ABC 13 March, https://www.abc.net.au/4corners/firestorm/8953390

Linn, R Winterkamp, J Weise, D & Edminster, C 2010, 'A numerical study of slope and fuel structure effects on coupled wildfire behaviour', *International Journal of Wildland Fire*, vol. 2, pp. 179-201.

Llausàs, A Buxton, M & Bellin, R 2016, 'Spatial planning and changing landscapes: a failure of policy in peri-urban Victoria, Australia', *Journal of Environmental Planning and Management*, vol. 59, no. 7, pp. 1304-1322.

Lönnermark, A Blomqvist, P & Marklund, S 2008, 'Emissions from simulated deep-seated fires in domestic waste', *Chemosphere*, vol. 70, pp. 626-639.

Lovelock, J 2006, *The Revenge of Gaia: why the earth is fighting back and how we can still save humanity*, Penguin, NY.

Lovreglio, R Leone, V Giaquinto, P & Notarnicola, A 2010, 'Wildfire cause analysis: four case-studies in southern Italy, *iForest - Biogeosciences and Forestry*, vol. 3, no. 1, pp. 8-15.

Lovreglio, R Ronchi, E & Nilsson, D 2015, 'A model of the decision-making process during pre-evacuation', *Fire Safety Journal*, vol. 78, pp. 168-179.

Löw, P 2019, *The natural disasters of 2018 in figures: losses in 2018 dominated by wildfires and tropical storms*, Munich Re, 8 January, https://www.munichre.com/topics-online/en/climate-change-and-natural-disasters/natural-disasters/the-natural-disasters-of-2018-in-figures.html

Lucas, CK, Hennessy, G Mills & Bathols, J 2007, *Bushfire Weather in Southeast Australia: Recent Trends and Climate Change Impacts*, Bushfire Cooperative Research Centre, Melbourne.

McCaffey, S Toman, E Stidham, M & Scindler, B 2014, 'Social science findings in the United States', in J. Shroder (ed), *Wildfire hazards, risks, and disasters*, pp. 15-36, Elsevier, UK.

McCaw, L 2013, 'Managing forest fuels using prescribed fire: a perspective from southern Australia', *Forest Ecology and Management* vol. 294, pp. 217-224.

McClelland, R 2010, 'Opening of bushfire arson prevention symposium', in J Stanley & T Kestin, (eds.), *Advancing bushfire arson prevention in Australia*, Monash University, Melbourne.

McDonald, K 2010, *Perspectives on effectiveness: What works in a juvenile fire awareness and intervention program?* Doctoral thesis, http://vuir.vu.edu.au/16037/2/kate_mcdonald_PHD_Final_Thesis1.pdf

McDonald, K et al. 2012, *Youth firesetting support guide: a resource for parents and practitioners concerned about fire risk behaviour in a child or young person*, CFA, Burwood East, Victoria, http://www.cfa.vic.gov.au/fm_files/attachments/plan_and_prepare/firestarters_v7-4_interactive.pdf

McEwan, TE & Ducat, L 2015, 'The role of mental disorder in firesetting,' in R Doley GL Dickens & TA Gannon (eds.), *The psychology of arson: a practical guide to understanding and managing deliberate firesetters*, pp. 211-217, Routledge, London.

McGee, T McFarlane, B & Tymstra, C 2015, 'Wildfire: a Canadian perspective', in D. Paton (ed.), *Wildfire hazards, risks, and disasters*, pp. 35-57, Elsevier, Oxford.

Macht, LB & Mack, JE 1968, 'The firesetter syndrome', *Psychiatry: Journal for the Study of Interpersonal Processes*, vol. 31, no. 3, pp. 277–288.

Maciak, B Moore, M Leviton, L & Guinan, M 1998, 'Prevention halloween arson in an urban setting: a model for multisectoral planning and community participation', *Health Education & Behavior*, vol. 25, pp. 194-211.

Macintosh, A 2012, *Coastal adaptation planning: a case study on Victoria, Australia*, Working Paper Series 2012/2, ANU Centre for Climate Law and Policy, Canberra.

MacKay, S Henderson, J Del Bove, G Marton, P Warling, D & Root, C 2006 'Fire interest and antisociality as risk factors in the severity and persistence of juvenile firesetting', *Journal of the American Academy of Child and Adolescent Psychiatry*, vol. 45, pp. 1077–1084.

MacKay, S Paglia-Boak, A Henderson, J Marton, P & Adlaf, E 2009, 'Epidemiology of firesetting in adolescents: mental health and substance use correlates', *Journal of Child Psychology and Psychiatry*, vol. 50, no. 10, pp. 1282-1290.

Mair, D Smillie, L La Placa, G Schwendinger, F Raykovska, M Pasztor Z & van Bavel R 2019, *Understanding our political nature: How to put knowledge and reason at the heart of political decision-making. Executive summary*, June, European Union, Luxembourg.

March, A 2017, 'Integrated education for resilient urban adaptation: wildfire risk reduction in Australia', *Planning Practice and Research*, vol. 32, no. 5, pp. 524-536.

March, A Nogueira de Moraes, L Riddell, GA Stanley, J van Delden, H Beilin, R. Maier, H 2018a, *Practical and theoretical issues - integrating urban planning and emergency management*, Melbourne: Bushfire and Natural Hazards CRC. https://www.bnhcrc.com.au/file/8951/download?token=u4pNzrhc

March, A Nogueira de Moraes, L Riddell, G Dovers, S Stanley, J van Delden, H Bellin, R Maier, H 2018b, *Australian inquiries into natural hazard events: recommendations relating to urban planning for natural hazard mitigation (2009-2017)*, Bushfire and Natural Hazards CRC, Melbourne.

March, A Nogueira de Moraes, L & Stanley, J 2020, 'Dimensions of risk justice and resilience: mapping urban planning's role between individual versus collective rights', in A Lukasiewicz & C Baldwin, *natural hazards and disaster justice: challenges for Australia and its neighbours*, pp. 93-115, Palgrave Macmillan, Australia.

Maron, M Griffin, A Reside, A Laurence, B Driscoll, D Tithie, E & Turton, S 2019, 'To reduce fire risk and meet climate targets, over 300 scientists call for stronger land clearing laws', *The Conversation*, March 11, https://the conversation.com/to-reduce-fire-risk-and-meet-climate-targets-over-300-scientists-call-for-stronger-land-clearing-laws-113172

Martin DA 2016, 'At the nexus of fire, water and society,' *Philosophical Transactions B* vol. 371, June 5, https://www.ncbi.nlm.nih.gov/pmc/articles/PMC4874410/

Martin, G Bergen, H Richardson, AS Roegar, L & Allison, S 2004, 'Correlates of firesetting in a community sample of young adolescents', *Australian and New Zealand Journal of Psychiatry*, vol. 38, pp. 148–154.

Martínez, R 2011. 'Políticas Públicas e innovación social', *Marcos conceptuales y efectos en la formulación de las políticas*, Universitat Autònoma de Barcelon Barcelona.

Martinez, J Vega-Garcia, C & Chuvieco, E 2009, 'Human-caused wildfire risk rating for prevention planning in Spain', *Journal of Environmental Management*, vol. 90, pp. 1241–1252.

Massola, J & Rompies, K 2019, 'Demand for action on roaring fires', *The Age*, September 18, p.20.

Masters, R & Waymire, J 2012, 'Oak savanna restoration: Oak response to fire and thinning through 28 years', paper presented at the *Proceedings of the 4th Fire in Eastern Oak Forests Conference*, United States Department of Agriculture & Forest Service, http://www.nrs.fs.fed.us/

McKenzie, F 1997, 'Growth management or encouragement? A critical review of land use policies affecting Australia's major exurban regions,' *Urban Policy and Research*, vol. 15, no.2, pp. 83-99.

McLaren, D Lefoe, G Ede, F Dugdale, T Steel, J Kwong, R Weiss, J Mahr, F Clements, D & Hunt, T 2016, 'Highlighting the complexity of interactions between peri-urban environment and weed management using case studies from Southern Victoria', in M Kennedy, A Butt & M Amati (eds.), *Conflict and change in Australia's peri-urban landscapes*, pp. 189-203, Routledge, London.

McLennan, B & Handmer, J 2014, *Sharing responsibility in Australian disaster management: Final report for the sharing responsibility project*, January, RMIT University, Melbourne.

McLennan, J Reid, K & Beilin, R 2019, 'Shared responsibility, community engagement and resilience: international perspectives', *Australian Journal of Emergency Management*, vol. 34, no. 3, pp. 40-46.

Meadows, D 1997, 'Places to Intervene in a System', *Whole Earth Winter*, https://www.bfi.org/sites/default/files/attachments/pages/PlacesIntervene System-Meadows.pdf

Mell, W Manzello, S Maranghides, A Butry, D & Rehm, R 2010, 'The wildland-urban interface fire problem – current approaches and research needs', *International Journal of Wildland Fire*, vol. no. 19, pp. 238-251.

Melvin, M 2018, *National prescribed fire use survey report*, Technical Report 03-18.

Mikkola, E 2008, 'Forest fire impacts on buildings', in J Heras, C Brebbia, D Viegas & V Leone (eds.), *Modelling, monitoring and management of forest fires*, WIT Press, Southampton.

Millar, J 2010, 'Land-use Planning and Demographic Change: Mechanisms for Designing Rural Landscapes and Communities', in *Demographic change in Australia's rural landscapes*, GW Luck, D Race, & R Black, eds., Dordrecht Springer, USA.

Miller, J 2017, 'The maximum criminal penalty for accidentally starting a Utah wildfire? A year in jail' The Salt Lake Tribune, https://archive.sltrib.com/article.php?id=5470610&itype=CMSID

Miller, C Abatzoglou, J Brown, T Syphard, A 2011, 'Wilderness Fire Management in a changing environment', in D McKenzie, C Miller, D Falk, (eds.), *The Landscape Ecology of Fire*, pp. 269-294, Springer, London.

Millennium Ecosystem Assessment 2019, *Overview of the Millennium Ecosystem Assessment*, Millennium Ecosystem Assessment, https://www.millenniumassessment.org/en/About.html

Milman, O 2015, 'Victoria seeks answers on preventing bushfires in changing conditions' *The Guardian*, 9 October, https://www.theguardian.com/australia-news/2015/oct/09/victoria-seeks-answers-on-preventing-bushfires-in-changing-conditions

Misni, F & Lee, L 2017, 'A review on Strategic, Tactical and Operational decision planning in reverse logistics of green supply chain network design', *Journal of Computer and Communications*, vol 5, no. 8, pp. 83-104.

Morgan, A & Homel, P 2013, *Evaluating crime prevention: lessons from large-scale community crime prevention programs*, Trends & Issues in Crime and Criminal Justice No. 458. Australian Institute of Criminology, Canberra, Australia.

Morse, S 1996, 'Building collaborative communities', *Leadership Collaboration Series*, Pew Partnership for Civic Change, www.pew-partnership.org/research/Ics/collabinex

Morton, S Sheppard A & Lonsdale, M 2012, 'Explainer: What biodiversity and why does it matter?', *The Conversation*, 12 October, https://theconversation.com/explainer-what-is-biodiversity-and-why-does-it-matter-9798

Muller, D 2008, *Offending and reoffending patterns of arsonists and bushfire arsonists in New South Wales*, Australian Institute of Criminology, Canberra, Australia.

Muller, D 2009a, *Using crime prevention to reduce deliberate bushfires in Australia*, Research and Public Policy Series 98, Australian Institute of Criminology Canberra, Australia.

Muller, D 2009b, *Patterns in bushfire arson*, Bulletin No.58, Australian Institute of Criminology, Canberra, Australia.

Muller, DA & Bryant, C 2009, 'Understanding and preventing bushfire arson', In J Handmer & K Haynes (eds.), *Community bushfire safety*, pp. 99-106, CSIRO Publishing, Melbourne.

Muller, D & Stebbins, A 2007, *Juvenile arson intervention programs in Australia*. Trends & issues in crime and criminal justice no. 335. Australian Institute of Criminology, Canberra, Australia. http://www.aic.gov.au/publications/current series/tandi/321-340/tandi335.html

Municipal Association of Victoria 2015, *Local government emergency management handbook*, Attorney General's Department, Victoria.

Munroe, T 2019, 'Embers under the earth: the surprising world of coal seam fires', *Global Forest Watch*, January 30, https://blog.globalforestwatch.org/fires/embers-under-the-earth-the-surprising-world-of-coal-seam-fires

Nanayakkara, V Ogloff, JR McEwan, TE & Davis, MR (in press b), 'Firesetting among people with mental disorders: differences in diagnosis, motives and behaviour', *International Journal of Forensic Mental Health.*

Nanayakkara, V Ogloff, JR & Thomas, SD 2015, 'From Haystacks to hospitals: an evolving understanding of mental disorder and firesetting', *International Journal of Forensic Mental Health*, vol. 14, pp. 66-75.

Nanayakkara, V Ogloff, JR McEwan, TE & Davis, MR (in press a). 'Applying classification methodology to high-consequence firesetting', *Psychology, Crime, and Law.*

NASA Earth Observatory 2014, *Fires in Indonesia*, March 7, https://earth observatory.nasa.gov/images/83304/fires-in-indonesia

National Association of State Foresters & Coalition of Prescribed Fire Councils, USA, https://inpfc.org/wp-content/uploads/2019/03/2018-Prescribed-Fire-Use-Survey-Report-1.pdf

National Emergency Management Committee 2011, *Australia: National strategy for disaster resilience*, Australian government, Council of Australian Governments.

National Institute of Building Sciences in the USA 2017, *Natural hazard mitigation saves 2017, Interim Report:* An independent study, December, National Institute of Building Sciences, Washington.

National Interagency Fire Centre 2019, https://www.nifc.gov/fireInfo/fireInfo _stats_totalFires.html

Natural Resources Canada 2019, *How various boreal species respond to fire*, Government of Canada, https://www.nrcan.gc.ca/our-natural-resources/forests-forestry/wildland-fires-insects-disturban/forest-fires/fire-ecology/13149

Nelson, N & Wright, S 1995, *Power and participatory development: theory and practice*, Intermediate Technology Publications, London.

Newman, O 1972, *Defensible space: Crime prevention through urban design*, Macmillan, New York, Macmillan.

New South Wales Government 2019b, 'Prevent bushfire arson', New South Wales Government, https://www.rfs.nsw.gov.au/fire-information/prevent-bush-fire-arson

New South Wales Office of Environment and Heritage 2017, *Threatened species profile search*, https://www.environment.nsw.gov.au/topics/animals-and-plants/threatened-species/about-threatened-species/key-threatening-processes

New South Wales Rural Fire Service 2013, *Ministerial releases*, 10 January, www.rfs.nsw.gov.au/dsp_more_info.cfo.cfm?CON_=8401&CAT_ID=1327

Nicolopoulos, N 1997, *Socio-economic characteristics of communities and fires*, NSW Fire Brigades Statistical Research Paper Issue 4, https://cata logue.nla.gov.au/Record/2518864?lookfor=NSW%20Fire%20Brigades%20Sta tistical%20Research%20Paper%20Issue%204.&offset=1&max=2421502

NIEIR (National Institute of Economic and Industry Research) 2013, *Firefighters and climate change: the human resources dimension of adapting to climate change: final and consolidated report*, February, unpublished report, Melbourne.

NIEIR (National Institute of Economic and Industry Research) 2014, *State of the regions 2013/14*, unpublished report, Melbourne.

Normille, D 2019, 'Indonesia's fires are bad, but new measures prevented them from becoming worse,' October 1, *Science*, https://www.sciencemag.org/news/2019/10/indonesias-fires-are-bad-new-measures-prevented-them-becoming-worse

Notzon, N & Damjanovic 2017, 'Wildfires believed to be deliberately lit by pig hunters burning near Darwin,' *ABC News*, 15 June, https://www.abc.net.au/news/2017-06-14/nt-fire-lit-by-pig-hunters-authorities-say/8618816

Nuccitelli, D 2017, 'California's hellish fires: a visit from the Ghost of Christmas Future', *The Guardian*, December 11, https://www.theguardian.com/environment/climate-consensus-97-per-cent/2017/dec/11/californias-hellish-fires-a-visit-from-the-ghost-of-christmas-future

Nugent, D Steven, W Leonard, A & Clarke, M 2014, 'Interactions between the superb lyrebird (Menura novaehollandiae) and fire in south-eastern Australia', *Wildlife Research*, vol. 41, pp. 203–211.

OECD (Organisation for Economic Co-operation and Development), IOM (UN Migration), UNHCR (United Nations High Commissioner for Refugees) 2018, *G20 International Migration and Displacement Trends Report*, September, http://www.oecd.org/els/mig/G20-international-migration-and-displacement-trends-report-2018.pdf

Office of Bushfire Risk Management 2018, *Report of the circumstances that led to the escapes of planned burns in the South West and Great Southern Regions of Western Australia on 24 and 25 May 2018*, https://dfes.wa. gov.au/waemergencyandriskmanagement/obrm/Documents/Final-Report-Circumstances-Escape-of-Planned-Burns-SW-and-GS-Region-24-25-May-2018.pdf

Office of the Auditor General Western Australia 2013, *Western Power's Management of its Wood Pole Assets*, November, http://www.parliament.wa.gov.au/publications/tabledpapers.nsf/displaypaper/3911155ad68b3bec3886867648257c29001fbc64/$file/1155.pdf

Ogloff, JR 2009, 'Shedding light on the unfathomable: the psychology of firesetting in the wake of Victoria's bushfires', *InPsych*, vol. 31, no.2, pp.16-17.

Ojerio, R Moseley, Lynn, K & Bania, N 2011, 'Limited involvement of socially vulnerable populations in federal programs to mitigate wildfire risk in Arizona', *Natural Hazards Review*, vol. 12, no, 1, pp. 28–36.

Oliveira, S Pereira, JMC San-Miguel-Ayanz, J Lourenco, L 2014, 'Exploring the spatial patterns of fire density in Southern Europe using geographically weighted regression', *Applied Geography*, vol. 51, pp. 143–157.

O'Neill, S & Handmer, J 2010, 'Responding to bushfire risk: The need for transformative adaptation', *Environmental Research Letters*, vol. 7, no. 1, 4018.

Padilla, M & Vega-Garcia, C 2011, 'On the comparative importance of fire danger rating indices and their integration with spatial and temporal variables for predicting daily human-caused fire occurrences in Spain', *International Journal of Wildland Fire*, 20, 46-58.

Palmer, E Caulfield, L & Hollin, C 1995, *Evaluation of interventions with arsonists and young firesetters*, Office of the Deputy Prime Minister, London.

Parés, M Ospina, S & Subirats, J 2017, 'Social innovation and relational leadership: opening up new perspectives on social change', *International Journal of Urban and Regional Research*, vol. 42, no. 5, pp. 958-960.

Parliamentary Education Office and Australian Government Solicitor 2010, *Australia's constitution*, Commonwealth of Australia, Canberra.

Parliament of Victoria 2017, *Inquiry into fire season preparedness: final report*, June, Victorian Government Printer.

Parsons, M Glavac, S Hastings, P Marshal, G McGregor, J McNeill, J Morley, P Reeve, I & Stayner, R 2016, 'Top-down assessment of disaster resilience: a conceptual framework using coping and adaptive capacities', *International Journal of Disaster Risk Reduction*, vol. 19, pp. 1-11.

Partington, A 2012, 'Police launch anti-arson program for summer', *The Age*, 19 November, http://www.theage.com.au/victoria/police-launch-antiarson-program-for-summer-20121119-29luw.html

Paschen, J & Ison, R 2011, *Exploring local narratives of environmental change and adaptation*, Monash Sustainability Report 11/1, Monash Sustainability Institute, Melbourne.

Patel, K 2018, 'Six trends to know about fire season in the western U.S.', December 5, *Ask NASA Climate*, https://climate.nasa.gov/blog/2830/six-trends-to-know-about-fire-season-in-the-western-us/

Paton, D Buergelt, P & Flannigan, M 2015, 'Ensuring that we can see the wood and the trees: growing the capacity for ecological wildfire risk management', in D Paton (ed.), *Wildfire hazards, risks, and disasters*, pp. 247-262, Elsevier, Oxford.

Paton, D Buergelt, P Tedim, F & McCaffrey, S 2015, 'Wildfires: international perspectives on their social-ecological implications', in D Paton (ed.), *Wildfire hazards, risks, and disasters*, pp. 1-14, Elsevier, Oxford.

Pausas, J & Fernández-Muñoz, S 2012, 'Fire regime changes in the Western Mediteranean Basin from fuel-limited to drought-driven fire regime,' *Climate Change*, vol. 110, pp. 215-226.

Paveglio, T Kooistra, C Hall, C & Pickering, M 2016, 'Understanding the effect of large wildfires on residents' well-being: what factors influence wildfire impact? *Forest Science*, vol. 62, no.1, pp. 59-69.

Pearce, D 1991, 'The global commons', in *Blueprint 2: greening the world economy*, in D Pearce, (ed), pp. 11-30, Earthscan Publications Ltd, London.

Pearce, D Barbier, E Markandya, A Barrett, S Turner, RK & Swanson, T 1991, *Blueprint 2: greening the world economy*, Earthscan Publications Ltd, London.

Pearce, D Markandya, E & Barbier, B 1989, *Blueprint for a green economy*. Earthscan Publications Ltd., London.

Pearce, D & Turner R 1990, *Economics of natural resources and the environment*, Harvester Wheatsheaf, London.

Pease, K 1998, 'Repeat victimisation: taking stock', *Police Research Group*, https://pdfs.semanticscholar.org/dd35/f369b91332ae9ca9fce929cbebfd7b0 cfc06.pdf

Pelling, M 2010, *Adaptation to climate change: from resilience to transformation*, Routledge, London.

Pendrey, C Carey M & Stanley, J 2012, *Extreme weather and the health of homeless people in Victoria, Australia: An emerging challenge for health equity*, unpublished report.

Penn, I 2017, 'Power lines and electrical equipment are a leading cause of California wildfires', *Los Angeles Times*, 17 October, https://www.la times.com/business/la-fi-utility-wildfires-20171017-story.html

Penman, T 2015, 'Saving homes, saving wildlife: Victoria ditches burnoff targets', *The Conversation*, November 25, https://theconver sation.com/saving-homes-saving-wildlife-victoria-ditches-burnoff-targets-51114

Penman, TD Bradstock, RA & Price, O 2013, 'Modelling the determinants of ignition in the Sydney Basin, Australia: Implications for future management', *Faculty of Science, Medicine and Health – Papers: Part A*, vol. 22, pp. 469-478, https://ro.uow.edu.au/smhpapers/991/

Pérez-Peña, R & Stevis-Gridneff, M 2019, 'Brazil's rainforest fires prompt alarm and anger in Europe', *New York Times*, August 23, https://www.ny times.com/2019/08/23/world/americas/amazon-fires-brazil.html? action=click&module=RelatedCoverage&pgtype=Article&region=Footer

Perry, R 2012, 'A review of fire effects on bats and bat habitat in the eastern Oak region'.

Proceedings of the 4th Fire in Eastern Oak Forests Conference, United States Department of Agriculture & Forest Service, http://www.nrs.fs.fed.us/

Pidot, J 2015, 'Symbolic, cognitive, and structural obstacles to formulating disaster policy', *Special Issue: Studies in Law, Politics, and Society*, vol. 68, pp. 33-64.

Plucinski, M 2014, 'The timing of vegetation fire occurrence in a human landscape', *Fire Safety Journal*, vol. 67, pp. 42-52.

Ponce, J Penalver, A Capdeferro, O & Burton, L 2015, 'The multi-level prevention and control of catastrophic wildfires in Mediterranean Europe: the European Union, Spain and Catalonia, Special Issue: Cassandra's Curse, *Studies in Law, Politics, and Society*, vol. 68, pp. 189-225.

Pooley, K 2018, *An evaluation of youth justice conferencing for youth misuse of fire*, PhD thesis, Queensland University of Technology.

Preece, N & Oosterzee, P 2017, 'Australia is a global top-ten deforester – and Queensland is leading the way', *The Conversation*, November 17, https://the conversation.com/australia-is-a-global-top-ten-deforester-and-queens land-is-leading-the-way-87259

Preiss, B 2019, 'Another recycling plant catches fire', *The Age*, April 25, https://www.theage.com.au/national/victoria/another-recycling-plant-catches-fire-20190425-p51h8c.html

Prestemon, J & Butry, D 2005, 'Time to burn: modeling wildland arson as an autoregressive crime function', *American Journal of Agricultural Economics*, vol. 87, no. 3, pp. 756-770.

Prestemon, J Butry, D & Thomas, D 2013, 'Exploiting Autoaggressive properties to develop prospective urban arson forecasts by target', *Applied Geography*, vol. 44, pp. 142-53.

Prestemon, JP Chas-Amil, ML Touza JM & Goodrickm SL 2012, Forecasting intentional wildfires using temporal and spatiotemporal autocorrelations, *International Journal of Wildland Fire*, vol. 21, pp. 743–754.

Prestemon, J Hawbaker, T Bowden, M Carpenter, J Brooks, M Abt, K Sutphen, R & Scranton, S 2013, *Wildfire ignitions: A review of the science and recommendations for empirical modeling*, United States Department of Agriculture, Forest Service, General Technical Report SRS-171.

Pretty, J Angus, C Bain, M Barton, J Gladwell, V Hine, R et al. 2009, *Nature, childhood, health and life pathways*, University of Essex, Colchester.

Price, O 2013, 'Reducing bushfire risk: Don't forget the science', *The Conversation*, 11 October, http://theconversation.com/reducing-bushfire-risk-don't-forget-the-science-19065

Price, O & Bradstock, R 2013, 'Landscape scale influences of forest area and housing density on house loss in the 2009 Victorian bushfires', *Plos One*, vol. 8 no. 8.

Prilleltensky, I & Prilleltensky, O 2006, *Promoting well-being: linking personal, organisational and community change*, John Wiley & Sons, Inc., Hoboken, New Jersey.

Prins, H 1995, 'Adult fire-raising: law and psychology', *Psychology, Crime and Law*, vol. 1, pp. 271-281.

Productivity Commission 2010, *Contribution of the not-for-profit sector research report*, https://www.pc.gov.au/inquiries/completed/not-for-profit/report

Productivity Commission 2015, *Inquiry report*, Australian Government, https://www.pc.gov.au/inquiries/completed/disaster-funding/report

Productivity Commission 2018, *Report on Government Services 2018*, Part D, Chapter 9, Emergency services for fire and other events, https://www.pc.gov.au/research/ongoing/report-on-government-services/2018/emergency-management/emergency-services

Putnam, R 1995, 'Bowing alone: America's declining social capital', *Journal of Democracy*, vol. 6, pp. 65-78.

Putnam, C & Kirkpatrick, J 2005, 'Juvenile firesetting: a research overview', *Juvenile Justice Bulletin*, January, U.S. Department of Justice, https://files.eric.ed.gov/fulltext/ED485846.pdf

Quay, R 2010, 'Anticipatory governance: a tool for climate change adaptation', *Journal of the American Planning Association*, vol. 76, no.4, pp. 496-511.

Queensland Councils of Social Services 2011, Submission to the Queensland Floods Commission of Inquiry www.floodcommission.qld.gov.au/_data/assets/file/0008/6983/Qld_Council_of_Social_Service_QCOSS.pdf

Quiggin P 2019, 'Explaining Adani: why would a billionaire persist with a mine that will probably lose money?' *The Conversation*, June 3, https://theconversation.com/explaining-adani-why-would-a-billionaire-persist-with-a-mine-that-will-probably-lose-money-117682

Quinsey, V Rice, M Harris, G & Cormier, C 2006, *Violent offenders: Appraising and managing risk*, American Psychological Association, Washington, DC.

Ransom, S 2007, 'A profile of motor vehicle theft related arson in New South Wales and South Australia', *Information Bulletin*, May, https://carsafe.com.au/docs/mvt_and_arson.pdf

Rayda, N 2019, 'Death toll rises as millions in Indonesia suffer from raging forest fires,' 13 September, *Channel New Asia*, https://www.channel newsasia.com/news/asia/death-toll-rises-as-millions-in-indonesia-suffer-from-raging-11902862

Read, P 2015, *Community attitudes towards reporting bushfire arson to Crime Stoppers in Victoria, 2009 – 2015: have patterns changed?* December, unpublished report.

Read, P & Stanley, J 2017, *Community attitudes towards reporting bushfire arson to Crime Stoppers Victoria 2012-2015*, Crime Stoppers Victoria, Melbourne Sustainable Society Institute, University of Melbourne.

Read, P & Stanley, J 2018, *Preventing wildfires through community reporting to Crime Stoppers: 2017 survey, Sixth report to Crime Stoppers Victoria*, Melbourne Sustainable Society Institute, Crime Stoppers Victoria.

Rebbeck, J 2012, 'Fire management and woody invasive plants In Oak ecosystems', *Proceedings of the 4th Fire in Eastern Oak Forests conference*, United States Department of Agriculture & Forest Service, http://www.nrs.fs.fed.us/

Reddel, T 2004, 'Third way social governance: Where is the State?' *Australian Journal of Social Issues*, vol. 39, no. 2 pp. 129-142.

Reid, K & Beilin, R 2015, 'Making the landscape 'home': narratives of bushfire and place in Australia', *Geoforum*, vol. 58, pp. 95-103.

Rice, ME & Harris, GT 1991, 'Firesetters admitted to a maximum security institution', *Journal of Interpersonal Violence*, vol. 6, pp. 461-475.

Rice, M & Harris, G 1996, 'Predicting the recidivism of mentally disordered fire-setters', *Journal of Interpersonal Violence*, vol. 11, pp. 364-375.

Ridge, T 2002, *Childhood poverty and social exclusion: from a child's perspective*, The Policy Press, Bristol, UK.

Rifkin, J 2011, *The Third Industrial Revolution: how lateral power is transforming energy, the economy, and the world*, Palgrave Macmillan, N.Y.

Rijksen, E & Dickman, C 2014, 'Predators get the advantage when bushfires destroy vegetation', *The Conversation*, 12 December, https://theconver sation.com/predators-get-the-advantage-when-bushfires-destroy-vegetation-32821

Ritchie, D 2011, *Sentencing matters: does imprisonment deter? A review of the evidence*. Sentencing Advisory Council, https://www.sentencingcouncil.vic.gov.au/sites/default/files/publication-documents/Does%20Imprisonment%20Deter%20A%20Review%20of%20the%20Evidence.pdf

Rix, KJ 1994, 'A psychiatric study of adult arsonists', *Medicine, Science and the Law*, vol. 34, pp. 21-34.

Roberts, D 2018, 'We are almost certainly underestimating the economic risks of climate change', *Vox*, June 9, https://www.vox.com/energy-and-environment/2018/6/8/17437104/climate-change-global-warming-models-risks

Robinson, M 2018, 'California fires maps LIVE: Fires won't be out until SEPTEMBER - 14,000 fight RAGING blaze', *Express*, August 10, https://www.

express.co.uk/news/world/999928/California-fires-2018-map-LIVE-updates-current-fires-northern-southern-California-latest

Roe-Sepowitz, D & Hickle, K 2011, 'Comparing boy and girl arsonists: crisis, family, and crime scene characteristics', *Legal and Criminological Psychology*, vol. 16, pp. 277-288.

Romps, D Seeley, J Vollaro, D & Molinari, J 2014, 'Projected increase in lightning strikes in the United States due to global warming', *Science*, vol. 346, pp. 851-854. http://www.atmos.albany.edu/facstaff/vollaro/pubs/Romps.et.al-SCI2014.pdf

Rook, G 2013, 'Regulation of the immune system by biodiversity from the natural environment: an ecosystem service essential to health', *Proceedings of the National Academy of Science*, vol. 110, no. 46, pp. 18360-18367.

Rossmo, D 2000, *Geographical profiling*, Boca Raton, Fl: CRC Press On-line, https://www.worldcat.org/title/geographic-profiling/oclc/42692068

Rozsa, M 2018, 'On climate change, it's time to start panicking', *Salon*, August 5 https://www.salon.com/2018/08/05/on-climate-change-its-time-to-start-panicking/

Ryan, R & Deci, E 2001, 'On Happiness and human potentials: a review of research on hedonic and eudaimonic well-being', *Annual Review of Psychology*, vol. 52, pp. 141-166.

Sagala, S Sitinjak, E & Yamin, D 2015, 'Fostering community participation to wildfire: Experiences from Indonesia', in D Paton (ed) *Wildfire hazards, risks, and Disasters*, pp. 247-262, Elsevier, Oxford.

Saillant, C 2007, 'Accidental wildfires draw aggressive prosecutions', *Los Angeles Times*, December 2, https://www.latimes.com/archives/la-xpm-2007-dec-02-me-firestart2-story.html

Salvador, R 2016, 'Jumping from the frying pan into the fire: a criminological study of forest fire-setting in Spain', in J Donnermeyer (ed), *The Routledge international handbook of rural criminology*, pp. 339-350, Routledge, London & New York.

San-Miguel-Ayanz, J Durrant, T Boca, R et al. 2018, *Forest fires in Europe, Middle East and North Africa 2017*, Report of the European Commission, https://www.researchgate.net/publication/329775375_Forest_fires_in_Europe_Middle_East_and_North_Africa_2017

Sapountzaki, K Wanczura, S Castertano, G Greiving, S Xanthopoulos, G & Ferrara, F 2011, 'Disconnected policies and actors and the missing role of spatial planning throughout the risk management cycle', *Natural Hazards*, vol. 59, pp. 1445-1474.

Saunders, B 2017, 'Words matter: textual abuse of childhood in the English-Speaking world, and the role of language in the continuing denial of children's rights, *International Journal of Children's Rights*, vol. 25, pp. 519-536.

Schilders, M & Ogloff, JR 2014, 'Review of point-of-reception mental health screening outcomes in an Australian prison', *Journal of Forensic Psychiatry and Psychology*, vol. 25, pp. 480 – 494.

Schulte, S Miller, KA 2010, 'Wildfire risk and climate change: the influence on homeowner mitigation behavior in the wildland–urban interface', *Society & Natural Resources*, vol. 23, no. 5, pp. 417–435.

Schumacher, EF 1973, *Small is beautiful*, Blond & Briggs Ltd, London.

Scott, A Bowman, D Bond, W Bond, S Pyne, S & Alexander, M 2014, *Fire on earth: an introduction*, John Wiley & Sons, Hoboken, NJ.

SCRGSP (Steering Committee for the Review of Government Service Provision) 2012, *Report on Government Services for 2012, Volume 1*, Steering Committee for the Review of Government Service Provision, Productivity Commission, Canberra.

SCRGSP (Steering Committee for the Review of Government Service Provision) 2016, *Report on Government Services 2016*, vol. D, Emergency Management, Productivity Commission, Canberra, Australia.

Secombe, M 2018, 'Love for a coal climate', *The Saturday Paper*, September 8-14, pp. 10-11.

Semega, J Fontenot, KR Kollar, MA 2018, Income poverty in the United States, 2017, Census Bureau, September, https://poverty.ucdavis.edu/faq/what-current-poverty-rate-united-states

Sentencing Advisory Council 2012, 'Arson and deliberately lit fires, Final Report no. 1, author, December, https://www.sentencingcouncil.tas.gov.au/__data/assets/pdf_file/0008/227906/Arson_and_Deliberately_Lit_Fires_Final_Report_No_1.pdf

Sentencing Advisory Council 2015, *Sentencing snapshot: sentencing trends in the higher courts of Victoria 2009-10 to 2013-14*, Sentencing Advisory Council, Melbourne. https://www.sentencingcouncil.vic.gov.au/sites/defau lt/files/publication-documents/Snapshot%20174%20Make%20Threat %20to%20Kill%20Higher%20Courts%20May%202015.pdf

Sharples, J Carey, G Fox-Hughes, P Mooney, S Evans, J Fletcher, M Fromm, M Grierson, P McRae, R & Baker P 2016, 'Natural hazards in Australia: extreme bushfire', *Climate Change*, vol. 139, pp. 85-99.

Siask, M & Värnik, A 2012, 'Media roles in suicide prevention: a systematic review', *International Journal of Environmental Research and Public Health*, vol. 9, no. 1, pp. 123-138, https://www.ncbi.nlm.nih.gov/pmc/articles/PM C3315075/

Sibthorge, C & Lowrey, T 2018, 'Residents urged to create bushfire survival plans as firefighters work to bring Canberra blaze and spot fires under control', November 4, *ABC News*, https://www.abc.net.au/news/2018-11-04/crews-still-trying-to-get-canberra-fire-under-control/10463648

Singer, SD & Hensley, C 2004, 'Applying social learning theory to childhood and adolescent firesetting: can it lead to serial murder?', *International Journal of Offender Therapy and Comparative Criminology*, vol. 48, no. 4, pp. 461–476.

Singh, R 2013, 'Spontaneous heating and fire in coal mines', *Procedia Engineering*, vol. 62, pp. 78-90.

Skinner, R 2010, 'Adaptation to climate change in Melbourne: Changing the fundamental planning assumptions', *Climate Change Impacts on Water Supply: An International Adaptation Forum*, Washington DC, 27 January.

Smith, K 2001, *Environmental hazards-assessing risk and reducing disaster*, 3rd ed., Routledge, New York.

Smith, RD 2004,' Community centred bush fire (arson) reduction'. Paper presented at 11th annual *AFAC conference and inaugural Bushfire CRC conference*, Perth, Western Australia.

Smith, H Cawson, J Sheridan, G & Lane, P 2011, *Desktop review – impact of bushfires on water quality*, March, https://www.waterquality.gov.au/sites/default/files/documents/impact-bushfires.pdf

Smith, M Kolden, C Paveflio, T et al. 2016, 'The science of firescapes: achieving fire-resilient communities', *BioScience*, vol. 66, no. 2, pp. 130-146.

Smith, R Vonberg, J & Miller, B 2018, 'Sweden struggling to contain dozens of drought-fueled wildfires', *CNN*, 18 July, https://edition.cnn.com/2018/07/18/europe/sweden-wildfires-intl/index.html

Soothill, KJ Ackerley, E & Francis, B 2004, 'The criminal career of arsonists', *British Journal of Hospital Medicine*, vol. 44, pp. 27-40.

Stacey, R Lintrup, K Notaro, F & Kokki, E 2010, *The ANSFER project final report: recommendations for improving fire risk assessment and management in Europe*, Northumberland, Northumberland Fire and Rescue Service, http://ec.europa.eu/echo/files/civil_protection/civil/prote/pdfdocs/2008_a nsfr_recommendations_en.pdf

Stahura, JM & Hollinger, RC 1988, 'A Routine Activities Approach to Suburban Arson Rates', *Sociological Spectrum*, vol. 8, pp. 349-69.

Stambaugh, M Guyette, R Stroh, Struckhoff, M & Whittier, J 2018, 'Future southcentral US wildfire probability due to climate change,' *Climatic Change*, vol. 147, pp. 617–631.

Stanley, J 2002, 'Preventing children & young people lighting bushfires in Australia', *Child Abuse Prevention Newsletter*, vol. 10, no. 2, NCPC, AIFS, Melbourne.

Stanley, J 2009, *Promoting social inclusion in adaptation to climate change: a discussion paper*, Commissioned by the Department of Sustainability and Environment, Victoria, unpublished report, Monash University, Victoria.

Stanley, J 2013, 'We know what starts fires; are we brave enough to prevent them?' *The Conversation*, https://theconversation.com/we-know-what-starts-fires-are-we-brave-enough-to-prevent-them-19323

Stanley, J 2015a, 'Social Resilience', paper for *Resilient urban communities: the new global imperative the future is now*, December 2, the Municipal Association of Victoria Annual conference, Melbourne.

Stanley, J 2015b, *Comments on fire report for gondola*, May, Peninsula Preservation Group, unpublished report.

Stanley, J 2020, How a failure in social justice is leading to higher risks of bushfire events, In A. Lukasiewicz and C. Baldwin, (eds.), *Natural hazards and disaster justice: how Australia rises to the challenge of a disaster-laden future*, Palgrave Macmillan, Singapore.

Stanley, JR & Banks, M 2012, *Transport needs analysis for getting there and back: report for Transport Connections: Shires of Moyne and Corangamite*, June, unpublished report.

Stanley, J Birrell, B Brain, P Carey, M Duffy, M Ferraro, S Fisher , Griggs, D Hall, A Kestin, T Macmillan, C Manning, I Martin, H Rapson, V Spence, M Stanley, C Steffen, W Symmons, M & Wright, W 2013, *What would a climate-adapted settlement look like in 2030? A case study of Inverloch and Sandy Point,* report for the National Climate Change Adaptation Research Facility, Gold Coast.

Stanley, JR & Goddard, CR 2002, *In the firing-line: violence and power in child protection work.* John Wiley & Sons, Chichester.

Stanley, JK, Hensher D, Stanley JR & Vella-Brodrick, D 2011, 'Mobility, social exclusion and well-being: exploring the links', *Transportation Research A,* vol. 45, no. 8, pp. 789-801.

Stanley, J & Kestin, T (eds.) 2010, *Advancing bushfire arson prevention in Australia,* Monash University and the Australian Institute of Criminology.

Stanley, J & Read, P 2013, Bushfire arson: prevention is the cure, *The Conversation,* January 10, https://theconversation.com/bushfire-arson-prevention-is-the-cure-11506

Stanley, J & Read, P 2016, 'Current and future directions for the place of community in the prevention of bushfire arson', in R Doley, G Dickens & T Gannon (eds.), *The psychology of arson a practical guide to understanding and managing deliberate firesetters,* Psychology Press and Routledge Academic, UK.

Stanley, JK & Stanley, JR 2018, *The value of getting there: mobility for stronger Australian regions,* Policy Paper 10, Bus and Coach Industry, Canberra, ACT.

Stanley, JR Read, P & Willis, M 2016, The Gippsland Arson Prevention Program: a review, Melbourne Sustainable Society Institute, University of Melbourne and the Australian Institute of Criminology, Canberra, unpublished report

Stanley, JK & Stanley, JR. & Hansen, R 2017, *How great cities happen: integrating people, land use and transport,* Edward Elgar, UK.

Statista 2019, Youth unemployment rate in EU member states as of May 2019 (seasonally adjusted), *Statista,* https://www.statista.com/statistics/266228/youth-unemployment-rate-in-eu-countries/

Steffen, W Alexander, D & Rice, M 2017, *Critical decade 2017: accelerating climate action,* Climate Council of Australia Ltd, Canberra.

Steffen, WK Richardson, Rockström, SE Cornell, et.al. 2015, 'Planetary boundaries: guiding human development on a changing planet', *Science,* vol. 347, no. 6223, pp. 736-748.

Steffen, W Rockström, J Richardson, K Lenton, T Folke, C Liverman, D Summerhayes, C Barnosky, A Cornell, S Crucifix, M Donges, J Fetzer, I Lade, S Scheffer, M Winkelmann, R & Schellnhuber, H 2018, 'Trajectories of the Earth System on the Anthropocene', *Proceedings of the National Academy of Sciences, PNAS,* vol. 115, no. 8252-8259.

Steiner, A 2011, 'Foreword', *UNEP 2011: Towards a Green Economy: Pathways to Sustainable Development and Poverty Eradication,* United Nations Environment Program http://www.unep.org/greeneconomy/greenecono myreport/tabid/29846/default.aspx

Stickle, TR & Blechman, EA 2002, 'Aggression and fire: antisocial behavior in firesetting and nonfiresetting juvenile offenders,' *Journal of Psychopathology and Behavioral Assessment*, vol. 24, no.3, pp. 177-193.

Stiglitz, J 2012, *The Price of inequality*, Allen Lane, New York.

Stopher, P & Stanley, J 2014, *Introduction to transport policy: a public policy view*, Edward Elgar, Cheltenham, UK.

Sukhdev, P 2012, *Corporation 2020: transforming business for tomorrow's world*, IslandPress, Washington.

Sullivan, H 2012, 'A Big Society needs and active state', *Policy & Politics*, vol. 40, no.1, pp. 145-148.

Summers, L Johnson, S & Rengert, G 2010, 'The use of maps in offender interviewing', in W Bernasco (ed.), *Offenders on offending*, pp. 246-272, Willan, Cullomption, UK.

Surette, R 2002, 'Self-reported copycat crime among a population of serious and violent juvenile offenders', *Crime and delinquency*, vol. 48, no.1, pp. 46–69.

Surette, R 2011, *Media, crime and criminal justice, images and realities*, (4th edition), Wadsworth, Belmont, C.A.

Sweetlove, L 2011, 'Number of species on Earth tagged at 8.7 million', *Nature*, 23 August, https://www.nature.com/news/2011/110823/full/news.2011. 498.html

Syphard, A Radeloff, VC Keeley, JE Hawbaker, TJ Clayton, MK Stewart, SI & Hammer, RB 2007, 'Human influence on California fire regimes', *Ecological Applications*, vol. 17, pp. 1388–1402.

Taylor, J 2013, 'Pathological firesetting and adults with intellectual and developmental disabilities', paper presented at the *International Conference on the Care and Treatment of Offenders with ID*, Northumbria University, Newcastle, UK.

Teague, B McLeod, R & Pascoe, S 2010, *2009 Victorian Bushfires Royal Commission: Final Report: Summary*, July, Government Printer, Victoria.

Tedim, F Leone, V Amraoui, M Bouillon, C Coughlan, M Delogu, G Fernandes, P Ferreira, C McCaffrey, S McGee, T Parente, J Paton, D Pereira, M Ribeiro, L Viegas, D & Xanthopoulos, G 2018, 'Defining extreme wildfire events: difficulties, challenges, and impacts', *Fire*, vol. 1, no. 9, https://www.mdpi.com/2571-6255/1/1/9/htm

Tedim, F Xanthopoulos G & Leone, V 2015, 'Forest fires in Europe: facts and challenges', In D. Paton (ed.), *Wildfire Hazards, Risks, and Disasters*, pp. 77-100, Elsevier, Oxford.

The British Psychological Society 2016, *The first comprehensive theory-based treatment of firesetting*, 26 September, https://www.bps.org.uk/news-and-policy/first-comprehensive-theory-based-treatment-firesetting

The Economist 2018a, 'In the line of fire: The world is losing the war against climate change', *The Economist*, August 4 to 10, p. 7.

The Economist 2018b, 'Burning out', *The Economist*, November 17, page 89.

The Economist 2018c, 'The new abnormal', November 17, *The Economist*, p.37-38.

The Guardian 2019, 'Indonesian forest fires putting 10 million children at risk, says UNICEF, *The Guardian*, 25 September, https://www.theguardian.com/

world/2019/sep/25/indonesian-forest-fires-putting-10-million-children-at-risk-says-unicef

The Prince's Rainforest Project 2009, Rainforests: the burning issue, *The Ecologist*, https://theecologist.org/2009/nov/09/princes-rainforests-project-keeping-forests-standing

The Royal Australian & New Zealand College of Psychiatrists 2019, *Suicide reporting in the media*, March, https://www.ranzcp.org/news-policy/policy-and-advocacy/position-statements/suicide-reporting-in-the-media

Thomas, D Butry, D & Prestemon, J 2012, 'Social disorder, accidents and municipal wildfires, Reframing shared responsibility in Australian disaster policy', *Proceedings of 3rd Human Dimensions of Wildland Fire*, April 17-19, Seattle, Washington, USA.

Thornton, J 2002, *Environmental impacts of Polyvinyl Chloride (PVC) building materials, a briefing paper for the Healthy Building Network*, http://mts.sustainableproducts.com/SMaRT/ThorntonRevised.pdf

Tidey, A (2019) 'Bolivia, like neighbour Brazil, battles intense wildfires that have so far burnt 500,000 hectares', *Euronews*, August, https://www.euronews.com/2019/08/22/bolivia-like-neighbour-brazil-battles-intense-wildfires-that-have-so-far-burnt-500-000-hec

Tomison, A 2010, 'Bushfire arson: setting the scene', in J Stanley & T Kestin, (eds.), *Advancing bushfire arson prevention in Australia*, Report from Collaborating for change: Advancing bushfire arson prevention in Australia symposium, Melbourne 25-26 March.

Townsley, M & Sudebottom, A 2010, 'All offenders are equal, but some are more equal than others: variation in journeys to crime between offenders', *Criminology*, vol. 48, pp. 897-917.

Trutnevyte, E Stauffacher, M & Scholz, R 2012, 'Linking stakeholder visions with resource allocation', *Environmental Science & Technology*, vol. 46, pp. 9240-9248.

Turco, M Rosa-Cánovas, J Bedia, J Jerez, S Montávez, J Llassat, M & Provenzale, A 2018, 'Exacerbated fires in Mediterranean Europe due to anthropogenic warming projected with non-stationary climate-fire models, *Nature Communications*, vol. 9, pp. 3821,

Turkewitz, J 2019, 'The Amazon Is on Fire. So Is Central Africa', *The New York Times*, 27 August, https://www.nytimes.com/2019/08/27/world/africa/congo-angola-rainforest-fires.html

Twenge, J & Baumeister, R 2005, 'Social exclusion increases aggression and self-defeating behavior while reducing intelligent thought and prosocial behaviour', in D Abrams, M Hogg & J Marques, (eds.), *The social psychology of inclusion and exclusion*, pp. 27-46, Psychology Press, NY.

Tyler, N Gannon, TA Ciardha, CO Ogloff, JR & Stadolnik, R (in press), 'Deliberate firesetting: an international public health issue', *The Lancet Public Health*.

Tyler, N Gannon, TA Dickens, GL & Lockerbie, L 2015, 'Characteristics that predict firesetting in male and female mentally disordered offenders', *Psychology, Crime and Law, https://www.tandfonline.com/doi/abs/10.1080/1068316X.2015.1054382*

Tyler, N Gannon, TA Lockerbie, L King, T Dickens, GL & De Burca, C 2014, 'A firesetting offense chain for mentally disordered offenders, *Criminal Justice and Behavior*, vol. 41. No. 4, pp. 512–530.

UNEP (United Nations Environment Program) 2011, Towards a green economy: pathways to sustainable development and poverty eradication, Foreword by Steiner, A.

UNEP (United Nations Environment Programme) 2012, *The Emissions Gap Report* http://www.unep.org/publications/ebooks/emissionsgapreport/pdf s/EMISSIONS_GAP_TECHNICAL_SUMMARY.pdf

UNISDR (United Nations Office for Disaster Risk Reduction) 2015, *Sendai framework for disaster risk reduction 2015 – 2030*, http://www.uni sdr.org/files/43291_sendaiframeworkfordrren.pdf

United Nations Department of Economic and Social Affairs 2017, *2017 world population prospects 2017*, Department of Economic and Social Affairs of the United Nations Secretariat, Population Division, https://population.un. org/wpp/

United Press International 2006, 'Africa leads globe in forest fires', *Phys.org*, April 2, https://phys.org/news/2006-04-africa-globe-forest.html

US Department of Agriculture 2015, *Forest service report: rising firefighting costs raises alarms*, Washington, August 5, https://www.usda.gov/media/ press-releases/2015/08/05/forest-service-report-rising-firefighting-costs-raises-ala

US Department of Agriculture 2019, *Cost of fire operations*, https://www.fs. fed.us/about-agency/budget-performance/cost-fire-operations

US Department of the Interior 2018, *New analysis shows 2018 California wildfires emitted as much carbon dioxide as an entire year's worth of electricity*, November 30, https://www.doi.gov/pressreleases/new-analysis-shows-2018-california-wildfires-emitted-much-carbon-dioxide-entire-years

US Fire Administration 2004, Fire in the United States 1992–2001, October, https://www.usfa.fema.gov/downloads/pdf/publications/fa-286.pdf

US Fire Administration 2014, *Vehicle* arson — a combustible crime, May, https://www.usfa.fema.gov/downloads/pdf/arson/aaw14_media_kit.pdf

US Forest Fire Services 2019, *Military partners*, https://www.fs.fed.us/ managing-land/fire/partners/military

US National Park Service 2017, *Wildland fire ecology resource brief wildland fire and ecosystems*, October 5, https://www.nps.gov/articles/wildland-fire-ecosystems.htm

Van de Velde, DM 1999, 'Organisational forms and entrepreneurship in public transport, *Transport Policy*, vol. 6, pp. 147-157.

Van Dijk, A 2019, 'Australia's 2018 environmental scorecard: a dreadful year that demands action', *The Conversation*, April 4, https://theconver sation. com/australias-2018-environmental-scorecard-a-dreadful-year-that-deman ds-action-114760

Victorian Bushfires Royal Commission 2009, *Fire preparation: response and recovery*, http://royalcommission.vic.gov.au/Commission-Reports/Final-Re port/Volume-2/Print-Friendly-Version.html

Victorian Bushfires Royal Commission 2010, *Final report*, July, Parliament of Victoria, Melbourne.

Victorian Bushfires Royal Commission Implementation Monitor 2012, *Bushfires Royal Commission implementation monitor: final report*. Melbourne: Government Printer for the State of Victoria.

Victorian Department of Sustainability and Environment 2009, *Advisory List of Threatened Invertebrate Fauna in Victoria – 2009*, Department of Sustainability and Environment, East Melbourne, Victoria.

Victorian Government 2015, *Safer together: a new approach to reducing the risk of bushfire in Victoria*, Melbourne, Victorian Government.

Virkkunen, M de Jong, J, Bartko, JJ Goodwin, FK & Linnoila, M 1989, 'Relationship of psychobiological variables to recidivism in violent offenders and impulsive fire setters: a follow-up study', *Archives of General Psychiatry*, vol. 46, no. 7, pp. 600-603.

Virkkunen, M Nuutila, A Goodwin, FK & Linnoila, M 1987, 'Cerebrospinal fluid monoamine metabolite levels in male arsonists', *Archives of General Psychiatry*, vol. 46, pp. 600-603.

Vreeland, R & Levin, B 1980, 'Fires and human behaviour' in D Canter (ed.), *Psychological aspects of firesetting*, pp. 31–46, Wiley, Chichester, England.

Wachi, T Watanabe, K Yokota, K Suzuki, M Hoshino, M Sato, A & Fujita, G 2007, 'Offender and crime characteristics of female serial arsonists in Japan,' *Journal of Investigative Psychology and Offender Profiling*, vol. 4, pp. 29-52.

Wang, Y & Anderson, K 2010, 'An evaluation of spatial and temporal patterns of lightning- and human-caused forest fires in Alberta, Canada, 1980-2007', *International Journal of Wildland Fire*, vol. 19, pp. 1059-1072.

Ward Thompson, C 2011, 'Linking landscape and health: the recurring theme', *Landscape and Urban Planning*, vol. 99, no. 3, pp. 187-195.

Watt, BD Geritz, K Hasan, T Harden, S & Doley, R 2015, 'Prevalence and correlates of firesetting behaviours among offending and non-offending youth', *Legal and Criminological Psychology*, vol. 20, pp. 19-36.

Watson, R & Albon, S 2011, *UK National Ecosystem Assessment: Synthesis of the Key Findings*, UNEP-WCMC, Cambridge.

Weatherburn, D 2001, 'What causes crime?' *Crime and Justice Bulletin: contemporary issues in crime and justice*, no. 54, February, https://www.bocsar.nsw.gov.au/Documents/CJB/cjb54.pdf

Weinhold, R 2011, 'Fields and forests in flames: vegetation smoke & human health', *Environmental Health Perspectives*, vol. 119, no. 9, September, https://ehp.niehs.nih.gov/doi/pdf/10.1289/ehp.119-a386

Weitzman, ML 2010, *GHG targets as insurance against catastrophic climate damages*, June 3, Department of Economics, Harvard University, https://scholar.harvard.edu/files/weitzman/files/ghgtargetsinsuranceagainst.pdf

Weitzman, ML 2012, 'GHG targes as insurance against catastrophic climate damages', *Journal of Public Economic Theory*, vol. 14, no. 2, pp. 221-244.

Wentz, J 2018, 'Six important points about the "affordable clean energy rule"', *State of the Planet*, August 22, Sabin Centre for Climate Change Law, Earth Institute, Columbia University, https://blogs.ei.columbia.edu/2018/08/22/affordable-clean-energy-rule/

Westerling, A 2016, 'Increasing Western US forest wildfire activity: sensitivity to changes in the timing of spring', *Philosophical Transactions B*, vol. 371, pp. 1-10.

Western Australia (undated) *Understanding bushfire: trends in deliberate vegetation fires in Australia*, https://aic.gov.au/sites/default/files/publica tions/tbp/downloads/tbp027_05_wa.pdf

Westley, F & Antadze, N 2010, 'Making a difference: strategies for scaling social innovation for greater impact. *Innovation Journal: The Public Sector Innovation Journal*, vol. 15, no. 2, pp. 1–19.

Whiteford, P 2019, 'Future budgets are going to have to spend more on welfare, which is fine. It's spending on us', March 7, *The Conversation*, https://theconversation.com/future-budgets-are-going-to-have-to-spend-more-on-welfare-which-is-fine-its-spending-on-us-111498

Wilkinson, R & Pickett, K 2009, *The spirit level: why more equal societies almost always do better*, Allen Lane, London.

Williams, LT 2011, 'The worst bushfires in Australia's history', *Australian Geographic*, November 3, https://www.australiangeographic.com.au/topics /science-environment/2011/11/the-worst-bushfires-in-australias-history/

Williams, D 2013, *Understanding the arsonist: from assessment to confession*, Lawyers & Judges Publishing, USA.

Williams, A Abatzoglou, J Gershunov, A Guzman-Morales, J Bishop, D Balch, J & Lettenmaier, D 2019, 'Observed impacts of Anthropogenic Climate Change on wildfire in California', *Earth's Future*, vol. 7, no. 8, pp. 892-910.

Williams, J & Hyde, A 2009, 'The mega-fire phenomenon: observations from a course-scale assessment with implications for foresters, land managers, and policy makers', *Proceedings from the Society of American Foresters 89th National Convention*, Orlando, FL September 30 to October 4, 2009.

Willis, M 2004, *Bushfire arson: a review of the literature*, Research and public policy series no. 61, Australian Institute of Criminology, Canberra, http://www.aic.gov.au/publications/current series/rpp/61-80/rpp61.html

Wilpert, J van Horn, J & Eisenberg, M 2015, Arsonists and violent offenders compared: two peas in a pod? *International Journal of Offender Therapy and Comparative Criminology*, vol. 61, no. 12, pp. 1354-1368.

Wilson, J & Kelling, G 1982, 'The police and neighbourhood safety: Broken windows', *Atlantic Monthly*, vol. 249, no. 3, pp. 29-34.

deWine, M 2013, *Ohio arson registry activated*. 1 June. http://www.ohio attorneygeneral.gov/Media/News-Releases/July-2013/Ohio-Arson-Registry-Activated

Wines, G Graham, M Scarborough, H Stanley, J & Wallis, A 2014, *Evaluation of Horizon 21's ConnectU social enterprise (Warrnambool and Surrounding Districts): Final monograph*, unpublished document, Monash University and Deakin University, Victoria.

Woods, R 2011, 'Opinion: Co-operative wildfire arson investigation: a new approach', *The Australian Journal of Emergency Management*, vol. 26, no. 2, pp. 11-14.

World Economic Forum 2019, *The global risks report 2019*, (14th edition), World Economic Forum, Davos.

World Commission on Environment and Development 1987, *Brundtland report our common future*, United Nations, Oxford University Press, UK.

World Meteorological Organization 2018, *WMO confirms past 4 years were warmest on record*, https://public.wmo.int/en/media/press-release/wmo-confirms-past-4-years-were-warmest-record

World Weather Attribution 2018, *Heatwave in Northern Europe, summer 2018*, 28 July, author, https://www.worldweatherattribution.org/attribution-of-the-2018-heat-in-northern-europe/

Wright, R 2004, *A short history of progress*, The Text Publishing Company, Victoria.

WWF (World Wildlife Fund) 2018, *Living planet report 2018*, https://www.wor ldwildlife.org/pages/living-planet-report-2018

Yocom, L Jennes, J Fulé, P & Thode, A 2019, 'Previous fires and roads limit wildfire growth in Arizona and New Mexico, USA, *Forest Ecology and Management*, vol. 449, no. 117440.

Yuen, E Jovicich, S & Preston, B 2013, Climate change vulnerability assessments as catalysts for social learning: four case studies in south-eastern Australia, *Mitigation and Adaptation Strategies for Global Change*, vol. 18, pp. 567-590.

Zhang, S 2014, 'World's oldest underground fire has been burning for 6000 years in Australia',

Gizmodo, Mar 11, https://www.gizmodo.com.au/2014/03/the-worlds-oldest-underground-fire-has-been-burning-for-6000-years/

Zukerman, W 2011, 'Mixed response to climate change on Australia's coasts', *New Scientist*, 31 March, https://www.newscientist.com/article/dn20321-mixed-response-to-climate-change-on-australias-coasts/

Zylstra, P 2016, 'New modelling on bushfires shows how they really burn through an area', *The Conversation*, August 22, https://theconver sation.com/new-modelling-on-bushfires-shows-how-they-really-burn-through-an-area-63943

Zylstra, P 2017, 'Forests, not fuels', paper presented at *Bushfires: balancing the risks* conference, July, Canberra, ACT, http://www.serca.org.au/research/20 17/zylstra.pdf

Zylstra, P 2018, 'Flammability dynamics in the Australian Alps', *Austral. Ecology*, vol. 43, pp. 578-591.

Index

www.ingramcontent.com/pod-product-compliance
Lightning Source LLC
Chambersburg PA
CBHW072052020426
42334CB00017B/1476